THE COMPLETE PADDLER

A Guidebook for Paddling the Missouri River from the Headwaters to St. Louis, Missouri

by **David L. Miller**

Dedication

For Max and Rose, my parents,
who had no idea what an adventure they would
launch when they went out for a little bike ride

FRONT COVER: *Photo of the author by Bryan Hopkins.*

ISBN 1-56037-325-3

Library of Congress Cataloging-in-Publication Data

Miller, David L., 1948-
The complete paddler : a guidebook to the Missouri River from the Headwaters to St. Louis / by David L. Miller.
p. cm.
Includes index.
ISBN 1-56037-325-3
1. Canoes and canoeing--Missouri River--Guidebooks. 2. Missouri River--Guidebooks. I. Title.
GV776.M83M55 2005
797.122'0978--dc22

2005006440

Created, produced, and designed in the United States of America.
Printed in Canada.

09 08 07 06 05 1 2 3 4 5

Acknowledgments

I paddled the Missouri over the course of three summers. My efforts along the way were assisted by the good will and acts of kindness by countless individuals. I also wish to acknowledge the help of numerous local, state, and federal officials who patiently responded to my questions, helped me mark up my maps with essential information, and assisted me with logistical support. A comprehensive list of those who assisted me is at the back of this book. Although many individuals have contributed to my effort to get the facts right, any errors are solely my responsibility.

By nature I am a solitary paddler. In part this is because it takes time to make field notes for accurate mapping. I paddled the entire river solo with the exceptions of the float between Coal Banks and Judith alongside members of the Montana Mountain Men Brigade going downriver in a replica pirogue; the section between Vermillion, South Dakota, and Sioux City, Iowa, with Chad Caldwell and MRE personnel; between Decatur and Omaha, Nebraska, with Matt Perkins; between Cooper's Landing and Jefferson City, Missouri, with Bryan Hopkins; and the Mississippi River float from the confluence to St. Louis, again with Bryan along with Scott Meyers. These were good companions.

I began my planning for this project with sabbatical support from the State University of New York College at Cortland. I owe a special debt to the following individuals for expedition support, critical assistance, and information: Cloudberry Corporation provided critical tech support–Dennis Clark, Stuart Grant, Jeff Sloane, Tom Rankin, Bill Ceglia, Ron Hawkins, Marc Bernard, and Joe Masso; Bob Bergantino, Montana Bureau of Mines and Geology, associate professor at Montana Tech, University of Montana; Gary E. Moulton, Thomas C. Sorensen Professor of American History at the University of Nebraska; Richard Williams, Midori Raymore, and Bob Pawloski of the NPS Omaha Office; Paul Johnston, Jeannie Nauss, and John Remus II of the USACE-Omaha District; Jeanne Heuser, technical information specialist USGS Columbia Environmental Research Center; Carol Bronson, executive director, Lewis and Clark Trail Heritage Foundation; Hunter Shoop, assistant product manager at Sierra Designs; Kimberly Hermes, editor, Small Craft Advisory, National Association of State Boating Law Administrators; and David Seidman, editor at *Boating Magazine;* Russ Martin, Norm Miller, and Bill Hammer, extreme paddlers; and Sandy Bramlette at Fort Benton.

I owe a special debt to Kathy Springmeyer, Shirley Machonis, Jessica Solberg, Caroline Patterson, my editor Peggy O'Neill, and my copy editor Ann Seifert, all at Farcountry Press.

Last and not least, I thank my Cortland, New York support team: Carl and Jeff Gambitta, my sons, Daniel and Michael Miller, and my friend and partner, Eline Haukenes. I would not have completed my odyssey and this book without their support and encouragement.

Table of Contents

Part I: The Preliminaries

WHY YOU SHOULD PADDLE THE MISSOURI RIVER AND WHY YOU NEED THIS BOOK

Get your facts first, and...then you can distort 'em as much as you please.

MARK TWAIN, AS QUOTED BY RUDYARD KIPLING IN *FROM SEA TO SEA*

With the exception of a few popular sections, most of the 2,321-mile-long Missouri River remains undiscovered by America's paddlesport community. Montana's 149-mile-long Upper Missouri section, which provides the only public access to the White Cliffs, is the lone section that sees regular and sometimes heavy paddler traffic. The remainder of the Missouri remains largely ignored. Although a handful of paddlers complete the entire distance every year, most of the Missouri, which is longer in length than the Mississippi, sees scant use. This is unfortunate. For those seeking a self-propelled long-distance adventure, the 2,300-plus-mile-long Missouri River presents a paddling challenge every bit as daunting as setting out to hike the entire Appalachian Trail.

At some point in the future, the Missouri River will be discovered as an ultimate paddler's challenge. The river provides a wonderful opportunity for long-distance voyaging. Those floating the river are charmed by long stretches of unspoiled beauty and the quiet solitude it affords. As the river carves its way down to the Mississippi confluence, it exposes millions of years of geologic history. Just beyond the riparian vegetation of the riverbanks, plant associations range from Montana's near desert of sparse grass and sagebrush to the lush prairie grasslands and aromatic pine stands of the Dakotas. Farther downriver, paddlers will encounter thick forests of cottonwood and oak. Of course, opportunities to view wildlife abound. On the Upper Missouri alone there are 49 species of fish, 60 species of mammals, 233 species of birds, and 20 species of amphibians and reptiles.

From a technical standpoint, the river offers a wide range of challenging trials. Depending on water levels, some short sections of the river offer fast and occasionally "white" water (Class I–III). Fortunately, these can be portaged around or otherwise negotiated safely. Other sections offer a gentle 2 to 4 mph current that allows a lazy float down a meandering channel. Where the Missouri is unconstrained by levees, the river snakes all over the bottoms. Whether levees are present or not, however, when a good wind is blowing these aspect changes require paddlers to continually work to reposition themselves in order to remain in the lee of the wind whenever possible.

Perhaps the greatest challenge that paddlers will face is traversing the three largest Army Corps of Engineers reservoirs–Fort Peck Lake, Lake Sakakawea, and Lake Oahe. Ranging from 134 to 231 miles long, these lakes are narrow at their upper ends and become progressively wider as you approach their dams. Because of the stiff winds that grace them, they require good seamanship, patience, and a carefully thought-out navigation plan. In addition, the upstream ends of these reservoirs present extended areas of braided channels replete with mudflats and dense marsh. Here the main channel can be very difficult to follow. Finally, long portages are required once paddlers reach the dams.

Other challenges are also present. Much of the river passes through remote and sparsely populated areas; opportunities to resupply are limited as are sources for drinking water. The river carries a heavy sediment load that quickly clogs filters, and water quality is problematic in some areas. And below Sioux City–more than 1,500 miles downriver from the Three Forks confluence–wing dams, barge traffic, flying carp, and fast-rising water associated with storm runoff create their own suite of issues. All these elements combine to make distance voyaging on the Missouri a magnum-caliber opportunity for great adventure. And, as Dallas Kropp, the owner of the K&S Bait and Fish Shop in Herman, Missouri, succinctly put it, "You get on this river and you better know what the hell you are doing."

Don't buy this book expecting a series of worked-out itineraries getting you from coordinate A to Z in X amount of time. When you are on the river, the temporal/spatial equation is buckshot by uncertainty variables generated |by current, wind, wave, and weather. What you will find between this book's covers are lessons from my passage, strategies and techniques that you can consider adopting, accurate information about where you can launch and take out, and general encouragement to get on the Missouri River to make your own voyage of discovery.

So what are you to make of this guidebook, and how can you use it? Use it to review the elements that you need to pay attention to, read it to help narrow down equipment choices and to think through daily routines, and study it for information to mark on your maps whether paper or digital. And then leave this guide at home when you set out for the river. Work on your own thoughts, avoid rigid itineraries and designated campsites whenever possible, and minimize your impacts. You will do fine.

RETRACING THE LEWIS AND CLARK EXPEDITION'S ROUTE ON TODAY'S MISSOURI RIVER

Everyone who has ever paddled a canoe on the Missouri, or the Columbia, does so in the wake of the Lewis and Clark expedition.

STEPHEN E. AMBROSE, *UNDAUNTED COURAGE*

According to some estimates, 20 to 30 million people will have attempted to retrace some or all of the Corps of Discovery's route from St. Louis to the Pacific by the end of the Lewis and Clark Bicentennial. Two-thirds of the outbound distance made by the original expedition–some 2,000 miles–was floated on the Missouri River. Modern-day explorers can follow highways that only roughly skirt, and occasionally cross, the expedition's path. They will visit museums, view displays, and attend celebrations at any number of cities and towns along the trail. For many, this will be a rewarding enough experience. More adventurous souls will attempt to more closely follow the Corp's tracks by actually voyaging on the Missouri River.

From my perspective, to really follow the Lewis and Clark trail you have to get on the Missouri River. There is perhaps no better way than a river trip to lend context to the expedition's story as told in the journals. Floating on the river, moving at 3 mph, rather than on a state highway doing 60, paddlers have a truly unique opportunity to connect the landscape with the written record of the expedition. It is still possible to locate and camp at many of the same places where Lewis and Clark camped. Few of these sites are accessible by car. Using the maps provided in this guidebook, paddlers can locate the areas where Lewis and Clark made their nightly journal entries by firelight. I can think of no better place to read the journals than where the events they describe took place.

Those choosing to retrace the expedition's route on the Upper Missouri River–from Three Forks to Sioux City–or paddlers simply looking for a quality distance adventure, will experience one of the last best opportunities to view a landscape much like that seen by explorers a century or two ago. Paddlers can make their way through more than a thousand miles of sparsely populated, remote, and God-awful rugged landscape. Opportunities abound to view wildlife. Slipping quietly along the water, paddlers will certainly see antelope, elk, mule deer, bighorn sheep, and perhaps even a cougar. Bird watchers also enjoy a special opportunity because the river passes through a range of eastern and western species. More than 120 species of birds have been observed on the Upper Missouri, in large measure concentrated in its narrow corridor of riparian habitat.

Perhaps the most compelling reason to paddle the entire Missouri is that there is no better way to understand the challenge of wilderness travel than to read the expedition's chronicles at the locations where the events took place. There is no better setting to understand what it was like to be sent upriver, to move into the unknown of distance. On a river expedition, in the fire-lit darkness under a canopy of stars, there is no better place to hear journal passages read and to feel them magically take on their authors' voices. Perhaps at this moment we understand most profoundly that we are truly on a common passage.

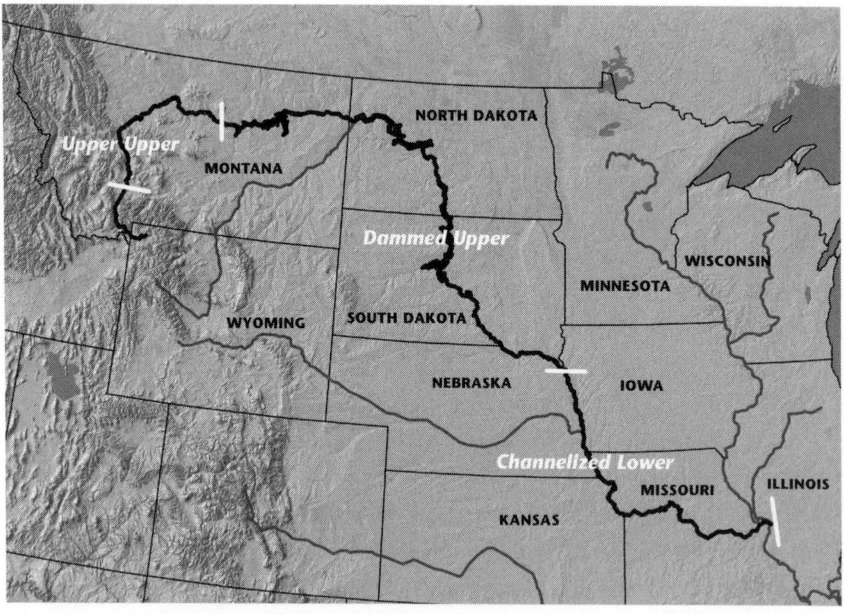

Map 0.0: Map of the Missouri River, from the headwaters near Three Forks, Montana, to the confluence with the Mississippi River.

THE MISSOURI RIVER—FOCUS OF THIS GUIDEBOOK

Rivers were America's first highways.... They're still highways, and they're my highways.

VERLEN KRUGER AS QUOTED BY JOE GLICKMAN IN *PADDLER MAGAZINE*

The Missouri River–stretching more than 2,300 miles before it joins the Mississippi above St. Louis–is the longest river in the United States. The Missouri is traditionally divided into two sections: upper and lower. Simply put, the Upper Missouri River ends where the Lower Missouri begins. Where exactly this occurs is, to some folks, a matter of opinion. Most consider the Lower Missouri to be the channelized stretch of the river from Sioux City, Iowa, to St. Louis. Everything above Sioux City is the "Upper" river. For the purposes of this guidebook, I've adopted this division.

Also for the purposes of this guidebook, I've made an additional division of the Upper Missouri. The first segment–from the headwaters confluence near Three Forks to the Kipp Floater's ramp at the Robinson Bridge (river mile 2,321 to 1,921)–I refer to as the "Upper Upper" This segment ends 400 river miles from the confluence, at the push-off point for Fort Peck Lake. Fort Peck is the first of several large Army Corps of Engineers (ACE) reservoirs. I've named this next segment–from the Kipp ramp to Sioux City (river mile 1,921 to 732) the "Dammed Upper." This makes sense to me and sounds right. After you paddle across Fort Peck Lake–the first of five reservoirs–you will probably want to insist that I change the spelling of the segment to more accurately describe your experience. More, of course, about this later.

The headwaters of the Missouri is at the confluence of the Gallatin, Madison, and Jefferson Rivers, near Three Forks, Montana. A river trip might begin at the nearby Missouri Headwaters State Park, or–to avoid having to portage around dams before and at Great Falls–paddlers may want to consider starting first with the Fort Benton to Robinson Bridge segment. The Upper Missouri National Wild and Scenic River corridor begins at Fort Benton.

Fort Benton is traditionally considered the upstream end of the navigable Missouri River. Before you decide to start at the headwaters, I suggest that you look over maps of the area. You will have to portage four dams and pull out above Great Falls. There are five additional dams in the Great Falls area. These dams are closely spaced, there is no easy access to the river, and sudden dam discharges can create hazardous conditions. For these reasons and because of

9-11 security-related concerns, these waters are off-limits to through-paddlers. There is today, happily, a portage arrangement to get you around these obstacles and in the water below the fifth dam.

When I started my expedition in the summer of 2002, I had no information about the portage situation at Great Falls, and one source warned me about dangerous rock shelves and large waves below the last Great Falls dam. Because of a lack of additional information, I decided to start at Fort Benton (river mile 2,074). Fort Benton is at the upstream end of the 149-mile-long Upper Missouri National Wild and Scenic River. There are numerous canoe and kayak trip outfitters at Fort Benton, and it is a neat little town. You can actually get a beer and a haircut at a main street bar. So if you are willing to consider doing the distance in segments, Fort Benton is a logical starting place for many paddlers.

I left from Fort Benton during my first summer of paddling in order to get to Virgelle in time for an early-June Lewis and Clark celebration. I then paddled on, ending my effort at West Whitlock, South Dakota, in early August. The following summer, I picked up where I had left off and reached Sioux City by the end of the season. I began my third summer of paddling in mid-June and completed the Three Forks to Fort Benton stretch (~ 248 miles) on July 4th. I then returned to Sioux City and completed the 733-mile distance to the Missouri confluence and then paddled down the Mississippi to St. Louis by early August.

ON TIME, DISTANCE, AND THE RIVER

Distance changes utterly when you take the world on foot. A mile becomes a long way, two miles literally considerable, ten miles whopping, fifty miles at the very limits of conception. The world, you realize, is enormous in a way that only you and a small community of fellow hikers know. Planetary scale is your little secret.

Life takes on a neat simplicity, too. Time ceases to have any meaning. When it is dark, you go to bed, and when it is light again you get up, and everything in between is just in between. It's quite wonderful, really.

Bill Bryson, *A Walk in the Woods*

According to the Army Corps of Engineers (ACE)—the agency that manages flows and navigation on the river—the navigable Missouri extends from its confluence with the Mississippi at St. Louis to the historic end of steamboat traffic in Fort Benton, Montana, a distance of 2,073 river miles. River miles are defined as the river's distance along a line at midchannel. From the river's start at the headwaters confluence near Three Forks, the total length is 2,321 miles. Experienced paddlers understand, of course, that these official distances are abstractions. That mile marks are an abstraction on many sections of the river obviously complicates the effort to provide mile-mark references in this guidebook. Where the river is spared from efforts to train its flow, the river's main channel meanders and its location occasionally shifts. How far you actually paddle depends on water level, current strength, and the path of an often winding and sometimes elusive channel. Thus, the actual distance that you travel cannot be gauged accurately by mile marks. After voyaging on the Missouri, you come to understand that the true distance between places is never accurately measured, or understood, until after passage is completed.

Many river sections are relatively wild and remote. As the railroad took commerce from steamboat traffic in the 1870s, settlement patterns changed fundamentally. Towns turned their backs to the river, many declined and were eventually abandoned, and new towns were sited along railroad lines on higher ground farther away from the Missouri's floodwaters. In some instances, whole towns were moved after catastrophic inundations. These circumstances mean that paddlers on the Missouri can still enjoy many opportunities to view the river as early explorers might have seen it.

THE ORGANIZATION OF THIS GUIDEBOOK

The first section of this guidebook provides basic information that is intended to help paddlers estimate their ability to safely complete a Missouri River expedition. Detail is provided about the risks involved, the equipment necessary, and what may best be thought of as tactical strategies. This information is based on my own experience, and the experiences of other modern-day voyagers. This guidebook begins with a basic premise: This is not a true "float." Making passage down most of the Missouri requires that you paddle more often than not. This is an active river; its twists and turns frequently require that you work actively to keep yourself positioned in the main channel to take advantage of the best current. Because of the river's changing aspect, you will frequently be going into the wind. The six large reservoir lakes–from 25 to 231 miles long–have little or no current to assist your progress. The wind is often in your face. More often than not, you will get nowhere if you do not paddle.

The second section of this book provides maps of sections of the river, trip divisions made based on my experiences and the recommendations of other voyagers. The most current information about landing sites is plotted on satellite image–based maps. My design is to provide information that would have been useful to me as I was working my way down the river. With the exception of the Bureau of Land Management's *Floater's Guide for the Upper Missouri National Wild and Scenic River* (149 miles from Fort Benton to James Kipp State Park), few good maps are available that have been designed for paddlers. This guide uses satellite images as a base for the section maps. These images can be downloaded from the Internet at no cost. Areas of the river can be zoomed-in on and copied as images or printed. I carried prints of the western delta areas of the reservoirs in a waterproof, clear plastic map envelope on the deck of my boat. These images provided me with detailed information about the shoreline and location of major channels, and a valuable "big picture" context.

To assist trip planning, I have characterized river segments to indicate my best estimation of the ability level required to make safe passage down each section. Information on the character of the shoreline, currents, prevailing winds, campsites, campgrounds, boat ramps, marinas, and opportunities for resupply are indicated. Portage paths around dams are described and information about portage services is listed. Also provided is information on areas where I was able to get cell phone and weather radio reception. In addition, I have included anecdotal information to assist paddlers through problematic areas or difficult circumstances that I encountered or that presented to previous voyagers. It bears repeating, however, that conditions on the Missouri change frequently. Given this circumstance, the information in this book can only help to prepare you to make your way safely down the river. A prudent paddler will seek updates from the many sources provided and will always seek local knowledge.

To further assist paddlers I have provided ACE river-mile-mark information for features such as ramps and campsites for the downstream paddle from the headwaters confluence to St. Louis. A typical statement of mile-mark information is "mile 2,319.7 right; 45.94021/-111.49097." This location translates to 2,319.7 miles from the Missouri confluence at the Mississippi, on the right as you paddle downstream ("right" or "left" refers to "descending river right" or "descending river left"), at the specified latitude and longitude stated in decimal degrees (more about this later). ACE mile marks are calculated along the river's thalweg–the deepest part of the channel. Since efforts to contain the free-running sections of the Upper Missouri are relatively modest, the river's main channel shifts periodically. Mileage figures here should be considered approximate, but can be used in conjunction with this book's maps and my expedition's tracks. When possible, I have included latitude and longitude coordinates of mentioned locations. These coordinates are based on GPS (Global Positioning System) waypoints that I fixed on my trip or that were later derived from computer-based map software or GIS (Geographic Information System)-processed imagery. Based on current estimates, these coordinates are accurate to within 3 to 10 meters. This is accurate enough to get paddlers to ramps or campsites that I used along the river and reservoirs.

A modestly priced handheld GPS unit–costing $140 to $180–can display your position over a relatively detailed base map. Thus, a river traveler can know his or her position at all times. Nevertheless, batteries die, units fail, and satellites fall from orbit. A prudent navigator will carry a backup unit and extra batteries stored in a cushioned dry box, and a compass attached securely to his or her lifejacket.

I have plotted the approximate locations of the Lewis and Clark campsites based on two sources. Bob Bergantino, of the Montana Technical University, graciously provided me with coordinates based on some 30 years of patient scholarship. For campsites in the state of Missouri, I also relied on the campsite data produced by James Harlan, of the University of Missouri Geographic Resources Center.

STARTING CONSIDERATIONS: WHEN TO GO, WATER LEVELS, AND HOW TO GET CURRENT INFORMATION

Had anyone ever retraced the Lewis and Clark expedition's tracks? I guessed that surely someone had. But, oh, wouldn't it be something to see the river they had. To travel through the heart of America and experience the river for the first time like so many other Americans had 150 years ago. The thought stuck in my mind and stayed there like a little pinprick.

CHRIS BECHTOLD, *A CURRENT ADVENTURE*

This guidebook is for paddlers intending to do some or all of the Missouri River. For those paddlers intending to paddle the entire 2,321 miles, this guide assumes a late May or early June start near Three Forks, Montana. With a good effort and some luck, by mid-August a paddler might be near Pierre, South Dakota, or perhaps Omaha, Nebraska. Those wishing to continue down the Lower Missouri–to make the entire trip to St. Louis–will be on the river another couple months, based on weather, water levels, and current. Another option is to break up the effort over the course of a couple summers, as I did. Two cautions: If you start before late May in Montana, you run the risk of a late-season snowstorm and accompanying frigid temperatures. You may have to hole up in your tent for several days. And if you start early in the spring on the Lower Missouri, you expose yourself to especially severe thunderstorms and possibly tornadoes. Serious numbers of tornadoes are spawned between April and June; weathering these in a tent is a bad choice.

Another caution: Water levels and strength of current are highly variable. Water levels on the free-running stretches of the Upper Missouri can become quite low by late summer. Virtually the entire length of the Missouri River is managed by the Army Corps of Engineers using a series of dams and reservoirs. Downstream user needs have historically received priority over the needs of paddlers, anglers, and others seeking water-related recreation. During drought years, drawdown from reservoirs is extreme. For those planning to paddle the entire Upper Missouri, six reservoirs–Fort Peck, Sakakawea, Oahe, Sharpe, Francis Case, and Lewis and Clark–need to be traversed. Annual changes in water levels can be dramatic, complicating the effort. Recent court battles have resulted in efforts to more equitably distribute the Missouri's waters among stakeholders, so more predictable flows may eventually result.

It is important to understand that much of the information about the Dammed Upper section was gathered during a voyage at relatively low water levels. In many respects this was fortunate, as voyaging is made generally more complicated by low water. A high water level on the river means a faster current; this helps you make more distance in a day. At low water levels, short sections of rapids intensify, long stretches of mudflats emerge, and opportunities to snag on some bottom feature are more frequent. Also, particularly on the reservoirs, low water levels mean that suitable campsites are farther up the shore, often only accessible after traversing a muddy approach. At the end of a long day of lake paddling, this circumstance presents an unwelcome and messy exercise.

When I paddled the Channelized Lower section of the river–from Sioux City to St. Louis–in the summer of 2004, water levels were generally high but receding. However, on two occasions, below Kansas City, the level rose substantially (2 to 4 feet) overnight. These rises were occasioned by heavy rains and flooding of tributaries that dumped into the Missouri. Besides complicating the issue of finding a safe place to camp along the shore, these events packed the river with debris, including many tree trunks and smaller snags. When levels were low, it was much easier to find nice campsites on sandbars and beaches. Locals will tell you that sudden rises in water levels can occur at any time of the year, but you can often count on high water and debris for a week or two in June.

Data are available to compare current conditions to the water level and discharge situation at the time that information was collected for this guidebook. I recommend that you do this. Real-time stream flow (short-term changes over several hours) and gage height are monitored at United States Geological Survey (USGS) river gauging stations and posted on the "Water Watch" website (http://water.usgs.gov/waterwatch/). At this site, you can view daily mean averages for discharge and gage height for the past seven days. More importantly, for a better perspective, you can generate a nice graph of daily discharge for the previous couple of months or up to a year and a half.

Paddlers and, for that matter, voyagers in any type of watercraft should also check the ACE's Missouri River Region–Water Management Information website (www.nwd-mr.usace.army.mil/rcc) for details on daily and monthly reservoir elevations, historic data, and the latest information on recreational facilities and boat ramps at Corps sites.

It is especially important to check this site before voyaging on the Upper Missouri. Current conditions and historic mean flow data (discharge measured in cubic feet per second) or gage heights can be compared with measurements taken during the time of my expedition. This will provide prospective voyagers with a better picture of what they can expect. To facilitate this, it would be a good idea to check the most recent information on the discharge rates and water levels and to compare this with the situation at the time I made my passage.

ON-LINE SOURCES FOR IMAGERY

Two interactive map services on the Web provide easy access to high quality images: *The National Map* (www.nationalmap.gov) and *TerraServer* (http://www.terraserver.microsoft.com). I've used both; the *TerraServer* is initially easiest to use, but you are able to produce custom maps with *The National Map*. With a GPS coordinate from this guidebook, you can secure useful imagery of the river at that location.

WHAT TO READ AND HELPFUL SOURCES OF INFORMATION

Missouri River Paddler's Guides

When I began research for my trip, I was surprised by the lack of information for those planning a "full-distance" expedition. To my knowledge, Keith Drury's *A Guide to Canoeing the Missouri River* (1999) is the only entire river source for information on making a downstream float trip from Montana all the way to St. Louis. However, Drury did not paddle the Missouri; he powered his square-end canoe downstream with an outboard. While useful, some of the information in this book is out of date.

There are two useful paddler's guidebooks for Montana rivers that include information about floating the Missouri. Curt Thompson's *Floating and Recreation on Montana Rivers* is a useful but somewhat dated (1993) source of information. Although this book provides only a page-and-a-half of commentary about floating options above and below Fort Benton, Thompson includes five black-and-white maps that show places along the river with mile-mark information. Hank and Carol Fischer's book, *Paddling Montana* (1999), provides much useful information about paddling in Montana, good advice, and a series of well-executed maps. For the popular 149-mile-long stretch between Fort Benton and Robinson Bridge, I highly recommend that you obtain a copy of *Montana's Wild and Scenic Upper Missouri River* (second edition) by Glenn Monahan and Chanler Biggs. This guide provides colorful detail about local history and is an excellent source for descriptions of the area's geology.

My efforts to gather useful guidebooks focusing on the Missouri River in other states yielded quite limited results. The Army Corps of Engineers small ring-bound publication, *Missouri River Traveler's Guide & Journal,* provides information on water safety, exotic and endangered species, cultural resources, and tribal nations. This publication also provides an extensive list of contact addresses. You can obtain a copy of this publication from the Missouri River

Information Center in Yankton, South Dakota (1-866-285-3219). Beyond this booklet, I located only a handful of sources for the state of Missouri. Although dated and out of print, the Missouri Department of Natural Resource's *Exploring Missouri River Country* by Don Pierce (~ 1982) is an outstanding source for information and local color. A few copies of Pierce's book may still be available, but you'll be very lucky to find one. Another out-of-print booklet is the MDNR publication *Canoeing in Northern Missouri,* by Mary Ann Pemberton (1978). Andy Cline's *The Floater's Guide to Missouri* (1992) is useful but dated. Oz Hawksley's *A Paddler's Guide to Missouri: Featuring 58 Streams to Canoe and Kayak* (2003) includes six nicely done Missouri River maps, river mile information for conservation areas and ramps, and a good page of river safety tips. If you are going to be paddling on any river in the state of Missouri, I highly recommend that you purchase this publication.

General Guides to Distance Paddling

Whether you are relatively new to paddling, or you have big distances under your spray skirt, you'll benefit from reading Cliff Jacobson's *Expedition Canoeing* (third edition), David Seidman's *The Essential Sea Kayaker* (second edition), and Joe Glickman's *The Kayak Companion.* Each of these publications provides well-tested and hard-won advice on gear, tactics, and safe navigation. There are other guides to paddling on rivers and open water that may be as good as these three sources; but there are none better.

Two additional sources deserve mention. First, although not a paddling guidebook, I recommend that you read Fletcher and Rawling's *The Complete Walker IV.* This thick volume presents the most comprehensive analysis of backpacker food/water/shelter systems available. For lack of a better explanation, I've often described expedition kayaking as backpacking on water. I am able to carry in my boat about double the weight that a backpacker might hump, and about twice the volume. I can go four to five weeks without resupplying as long as my water filter does not clog on the Missouri's often muddy water.

A second useful book is Tony Kellar's *Camping and Cooking with the Bare Essentials.* When you paddle you burn calories. Most of the time you make a quick meal and wolf down the fare. Every now and then, perhaps when you are pinned to the shore by bad weather, it's good to prepare something beyond edible. This book contains cooking tips and excellent recipes that will help you prepare memorable meals. Where else can you find a recipe for grilling chicken involving a can of root beer inserted up the hind end of a chicken? This is truly a river rat's gourmet cookbook.

Finally, I also recommend three recent publications–although not "paddler's guides"–that will provide you with useful information and good context. Trapper Badovinac's *Fly Fishing Montana's Missouri River* provides useful information for paddlers who may want to fish the blue ribbon trout section of the Upper Missouri. Tom Mullen's *Rivers of Change: Trailing the Waterways of Lewis and Clark* provides a section of thoughtful essays dealing with the changed character of the Missouri River ecosystem. His material is well researched, and his stories demonstrate that one can learn a great deal of useful information by listening to people living along the river. Also, I suggest you consider purchasing Brett Dufur's *Exploring Lewis & Clark's Missouri.* You should have this with you when you paddle the river in the state of Missouri. Brett is a member of the Discovery Expedition of St. Charles, the group doing the "official" reenactment of the Lewis and Clark Expedition. He is a river rat historian, and his book provides accurate information and colorful detail about places along the river.

Other Recommended Readings

There are a host of sources about trips up or down the Missouri River. A search engine–based query on the Internet will produce a long list. However, among the most recent publications, and one of my favorites, is Chris Bechtold's *A Current Adventure: In the Wake of Lewis and Clark* (2003). Another personal favorite, focusing in part on the Missouri River, is William Least Heat-Moon's *River-Horse* (1999).

I also recommend that you read two classic accounts written in the early 1900s: James Shultz's Floating on the Missouri ([1902] 2003) and John Neihardt's *The River and I* ([1910] 1997). In addition your library might include the journals of Lewis and Clark. These are now available in a very affordable paperback edition as a seven-volume set: *The Definitive Journals of Lewis and Clark* by Gary Moulton (2002). You may also want to look over Martin Plamondon's *Lewis and Clark Trail Maps: A Cartographic Reconstruction* (available in paperback as a three-volume set; see, for example, Volume II North Dakota to Washington). For the Missouri state segment of the river I suggest that you get the *Atlas of Lewis and Clark in Missouri* by James Harlan and James Denny. Integrating today's high-tech mapping technologies with the best traditions of scholarly cartographic research, this work sets a new and very high standard for historical atlases. Besides locating expedition campsites, Indian settlements, and forts in relation to present-day features, the maps show a great deal of additional information including overlays of the current course of the river. You will want to carry this one with you as you paddle the Missouri in Missouri.

And finally, I recommend that you read David Peck's *Or Perish in the Attempt: Wilderness Medicine in the Lewis and Clark Expedition* (2002). This book is well written and presents a fascinating analysis about medical knowledge at the turn of the nineteenth century. Peck also provides a great deal of information about current-day medical treatment. Missouri River paddlers who read this book will never complain about a few mosquito bites.

BEGINNING CONSIDERATIONS: SOLO OR ACCOMPANIED?

> *. . . there is that old saying about safety in numbers. Don't believe it for a minute, or doubt it for a second. No matter how big a crowd you have around you, in the end you are on your own; but if you can, never forgo the company of others on the water. It is not that it is unsafe to paddle alone, it's just that it is much safer if you are not. Once away from land, a group becomes a team, a team whose purpose is added security, plus (and this can never be discounted) the pleasure and support of companionship in an alien environment.*
>
> DAVID SEIDMAN, *THE ESSENTIAL SEA KAYAKER,* 2ND ED.

Before serious planning gets underway, you must decide on the most fundamental character of the trip: solo or accompanied. I chose to do a solo trip. This was a decision that I made during the earliest stage of my thinking about my expedition. Early on I was asked, "Why solo?" I remember that my answer was not entirely articulate. In response to the question I typically volunteered something along the lines of mapping being a time-consuming business, and not wanting to have others locked to my timetable of activity. I also wanted to make a quiet passage, with time for reflection and opportunities for long periods of silence. In retrospect, although my early rationale was fuzzy, my decision to go solo was intuitively right.

Besides reading the expedition's journals, I read a number of books as I was assembling my gear for the trip. Generally these involved a long-distance travel component, most featuring some passage on or along the Missouri. The journeys described in these books were made with company. With one exception: John Steinbeck's *Travels with Charley*. An old, yellowed, paperback copy of the book found me when I pulled it from a bookshelf filled with old paperbacks, remembering that I had read it as a senior in high school, and that it had resonated. Halfway through the book, Steinbeck muses on what he calls the "nature and quality of being alone." Here I found a more eloquent articulation for my decision to go solo:

Having a companion fixes you in time and that the present, but when the quality of aloneness settles down, past, present, and future all flow together. A memory, a present event, and a forecast all equally present (Travels with Charley).

Of course, from a practical standpoint, the decision to go solo requires that you carry your expedition's entire load. Larger items such as the tent, stove, fuel, and cooking gear cannot be parceled out among trip mates. And since opportunities to reprovision are limited, a two- to three-week food supply must be carried during the first and most remote segments of the trip. Freeze-dried food, while light, is relatively bulky. Even with careful packing, the start-out volume of the food supply–dried food and otherwise–will fill two sleeping bag–sized dry bags. So with a kayak, at least one deck bag will probably be necessary. This increases the craft's silhouette and raises its center of gravity–factors that need to be minimized when paddling into the wind and working across the big water of reservoirs.

And there are other safety considerations. In the event of illness, injury, or the general unforeseen, there is no partner to assist or to go for help. In this vein, I particularly like Daniel Botkin's contemplation that a wilderness hiker would today "fare no better from a ruptured appendix" than Sergeant Floyd, the Lewis and Clark Expedition's only fatality. In a paragraph that follows his rumination, Botkin writes about acceptance of risk:

If you choose to seek a wilderness experience as close as possible to that of Lewis and Clark, you would have to forgo the availability of modern medical assistance, and accept Floyd's risk of death. The alternative, often accepted today even among the most physically rugged of us is to have society support the search and rescue of sick and injured mountain climbers and wilderness seekers. Increasingly, hikers equipped with GPS satellite positioning devices and cellular phones have been calling in to ask for helicopter assistance when they find it nearing dusk and themselves not yet home or lost. This have-it or not-have-it-wilderness experience is spiritually much different from the travels of Lewis and Clark (Passage of Discovery).

Paddlers of the Upper Missouri need to understand that much of the river passes through remote areas, and that this is a "have-it" wilderness experience. A handheld GPS device will give you a position virtually anywhere on the

Missouri, but don't count on the use of a cell phone to be able to relay the information to anyone, especially in an emergency. Cell phone coverage is generally nonexistent to infrequent for the first several hundred miles, and very spotty thereafter. To be solo on long and remote stretches of the river and the big reservoirs is to be out of touch and totally alone for days at a time. This may be a bit more of a spiritual experience than many seek or are prepared for.

Voyagers planning to make an extended trip with a partner or in a group need to consider carefully a number of issues. Perhaps the most important issue is that of compatibility. Going long distance on the Missouri is hard and, at times, exhausting work. Persistence, patience, and grace are required. Paddlers should carefully consider the match of their skill sets. Leadership and division of labor will need to be worked out. The tasks–camp setup, meal preparation, and so on–can be rotated. Since freeze-dried food preparation is not rocket science, meals should not be a problem. Even if an individual has a particularly strong skill, the task rotation strategy will improve the skill set of other group members. If someone becomes ill, another member of the group can handle any task.

With respect to the issue of group size, I like David Seidman's advice:

It is an axiom of life that, although it may take only one person to get into trouble, it usually takes several more to get out. Three boats now offer two to help the one, or, one to help and the other to go for assistance. The odds are improved with three and stay that way until you reach six, with eight being the upper limit. Above this the numbers become unwieldy with too many people to be looked after or to look after others, so smaller subgroups should be formed (The Essential Sea Kayaker).

The environmental impact of a larger group must be considered, too. Given the promised increase in river traffic, minimizing the environmental footprint of voyagers must be an absolute priority. It is difficult to erase the evidence of passage of many feet at a campsite. And riverfront property owners will not long tolerate slobs. Downstream from Garrison Dam, before Washburn, North Dakota, I found a long stretch of riverfront posted against trespassers. I had been warned that I would see this by a park ranger at Cross Ranch State Park. He told me that the posting was the result of a mess left at a campsite by a group of canoers. He knew about this situation because the property owner had written a rather heated letter describing the problem to the editor of the local newspaper. Unless impacts are minimized, I have no doubt that additional areas will be posted. So traveling in smaller groups is recommended. And a "zero-impact" attention to policing a campsite is in order.

Whenever possible, voyagers should obtain permission to camp on private land from landowners. Smaller groups will have an easier time obtaining permission to camp. Property owners can do the math: A small group has a smaller impact. If you cannot locate the owner and must set up camp because of approaching weather or impending darkness, do everything possible to minimize your environmental footprint. If you are on private land and do not have the landowner's specific permission to have a campfire, do not build a campfire. If you have permission for a campfire, keep it small, put it out before you go to bed, and erase all evidence of it in the morning. Leave the site better than you found it.

An additional point about campfires: Notions about getting the group around the campfire every night and reading historical journals may at times have to be put on hold. Much of the region surrounding the river is frequently in drought. When fire hazard is high, campfires are prohibited, even at campgrounds with metal fire rings. Great care needs to be exercised even where fires are permitted. The wind can pick up incredibly fast in Montana and the Dakotas. At one point when I was camped at Tobacco Creek along the shore of Lake Sakakawea, the wind went from 0 to more than 70 mph in a matter of minutes. Fires should be kept small, watched carefully, and put out completely. I have no doubt that a rancher, upon finding a smoldering campfire on his land, would go ballistic. And rightly so.

PREDICTION, FORECASTING, LUCK, AND FORTUNE

Searching for the correct fork is inherently a different problem from trying to avoid slipping on wet clay and falling into the river. The second kind of uncertainties are referred to today as problems of risk, because the event has not yet happened and its occurrence has to do with inherent chance or with process whose causes, for all practical purposes we cannot distinguish from true chance events. Translated into human events, risk becomes a matter of prediction, forecasting, luck, and fortune, the latter two of which were also constant companions of the expedition.

Daniel B. Botkin, *Passage of Discovery*

I like Botkin's statement–his division of luck and fortune from prediction and forecasting. But I'd also observe that accurate prediction and forecasting no doubt enhance luck and fortune. Voyagers need to keep this in mind. There is no substitute for good preparation, exercised intelligence, and the ability to adapt to local conditions.

Many writers have commented on the numerous instances where luck and fortune seemed to have charmed the Lewis and Clark Expedition. My impression, after reading the original accounts, is that the expedition succeeded because its leaders selected good companions and good equipment. And, that they generally proceeded with prudence. They scouted ahead, constantly gathered local intelligence, and modified their plan as they were underway. Personnel assignments were shifted, clearly based on performance. And these men were competent frontiersmen. By today's standards, they were iron men—hardened by a life outdoors, resilient and resourceful soldiers. The men functioned as a unit because they understood that there was no other option. Sergeant Floyd's random death and his lonely gravesite must have sobered and powerfully crystallized the attention of everyone in the party.

CLOTHING, GEAR, HARDWARE, WATER, FOOD, AND SHELTER

There is something very satisfying about equipment. It is almost as if you were buying security. Most of it looks so dependable and reassuring, and when used wisely it can be. But very often the passion for equipment is the hiding place of those hoping to purchase what can only be achieved through skill. Choose products with discretion, use them wisely, but don't depend solely on your equipment to save you in an emergency.

David Seidman, *The Essential Sea Kayaker*

You need to think very carefully about your selection of gear. In essence, you want to reduce what you carry to just the rugged basics. There are a series of portages on the Dammed Upper Missouri. On the Lower Missouri, you will frequently have to pull your boat up steep banks or boat ramps. Experienced distance paddlers will already have their gear list and preferences. Less experienced paddlers should consult equipment lists found in distance paddler's guides such as Cliff Jacobson's *Expedition Canoeing.*

Remember the golden rule of boat packing: Gear takes space and adds weight. So minimize stuff. The three rules regarding equipment are: Simplify, simplify, simplify. I followed these rules to a T during my first year of paddling from Fort Benton, Montana, to Pierre, South Dakota; on three occasions I mailed packages of unnecessary gear home. Over time I have whittled down my equipment list to the basics. My rule was that if I wasn't using it, and it did not materially or potentially contribute to my safety, it went away. After I settled down into the rhythm of the trip, it became easier to sift to the essentials. The equipment list that follows is my distillation after more than 2,300 miles paddled over the course of three summers.

Clothing

Clothing should be lightweight, still function as an insulator when wet, and be able to dry quickly. Select well-constructed and hard-wearing clothing that you can layer and that is appropriate to weather and climate.

Parka or Paddling Jacket

Wind is an issue, and it will steal body heat at a brutally unforgiving rate, so one of your most important items will be a Gore-Tex, or other breathable fabric, parka. If you already have a true paddling jacket (with rubber gasket at the sleeves and neck), it can serve the same function. I carry both; the parka is perhaps a bit of a luxury, but it has a full-length zipper that allows for better venting, and it serves as somewhat more appropriate outerwear when I visit a town. Not that style is an issue, but when I visit a bar or restaurant I like to just sit quietly, watch the goings on, and listen for stories. My bright yellow paddling jacket would be out of place and might attract attention. By the way, my paddling jacket is yellow so I have a better chance of being seen by powerboaters; my parka is a dull green that blends into the woods or woodwork at a local watering hole.

For layering, a light- or medium-weight fleece jacket is a good idea. To this I would add a fleece or insulated fabric vest if I expect to be paddling in cold weather. If you wear this under a paddling jacket that has neck, wrist, and waist seals, you can paddle through waves and spray or take a dunking and still not saturate what's underneath and lose the value of your insulation. Also, your fleece jacket should have a full-length zipper to allow for best management of ventilation.

Clothing for General Use

I rely exclusively on well-constructed, lightweight Supplex–a nylon-like clothing with a sun protection factor (SPF) of 30 or 40. This material cleans up well, dries fast, weighs little, packs small, and gives you the additional benefit of some protection from the sun. Also, I carry two sets of polypropylene undergarments–underwear and T-shirts. If I am expecting cool or cold weather, I take along two long-sleeved tops.

Pants: Do not get the trendy kind with legs that zip off to make shorts. When the mosquitoes attack, you will not find the missing parts fast enough. And trying to zip everything together as swarms of biting insects zero in on you is a no-win situation. Besides this disfunctionality, the zipper is easily jammed by mud and dried sediment. Just get a couple pairs of well-constructed pants made of lightweight, quick-drying material. Use a pair of nylon boxer-style swim trunks for shorts.

Shirts: I took two khaki-colored, long-sleeved collared shirts, again made of lightweight, quick-drying synthetic material. The khaki/tan color reflects light and is cooler; it also does not show mud. I carried one dark green, short-sleeved, collared shirt. This was for wear in town.

Hats: A big-brimmed (not floppy) hat with chinstrap is a must when you are paddling on the river. I have yet to find the perfect hat; after most hats are worn in, their fronts tend to fold back on your forehead in a strong wind. So in addition I carry a ball cap, which I wear for three reasons: I feel comfortable in it; when in town or hanging with local river rats, I don't feel like some kind of out-of-place nimrod; and when it is really windy or raining hard, I wear my ball cap under the big floppy hat to stiffen the brim. With the chinstrap tightly cinched, this tactic minimizes the brim flopping and gives me the protection that I need from driving rain.

Sandals: Tevas or a similar type with "hold-tight" ankle fastening. Missouri River mud can be tenacious. Get a pair with a relatively thick sole and a strapping system that locks tightly to your foot. If you plan to do extensive hiking, you should consider a lightweight hiking boot. I also carried, and wore while paddling, a pair of water slippers–neoprene booties with some thickness to their soles.

Other Items: Life vest with attached strobe light; small boat horn or whistle; compass; sunscreen; lip balm; one pair of wool or thick, fleece socks; wool or fleece watch cap; and three bandanas. The latter serve as washcloth, dewrag, glasses wipe, and potholder.

What to Wear When Paddling

Wear comfortable clothes. For the most part–with the exception of safety gear–decisions about equipment are personal choices. What follows should be recognized as my own preferences.

- I always wear a life vest with survival and signaling gear: waterproof lighter, compass, knife, quarters for phone calls, small boat horn or whistle, and a marine band radio with NOAA weather channel.
- Most of the time I paddle wearing a polypropylene athletic shirt under a long-sleeved Supplex shirt, Supplex pants, neoprene paddling slippers, and a floppy hat. And I always have a bandana around my neck or stuffed in a pocket.
- A paddling jacket is another essential piece of gear; I have a Gore-Tex pullover that is highly breathable and waterproof. It has seals around the wrists, waist, and collar.
- I consider paddling pants–Gore-Tex or a (cheaper) impermeable fabric–optional. A Farmer John wetsuit, full- or three-quarter-length, might be a good substitute. If you are making a long-distance trip, you could send these back by midsummer when water temperatures rise. In Montana, the spring meltwater is, of course, cold, very cold. Neoprene gloves are a godsend. I initially carried a pair of pogies–special neoprene mittens to use with a kayak paddle. I did not use them; the gloves worked out just fine. Finally, I carried a half-length, closed-cell foam backpacker pad–the kind that folds like an accordion–that I laid in the cockpit under my legs and heels for extra cushion. This turned out to be a really outstanding addition to my equipment list. I used it as extra cushion and insulation under my self-inflating sleeping pad.

Camp Gear

Tent
Plastic tarp for use as inside tent liner
Bivy bag (optional)
Extra nylon parachute cord and tent stakes
Small tube of seam sealer
Sleeping bag
Lightweight fleece bag (to be used as a liner or alone on warm nights)
Self-inflating pad with repair kit
Gasoline (or multi-fuel) stove
Fuel bottles
Cook kit: nesting pots, with one cover
Large spoon

Large pocketknife
Biodegradable soap for washing, doing dishes, general cleaning
Flashlight with an extra set of batteries
Water purifier with extra filters
Small plastic shovel or toilet trowel
Small pruning shears or small machete
Clothespins and line
Water bags and bottles
Collapsible water bucket
Backpacker's towel
Seasonings, pump-spray margarine, and small bottle of olive oil
Backpacker's freeze-dried fare
Bag meats: tuna, chicken, salmon
Energy snacks, breakfast bars
Powdered drink mix
Coffee and/or tea, powdered milk/creamer/sweetener
Plastic tub of baby hand-wipes, toilet paper
Bathroom bags for areas where paddlers must manage their own waste

Miscellaneous Gear

Glasses (two pair), reading or prescription
Sunglasses (two pair)
Eyeglasses strap
Map case for kayak deck
Waterproof watch with alarm
GPS unit with spare batteries
Marine band two-way radio with NOAA weather band (waterproof)
Dog tags (www.id-ideas.com) with name, address, phone number, and blood type
Camera (water resistant/proof) and film
First-aid kit, snakebite kit
Medications: antibiotics, ear drops, and eye drops
Cell phone in small dry box with charging equipment
Medium-sized dry box for odds and ends
Assortment of small and medium carabiner clips
Binoculars

Duct tape, tube of Goop, tube of marine hand-moldable epoxy, multipurpose tool

Dry bags for deck: light, solid color, one with backpack straps

Small stainless steel thermos

Fishing pole and reel, tackle including a small lure assortment, salt minnows

Extra lighters/fire starters

Life vest with compass, survival gear, small boat horn

Kayak or canoe with all the essentials: bilge pump, paddle float, sponge, bailer, throw line bag, flotation bags, and extra rope (two 50-foot sections), bike cable and lock with extra keys

Additional Thoughts about Camping Gear

The best advice is to take the best tent that you can afford. I bought a Sierra Designs Orion AST3 ("Arch Support Technology") for the trip. Advertised as a three-person tent, it is actually a very comfortable two-person tent. Traveling solo, I probably could have done well enough with a smaller tent, but the extra space allowed me to empty out the kayak, put all my gear inside, and still have room to lay out my self-inflating pad and extra-long sleeping bag. This tent, as many in the $200 to $300 range, is relatively bombproof.

Go with bombproof. At some point–probably in July in North Dakota–you will need it. My tent held up to a Lake Sakakawea storm with sustained wind gusts that measured more than 70 mph. One of the tent's main arch poles bent during this storm. Almost a month later, after several more storms, this bent pole snapped below a joint during a long night of thunderstorms (50 mph winds) at Indian Creek State Campground near Mobridge, South Dakota. The tent was crippled but still held up. I spliced the pole together quickly and managed to stay dry, while other tents in the campground were flattened. It took me five days to get a replacement tent from REI. The lesson here is to travel with some extra pole sections for repairs or a pole repair kit.

Given the nature of the winds in this region (locals say to add the 20- to 30-mph NOAA estimate together to get what's probably coming your way), you may want to consider a four-season tent. When I was camped at Little Bend on Lake Oahe, I was caught in a supremely violent thunderstorm. Windblown rain slammed into my tent like someone had turned a fire hose on it. Sustained wind gusts literally flattened the tent to the ground, and held it there for more than 15 minutes. I was completely pancaked; the wind pressed the tent fabric down on me so tightly that I could barely breathe. But my tent held because it has a relatively low profile, is flexible and well constructed, and because I put heavy rocks on top of each stake to anchor my storm lines. Farther downriver, I related this story to a kayak outfitter who told me that this kind of storm is not uncommon, and that three- or four-pole tents are the only ones that can handle the wind.

Here are my thoughts about tent stakes. The thin metal stakes that come with most tents are inadequate. I carried four cheap, yellow, plastic stakes that I bought at Kmart. These eventually broke, but I purchased replacements along the way. During the second summer, I took six longer, tempered metal stakes to use with my storm lines. These stakes are wide at the top and taper to a point. The storm lines attach to the fly on the corners of the tent and run out at least 7 or 8 feet to the "premium" stakes securely set in the ground.

BOAT, INFLATABLE RAFT, KAYAK, FOLDING KAYAK, OR CANOE?

Depending on the nature of the trip–self-sufficient solo or group, with or without a support vehicle–my recommendation varies. For an unsupported solo trip, my advice is to go with a long and comfortable sea kayak with rudder. I made the trip in a Perception Vizcaya, a 17-foot sea kayak that comes pretty much expedition rigged. This kayak is a good compromise between fast and stable, and has good storage space and a very comfortable seat. I tried several brands and styles of kayaks before I settled on the Vizcaya model; it moved well through the water and fit me. It proved a good choice. By the time I reached North Dakota, I was paddling ten-hour days. I was able to paddle from 6 A.M. to about noon, rest and take lunch in the shade if I could find it, and then continue on. Most days, wind permitting, I paddled an additional three or four hours.

Attempting to float the entire Upper Missouri in an inflatable raft, a boat, or an uncovered canoe is, in my opinion, a prescription for disaster. Although experienced, skilled, and determined canoers have completed the distance from Fort Benton to St. Louis, the large reservoirs present an especially severe test of talent. Stiff headwinds, sudden storms with large waves, lack of safe landing places along shore, miles of shallow water replete with snags, and treacherous mudflats all present difficulties. At higher water levels than I experienced, it might be possible to make most of the passage in a powered boat or an inflatable dingy. But rocks, hidden stumps, and sharp-edged junked automobiles or agricultural equipment lurk along some areas of the river bottom. Higher water levels may simply conceal many of these impediments. Also, in Montana, motors are banned from some sections of the river.

Several have made the entire distance in square-ended canoes or johnboats powered by a small outboard motor. This might make the passage across the big reservoirs much less of an effort, but it would still be necessary to stay near the shore and exercise a great deal of caution. And because of the wind and waves, adequate flotation and bow, belly, and stern covers, or spray shields, are essential.

Based on my experiences, a kayak with a rudder makes better headway into a headwind or crosswind, is more seaworthy, and is more efficient. In addition, a hard-body kayak tends to slide past a snag rather than pin on it. For these reasons, I would argue that a kayak's lack of cargo space relative to what you get in a canoe is an acceptable trade-off. At the populated ends of the big lakes, there are opportunities to arrange supply drops. On the Lower Missouri I met Steve Campbell paddling his way upstream on a sit-on-top–sort of a cross between a kayak and a surfboard. A professional guide in triathlon shape, Steve explained that his sit-on-top had under-deck cargo space, was unsinkable, and allowed him to hop off quickly when he had to line his boat around some obstacle or section too difficult to paddle. Steve was making 15 to 20 miles a day paddling against the current, so this craft worked for him. My only reservation about an open-deck boat is the additional body area exposed to the elements, particularly the very hot sun. With attention to this aspect, however, an open-deck boat seems to be a viable alternative. Certainly you can more quickly crawl aboard this boat than a kayak if you have to bail out or are knocked over.

Whatever craft you select, understand that it will take a beating. I have put more than 2,000 river miles on my kayak, and the bottom of my boat shows a great deal of wear–it is scratched, scraped, and scarred. The Missouri can be very hard on your boat. The rocks in the shallows and along the shore are jagged. On the Lower Missouri, there is rebar among the riprap. In my opinion, if you choose to make the entire trip in a kayak or canoe, don't use a high-end, skinny boat made of exotic materials. This is not a place for a race boat. You need a boat that is stable and rugged, not pretty. So consider a well-designed, roto-molded polyethylene or thermoformed composite boat. And bring a roll of high-quality duct tape and a couple of tubes of hand-moldable marine epoxy putty sticks.

Boat Color

Most kayaks are brightly colored, making their low profile more visible for obvious safety reasons. But this can create an issue. Often it is necessary to leave the boat near the shore when your campsite is on higher ground. The boat remains relatively full of gear; only a deck bag is removed and perhaps one compartment is opened for gear and provisions to set up camp. So the boat sits along the shore, highly visible. It may attract unwanted attention. In most instances, this is not a problem; however, there will be times when it is advisable to be in "stealth" mode. Near towns and on some reservation lands, you might not want to attract attention to yourself. Sometimes it is possible to pull your craft into the weeds or bushes for concealment. However, where vegetation is sparse, a brightly colored boat does nothing to make your presence less apparent. I chose a gray-white colored kayak. From a distance, when I have pulled on shore, my boat looks like the sun-bleached trunk of a tree. Finally, if your boat is not in sight of your camp, lock it to a tree.

A DAY ON THE RIVER: WORKING OUT A SYSTEM

On long journeys, it can take us a couple of weeks to become completely submerged, to relinquish the clutter and adjust to living each day as an open slate. It is a time of decompression, of body break-in, or reorienting out ebb and flow to the wind, waves, and tides. It is a time to remember or to develop systems.

JILL FREDSTON, *ROWING TO LATITUDE*

What follows is intended to help the reader better understand, step-by-step, what a day on a long river passage might be like. Obviously every paddler will develop their own routine, but the basic tasks are the same, whether you are solo or in a group. The important thing is to work out a functional sequence to the tasks. You need to make and then break camp efficiently. You want to establish a secure camp, you don't want to forget anything when you leave, and you don't want to make additional work for yourself. And you want to erase all evidence of your passage. So you need to think about the tasks and how you will handle them. Although I refined my system over the course of three summers, by the second or third week my routine was pretty well set.

By that time, I was able to make or break camp within about 15 minutes.

Morning

The morning's basic tasks pretty much remain the same: evaluate the weather and water conditions, eat and drink, fill water bottles, review maps, and make a tentative plan. If the day is a go, break camp, load gear, and push off.

Whenever possible, I orient my camp so that the early morning sun will light and dry my tent. I can generally do this since, in most areas, prevailing winds are from the northwest. The first rays of sunlight serve as my alarm clock; if the sky is overcast and the wind is blowing, I typically extend my sack time, hoping that conditions might improve in another hour or so. When it seems about time to get up, I turn on my small portable weather radio in an attempt to get the forecast. On the big reservoirs, reception is poor or nonexistent. With or without the NOAA weather forecast, I crawl out of my sleeping bag, do a quick check for ticks, pull on a pair of pants, and put my sandals on. Ready to go outside, I unzip the tent door, exit, and zip the door shut to keep the bugs out. At this point I typically look out at the water and sky, and try to gauge conditions for the day ahead. If a bluff or rise is nearby, I might climb it to see if I can get a better view of any approaching weather and the general lay of the land. I might also try the weather radio at the higher elevation to see if I can get better reception.

Upon my return to the tent, I crawl back in, remove my sandals, again make a quick check for ticks, and gather my breakfast gear. If I need to make a quick start to take advantage of an early morning calm, I eat two breakfast bars and make instant coffee using hot water from my thermos. If there is no need to hurry, I fill a pot with water from my folding bucket, light my backpacker's stove, and put the water on to boil. While the water is heating, I assemble my water filter and pump water through the unit to fill my three water bottles. Next, I mix powdered sports drink in my two 1.5-liter bottles–I will drink these during the day. I fill the third bottle, drink as much as I can, and then pump more water into it to top it off. My goal is to be completely hydrated. This bottle will go into the small "day-hatch" behind my seat, and I will use this water when I prepare the evening's dinner.

When I finish my coffee, I splash some boiled water into the cup to rinse it out, then I mix up some instant oatmeal in the mug. I usually add some raisins or dried apple chunks to vary the fare. I eat this, then splash more hot water into the mug to clean it out. The idea is to minimize cleanup chores. When breakfast is complete, I begin to pack my camp. I stuff my sleeping bag into its dry sack, and deflate and roll up the sleeping pad. Next, I put the cooled-down cookstove and pot away. Before I seal the food sack, I pull out a handful of breakfast bars and a package of instant soup or an envelope of tuna fish for lunch. I also look over the choices of freeze-dried dinners and put one at the top of the food bag for dinner that night. I typically carry about three or four day's provisions in a transparent dry bag that I store between my legs in the kayak's cockpit.

Before the tent can come down, I stuff the sleeping bag, cook gear, toiletries, and clothes into the rear deck bag, a waterproof Boundary Bag with backpack straps. I place this and the remaining items (a couple of dry boxes containing electronic equipment, a bag containing my maps and journal, trash bag, closed cell pad, and my weather gear sack) outside the door of the tent. Sandals go on, and I exit the tent and take it down. The tent, ground cloth, rolled sleeping pad, and a lightweight fleece sleeping bag liner go into the smaller front deck bag. I carry this deck bag, still unsealed, and the dry boxes to the kayak.

My design is to have accessible everything that I need to quickly pitch camp at the end of the day. Between the two deck bags and the food bag in the cockpit, I can set up quickly. I do not have to rummage below deck for anything additional. One bag contains my tent and sleeping pad, flattened to lie politely on the forward deck. This one deck bag should be adequate for most paddlers.

Having two deck bags is an issue. The second bag further raises the boat's center of gravity and increases the profile to the wind. The extra bag also makes it harder to roll back upright in the event of an accident. I carried the second deck bag because of the space taken by the tracking system battery pack that I stored below my kayak's rear hatch. Few paddlers will carry a tracking system like my Cloudberry unit. No doubt tracking/satellite uplink systems of the future will be considerably smaller and lighter, so the contents of my second bag–sleeping bag, stove and cook kit, underwear and T-shirt, parka, and personal essentials kit–should then fit under the rear hatch.

I return to the camp, set out a package of moist hand towels and my pack shovel for my latrine effort, and truck the rest of my gear to the kayak. I make a final trip back to my campsite, police the area, dig a cat hole nearby, and go to the bathroom. I clean up with the hand-wipes and make sure all evidence is adequately buried. Then I inspect the tent site one last time to make sure that I have removed all signs of my occupation.

Back at my kayak, I put the shovel and trash bag into the smaller deck bag, and I lay on it to force the air out. When it is flattened, I seal it up and secure it to the forward deck area. I lay the foam pad in the cockpit. Then I put the provision dry bag in, against the transom and between the rudder pedals. Finally I secure the aft deck bag. At this point, I clip my map case to the front cockpit area and set my GPS unit up for the next leg of the trip, securing it with a clip to the deck. I put on my dry top if necessary, slip into my spray skirt, and change to my paddling shoes. I place my sandals under the rear bag straps. Ready to go, I look behind to make sure that I've left nothing behind, untie my kayak and pull it into launching position, climb in, attach the spray skirt, and push off.

The Day's Paddle

The on-the-water routine consists of paddling; on the reservoirs you get nowhere unless you paddle. Pacing yourself, keeping your energy level up, and staying hydrated are tasks that must be attended to.

My routine for morning paddling typically has me paddling until about midday. Early in the trip, I was only able to go no more than two hours without stopping and getting out of the boat. After a couple weeks I was able to paddle for three or four hours at a stretch. Besides keeping pointed in the right direction, nothing is more important than keeping hydrated. I make it a point to drink frequently. If conditions are moderate, I keep my drink mix bottle on the spray skirt in front of me; at any point when I pause my paddling, I drink. A hydration pack may work for some, not for me. As far as I am concerned, this is just a piece of trendy gear. It's better to have a bottle in front to serve as a reminder to drink and to let you know exactly how you are progressing in the effort to keep hydrated.

As I write this, I am thinking that I may be sounding like the kayaker curmudgeon. But the need to stay hydrated is absolutely critical. Much of the area that you will be paddling through is extremely dry and frequently in drought. By midday, the sun is burning hot. If you wait until you are thirsty to drink, you have screwed up. Your thinking can quickly get fuzzy when you are dehydrated. You need your wits about you to read the river, understand your options, and make good decisions. To remind myself to stay hydrated, I have come up with the "drink what you pee" rule. This works very well, but when I stated the rule to a reporter in Mobridge, South Dakota, I got a funny look. I then realized that I needed to explain that the rule actually refers to drinking enough water to replace the volume that you pee. In practice, I always try to drink a bit more. Along this line, keep in mind that if your pee is yellow, you are probably not drinking enough water.

Of course, because I am drinking frequently, the need to pee arises. Rather than making for shore, I pee into a collapsible plastic canteen that I carry for this purpose. With a bit of practice, I learned to accomplish this without a misfire. The technique has the additional advantage of being discreet–everything is done under the spray skirt. The alternative, at least the only other one that I am good with, is to make for shore. Since appropriate landing sites are sometimes farther than your bladder thinks reasonable, the bag option is the most attractive. The issue for women involves a different geometry. Some kayak guidebooks suggest women take along an external catheter. While I have no acquaintance with this hardware and its technique, I know it is possible to lift oneself a bit off the seat, so it seems reasonable to assume that women can get the required angle. In any event, deciding how you are going to handle this issue is important–if you are going to make distance, you have to paddle for long stretches without making frequent stops.

By midday, I begin to look for a landing place with shade for lunch. By now I am hungry, even though I've probably eaten one or two breakfast bars to keep my energy level up. My first water bottle is nearly empty. I look for a landing site on the downstream side of a point. Usually, by paddling around the point, I am able to find a suitable place to beach my kayak. Ideally this will be a sandy area with some shade, which is critical by midsummer. When I pull in, the first thing that I do is drag the boat above the waterline, if possible. In any event, I securely tie the boat to a tree, a branch, or a stake that I have driven into the shore.

When you are in a remote area of the river, you can get a bit paranoid about the security of your boat. This is not a bad thing; large trees do occasionally float by, and one could easily snag your boat. Also, water levels can rise suddenly as increased flow is released from power stations at dams. For example, when I stayed at Cross Ranch State Park, downstream from Garrison Dam, I observed the river rise and fall more than 2 feet in a matter of hours. Some islands in the center of the river were completely submerged. When you stop for anything more than a quick lunch, pull your boat completely out of the water. And always tie up your boat.

With my boat secure, I finish my remaining sports drink. I remove my provision bag, the second water bottle, my thermos, and the pad from the cockpit. If it is cold or wet, I keep the spray skirt on for warmth. I pull the cockpit cover out and attach it to my boat. This discourages unwanted guests–bugs and snakes. Carrying my gear, and stepping carefully, I make my way to whatever shade is available. If there is a log, I'll put my pad on that to serve as a chair. From the provision bag, I'll remove a packet of instant soup and prepare it in my mug using hot water from the thermos. On a cold day, if the paddling is not going easy, I might fix a double batch of soup or oatmeal. Either meal is quick, nourishing, and a good stick-to-the-ribs energy source. After I eat, I lay the pad on the ground and try to nap for a while. Regardless of how I am feeling, I will rest at least one hour, unless the weather looks like it might turn worse. When I am ready to go, I stow my gear, put a couple snack bars in my life vest pocket, and shove off.

Finding a Campsite

A good campsite is level, sheltered, and has shade when you need it. You can see your beached boat from the entrance of your tent. Don't expect to find many really good campsites.

At some point during your trip, when you are resting on shore, the weather will certainly get nasty. So a good rule to follow is to select a resting site where you can camp if necessary. Summer storms bring high winds and possibly damaging hail. So being near a clump of young trees, against or alongside some feature in the lee of the prevailing wind, or near some decent shelter is important. When you are evaluating a place to pull in, look it over with the thought that the weather could turn bad and that you may need to camp there. Always ask yourself, "Is this site appropriate?"

Unless you are intending to stay at a particular campground, it is a good idea to start looking for a campsite in the late afternoon. You might consider adopting my four o'clock rule: take the first decent-looking campsite that you find. On more than one occasion, I felt like kicking myself repeatedly for ignoring this rule. One late afternoon after I had navigated through the marshes south of Williston, North Dakota, I passed by a couple of adequate campsites. I assumed that there would be another around the next bend. No luck. No campsite, only miles of shoreline consisting of mudflats and flooded woods. I had to paddle several more miles than I should have. I slowly threaded my way along a channel through a very complicated maze of mudflats. Finally at dusk I found a marginal campsite. Fortunately the weather was clear that night.

Making Camp

On landing at a site that looks good for the night's camp, I first secure my boat. Then I pick up a long stick and carefully scout the area. Keeping an eye out for snakes, I look for a level, sheltered site with good drainage. Even in the late afternoon the sun is quite hot, so some shade is a consideration. But being among trees–frequently cottonwoods–has a downside. I examine the trees for "widow-maker" snags or overhanging branches that might break away during a windstorm. I won't place my tent too close to any of these.

I also look for evidence of cattle. One lesson that I learned is not to assume they are all cows. Bulls are frequently in the herd. One morning I spent an extra hour and a half waiting for a rather agitated bull to decide that my tent was not going to move. He stamped his hooves, tossed dirt, and generally sounded as if he might charge my tent. I stayed inside, silent. Eventually he wandered off.

If I am satisfied that the area is an acceptable campsite, I return to my kayak, remove the forward deck bag, and truck it to the tent site that I have selected. I police the site, removing stones and twigs to clear an area for my ground cloth. Then I pitch my tent, oriented so that the rear of the tent is facing the direction of the area's normal storm track. Regardless of how good the weather looks, I put out storm lines–6-foot-long, 0.25-inch nylon lines attached to the corners of my tent's storm fly. I stake these well, or tie the lines to nearby trees. On numerous occasions during my passage, I was awakened in the middle of the night by an unexpected and bad thunderstorm. The high winds that accompanied the storms made me glad that I had secured my tent with the extra lines.

With the tent up, I return to the kayak and haul it safely up the beach. In some instances, because of the low water level, I will have to drag the boat 20 to 30 yards. If sticks or tree limbs are available, I use these as rollers to make the task easier. When I am satisfied that the kayak is far enough from the waterline, I drive a stake into the ground ahead of the boat and tie the bowline to it. I remove the second deck bag, my map case, and GPS hard case. Next, I set a waypoint for the campsite. I then remove the remaining things that I will need from the cockpit. This includes the provision bag kept by my feet, the half-length sleeping pad, two small dry boxes, bug repellent, and the collapsible water bucket. I put the smaller items in the bucket and carry it all to the tent.

On my final trip to the kayak, I put my life vest and spray skirt in the cockpit, change my paddling booties for nylon sandals, and attach the cockpit cover to prevent snakes, spiders, and other creatures from crawling into the cockpit.

If it seems prudent, I pull a bit of vegetation and driftwood over my boat to make it appear less obvious and then take my paddle with me to the tent.

Returning to camp, I place my gear inside the tent, set up the sleeping pads, and stretch out my sleeping bag. I take out my cooking equipment, set up my kitchen outside the front door of the tent, and heat a pot of water for a freeze-dried meal. While I wait for the water to boil, I pull out my maps and journal to begin making my notes for the day. When the water boils, I mix the night's fare, set it aside to inflate, and set a second pot of water on the stove. I will use this water to make tea, to fill the thermos, and for general cleanup. After I finish my meal, I clean my food pot and spoon and pour boiling water over them to sanitize them.

The last chore is to fill the water bucket. I carry it to the shore, wade out to clear water, and fill it three-quarters full. I take this back to the tent and set it inside the vestibule. Much of the suspended sediment in the water will settle out overnight. I will use the filter pump to make drinking water in the morning. If the bugs are not bad, I might sit by the shore for a while. But I hit the sack by dark, and quickly fall asleep.

STARTING AND STOPPING: ESTABLISHING A SCHEDULE

Once a journey is designed, equipped, and put in process, a new factor enters and takes over. A trip, safari, an exploration, is an entity, different from all other journeys. It has personality, temperament, individuality, uniqueness. A journey is a person in itself; no two are alike. And all plans, safeguards, policing, and coercion are fruitless. We find after years of struggle that we do not take a trip; a trip takes us.

John Steinbeck, *Travels with Charley*

Steinbeck knew what he was talking about. I suggest that you think carefully about the kind of experience you are seeking before considering a long-distance paddle on the river. Trying to meet some daily distance objective on the Missouri will result in a good dose of pain, accompanied by great frustration.

My best advice has three elements: First, plan to stop when you need to rest. This is not a race. I am reminded of one of the best pieces of advice that my dissertation advisor gave me when I was preparing to drive my VW camper van to

Mexico for a year of fieldwork along the Mexican Caribbean. He told me, "There are three rules for survival when driving in Mexico: Never race a bus; never race a bus; and never race a bus." This river, like some Mexican bus drivers, can be totally unforgiving. Safe navigation of the Missouri River requires good judgment based on careful observation. If you allow yourself to become exhausted and/or dehydrated when you are on the river, your thinking gets fuzzy, you begin to miss things, and you make mistakes. At some point the cumulative effect of your errors will reach something like a tipping point that, when exceeded, can result in a serious lessening of your chances for survival.

Second, stop well before conditions deteriorate. In Montana and the Dakotas, high winds seem to come out of nowhere, and the wind can change direction fast. You learn to paddle with one eye on the sky–front, side, and back. Because you are in the "bottoms," high banks and vegetation often obscure your view, effectively cloaking weather changes. Often the first sign of an approaching storm will be the rumble of thunder. You'll ask yourself, "Where did that come from?" It is always a good idea to be constantly evaluating the shoreline ahead for suitability as a place to pull off and seek shelter. You do not want to be offshore on a reservoir or at midriver with bluffs on both sides in a violently fast wind or in a hail-laced thunderstorm.

Third, start when conditions are appropriate. Joe Glickman's account of his nine-day ordeal in crossing Lake Oahe underscores this wisdom:

I had made my passage on the lake into a contest, as if the wind were somehow against me, when in fact it was doing what wind in the Dakotas often does; blowing like hell for days or weeks at a time. The only way to maintain a positive attitude, I realized later, was to allow the wind and waves to define my path. So what if I wanted to log 30 to 40 miles a day? If the wind said, "No," that meant don't go. That's an important truth. Often, Mother Nature sets your course. Being flexible and respecting the forces of nature is a real life skill to master (The Kayak Companion).

On the large reservoirs, there will be many mornings when whitecaps are blowing before dawn. Settle back and read a book. Do maintenance, clip your toenails, and then go for a hike. The injunction to "start when conditions are appropriate" also applies to pushing off on both the "wild" stretches of the Upper Missouri River and the channelized sections of the Lower Missouri. If you round a bend and expose yourself to a 30- to 40-mph headwind, you will soon be blown backwards no matter how hard you paddle.

Finally, unless you allow the "trip to take you,"–Steinbeck's wisdom–the Missouri River will hammer on you. To make a safe passage, you must accept what the river presents. If you paddle yourself into exhaustion, you put yourself at risk. And when you do make it to shore, you are too beat-up to feel, see, and think clearly about the cost of your progress, and about the beauty underfoot.

GPS-BASED NAVIGATION

The importance of the magnetic compass cannot be overestimated. Today, seven hundred years after the emergence of the compass with a compass card indicating directions, and a millennium or longer since the invention of the simpler needle compass, every ship carries a magnetic compass at least as a backup for its electronic instruments.

AMIR D. ACZEL, *THE RIDDLE OF THE COMPASS*

I began my summer 2002 trip with two moderately expensive, handheld GPS devices. These were Garmin's Emap™ model, which cost about $300 each at the time. For the next two summers I used Garmin's eTrex Legend model, which cost less than $200. This unit has a larger memory aid, is relatively waterproof, and can be com-port linked to a computer and uploaded with relatively detailed base maps. Saved waypoints (latitude and longitude position coordinates) and tracks can be downloaded to a computer and positioned on base maps generated by Garmin's relatively inexpensive MapSource™ software. I purchased the "Roads and Recreation" CD, which provided relatively detailed lake shoreline, park, and boat ramp information. I kept my GPS unit in a dry case with a clear plastic top on the deck of my kayak. The spare unit was held in reserve, along with a good supply of AA batteries, below deck in a dry box.

During my first two summers, because I was traveling solo through remote areas, I also carried a GPS-based tracking system provided by the Air-Trak Corporation (www.air-trak.com). This tracking system ("Cloudberry DualTrak+ Mobile Hardware and Software") provided automatic hourly tracking of my boat and a satellite uplink for two-way messaging. A support team at Air-Trak in San Diego provided me with a TDS Ranger Model handheld computer. I mounted the GPS receiver/satellite transceiver, about the size of half a volleyball, on the kayak's front hatch. A dozen prototype batteries in a watertight dry case powered the unit.

Author with kayak, showing satellite uplink unit mounted on forward hatch, Ranger handheld computer, and Tadiran battery power pack in opened dry case. Photo taken by Don Hatfield, USACE park ranger at Beaver Creek Campground, North Dakota.

GPS Navigation: Why or Why Not?

Why use a GPS? With a relatively inexpensive unit that can show your position over a base map, it is relatively easy to establish your position on a map, air photo, or satellite image. On the Dammed Upper's big reservoir lakes, many bays are so large that they could be easily confused as the correct way up or down the lake. Also, because the shoreline at low water levels can present a much different picture than what you see on the map, a GPS unit set to track and display your progress can provide confirmation that you are indeed on the right course. After I had successfully crossed Montana's Fort Peck Lake during my first year of paddling, I heard a story about another paddler who had paddled several hours up the Musselshell River instead of turning east around the UL Bend. Does this sound like an absolutely boneheaded mistake? Perhaps, but having paddled through that area I can understand how someone with an inadequate map might make such an error. A GPS unit would also be helpful whenever the way is obscured by fog, or smoke from a prairie or forest fire. Lastly, in an emergency, if you are able to connect to a cell service, you can accurately describe your location to rescuers.

Why not use a GPS? In an emergency, knowing your GPS latitude and longitude coordinates is of little value if there is no way to communicate your position fix to rescuers. On much of the Upper Missouri, cell phone coverage is nonexistent; coverage is also spotty along much of the Lower Missouri.

There is also something to be said in favor of just not knowing your location with precision. It may be that without a GPS you pay closer attention to the landscape, map, and compass–and closer attention to the river. On the river your primary task is to read the river to follow the channel and avoid shallows and obstructions. The current, waves, and eddies will guide you if you know how to "read" them. You cannot see any of this on the GPS screen. You cannot deduce any of this from latitude and longitude coordinates.

My own bottom line is that this is a well-tested technology, not a trendy device for gearheads. There are sections of the Missouri River, particularly on the larger reservoirs, where a mistake in dead reckoning might get you dead. Also, you can use a GPS to help you learn to judge distance better and to help you make course corrections when wind and waves push you off track or require you to change your heading. You can also use a GPS to measure your actual moving speed and estimate the strength of the current; this information can help establish where you should position yourself when paddling against a stiff headwind. Finally, if you have the coordinates for a poorly marked boat ramp or a channel in a willow thicket or purple loosestrife marsh, you can use the GPS "find" function to locate the feature.

Navigation with the handheld Garmin GPS unit was relatively straightforward. Prior to setting out, I uploaded both units with base maps from the "Roads and Recreation" MapSource CD. Each GPS unit has an 8-megabyte memory module, sufficient for holding river corridor base map coverage for about half the trip. I loaded my "deck" GPS with maps from Fort Benton to Pierre, South Dakota. For extra security, I purchased a 16-megabyte module and uploaded the entire set of river base maps–all the county maps along the river from Fort Benton to St. Louis–on my backup machine. In addition, using the MapSource software on my home computer, I printed out 1 inch = 2 miles scale (approximately 1:126,720) sheets of the route from James Kipp Recreation Area to Pierre, South Dakota. I did not print out sheets for the distance between Fort Benton and Kipp (the Upper Missouri National Wild and Scenic River section) since a very good set of waterproof maps of the river is available from the Bureau of Land Management.

I also downloaded to my home computer Landsat satellite images of the area that I would be paddling. These, and a link to download a trial version of GeoExpress View software, can be obtained from the University of Montana's Lewis and Clark Education Center (www.lewisandclarkeducationcenter.com). I examined these images for information that might be useful. In particular, I was concerned about the west ends of the big reservoirs, where the river current slows and sediment is deposited. Examination of the imagery revealed a braided stream pattern–in effect a maze of interwoven channels–in these areas. I zoomed in on these images and printed copies to have on deck when I worked my way through these sections.

Although these satellite images were nearly a decade old, most of the main channels shown were still present when I paddled through the area in the summer of 2002. Thus the imagery was an invaluable aid to my successful navigation through the west ends of Fort Peck Lake and Sakakawea Lake. I did discover, however, that considerable additional sedimentation appears to have accumulated since these images were taken. For example, at the Musselshell River and UL Bend area of Fort Peck Lake, during low water level when I worked my way through, I could find no channel. The area appeared almost completely silted in. I managed to get through by paddling and knuckle-sliding my kayak through mere inches of water on the top of mudflats. Maybe there was a channel in there somewhere, but at the time I made my way through, a stiff wind from the northwest was pushing the water to the southeast, in effect draining the area. This further complicated the situation and made for a very difficult and muddy passage around the bend.

Using the Latitude and Longitude Coordinates with Your GPS

I have elected to provide location coordinates in decimal degree format. Over the years I have trained many students to navigate with GPS; I have observed that latitude/longitude data in this format has proved easiest to use from the standpoint of entering data into handheld units. Coordinates in the more familiar Degrees/Minutes/Seconds (DMS) format are converted to decimal degrees by: (1) dividing Seconds by 60 and adding the result to Minutes to create "decimal minutes"; (2) dividing "decimal minutes" by 60 and adding the result to Degrees to create decimal degrees (DD). Latitude and longitude converters are available on-line. You can see an example at either www.directionsmag.com/lat long.php or www.fcc.gov/mb/audio/bickel/DDDMMSS-decimal.html.

For purposes of navigation, DD coordinates provided in this guide can be keyed into moderately priced handheld GPS units such as the Garmin Legend. This unit is a personal favorite; it is rugged, waterproof, "moderately priced" (less than $180), and has WAAS capability, an accuracy enhancing feature. This model comes with a base map; additional and more detailed base maps can be uploaded to the unit via a data cable connected to a computer. I have found the more detailed (~ 1:100,000) digital topographic maps on Garmin's United States TOPO CD (~ $120) to be useful. All coordinates in this guide are north latitude and west longitude. For example, Montana's Fort Benton "Floater's Camp Launch" has the DD coordinate 47.80481/-110.67950; this means N 47.80481 and W 110.67950. You will need to make sure that your GPS is set up to display "units" as hddd.ddddd, the DD (decimal degree) format; the default on most units is DMS.

Two manuals that provide good background on using GPS units in the field can be downloaded from the Garmin website (www.garmin.com/aboutGPS.manual.html): "GPS Guide for Beginners" and "Using a Garmin GPS with Paper Maps." I recommend that you look at these sources. The process of entering a coordinate into a GPS unit is termed "creating a waypoint," and the steps involved are covered in the owner's manual. Once you have created a waypoint, it will display on the base map. This is useful because your GPS will show your current position and the location of nearby waypoints. Given this information, you can literally view your progress as you near a ramp or other feature that you are trying to locate. You can also query the unit to identify the nearest waypoints, and set it to maintain an on-screen pointer that indicates the course that you need to maintain to get to a selected waypoint.

A final feature deserves mention. Most GPS units have the ability to record what are known as "track logs." In essence, the unit keeps a record of your progress as a line constructed from "digital breadcrumbs." You turn this feature on when you start out and then turn it off when you stop moving at the end of the day. Your progress is stored, can be displayed on the unit's base map, or can be uploaded to a computer to be displayed on maps produced by Garmin's TOPO software or Delorme's popular TOPO USA mapping software. This feature also calculates your total distance and average moving speed. You may want to record this information in your trip journal. Or, maybe not. These numbers are just numbers; they tell you nothing about whether or not you had a good day, what you saw or thought about, or what you learned. All this technology has its place; keep it there.

READING THE RIVER

Piloting proved to be more art than science. It was taught by word of mouth and reinforced by hands-on training. A pilot would tell his cub that the only book to read was the river itself. "Reading" the river meant the ability to discern the water's depth by careful observation of the motion and appearance of the river's surface. The clues were subtle and easily misread by an inexperienced pilot.

GILLESPIE, *WILD RIVER, WOODEN BOATS*

Experienced paddlers know that going downstream with the current is not as easy as it sounds. Around sharp bends and when upstream dams are releasing water, you can find yourself pulled along in a 5- to 10-mph current. Paradoxically, although you gain speed when you run with the current, where it pulls you along fast you will frequently need to paddle to increase speed to maintain control of your boat. Where this occurs, you have less time to read the river to follow the best line to deeper water. And less time to avoid hazards.

From riverboat pilot lore we can gain some wisdom about electing the best course. What follows draws on Gillespie's useful summary. Water is often deepest where waves are higher when the wind is coming from upstream. When the wind is coming from downstream, high waves mean shallow water. The upstream side of an island, reef, or shoal generally inclines gradually to the surface, while a steep drop-off is usually present on the downstream side. Shallow water extends only a short way out from the end of a point, but the "rainbow reef" is an exception to this rule:

...[the rainbow reef] derived its name from the long arc that it formed as it extended all the way across the river. There was always a "break" in the reef–something akin to a miniature mountain pass–through which a boat could pass without striking the reef. The difficulty was in finding the break.... (Gillespie, *Wild River, Wooden Boats)*

Where the river channel crosses over to the other side of the river, you need to be alert for "slick, flat looking places on the water" and "rolling, boiling" areas. The former means a sandbar or mudflat just below, and the latter a bar being carved away by a shifted current or the location of a submerged snag.

You need to be able to see the river in order to read it. Steamboat pilots were perched in a pilothouse some 60 feet above the water. They had a much better view of the river than you will in your smaller craft. But even with their better vista, pilots did not often venture forward when they could not read the water:

The Missouri River so frequently changed its course that the pilot could not rely on memory alone—he had to see the water, clearly. For this reason steamboats seldom ran the river at night except in a very bright phase of the moon. It was considered unwise to run during a rainstorm, for the rippling pattern of the raindrops camouflaged all the signs on the surface. Nor would a boat run in the fog (Gillespie, *Wild River, Wooden Boats)*.

Of course, a kayak or a canoe has very little draft relative to that of a steamboat. So, often you can coast over shallows that would stop larger craft dead in the water. Still, you must proceed with caution. You don't want to take an unplanned bath, lose or damage gear, or become pinned against a snag. Common sense suggests that you postpone starting out until you have good visibility, and that you retire from the river before you can no longer read the signs.

PADDLING ISSUES AND TECHNIQUES ON THE UPPER UPPER MISSOURI

The narrow canyons of the river can hide the approach of storms until the last minute. Watch the weather both in front of and behind you. Sudden, violent thunderstorms can whip the river's surface into dangerous whitecaps. Get off the water and take cover when you see a storm approaching.

BLM LEWISTOWN FIELD OFFICE'S RIVER SAFETY WEB PAGE (WWW.MT.BLM.GOV/LDO/FBTRIP.HTML)

Dealing with the Wind

When the wind is blowing, getting around a long river bend can be a problem. The trick is to get on the side of the river that shelters you from the wind. For the most part it's easy to know where you should be. Getting there, however, is the issue. Wind direction, changes in the aspect of the river, and the location of the main channel are variables that need to be taken into account. It's a rather complex calculus that determines just how much effort you will need to expend at any given moment.

When the wind is blowing and you are on a winding stretch of river, take time to study the map before starting out. Consider wind direction and note the changes in aspect of the river. Reflect on what you see. You should be able to predict where paddling will be the most difficult. Winding stretches will be less difficult if you keep yourself positioned to take maximum advantage of the current. If you can stay in the current and on the sheltered side of the river as much as possible, a moderate in-the-face wind will not rob you of much more than the current's assist.

Sharp Bends, Snags, and Caution

When coming around sharp bends on the river, it is often a good strategy to stay on the inside and then to swing wide. Downstream of the point, on the outside of the bend, you can expect to find the channel and fast water. Where the landscape creates a pinch, you can expect a short section of modest rapids. So come around points with caution. Watch for snags; you may only have a few seconds to locate the channel. As a general rule, you'll be best off if you swing wide to the outside bend of the river. This may help you to avoid possible snags, rocks, and shallows.

Another general rule is to not get too close to steep banks. These banks are unstable and prone to collapse where they are being undercut by the river. When part of a bank cuts loose, tons of material drop into the water. This creates the danger of a large wave. Also, trees fall as the bank holding them gives way. Snag piles, known to pilots as "embarras," develop as fallen trees capture other debris, and extensive snag fields are created. These often have hidden underwater extensions that may not always show a telltale swirl in a very rapid surface current. Snag fields are the paddler's equivalent of a mine field, and should be navigated with caution.

If water levels have been low for some time, the main current may meander and be hard to track. More than once the channel that I was following petered out, and I was forced to work my way across a sand- or mudflat to the other side of the river, bumping along the bottom, in my effort to regain a deeper channel. When you can find it, look for the freshest cut along a sand bank and work in toward it. Here you will find deeper water and more current.

When in doubt, pick the freshest looking cut bank to follow the channel. Sometimes old channels present, and things become confusing. Look at your imagery or map. Always be conservative. A way may appear to be a shortcut; most often it is not. Go with the main stream of current if you can find it. Look for the most disturbed, freshest cut on a bank or along the side of an island. Generally you will have the best luck finding the channel if you do not gamble. Where the river widens out, or backs up before going around some pinch or turn, it is easy to lose the main channel. There may be, in fact, a number of major channels. When you have followed the river for a while, you'll get a better feel for this. But remember: when in doubt, be conservative. If you can stop, do so. Get out and scout. If this is not possible–if the banks are too steep, or the shore is too muddy–try back-paddling for a few minutes to hold your position; give yourself a bit more time to examine what the river presents.

More often than you would imagine possible, you will get yourself into shallow water. Hopefully this will occur on sandy bottom. You can generally push, knuckle, or bounce yourself over shallow, sandy areas. This is not the case when you hang up on a mud bar. If you run aground, you may have a very strenuous time getting back to deeper water. First, keep your craft from being turned in the current; in other words, keep yourself aligned parallel with the current. Try to locate the best course to deeper water. If you are coming to a dead end, your efforts may scare some large carp. They are probably being trapped like you. If you watch their escape route, you can sometimes better determine the best line to deeper water.

Extracting yourself from a mudflat slew can be a real workout. In late July, upstream from North Dakota's Beaver Creek Campground, I thought I saw a good shortcut through a mudflat and tried to take it. It looked like it would save me a mile or so of paddling around a big arc that the river made to the east. As I entered the channel, I remember thinking, "Hmmm, maybe I shouldn't do this." Attempting to take this shortcut turned out to be a real mistake. Although a current was running through the flat, and there was some recent evidence of "bank cutting," it soon became apparent that the water level had also recently gone down. It turned out that there was not enough water to allow me to float through. I knew I was in trouble when I started seeing numerous carp wallowing in the shallows. The channel braided out; I picked the best flow of water that I could find, but soon I was brushing along the muddy bottom. I startled the carp, and shortly they became so thick and the channel so narrow that I ran over some of them. It appeared that they were in the process of being trapped by the receding water. I bumped along the bottom, carp darting around me, their bronze backs zigzagging back and forth. I managed to keep my kayak in the deepest area and knuckled along in an inch or two of water.

Eventually, I found a shore that looked as if it might be firm enough to stand on. I got out of my kayak and pulled it along to the shore by walking on my knees. In effect, I used my lower legs as snowshoes–holding on to the bow of the kayak to keep from sinking in too deeply–to work my way to an area covered with short grass that was firm enough to walk on. I lined my boat just offshore for some 50 yards, slogging through ankle-deep muck. Ultimately I found deeper water, and I was able to get back in the boat and resume paddling.

After nearly two months on the river, this was a mistake that I should not have made. The message here is that there are no shortcuts to the main channel. The main channel is the shortest route to getting downstream. Do not gamble on the possibility of finding a quicker way through. Locate the main channel; follow it. Don't get cute and try to outguess the river. When you are faced with a choice or when the main channel location is uncertain, slow yourself down to buy time to examine the clues. Look for evidence of the most recent cutting of the current. If you see shallow weeds and snags in the shallows or fresh grass growing along a shallow shoreline, then odds are that is not the way. If an island presents, look for the channel along the side with the steepest cut bank, even if it is only a few inches high. In large, open areas where the river widens out, it is not uncommon for the channel to braid around a series of flats and low, willow-infested islands. These are challenging sections, where the clues to best passage must be studied carefully.

Although wing dams are commonly found after North Dakota's Garrison Dam, there are a handful on the Upper Upper. There is no real trick to getting along with these features–simply remember that the riprap or junked autos probably extend farther out in the direction that they point, and that there will be a swirling countercurrent on the downstream side. Backeddies, or "sucks"–inshore back currents resembling slowly rotating whirlpools–are often present. Large ones should be given berth. If you find yourself heading into a whirlpool, you need to paddle to pick up speed to get across it.

Backeddies are also found around areas of snags and where the river is cutting deeply into a riverbank. Often, in areas of steep–8 to 10 feet high–banks, irregular blocks or sections of bank are washed away where the river is most actively carving at the shore. Sometimes large indentations are made, creating very irregular shoreline. Serious countercurrents swirl along these sections, so you need to stay well away from them. If you find yourself in too close, remember that you can maintain better control of the situation by paddling hard to increase your speed.

Partially submerged trees (sawyers) sometimes bob up and down in the river current. Occasionally, these are trapped in back current areas downstream from where a large block of bank has fallen into the river. Fresh slides should be given a wide berth, as should snag-filled areas that frequently occur along the upstream inside bend of a sharp turn in the river. Beavers seem to delight in dropping trees in these areas, and their dens sometimes extend well out into the river. Also, along steep banks where the river is undercutting a grove of cottonwoods, some trees hang perilously over the bank. Sooner or later these trees will tumble into the river. Common sense suggests that paddlers should avoid passing near these potential hazards.

Finally, there are three ferry crossings below Great Falls that must be approached with caution. According to Gil Payne, an experienced Montana paddler, there are good reasons to give ferryboats wide berth:

We recommend that paddlers never make a landing upstream near a ferryboat. It is an annual event to hear of a canoe (I haven't heard of this happening to a kayak) pulling in upstream and drifting against the side of the ferryboat docked at the riverbank. The river current hits the side of the ferry and rolls under it; this can roll a canoe and suck it under the ferry. This usually happens to inexperienced paddlers. We have seen many inexperienced paddlers on this stretch of the Missouri River. I have never heard of any serious injuries resulting, but it is scary. I would guess it is hard to get the occupants back into a canoe to continue the trip after the experience.

PADDLING ISSUES AND TECHNIQUES ON THE LAKES OF THE DAMMED UPPER

When I look at Mr. McCreery's boat, when I imagine the oar blades plunged in the green transparency of a storm-raked sea, the boat cranking off a wave crest, six men straining in drenched motley wool and oilskins, their mouths agape, I know that life is wild, dangerous, beautiful.

BARRY LOPEZ, *ABOUT THIS LIFE*

The large reservoirs behind the Army Corps of Engineers–managed dams present their own suite of issues. The largest lakes–Fort Peck in eastern Montana, Sakakawea in North Dakota, and Oahe, spanning both North and South Dakota–are big water challenges. Wind is the main issue. The wind howls across the plains, and its speed seems to intensify as it rushes across the reservoirs. Sometimes it seems to come out of nowhere. You cannot appreciate what a barrier to paddling the wind can be until you get on one of these lakes. A Dakota headwind can blow so hard that you are driven backward no matter how furiously you paddle. Trying to fight the wind can make you crazy.

A main issue on the lakes deals with changes in aspect as you make your way "downstream." Because these lakes are often more than a mile across, and because of the danger of sudden squalls, it is safest to paddle near the shore.

You follow the shoreline because opportunities are limited to cross over to the opposite shore to gain shelter from a headwind. For very long stretches, and in some instances for the length of the lake, you pick a side of the lake to paddle along and stay on that side. If the lake turns down to the southeast and a southeast wind is blowing, you are pretty much stuck with a headwind until the lake's aspect changes.

According to many locals, the really dangerous blows come from the northwest. These can move in fast, with wind velocities of 60 to 80 mph. When one of these "howlers" comes ripping across the water, you do not want to be at the center of a lake. It is absolutely critical that you regularly monitor NOAA weather reports, when you can get them. However, on the biggest lakes you will find times when you cannot get good reception; of course, you need it most in these circumstances. Where this is the case, you really need to remember to pay regular attention to the sky at your back. Bad weather can run up very fast behind you. The situation is compounded by the fact that there are often hills and bluffs on either side of the lake that obscure your view of the sky. When I was on Fort Peck Lake, there were several times when absolutely nasty-looking, tall, anvil-shaped thunderclouds seemed to pop out of nowhere. Although I had been–or thought that I'd been–watching for weather changes, my first notice of the approaching weather was a long, grumbling roll of thunder that completely surprised me. You get on these lakes and you will have more than one "now where did that come from" experience.

When you are surprised by weather moving in fast, you need to locate a place to pull ashore as quickly as possible . If you are paddling along a rocky shore, you will have limited options. Ideally, you will find a place to pull out where you can also camp. If circumstances permit, look over your map for the closest bay or inlet where you might find shelter from the wind. Consider the distance, estimate the time you have before the storm breaks, cut your estimate in half, and decide whether you can make it to a more promising area. If not, get to shore wherever you can safely. Pull your boat well up the shore, out of the area where storm-generated waves will break. Secure your boat, and grab your sleeping pad and you weather gear if you don't already have it on. Find shelter if there is any, seal yourself up, and hunker down. Thunderstorms are sometimes accompanied by hail; put the pad over your head if you get caught in a hailstorm. You won't be comfortable, but you will survive your "50-yard-line seat" at nature's game to stone you senseless with ice pellets.

Is this starting to sound like a catalog of horrors? There is more, of course. But forewarned is forearmed: I relate these issues because I am convinced that they can be managed by making intelligent choices and acting in a timely manner.

Fast-moving wind associated with frontal activity can drive a cloud of dust and sand into the air, creating a sandstorm. If you see one of these coming at you, get to shore and get behind cover, even if you have to lie beside your boat. Use a handkerchief to cover your mouth and nose so you don't breathe in the debris. Yep, cowboys didn't wear these just as a fashion statement or to rob stagecoaches.

One final note about wind: Wind-driven waves will swell when they pass over submerged features such as points or rocks in shallower water. If there is some wave action, stay a bit farther offshore whenever you cross in front of a point. Very often, it extends for some distance underwater. Where this is the case, you may see waves breaking farther out from the shore. Or as you paddle over a submerged point, you may feel a sudden uplift, like you feel when you crest a hill in a fast-moving car.

Lastly, a word on camping on the Dammed Upper: You can generally find a place to camp on the shore near boat ramps. Many of these are barren, windswept places without facilities except for a vault toilet. Site your camp off to one side, away from the traffic pattern. If you search around, you can usually find a good place that has been used by paddlers before you. At many campgrounds, you will find the choice waterfront sites are allocated to RV campers, and that tent sites are truly second-rate campsites. Occasionally, you will run into a campground manager who is totally inflexible in his insistence that you camp in a "tenter"-designated site. Often these are second-rate, shadeless areas; but at least look over what is being offered. If it's a bad site, make your feelings known to the host and depart–after refilling your water bottles. Many campgrounds have reservation systems that, for a fee, allow campers to book good sites a year in advance. Most campsites are totally booked up, although there are typically a token handful of "drive-up" designated sites. This system fails miserably to satisfy the needs of paddlers, whose pace is determined by the vagaries of weather, wind, and current. Hopefully, the planners will recognize this issue and designate areas near the water with shade for "paddle-up" campers.

PADDLING ISSUES AND TECHNIQUES ON THE CHANNELIZED LOWER MISSOURI

Contrary to popular belief, the Missouri River is not too hazardous for canoeing. The current may be swift (about three miles per hour average), but the river does not have dangerous rapids. An experienced boater finds no problems with barges, buoys, floating debris, and submerged wind dikes frequently encountered on the river. And those boils that look and sound so treacherous from the bank do not have the power to tip or engulf a canoe.

DON PIERCE, *EXPLORING MISSOURI RIVER COUNTRY*

The Channelized Lower Missouri has been engineered for barge traffic; the Army Corps of Engineers (ACE) maintains a channel that is 300 feet wide and 9 feet deep. The river's meanders and its outside bends are typically lined with riprap, and the main channel runs along them. The inside bends are lined with wing dikes that extend nearly perpendicular into the river. These features constrain most of the river's flow between them, maintaining the channel. Many dikes have an "L-head" at their end, which angles downriver. The rock piles making up the end of these dikes run parallel to the channel and can be submerged. These are the most difficult to see. You need to stay in the main channel.

You will find the best current in the main channel. When you come to a long, straight section, the fastest current will be toward the center of the channel. Around river bends, the best current is closer to the outside shore. If you carry a GPS unit, you can set it to display your speed and experiment to see where you get the best "boost" from the current.

When you get on the Channelized Lower, you will see immediately that the main channel's position changes as the river bends back and forth. As a general rule, you will find the channel along the outside of a river bend. The Coast Guard is responsible for the placement and maintenance of aids to navigation (signs, markers, buoys) on the Lower Missouri; if you know how to read the signage, you will know exactly where the main channel is, and you can stay in it. Also, you can avoid barges because the channel markers and crossing beacons tell you the path an approaching barge has to take, and thus where you need to go to get out of their way.

What follows is a synopsis of what you need to know. You will see channel-related signage ("beacons") along the shore that tells you when to cross and when to stay along the shore. Red channel markers are on the left descending shore, green on the right. A crossing beacon is diamond shaped and indicates that you should cross the river, heading for the crossing beacon on the other side. Passing beacons (left bank, a red triangle; right bank, a green square) are at the start and finish of a bend. Stay on the side with the passing beacons until you come to a crossing beacon. After you have followed this signage for a couple bends, you will get the hang of this. The main thing to remember is that you want to swing back and forth with the bends of the river, staying in the main channel along the outside bend. Red buoys mark the left side of the descending channel; green the right side. Stay between the buoys. Understand, however, that buoys are frequently out of position; do not rely on them. Also, give buoys wide berth, as tree limbs and other debris hang up on them. A black buoy marks an obstruction in the channel, so give it extra wide berth.

With respect to towboats and barges, get out of their way. Barges have absolute right-of-way; it can be a mile before they can come to a stop. Move to the inside of a bend if one is approaching. Find shelter if you can, put on your spray skirt, and point your boat toward the oncoming wake. Pilots have a blind spot at the front of their barges. If you have a marine radio, you might hail the boat captain to let him know that you are out front. Towboats monitor channel 13 (also 16, the emergency channel). Tell the captain that you are in a canoe or kayak and give your approximate location by mile mark. Let him know that you are moving to the inside of the bend. If you are uncertain about which side you should be on, ask the captain whether he would like you on the descending bank right or left. Paddle to that side. Often, with this information ahead of time, the tow captain will be able to reduce his power as he passes you. This produces less wake.

The wake generated by barges can be considerable. Towboats don't tow; they push barges upstream or downstream. Towboats pushing barges upstream create the largest wake. The water behind a boat pushing barges can be extremely rough for more than 0.5 mile downstream. If you have pulled over to one side for shelter, it is best to wait for 20 to 30 minutes for the water to calm after the passage of an upstream working towboat with barges. If you are unable to find shelter, you will need to deal with the boat wake, which often generates a very confused "sea." This condition may conceal dikes and other hazards, so do not get too close to shore.

It goes without saying that you should not closely approach the front end of a barge. As one ACE publication states, "The hydraulics generated by barges can suck under objects including smaller craft." What you may also not appreciate is that the same is true for the front ends of moored barges. As Don Pierce cautions in his book, *Exploring Missouri River Country,* "Never approach a moored barge from upstream. Water flowing under such barges creates a tremendous suction. Nothing interesting can be seen under a barge."

There are other issues for paddlers here. The levees that contain and direct the river literally fence off paddlers from long stretches of the river. Attempting to land along a shore lined with riprap and in a fast current is a dicey proposition. It can be done, but I don't recommend that you try. So pull-out opportunities are more often than not on the downstream side of dikes, at remediation sites (where the ACE has modified the levee for fish and wildlife habitat), or at ramps. Boat ramps are good; you can pretty much count on being able to pull out at them. However, many of them function as sediment traps in addition to boat launches. Their lower ends may be clogged with a foot or more of mud. You will probably see a backhoe or loader scraping away at a ramp at least once during your trip. Also, many ramps have a dike just above them to create slack water at the ramp. More often than not you need to swing to the outside, around the dike, and then turn back upstream and paddle to the ramp. You need to read the water carefully as you approach a ramp. High water will conceal rocks and debris just below the surface. Along the downstream side of many ramps, there is an area where you can pull in or pull your boat to one side. This will keep you out of the traffic pattern.

Remediation sites are initially problematic. These areas have been created in response to a court order to create habitat for endangered species and as part of a plan to restore game fish spawning areas. Sections of levee have been "cut" in order to create small bays and backwater areas. In effect, big "bites" have been taken out of the containment walls. This is a work still in progress. ACE has initiated the effort, and the river will ultimately reshape these areas to its own designs. At these sites there can be a great deal of unconsolidated material that is collapsing or washing into the river. Where this is the case, the muddy sediment along the shore is deep. John Skelton, of ACE's Missouri River Area Office at Napoleon (Missouri), told me about a visitor who attempted to walk on the shore at one of the new sites; he sunk into knee-deep mud and had to be helped out. In a more recent communication, John has related that some of these sites are stabilizing, that nice sandbars are forming, and that–at least at low water–there may be suitable campsites.

Pulling out on the shore below a dike requires that you read the water well. Dikes come in different shapes and sizes; most stick out toward the channel and angle downstream. L-Head dikes stick out and have extensions that run parallel to the shore. You will paddle by a series of these L-Head dikes that effectively wall you off from the shore. Occasionally you will see breaks in their line, but often there are rocks just below the surface at these cuts. The upstream ends of many sets of dikes collect debris; stay well away from these areas. Sometimes, after you get by several dikes of a particular set, you will come to a couple with a wider interval between them. Here you can sometimes find an entrance that you can paddle into. The shore may or may not be suitable for a pullout, but if a barge is approaching, these areas might provide you with a safe harbor. When I discussed this with Captain Bill Beacom, a riverboat pilot for more than 30 years, he cautioned that when a towboat with barges passes a wing dam, the boat's props can suck water away from the shallows. If you are too close to the wing dam, you could be pulled onto the rocks. So if you seek shelter inside one of these areas, get close to shore if you can, stay well away from the rocks, and expect to observe some interesting hydraulics.

If you decide to put ashore to wait for the towboat to pass and the water to settle down, you should be able to find a suitable place. Ideally, this will be a sandy shore, but look things over carefully before you get out of the boat. You do not want to step off on a shelf of sand undercut by the river. Captain Beacom cautioned me that several drownings occur every year when overhanging banks collapse underfoot, depositing the unwary into deep and fast-moving water. If the edge of the sandbar is not touching the water, it probably will not support your weight. Keep your lifejacket on when you come ashore.

Another caution: Avoid log jams and do not paddle too close to bridge piers. As Bryan Hopkins, an experienced paddler and an environmental education specialist for the Missouri Department of Natural Resources puts it, these are *"probably the only real killer on the lower river… do not tarry above these (usually piled up on a wing dam or bridge piers)… if you would flip or break a paddle above one you could be sucked under the mess of jumbled trees and in real trouble. It is important to understand that the Lower Missouri is a river with many faces depending on its level. When the river is very low there are sandbars everywhere, both inshore and at midriver and as a result there are camping areas right, left, and center. However, the river can easily rise 9 feet in a week at any time of year. When this happens, all the campsites are blown out and shoreline camping becomes problematic. The bottom line is that at low water, the river is camper friendly and a very interesting float. However, at high water the river becomes more monotonous, sandbars are washed-out, and ramp areas may offer the only campsites."*

Extreme changes in water level can also occur overnight. It is not uncommon for water levels to rise more than 5 feet after upstream storms. Monitor NOAA weather radio and select an appropriate campsite. If flooding is in the forecast, a campsite with appropriate elevation is essential; a site well above a boat ramp may be your only safe choice.

MISCELLANEOUS ISSUES

With respect to West Nile virus, Rocky Mountain spotted fever, giardia, and brown recluse spiders: Use insect repellent, inspect yourself regularly for ticks, and remove them. If there are cattle or cattle sign at your campsite, expect ticks. Filter or boil your water. Keep a watch out for spiders when you use vault toilets. If you are not a gambling person, you probably should inspect under and around the toilet seat before sitting down.

Rattlesnakes

Rattlesnakes are found throughout the Upper Missouri region, and you will see some. Use caution when launching or coming ashore. Carry a stick when you hike and watch where you put your feet. Carry a snakebite kit and review its instructions before going into the field. If you come across a rattlesnake, remember that most snakes simply want to get away from you; if given a chance they will retreat, which is what you should do once you determine a safe exit path. Common sense suggests that you should zip up your tent at night and seal your cockpit if you have a kayak. If you have a canoe and have turned it upside down for the night, use caution when righting it in the morning.

Flying Carp

Paddlers on the Lower Missouri need to be aware that "flying" Asian carp pose a significant hazard. Silver carp in the 10- to 12-pound range are abundant and go airborne when disturbed; if one collides with you, there is a good chance you will be injured and probably capsize. However, the locations of these fish are predictable, as USGS fisheries biologist Duane Chapman relates:

A downstream canoeist who stays in the middle of the Missouri River will never see one of these fish. Canoeists should be aware that the fish are most abundant in water with low velocity, especially deep water or shallow water on the edge of deep water. In the Missouri River, most of the time, these fish like to be near water that is at least 8 foot deep–although I have seen huge concentrations of silver carp in the Chariton River in water that was less than 3 foot deep for miles. The Chariton, like most other tributaries of the Missouri, holds many silver carp. The silver carp tend to inhabit the portions of the tributaries that cross the floodplain of the Missouri. These sections tend to be low velocity and have plenty of the plankton that silver carp like to eat. Paddlers often like to use boater accesses that are on the tributaries rather than on the mainstem, because they can launch into slow-moving water. Paddlers should be especially careful of silver carp when using these sections. On the Missouri River, silver carp spend most of their time in the slack water behind wing dikes, and sometimes in the eddies in front of and just behind the tip of wing dikes. If you stay out of these areas, you usually won't see many silver carp. Some paddlers like to shoot through the notches in the dikes for excitement. Moving quickly into an area full of silver carp in that way will increase the likelihood that they will jump.

When moving through areas of calm water that will harbor silver carp, one will often see the large wakes of the fish as they scoot away from the boat. Often, but not always, these wakes can alert a boater of fish about to jump. If the fish encounters an obstruction (for example, a wing dike or boat) or very shallow water, the fish will either jump or turn sharply around and go the other way. If the fish is caught between two barriers (like your boat and a shallow area), the chance that it will jump is very high. If you see such a wake moving toward your boat, watch out! Guard your face with your hands. Also, the fish make a characteristic "schoomp" sound as they leave the water. If I hear that sound outside the range of vision, I duck.

So when you approach slack water or paddle up a tributary on the Channelized Lower, be aware that "flying" carp are an issue. Watch for the wakes of running carp, and be prepared to duck. More information on the exotic species–bighead and silver carp–is available at www.cerc.usgs.gov/pubs/center/pdfDocs/Asian_carp-2-2004.pdf.

Meth Labs

On two occasions I was warned to be careful about paddling near areas where methamphetamine labs might be operating. "Meth" labs are sometimes set up in abandoned structures in secluded areas or just at a campsite in the woods. If you smell a strong ammonia or cat urine smell, or see antifreeze containers, drain cleaner cans, empty boxes of allergy tablets, acetone, or brake cleaner containers, get away from the area as fast as you can. Do not stop to talk with anyone in the area. If you can, note the general location. Meth production can cause serious soil and water contamination; when it is safe to do so, contact appropriate authorities.

Reservation about Reservations

As a general rule, you should not camp on reservation lands without permission. On some reservations you will be treated as a respected guest; elsewhere, your reception will be less than cordial. Shots have been fired in the direction of paddlers, but my impression is that this was done to scare or warn them off. Recently (summer 2004), a solo paddler was beaten rather badly by a group of young toughs at Wolf Point, Montana. Do not expect to be welcomed there. My advice is to paddle by at least that reservation as quickly as possible, maintaining a low profile. Unless you have grown up in the area or have contacts, you do not know how to read the cultural landscape. You are, for all intents, in foreign country and some consider you an unwelcome presence.

Cottonwood Trees

If you are thinking about camping in the shade of a cottonwood tree, carefully inspect the tree for dead branches, snags, or overhanging limbs. Aging cottonwoods have a bad reputation for dropping parts and toppling over during high winds. I have been told that campers have been killed by falling trees, but have been unable to verify the information. Judging from the number of toppled trees and numerous fallen branches that I encountered, I have no reason to doubt that fatalities have occurred. Enjoy the shade of a towering cottonwood, but locate your campsite away from aging trees with suspect limbs.

Cold Water and Hypothermia

No paddler's guide should neglect mention of cold water–related issues. In the spring, snowmelt runoff fuels the Missouri's current; throughout the summer, dams release chilly water drawn from below lake thermoclines. Your motor functions are quickly degraded by cold water, so you need to be dressed appropriately, as if you expect to be dumped into the water. My choice for cold-water gear is a neoprene Farmer John wetsuit and booties, with a light- or midweight fleece top covered by a paddler's jacket that seals tightly at the waist and has gaskets at the wrists and neck. And always wear a lifejacket. You cannot truly understand how quickly cold water debilitates you until you have actually experienced an icy water dunking. But perhaps the account of my friend Bryan Hopkins' cold water accident will best help you to appreciate the issues:

It was to be an amazing day, with a predicted high of 50 degrees by noon...very unusual for January. Ice had choked the Big Muddy until just the week before and I was really itching for a "river fix." By midmorning we had the shuttle set up and were enjoying a warm south breeze as we paddled downstream. The wind continued to pick up and the waves were now awesome...this was fun! My kayak was in its element, with water breaking over the bow, as it sliced through the now 3-foot waves.

Then, with no warning, everything changed. My paddle was caught sideways by a particularly severe gust of wind, and, to my utter disbelief, I began to capsize in what seemed like slow motion.... The cold water swallowed me and it was like being hit by a solid brick wall! Not once was I even able to think about rolling the boat. My body recoiled from the frigid water and the air burst from my lungs. Instantly overwhelmed with shock and panic, I clawed with numb hands to grab the pull loop and release my spray skirt. Over and over, I struggled as my panic swelled. 'Where is the dam loop?...Come on man, get out!, get out!' I finally located the pull loop, ejected, and burst to the surface, choking and swallowing water. I felt as if I were on fire. A massive adrenaline dump to my system had me hyperventilating and my heartbeat was way out of control. I quickly glanced through the waves toward the faraway shore and I realized that I was in trouble, real trouble. 'Calm down, you have got to calm down...slow your breathing down...get control...calm down!' My mind was in a battle with the physical response to the cold.

I managed to flop myself across the bouncing kayak and start awkwardly paddling toward a distant sandbar. My progress was pathetic and I was mostly being swept down the river with the current. My fear reached even greater heights as I noticed that my arms were mysteriously starting to lose power! I was now forced to concentrate to keep my hands closed around the paddle. I wildly considered abandoning the boat and swimming for it, but rejected this option when I remembered my change of clothes in the boat. I had no option but to keep working toward the sandbar with increasingly feeble strokes.

Finally, in the shallow water, I slipped off the kayak and stumbled to shore with boat in tow. I remember being overwhelmingly tired and simply wanting to lie down and go to sleep. I shook this off and fumbled with the latches on my boat's storage compartments. I felt as weak as a kitten as I struggled to pull off my wet fleece pants and paddling jacket and put on dry clothes. It was surrealistic to be now standing in a warm 50-degree breeze, only a few feet away from the frigid water that had attacked me. Warming up in the balmy air, I looked about me with the sharply renewed vision and senses that come after a brush with death. I was acutely aware of the softness of the sand under my feet, the feel of the wind, the sound of the water, the depth of blue in the sky. Man that was close...so close!

Experience on the water does not by itself neutralize risk. I had a "bombproof" kayak roll from years of whitewater paddling...and this proved of no value during the shock-inducing stupor of January waters. I had dressed more for the day, not the water, a stupid mistake. Since then I have adopted a rule of thumb concerning cold water paddling: If you are not wearing enough clothes that you would be willing to jump in the water at any time...then you are not wearing enough clothes. As a result of my experience that January day, I am now much more mindful when on big rivers or open water. What would be the consequences of conducting a ferry across the river upstream of that logjam or parked barge? What are the consequences to my campsite if the river rises overnight? Can I find a landing if the waves kick up? Do I have more than one backup light when on the river at night? While certainly winter paddling is especially dangerous and hypothermia is a real killer, I now believe the real lesson of this day on the river is that complacency kills. I love this river, but this river can kill me.

Should You Carry a Weapon?

On several occasions as I talked with people that I met along the way, I was asked, "Do you carry a gun?" I did not carry a firearm. At one point when I was talking with a North Dakota sheriff, he asked me if I had a gun. I said, "No," and he said, "You should carry one. Come with me down to the office and I'll lend you one." I declined the offer as graciously as possible. I am convinced that he was very serious about providing me with a handgun. I am a hunter and am proficient with a pistol, rifle, or shotgun. But I prefer to rely on my wits and ability to quickly size up a situation and back away fast if necessary. And, besides deliberately maintaining a low profile and not camping at remote sites that have vehicle access, I carry a large knife.

Part II: Sailing Directions for the Missouri River in Three Trip Segments

Because many floaters will attempt only a section of the 2,321-mile-long Missouri River, I have divided the distance into three main trip sections beginning with the Upper Upper Missouri, which starts at the Missouri Headwaters State Park near Three Forks, Montana, and extends to James Kipp State Park, some 400 river miles downstream. Beyond Kipp is Fort Peck Lake, the first of six large reservoirs created behind Army Corps of Engineers (ACE) dams. I have named this next segment, which stretches for 1,198 river miles to Sioux City, Iowa, the Dammed Upper Missouri. This is followed by the Channelized Lower Missouri, which extends for 732 miles to the confluence with the Mississippi. For those desiring to complete their expedition at St. Louis, I have included directions for the 16-mile paddle to the Gateway Arch. Each section is divided into segments that provide detailed sailing directions for an area of the river.

These sailing directions assume that paddlers will go with the current. Riverbank side information given as left or right refers to "descending left" or "descending right" (what you would see on your left or right as you faced downriver), as is the customary practice for providing river navigation instructions. Those intrepid souls working their way upstream will need to make appropriate conversions.

Downstream or Upstream?

In recent years, a handful of paddlers have worked their way upstream for all or most of the river's 2,321 miles. The folks accomplishing this feat are expert paddlers. With few exceptions, those going upstream have paddled kayaks. On the free-running sections of the river, they had to battle against a stiff current. In years when water levels are low, paddling up many sections of the Upper Missouri may be somewhat easier because there is less current and the shore at the river's edge may be easier to walk when lining your boat.

On the Dammed Upper's larger reservoirs, there is little current to contend with, so working "upstream" is not an issue; upstream paddlers deal with the same elements that downstream paddlers have to contend with. Prevailing winds are generally from the northwest or southeast, so about half the time you can expect a headwind whether you work upstream or down. However, those going upstream may have an advantage if southeast winds prevail, as was the case when I worked across Fort Peck, Sakakawea, and Oahe in 2002. If lake levels are low, facilities can be more than a mile from the channel; many will be closed due to low water. Paddling up to downstream dam takeout points is easer if your approach is made when water releases are low. In the summer, additional dam-generated power is required for air-conditioning, so releases significantly increase by late morning. Finally, one very big disadvantage to working upstream on the Dammed Upper is that the upstream ends of the reservoirs are heavily sedimented; most have long areas of braided channels, marsh, and mudflats. In my experience, it is easer to navigate through these mazelike areas if you are paddling downstream.

Paddling upstream on the Lower Channelized Missouri has a suite of issues that should be attempted by only experienced paddlers. Ironically, having to paddle against a strong 3- to 6-mph main channel current is not the most challenging issue. More problematic is working around wing dams, logjams, and debris washing downriver after storms. These elements require endurance, polished technique, prudent decision-making, and the acceptance of an elevated level of risk. Norm Miller, who paddled up the Missouri in 2004, provides detail to be reflected upon by those considering going against the current:

Regarding the lower portion of the Missouri that is channelized, a paddler needs to stay away from the swift current, which means paddling very close to shore. One would tire rather quickly if he or she were to try to beat the opposing force of the river and paddle in the main channel. The U.S. Army Corp of Engineers constructed thousands of wing dikes from Sioux City, Iowa, all the way to the mouth of the Mississippi. These wing dikes...create large eddies and slack water pools on the downstream side below each dike. These slack water pools can be ideal for the upstream traveler since there is no opposing current. In fact, at times the current is actually flowing "upstream" the closer to shore you are, giving you an extra little bit of push up the river. These wing dikes are placed on the inside of every bend or on both sides of long straight sections of the river. There is one wing dike approximately every 150 feet for nearly 700 miles!

For the upstream paddlers these wing dikes can create a very dangerous situation. Depending on water levels these wing dikes will be totally submerged, barely submerged, or completely out of the water giving the appearance of a large cement wall. The ones that can be the most dangerous are the ones that are barely visible. The reason for this is because in order to get around each one you have to paddle as close to it as possible, aiming the bow directly at the fast water pouring around the very end of each dike. As you take advantage of the slack water below each dike, you will need to quickly get your boat in an all-out sprint. As the bow crosses over the eddy line and as the current is about to push you back downstream, you need to turn your boat toward the dike, continuing to sprint for approximately 20 more feet beyond the end of the dike. The reason is that as the water hits the dike, it accelerates and bulges up. You need to literally pop the boat up above this bulge and sprint to the area of the water before it begins to accelerate and this is usually a little more than a boat length above. (All canoes and kayaks will actually rise up in the water in a sprint due to the fact the boat will be riding on the forward wake created by the bow.)

Once you're free and clear of the wing dike you need to paddle back toward shore to the calm slack water behind the next dike. This sounds like a complicated process but after a few trial and errors you will quickly learn the characteristics of the wing dikes.

The reason they are so dangerous is because you can high-center your canoe or kayak on a submerged portion of the dike as you attempt to go around the tip of it. Once your boat is stuck on the dike the opposing current can literally flip you over. This happened to me the second week of my six-month solo trip following the Lewis and Clark trail to the Pacific. I was in an all-out sprint to get around the dike and as my boat crossed over the dike it became lodged on a log that was no more than an inch underwater. The log held my boat in place while the opposing current flipped it over and pushed it against the other submerged logs. I was quickly washed away from my boat and struggled to maintain my position with it while keeping it from being washed downstream. I was able to climb up on the wing dike from the downstream slack water side. I quickly grabbed the bow rope and tied it off to a log so the current could not completely push it under and against the dike. Only a foot of my boat was remaining above the water. I used a large driftwood log to pry and pop the boat out from the wing dike to the slack water behind the dike. I was fortunate enough not to lose my boat and most of my equipment, but it was a very close call.

At times you will encounter wing dikes where the water is too swift to paddle around. You will then need to pull or drag your boat over the top or around the wing dike. This can be very time-consuming and exhausting work. I had to do this on many occasions. Sometimes there would be a small channel of water pouring over the middle of the dike that was deep enough for me to drag my boat through. Other times I had to lay down logs horizontal to my boat and pull the boat across over the top of the logs to the water above the wing dike. The water is typically too strong to pull a boat around the end of the wing dike.

Consider carefully the above commentary and that you will need to traverse as many as 75 wing dikes a day for the first 700 miles of an upstream journey. If you are still entertaining the notion of going up the Missouri, factor into your thinking that you can expect to make some 13 to 17 miles in a 9- to 12-hour day's paddle on the Channelized Lower, an average of 25 to 35 miles a day on the Dammed Upper reservoirs, and 15 to 23 miles a day on the Upper Upper, where Norm relates that he was "in and out of his boat 30 times a day for three weeks."

Go downstream. There is adventure, risk, and pain enough when you go with the flow; an upstream effort may increase the caliber of the adventure, but elevates risk to an unacceptable level for all but the most skilled and accomplished paddlers.

The Organization of Sailing Directions

Each chapter that follows covers a trip section broken into segments. A small-scale (1:350,000) satellite-based infrared image is provided that displays each segment's start and end points and other significant route features. This is followed by commentary that appraises the character of the segment based on my field notes, discussions with other voyagers, and additional information that I gathered related to the area. Suggested publications and their sources are listed. This is followed by more detailed images (larger scale–typically 1:200,000) that divide the trip into 30- to 40-mile views that display the average distance that most paddlers might make on a fair day. The approximate locations of Lewis and Clark campsites are shown on these images.

These large-scale images are refined versions of those that I carried on the deck of my kayak in a waterproof, see-through map case. I consulted them frequently, and they often provided critical information that assisted my successful passage through numerous areas of shallow, mazelike channels. Whenever possible, I made notes on the margins of these views, recording GPS coordinates, possible campsites, rough water, and sections of particularly problematic shoreline. I transcribed these notes and included the information in the appropriate segment descriptions. When relevant, I also provide quotes, commentary, and anecdotal material from a variety of sources.

SECTION 1: THE UPPER UPPER MISSOURI (RIVER MILE 2,321 TO 1,921)

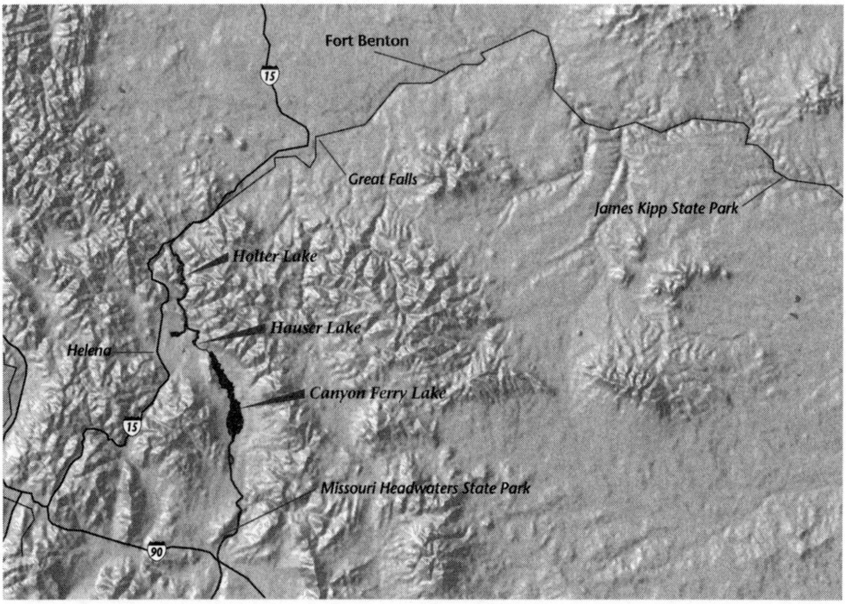

Map 1.0: Section 1—The Upper Upper Missouri River from the Missouri Headwaters State Park (Three Forks area, mile 2,321) to James Kipp State Park (mile 1,921).

> *...The confluence of these rivers form the Missouri on a semi-flat plain, ringed by limestone cliffs at its source. Explorers, fur traders, mountain men and pioneers made this a rendezvous point in their journeys. From this area the Missouri heads north and picks up waters from several other streams on its way.*
>
> DAVID A. MILLER, *CALL OF THE HEADWATERS*

There is no better place to start than at the beginning. The Missouri River begins at the confluence of the Jefferson, Madison, and Gallatin Rivers, north of Three Forks, Montana. From here to the far eastern side of the state where the river escapes into North Dakota, it is some 380 "as-the-crow-flies" miles. In river miles, paddlers will have to float a few miles short of twice this distance to get to the North Dakota border.

To complete the entire distance of the Upper Upper Missouri section–from the Missouri Headwaters State Park put-in to the Kipp Floater's Camp take-out–you will paddle exactly 400 river miles. You will see varied landscapes of incredible beauty, paddle through the Gates of the Mountains, and pass through the White Cliffs section of the Missouri Breaks. In the section below Holter Dam, you will cruise over water that is home to as many as 3,800 trout per mile–big trout; bring your rod.

Downstream from the headwaters confluence, you will need to portage four dams before reaching Great Falls, where you can get a courtesy shuttle around the city to a put-in site below the last dam. The five dams in Great Falls are close together, there are virtually no portage routes around them, and sudden water releases are the rule. For these reasons and 9-11–related security concerns, the waters are off-limits to through paddlers. If it is any consolation, the Lewis and Clark Expedition also had to portage around the Great Falls area.

Downstream from Great Falls, the land is sparsely populated, and the surrounding landscape begins to transition to the ragged character of the Missouri Breaks. Fort Benton, at the historic upstream end of steamboat navigation, is the only town of consequence along the river and a great stop for resupply, refreshment, and local color in general. Two day's paddle from the town is the wild and scenic White Cliffs area. A couple days beyond that is the end of the Upper Upper Missouri at the Kipp Floater's Camp just beyond the Highway 191 bridge.

Information/Maps/Resources

Good maps are available for this section of the Missouri River. I recommend that you go to the Montana Bureau of Land Management (BLM) website (www.mt.blm.gov/faq/index.html). This will display a link for a map coverage index for Montana. Here you can select the maps you need for $4 each. The following maps contain sections of the Missouri river:

Bozeman	43	Great Falls South	40
Townsend	42	Great Falls North	39
Canyon Ferry Dam	41	Fort Benton	49
Elliston*	31	Winifred	58
Dearborn River*	30	Zortman	67

*only a corner portion of the map displays the Missouri River; you may be able to do without this map.

At this site you can also purchase the *Upper Missouri National Wild and Scenic River Floater's Guides,* a two-part series, for $4 each. If you are going to paddle the NWSR, don't get on the river without both maps. High-resolution imagery of areas around dams can be downloaded as PDF files at http://nmviewogc.cr.usgs.gov/viewer.htm.

SEGMENT 1.A: Missouri Headwaters State Park near Three Forks, Montana (mile 2,321), to Fort Benton, Montana, take-out (mile 2,074.3)

- **River miles:** 246.7
- **Difficulty level:** Medium
- **Typical time to complete:** 14 to 20 days

Montana's first "Dude Ranch" was located at Three Forks in 1884 when an enterprising Englishman by the name of Henry C. Chater bought about 7,000 acres surrounding Bridgeville (near "Old Town," Three Forks). He had built a number of log cottages with the plan to develop a guest ranch for the British nobility to "farm out" their wild sons until they were mature enough to settle down in the mother country without embarrassment to their parents from their wild and youthful escapades. Chater figured that it would be worth fifty pounds to the nobleman to not have that responsibility for a year. That figured to $250.00 in American money, and Chater reasoned that many English first families would gladly finance their irresponsible heirs, who were continually getting into trouble in England, for a number of months or even years in the American wilds.

David A. Miller, *Call of the Headwaters*

Suggested Readings

More than 30 Lewis and Clark campsites are in this section. Information about what transpired here during the trip west (June 13 to July 27, 1805) can be found in Vol. 4:283–439 (*Journals,* [Moulton, ed.]). Return trip event detail (July 11 to 12, 1806) can be found in Vol. 8:104–107 of the same source. Context about the events can be found in Stephen Ambrose's *Undaunted Courage* in chapters 19:236–237 and 31:381–384. A very useful map, *The Route and Campsites of Lewis and Clark in Montana: A Geologic Perspective,* can be purchased by following links at www.mbmg.mtech.edu.

Paddler's Notes and Cautions

First of all, do not let the fact that there are dams littered across the first two-thirds of this section discourage you. Three of the four dams above Great Falls are reasonable distance portages. Only the Canyon Ferry Dam portage is beyond "humping your own gear" distance. But here you can easily arrange for someone to haul your gear to the downstream side. At Great Falls there is a designated pullout site, with phone numbers posted for a complimentary shuttle to a put-in below the last dam. With enough time and care, you can easily do this section. You'll paddle through remote canyons that burn with color in the late afternoon light, see mountain goats and mule deer close up, hear a cougar scream, watch expert fly fishers land trophy trout, and observe more bald eagles and ospreys than you ever thought possible. And finally, all along the way you'll be treated with great Montana hospitality.

◆ Missouri Headwaters State Park put-in (mile 2,321.5) to Toston Dam portage take-out (mile 2,299): 22.5 river miles *(Map 1.A.1)*

The Missouri Headwaters State Park is less than 5 miles from Three Forks on Trident Road. There is an information station and a campground host. When I began my paddle of this section in 2004, everyone at the park was very helpful. I was able to park my truck in a secure area here for the two-week period that it took me to navigate to Fort Benton. The actual campground is not on the river; however, there are shaded sites, potable water, and clean vault toilets. Mosquitoes can be troublesome.

There has been discussion about creating a floater's camp area closer to the river, so check with the ranger or campground host. The recommended put-in (launch) site is 0.5 mile up the road (north) of the campground on the left (45.92599/-111.50360). No camping is permitted at the put-in area, but a nicely mowed walking trail connects it with the campground. You'll need to scout for the best place to put your boat in the water. Once you shove off, you'll be in good current. And for the next several hours, you'll be on a very pretty float.

Technically, you are at the confluence area. You begin on the Madison, just below the confluence with the Jefferson. The Gallatin joins the flow about 1.5 miles downriver. Purists will want to know that the confluence put-in is 0.25 mile above the Army Corps of Engineers "2,321-start-river-mile-count-point." But who is counting? If it is early in the summer, you should not have to worry

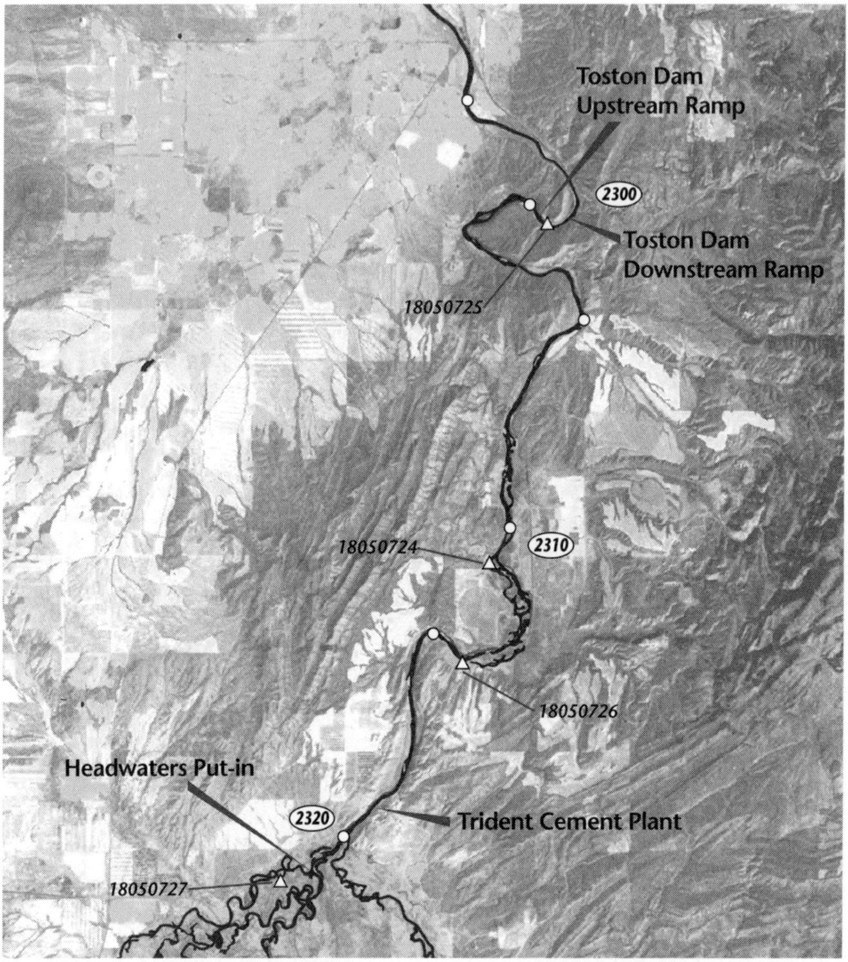

Map 1.A.1: Headwaters confluence (mile 2,320) near Three Forks, Montana, to Toston Dam area (mile 2,299).

about low water. In a dry year, however, low levels will slow your progress. Before you start out for the confluence, call the ranger's office for information about water levels.

A boat launch is on the right (descending river right), about a quarter mile beyond the Gallatin confluence (mile 2319.7; 45.94021/-111.49097). A railroad line joins the river from the right; this line mostly parallels the river all the way to Townsend. The cement plant at Trident is also on the right just downstream from mile 2,319. From here, the river flows to the north for almost 4 miles before turning sharply to the southeast at mile 2,315. Before this bend you'll encounter a series of small rapids with fast water all the way around the bend.

At mile 2,314, where the river cuts back to the east, you'll see a large colony of swallows and their mud huts tucked along the side of the rocks. It is generally smooth sailing for the next 7 miles to the abandoned railroad bridge crossing the river near mile 2,304. There are a couple possible campsites between mile 2,307 and 2,305. The river begins to widen about a mile beyond the railroad bridge. Stay right, pass an island on your left, and then work around a sharp bend to the northeast. On your left, you will see the Toston Pumping Station. This area is unaffectionately known as "The Devil's Bottom," probably because the wind can blow like hell here. Locals report that this area can get extremely rough because the canyon walls funnel the wind right into this stretch. There are few places to pull out before the dam.

Once you paddle beyond the pump station, it is 1.7 miles to the Toston

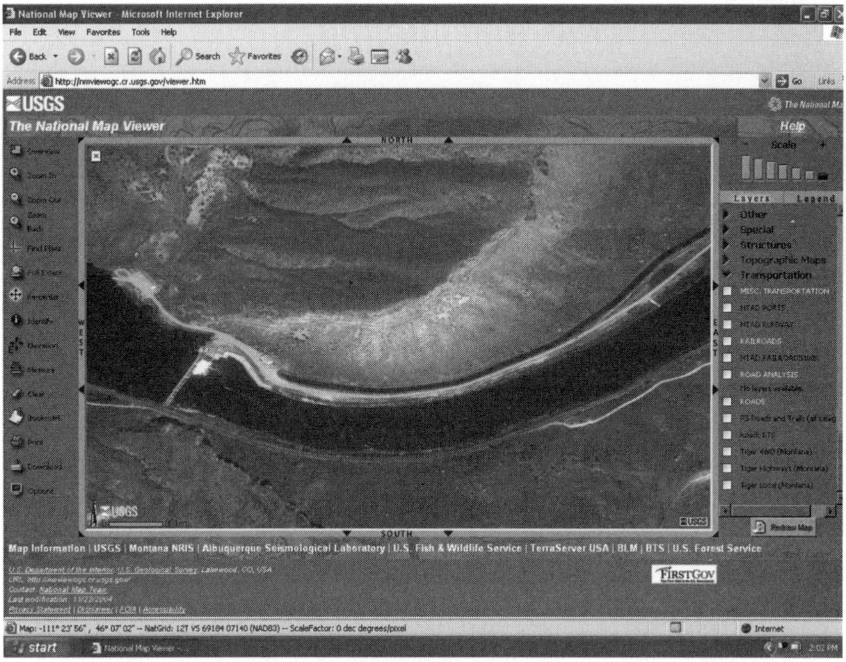

Map 1.A.2: Toston Dam area image downloaded from the USGS National Map website (www.nationalmap.gov). By entering in latitude and longitude coordinates of the upstream ramp (46.12210/-111.40975), you can view and print imagery that will show the area to be portaged.

Dam upstream ramp (mile 2,299.7 left; 46.12210/-111.40975). You must take out at the ramp (see Map 1.A.2). At the ramp is a picnic shelter and some campsites, but there is no source for drinking water. Below the dam the water is clear, cold, and filters out nicely. As I made my landing, an older gentleman walked up and asked how far I was going. I replied, "All the way," and went on to explain that I'd already paddled from Fort Benton to Sioux City over the previous two summers. The man turned out to be Sonny Weldon, the BLM campground host. He said, "I'll bring my truck over and take you to the downstream ramp. I don't want to be giving anyone CPR."

Sonny backed his dusty red Ford pickup truck down the ramp, and I loaded my gear and kayak in the back. He drove me down a hill to a small camping area near the downstream ramp. He helped me unload and then invited me up to his trailer for a cold drink once I got my camp set up. I could not believe my luck. From the ramp to the downstream camp, it is 0.6 mile and takes 12 minutes to walk. Although mostly downhill, there is no shade. After I set up camp, I walked up to Sonny's trailer. On the way, I scouted for anywhere the portage distance might be shortened. About a quarter mile below the dam, it might be possible to work your way down the bank, but it would not be easy. All in all, and since there are rattlesnakes in this area, it would be prudent to stay on the road and put in at the downstream ramp.

I knocked on the door of his trailer. Sonny invited me in, and I introduced myself and filled him in on my project. It turned out Sonny had been the campground host for several years. Over a couple beers and a glass or two of Lambrusco, he told me about other paddlers that he'd helped with the portage. He talked about a variety of voyagers, some whom he thought would never make it. Most of them were not well equipped and lacked the expertise necessary to safely manage on the river. I couldn't help but nod my head in agreement. For two summers I'd heard descriptions and stories about some of the same paddlers. Somehow they'd managed to stay alive and recover from mishap after mishap as they bungled themselves down the river. According to Sonny, most of these folks were in over their heads the first time they got in their boat.

Sonny and I talked almost until dark. He told me stories about folks that had been lost on this section of the river, and about the time that they'd fished a body out of the catchment area in front of the dam. And a sad story about a dog owner whom he'd warned to keep her dog on a leash because of park regulations and rattlesnakes. She ignored his request. A little while later he heard a yelp, and the dog was dead in minutes from a rattlesnake bite. "You killed my dog," the lady had screamed at him.

Before I left, Sonny filled my water bottle. I got his address and promised that I would let him know when I completed my trip. And I did.

As I walked down the gravel road to my downstream camp, I reflected on our conversation. Over a few drinks, we strangers recognized each other as kin-

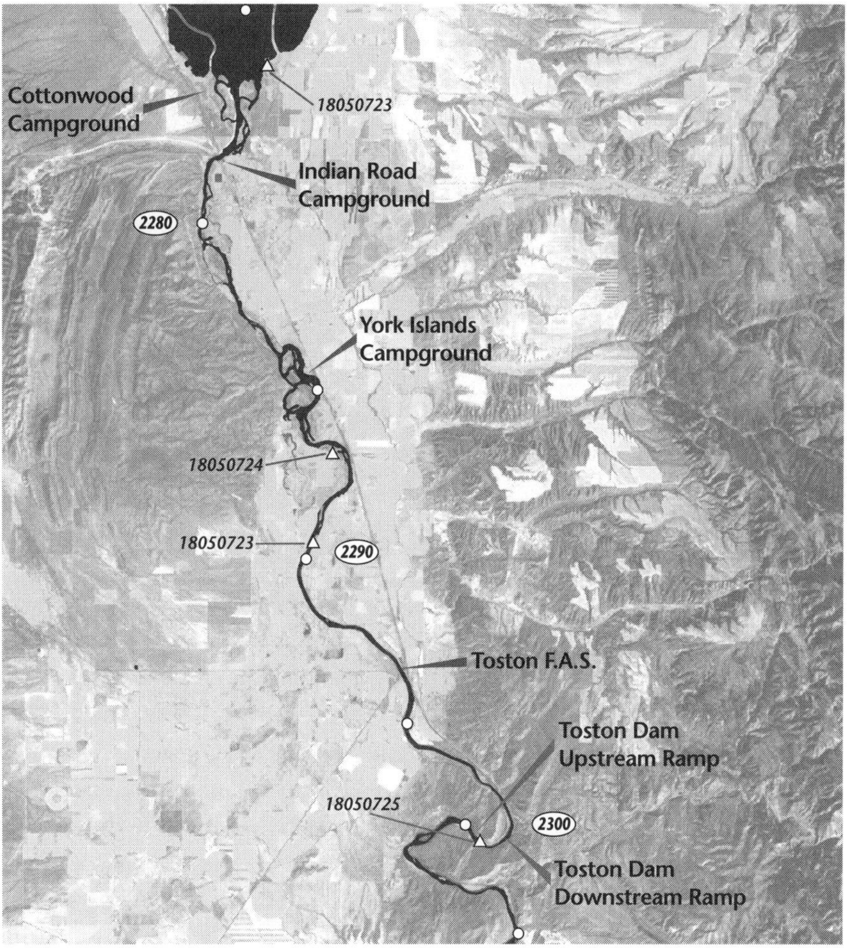

Map 1.A.3: Toston Dam downstream (mile 2,298.8) put-in to Indian Road Campground, near Townsend (mile 2,278.5). The absolute last chance to get off the river before you are committed to the open water of Canyon Ferry Lake is at the Cottonwood Campground, but I recommend that you stay at Indian Road Campground, on the right at mile 2,278.5, just after the Highway 287/12 bridge.

dred spirits on passage. Sonny, long in the tooth and nearing the end of his expedition; and me still at midpassage, but also aware of some horizon in sight. In tripspeak, with less in front than behind. On a river passage like this, there is lots of time to think; metaphors abound. You flow with the river, and although you are constantly moving, you find a stillness that anchors itself to you.

- **Toston Dam downstream put-in (mile 2,298.8) to Indian Road Campground, near Townsend (mile 2,278.5): ~ 20.3 river miles *(Map 1.A.3)***

The Toston downstream camping area is next to the boat ramp (mile 2,298.8; 46.12148/-111.39840. The site has picnic tables, fire rings, and a vault toilet. This can be a dusty site when there is any traffic on the gravel road that fronts the campsites. Nevertheless, if you want a good start in the morning, it is probably a good idea to complete the portage and camp here. Road traffic diminishes by early evening, so if you can, delay setting up your tent until then.

After you push off from the ramp, get quickly to the right. The river bends sharply around to the northwest, and you'll encounter several stretches of fast water in the next couple of miles. After about 1.5 miles you'll cross under a bridge that is actually a large pipe suspended across the river. Two-tenths of a mile beyond this on the left (mile 2,297.5) is a nice campsite. According to the BLM map, this is public land. Just before mile 2,296, you'll cross under a power line. From this point it is about 2 miles to the town of Toston.

There is a dirt ramp and fishing access site on the left (near mile 2,294), near Toston. This ramp is within a few dozen feet downstream of the old iron bridge that you pass under before the new Highway 287 bridge at mile 2,293.7. Beyond the town, the area opens up to a wide, flat plain. For the first time you can see evidence of large-scale agricultural activity; to the northeast (ahead right) you'll see the Big Belt Mountains and to the northwest are the Elkhorn Mountains.

Keep your eyes open for bald eagles after you pass Toston. The river bends gently to the northwest for about 5 miles and then back to the northeast. After mile 2,288, you'll see Highway 287 on the right. After mile 2,286 you should stay to the right, as you'll begin to encounter a series of islands that you need to work around. Three-and-a-half miles downstream (mile 2,284.5 right; 46.26600/-111.49263) is the Yorks Islands ramp and campground, where you will find nice shady campsites, picnic tables, fire rings, and a vault toilet. There is no source for drinking water.

Beyond Yorks Islands there are several areas of shallows and some areas of fast water and boulders, so you'll need good light to read the water correctly. At the time I paddled through, the gravel shallows had a distinct rusty-brown cast and the water splashed up in the area above them like little dancing pixies. Work with me here; paddle this section and you will see what I mean.

About 6 miles farther downstream you'll reach Townsend. You won't see the town since it is not on the river, but you will see homes along the left shore

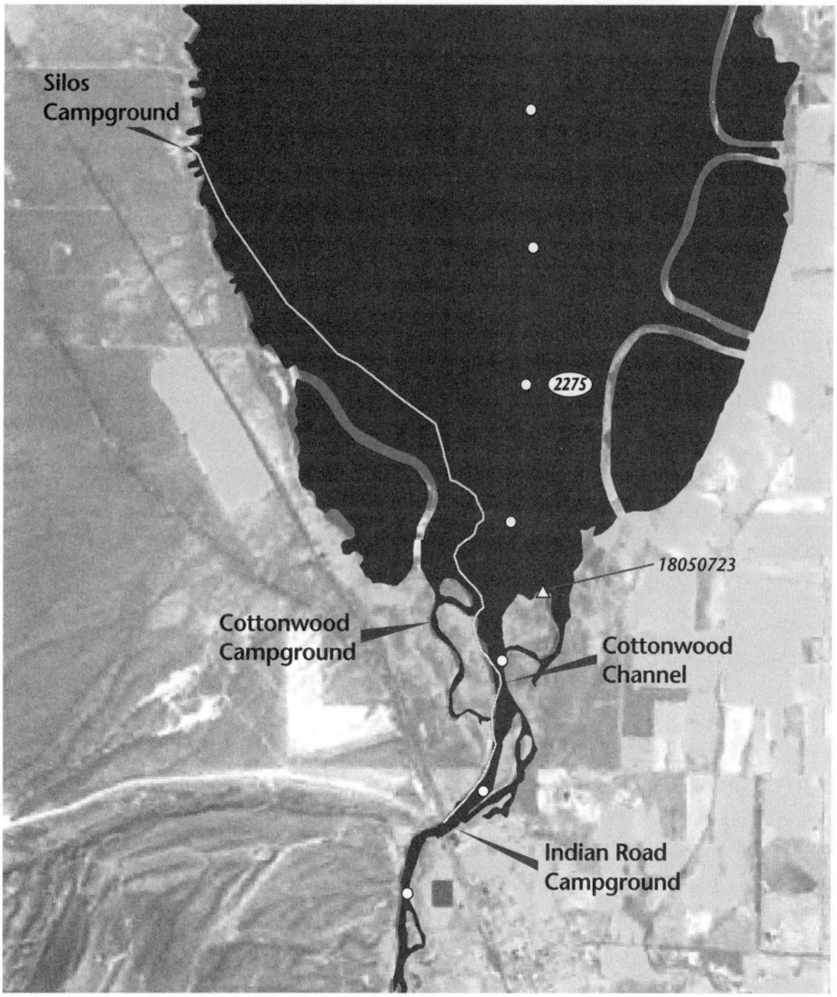

Map 1.A.4: South end of Canyon Ferry Lake, showing area of braided channels at delta. My June 2004 GPS course track is shown as a white line.

as you approach the two Townsend bridges. If you want to put in at the Indian Road Campground ramp (mile 2278.5; 46.3349/-111.52987), you must get right immediately after the railroad bridge and then cross under the Highway 287/12 bridge. The ramp is along the right shore, just downstream from the highway bridge. Above the ramp it may be very shallow; you might have to get out of your boat to tow it over the shallows to reach the ramp. There is a channel to the ramp a bit farther downstream, but you have to be looking back upstream at just the right moment to see the take-out; it is easy to miss.

A word of warning: Do not continue on to Canyon Ferry Lake unless you have good weather. Depending on the water level, you may have to thread your way through more than 1.5 miles of river delta consisting of shallow braided channel and mudflats. You are absolutely exposed to the elements during this passage and will not have any easy pullout until you get to Silos Campground, 3 miles up the west (left) shore. Locals will tell you that this end of the lake can be absolutely treacherous because the water is very shallow and big waves generate when the wind kicks up. I strongly recommend that you stop at the Indian Road Campground. It has nice campsites, vault toilets, and drinking water. You can easily get a ride into town for supplies.

The absolute last chance to get off the river before you are committed to the open water of Canyon Ferry Lake is at the Cottonwood Campground. However, the channel leading to the Cottonwood ramp can be difficult to locate. Examine Map 1.A.4. The channel entrance is about 2 miles downstream from the Highway 287/12 bridge (mile 2,276.4; 46.52758/-111.35753). To find the channel, you must get to the left after mile 2,277. If you can find the entrance, you will paddle a 0.5-mile-long, winding back channel that eventually works you to the west. The coordinates for the Cottonwood ramp are 46.35626/-111.53436; here you'll find campsites and a vault toilet but no water.

◆ Canyon Ferry Lake–Indian Road Campground (mile 2,278.5) to Yacht Basin Marina (mile 2,253.5): 25 miles *(Map 1.A.5)*

A note on campsites and beaches. There are fewer choices when the reservoir is at full pool (3,797 feet). In fact, beaches are nonexistent and steep slopes limit take-out sites, especially in foul weather. Although full pool was not reached in 2004, it was in 2003 and most previous years. Full pool is usually reached by the end of June, then the water starts dropping. Beaches become more plentiful in July and August.

DEAN CULWELL, USCG AUXILLARY

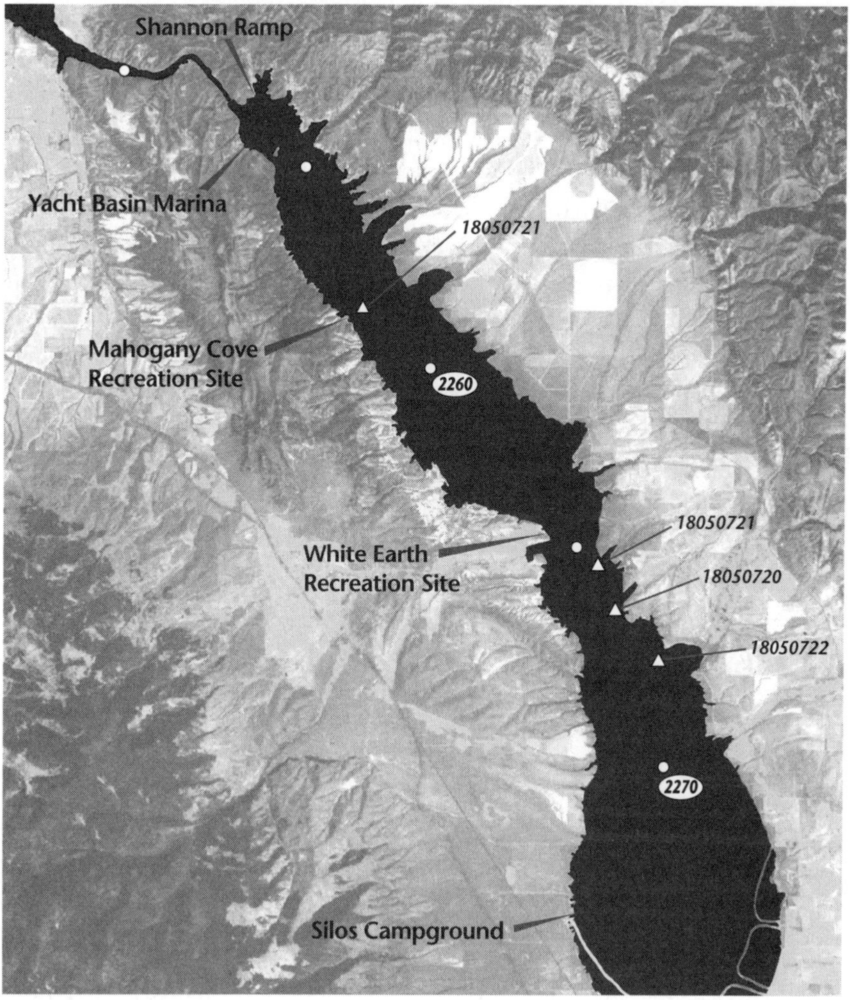

Map 1.A.5: On Canyon Ferry Lake, paddlers will find the best protection along the left (west) side of the lake. This lake can blow up very fast so get the NOAA weather radio forecast before setting out. White dots are 5 miles apart.

Put on your spray skirt; this lake can blow up fast. Although the lake is less than 5 miles wide, it is nearly 25 miles long. The north-south aspect of the lake, and the fact that the south end of the lake is shallow, combine to make passage rough even during a modest breeze. In addition, summer thunderstorms move in fast. Do not proceed out onto this lake unless you have good weather and a good forecast; check your weather radio frequently.

The delta at the south end of Canyon Ferry Lake will test your ability to read the water. Twice as I worked my way through the braid of channels, I couldn't decide which fork to take. On both occasions I stared at what looked to be two bad choices. Adding to my angst were the facts that (1) thunderclouds were beginning to build to the south and (2) both the channels that I had to choose from angled to the northeast. I wanted to get to the Silos Campground on the west side of the lake. Eventually, I had to work more than 0.5 mile to the northeast (~ mile 2,276) before I was able to cut back to the northwest.

Essentially, there is nowhere to pull out before Silos. A steep, 1.8-mile-long levee surrounds the "Duck Pond," effectively closing off that shore for a pullout. It is a 3-mile paddle from the end of the delta to the Silos Campground ramp (~ mile 2,273; 46.40555/-111.5798). There are at least three ramps to choose from; I chose to pull out at the second one that I encountered, where there was a high-water ramp that was not in use. The end of the ramp was some 30 yards above the waterline, and there was a nice sandy beach at the shore. One bay up is the entrance to a nicely sheltered cove with a new ramp that sees constant traffic.

When you get to a large campground like this, finding a good site is a bit of a crapshoot. You never know if you will be able to get a site near the water by your boat with a bit of shade. Most waterfront sites are set up for RV units. Those with any shade are the first occupied, and tenters are often relegated to open field. Fortunately, that's not the case here.

I spoke with the campground host, Ron Lloyd, who turned out to be very helpful. I explained that I was in a kayak, and that I would like to set up my small tent along the shore near my boat. Ron had no problem with that; he just asked me to let him know where I was and to fill out a permit/fee form. As the campground host for eight years, Ron is a good source for accurate information about conditions. I discussed my intention to stay along the west shore as I worked my way toward the dam, and Ron agreed that this was the best approach, as it would give me good shelter from winds from the northwest and west. He said that there are more small coves along the west side of the lake, making it easier to find refuge. Ron also warned me that the wind can come up very quick, and told me that several boats had swamped when a storm moved in quickly during a walleye-fishing tournament two years ago. "Lucky that we didn't lose anyone that day," he said.

With good weather you should be able to make the 20 miles from Silos to the Canyon Ferry Dam in one full-day's paddle. However, the shoreline becomes increasingly prettier as you get closer to the dam; I suggest that you take two days to make the crossing. If you have any weather, or if there is a wind from the northeast, you should plan on a two-day passage.

White Earth Recreation Site is 8.5 miles north of Silos (mile 2,264.5; 46.52205/-111.58730). The ramp is inside a bay that provides good shelter. This is a nice campground; there is a vault toilet, and you can fill your water bottles here. If you are planning to camp, I suggest you continue on an additional 6.5 miles to Mahogany Cove Recreation Site (mile 2,258; 46.58373/ -111.67297). Mahogany Cove can only be reached by water; it is a "boater's camp." You'll see colorful rock cliffs as you approach the area. This is a beautiful cove with several nice, sheltered campsites. There is a nice beach, and you can climb a trail up to a scenic lake overlook. I left Silos at 9 A.M. and pulled in here at 2:30 P.M. Dealing with a headwind, I averaged about 3 mph. I could have continued on and made the dam in a couple more hours of paddling, but this was so nice that I decided to stay. As I was setting up my tent, a mule deer and her two fawns came out of the pines and watered within 30 yards of my kayak. It was a weekday, and there were no other campers at the site. On a weekend this is a very popular place.

From Mahogany Cove to the dam is just 5 miles. You will begin to see cabins along the shore, and the effects of large forest fires, which burned along both sides of the lake in 2000. There are several picnic areas along the way with vault toilets and picnic tables. Once you pass through the channel between the shore and Cemetery Island (~ mile 2,254.3), you'll see a couple nice sandy bays, then come to the Yacht Basin Marina (mile 2,253.5; 46.63596/-111.72105). There is a great community of boat people here, and a good restaurant and bar just up the hill. The marina has a nice quiet beach where you can camp for a small fee. There is a Coast Guard Auxiliary Unit at the marina. The auxiliary has a VHF marine radio base station at the marina that montiors channel 16. Almost every boat with a marine radio also monitors channel 16. There is limited cell phone reception on this lake.

If you ask at the marina, you should be able to arrange a portage to the put-in area below the dam. This is the one dam that you cannot easily portage around. Another take-out site is at the Shannon ramp, about a mile to the northeast (mile 2,253; 46.64941/-111.71796). If you get there by midday, you should not have much trouble finding someone with a truck or boat trailer to help you get to Riverside, the downstream ramp and campground. Offer to pay for their time and gas. From Shannon to Riverside it is almost 2 miles. Twenty dollars or so will save you enormous pain.

- **Riverside Campground and ramp, below Canyon Ferry Dam (mile 2,252) to Hauser Dam take-out (~ mile 2,237.5): ~ 14.5 river miles *(Map 1.A.6)***

The put-in below Canyon Ferry Dam is at the Riverside Recreation Area. This

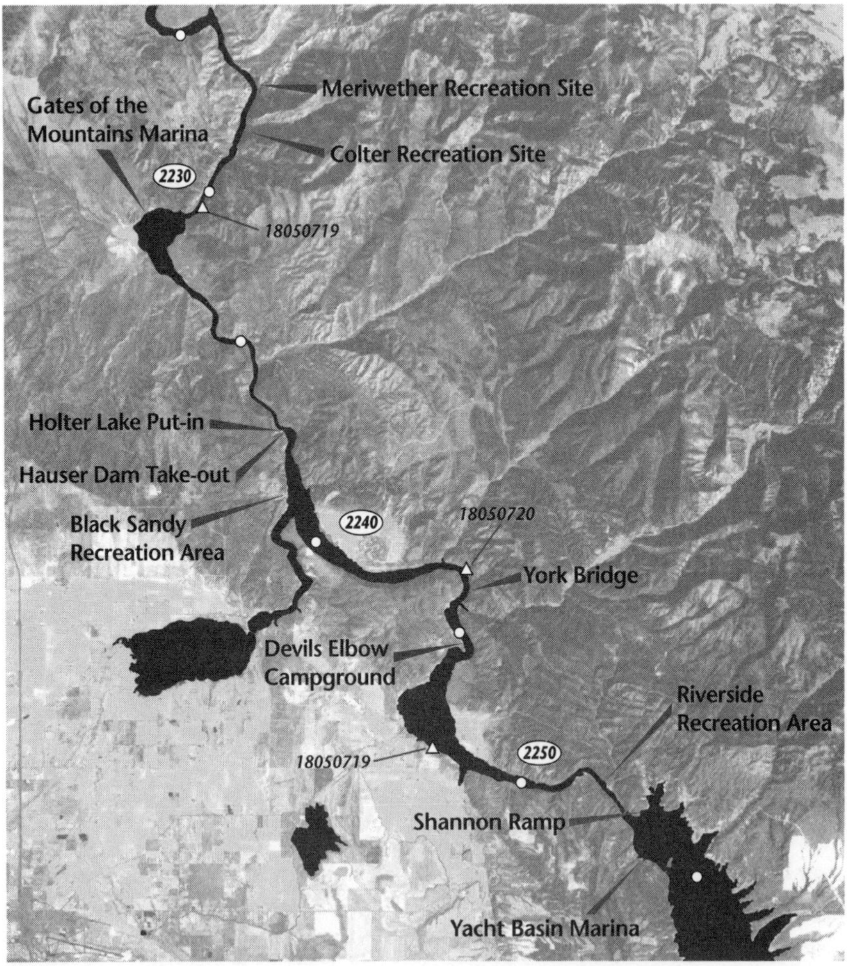

Map 1.A.6: Downstream end of Canyon Ferry Lake to the Gates of the Mountains area on Holter Lake.

is a nice campground with fire rings, vault toilets, and friendly campground hosts (Frank and Bonnie Nance) who like to keep track of paddlers coming through. They keep a scrapbook of voyagers' photos, so you may be asked to pose for a shot. Frank and Bonnie are a good source for information about downstream conditions and local lore. We talked as I loaded up my kayak, and I learned that the dredge across the river from the ramp had been used to mine sapphires from the riverbed gravel. According to Frank, the largest sapphire ever found in Montana came from this section of the river. The dredge operation is shut down because its permits have not been renewed. Maybe you should keep your eyes open for blue sparkles on the riverbed as you paddle downstream.

This is a popular campground, often filled on the weekends. Frank told me that he always tries to make room for paddlers wanting to camp and that he understands they like to be near the ramp to make loading easier. Before I arrived here, I had incomplete information about the portage at Hauser Dam; I had been told that 9-11–related security concerns had resulted in the closure of the portage route. Frank provided the more accurate information that the portage is now open and that paddlers can work their boat under the rope marking the security perimeter if they stay far left, along the shore, and pull out near the dam.

After you shove off, you'll paddle for about a mile to a point known as French Bar. After another mile, you'll see some cabins on your right, and the river begins to widen into Upper Hauser Lake. Just before mile 2,249, you'll see a pump station on the right; an osprey nest is nearby. A mile farther downstream, on the left, is Lakeside.

At Lakeside there are houses, a marina, a launch, campground, bar, and restaurant. About a mile farther downstream is BLM's Clark's Bay, a day-use site with a ramp. A half mile farther downstream on river left is BLM's Devils Elbow, with a campground, launch, and boat slips. Finally, on the left immediately above the York Bridge, is the York Bridge Fishing Access Site, a day-use area with launch and vault toilets.

As you get closer to the York Bridge, you will see homes and cabins. When I paddled this section, there were powerboats towing water-skiers at midlake, so I stayed close to the right shore. The water here is shallow and clear, and the bottom is weedy with occasional bare sand spots. If you paddle through here quietly, you'll see monster-size carp. I guarantee that more than one of them will startle you when your approach spooks them.

After mile 2,247, the lake begins to pinch in, and after another mile you will work your way around a point. There appeared to be a couple possible campsites on the right before you round this feature. Once around the bend you will come to a ramp and campground on the left (mile 2,245.2; 46.70085/-111.80353). From here to the York Bridge Fishing Access Site and ramp (also left) is about 0.7 mile. Trout Creek joins the lake on the right just before the bridge (mile 2,244.3). Less than 8 miles up that creek is the improbably named Vigilante Recreation Area, just above Goodman Gulch. Nice to know these guys have their own place.

Soup Creek joins you on the right just above mile 2,243. Downstream from here is the first stretch of shoreline that I saw posted with no trespassing signs. A mile below this is a power line that crosses the river almost exactly at mile 2,242. From here to the Hauser Dam take-out is about 4.5 miles. You'll want to work over to the left in the next mile or so as the lake begins to widen. Prickly Pear Creek, leading to Lake Helena, comes in on the left near mile 2,241. The Black Sandy State Park is also on the left, 0.25 mile downstream (46.74542/-111.88622). Here you will find nice, shaded campsites and bathrooms with running water. The ramp is wide, and there is space along the side to pull your boat out of the way of folks launching their boats.

The Hauser Dam take-out is on the left, just a mile farther downstream (~ mile 2,237.5; 46.76396/-11188779). As you approach the dam stay left. The shore is steep and rugged here. You will come to a line stretched across the river that marks the dam's restricted access area. At the time of this writing, I was told that paddlers had permission to slip their boat under this line and to proceed carefully along the left shore to the take-out, a cleared gravel area on the far left side of the dam. You will have to pull your boat up a 5-foot bank that's a bit steep but workable.

If for some reason this route is closed, you will have to pull out before the security rope, about 150 yards before the dam. The bank is extremely, almost impossibly, steep, and you will have to somehow pull your boat up the bank. Once you are up on the road, watch for traffic. There have been automobile accident–related fatalities on this road.

From the left side dam take-out to the downstream put-in is less than 0.2 mile and downhill. In half an hour, I managed to hump all my gear to the launch site and then rolled my kayak down on the folding wheel cart that I carried. You will see a road leading straight down to some buildings and a home on the left. About halfway down, a trail leads to the river; this will get you to a flat shoreline area. You can put in where convenient (~ 46.76576/-111.89073).

◆ **Holter Lake put-in, below Hauser Dam (mile 2,237.3) to Holter Dam take-out (mile 2,211.1): 26.2 miles** ***(Maps 1.A.6 & 1.A.7)***

This is such an absolutely spectacular paddle that a few words of introduction are in order. Holter Lake has an upper and lower section separated by a narrow 5-mile stretch that threads through an area of towering cliffs known as the Gates of the Mountains. Most of the land along the east side and large tracts along the west are public lands. Once you enter the Gates, you don't have to hike very far away from the river to get the feeling that you have entered wilderness. With good weather, you probably could paddle from the Holter put-in to the Holter Dam take-out in a day. But you'd be crazy to do so. Plan on camping a night just inside the Gates because its sheer beauty, especially at sunset, will leave you speechless. For spectacular views and to pay your respects to fallen smokejumpers, take time to hike from the Meriwether Landing up to the Mann Gulch overlook.

Below Hauser Dam at the Holter put-in, you'll probably see fly fishers casting from the shore for trout. You'll want to navigate by them with care. Before you shove off, let them know that you are going to be coming through, then give them a decent interval to complete a series of casts. You should study the water carefully before you put in, as there are some shallows and boulders in the channel. I had to stay to the left and then swing hard to the right before I could get to open water. For the next 1.5 miles, you'll see steep bluffs on the west side. You'll pass Beaver Creek, on the right at mile 2,235.8. You'll see an observation point just downstream from the creek entrance. There is a vault toilet at Beaver Creek, and trout fishing is excellent in this area.

The lake begins gradually to widen once you are past Beaver Creek. In a couple miles, on the right, you'll see several homes and cottages along an area known as American Bar. I stayed along this shore until it began to angle to the northeast, at which point I crossed to the opposite side, over to the ramp at the Gates of the Mountains Marina (mile 2,231.2; 46.83164/-111.95177). You can see the large tour boats docked near the ramp from the far side of the lake. The actual Gates begin 0.8 mile due east from the marina.

I reached the marina in the late afternoon, having paddled about 40 miles from Canyon Ferry Dam. I pulled my kayak in at the ramp and hauled it off to the side. Here I met Tim and Doris Crawford, who run the tour boats. They had just set out a nice banquet for an Elderhostel group about to take the tour.

Tim invited me to have dinner with him and Doris. I asked about a place to camp nearby, and they recommended either just before the entrance to the Gates or, better yet, about a 1.5-mile paddle past the entrance to a nice camping area on the left. Tim suggested that this would be the best plan as it would be quieter, and there would be a good early morning sun. The right side is in shadows until later in the morning. I decided to camp inside the Gates. Before I left, Doris fixed me up with a couple days' food supply including a big chunk of roast beef, corn on the cob, salad, and cookies. Both Doris and Tim warned me to stay to the side as I made my passage through the Gates. The channel is quite narrow, and powerboats race through here with little regard for anyone in their wake. Tour boats put up a big wake so give them wide berth.

I found a great campsite on the left about 1.5 miles inside the entrance to the Gates of the Mountains (46.84846/-111.91633). This is the first area that you come to that is relatively level. You will see the stones of a fire ring. Just beyond this is a low and level area where you can pull out. Here you will find several nice tent sites. Another nice campsite is 0.3 mile farther down the shore. Once the last powerboat has passed for the evening, this place takes on an incredible stillness. If you watch the upstream cliff sides on the opposite side of the canyon, you might see the setting sun briefly paint the limestone walls with golden light.

Farther on is the Colter Recreation Site on the right at mile 2,228.3. There are campsites with fire rings here, a vault toilet, and a hand pump for drinking water. Just 0.25 mile up from this, on the left, is another campsite. Camping on the left shore gives you the early morning sun. The Meriwether Recreation Site is on the right at mile 2,227.5 (46.86964/-111.90223). Tour boats dock here, so there is often a crowd of people on shore, but there is a nice shelter, picnic tables, and a water pump. The monument to the smokejumpers that died in the Mann Gulch Fire in 1949 is here.

If you hike up to the Mann Gulch overlook, at a couple places along the way you'll have great views of the Gates, and once you get to the overlook, you'll be able to better understand how the topography of Mann Gulch might have contributed to the deaths of the 13 firefighters. As the crow flies, it's 0.6 mile to the overlook. But hikers follow a steep 1.2-mile-long trail up a canyon, replete with switchbacks and some loose rocks, to gain the vista. The round trip will take at least two hours. Take a water jug and wear decent shoes.

Once you get back on the water, you'll get a good look up Mann Gulch when you get just less than a mile downstream from Meriwether Landing.

View of Gates of the Mountains as seen from the downstream approach. The river appears to dead-end at a curtain of rock cliffs.

Looking downriver from here, you'll see a point, and about halfway to this point on the left is a campsite (mile 2,226.4). Before you round this point, you should look back at the way you came. Look again after you round the point, and you'll understand exactly why Lewis called this place the Gates of the Mountains. As you approach this area from downstream, the river appears to dead-end at a curtain of rock cliffs. As you get closer, however, the through channel suddenly appears.

The Beartooth Landing Recreation Area is on the left just downstream from the 2,225-mile mark. There are several campsites with fire rings along the shore and a vault toilet, but there is no source for drinking water. Signs warn campers about rattlesnakes in the area. Take these warnings seriously. The broken rock on the hillsides surrounding the campground provides snakes with great habitat. From your camp along the shore you can see Beartooth Mountain to the northwest. It really does look like the lower jaw of a bear, teeth intact. Which reminds me: I noticed black bear scat in the area above the campground, so if you camp here, take appropriate precautions.

After spending the night at Beartooth Landing, I crossed to the other side and paddled around Ming Bar. The water is shallow here and the bottom sandy.

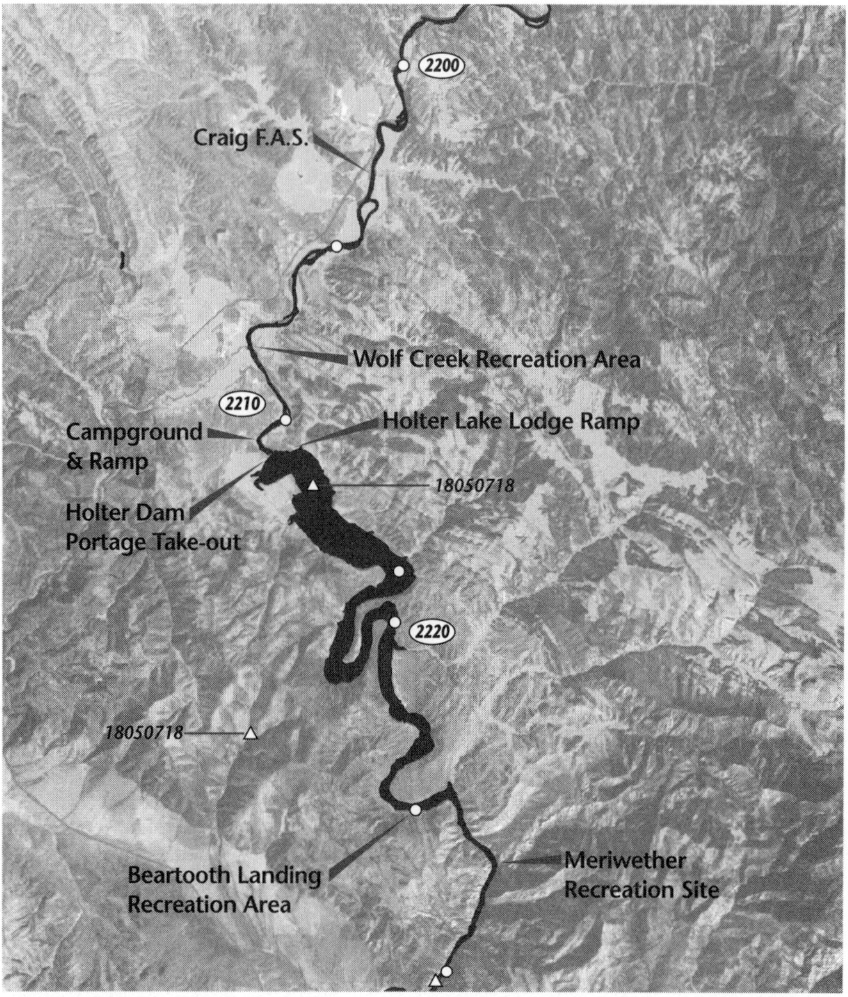

Map 1.A.7: Meriwether Recreation Site (mile 2,227.5) to Craig Fishing Access Site (mile 2,203). The scenery in this section is spectacular.

Once I got about halfway around the downstream side, I angled back over to the left shore. Just before I made my crossing, I saw two nice campsites near mile 2,223.5. When you get across to the left, look carefully at the rock formation above you. You will see a large pair of eyes staring out at you (46.90209/ -111.94269). Here it is easy to imagine that the mountain is watching you.

As you work to the north along the left shore, you'll round a point. Before the tip of the point, there is a possible campsite. Once around this point you will pass a large colony of swallows housed in the bank and then come to a very pretty small bay. There is a nice campsite on the downstream side of this bay (~ mile 2,222.1). With the swallows nearby, bugs will not be an issue. Another campsite is about 0.4 mile down the shore, also on the left. Holter Lake turns almost due north beyond this campsite for a distance of about 2 miles. Keep an eye out for wildlife in this section. I saw a pair of goats on the steep slope above the shore at mile 2,221. A bit farther down the shore, I also observed a pair of bald eagles and their nest. Also, if you are keeping track, and you started at the confluence, you have now paddled 100 miles.

As you work farther downstream, you approach Oxbow Bend. On the far shore you will see what appears to be a possible portage route across a low saddle at the start of this 2-mile-long peninsula (~ mile 2,219.8). The distance may be less than 0.8 mile. I did not investigate this possibility, but if the wind is blowing hard, you might want to scout this area for a possible portage. Of course, watch where you put your feet and keep an eye out for snakes.

There are a number of campsites in the vicinity. There is a camping area on the right at mile 2,220.5, near the mouth of Cottonwood Creek. Another site is 0.5 mile down on the same side. On the left side, you will find a very nice campsite once you round the point and begin to work your way south at mile 2,219.3. Another campsite is 0.4 mile down this shore. At the bottom of the bend, the lake widens to 0.5 mile across. There are homes and cabins along the left shore. The Indian Trails Bar is along here, and I was told that it is a good stop ("Beer is cold and burgers are good"). However, because it was windy, I stayed on the right, worked around the point, and then crossed over to reach the left shore at about mile 2,217, about 0.5 mile before a power line crosses the lake.

There are numerous cabins and homes along this left shore but few places to pull out until just after you work your way around a small point at mile 2,215.6. Just beyond this point is a marginally acceptable campsite. After this, you are committed to working around the next point, which brings you onto the main body of Holter Lake, where you will have to paddle for almost 2 miles to get to a decent campsite. On the north side of this point, the water can get quite rough. Nevertheless, locals recommend that paddlers stay on this west (left) side. Initially you may have to deal with relatively rough conditions, but as you work farther down the shore, you'll get to more sheltered paddling. Also, you'll find a couple shady places where you can pull out or camp just after mile 2,213.5. If you opt for the right shore, there are BLM campgrounds with all the amenities at Departure Point and Juniper Bay.

Before you reach Holter Dam, you'll work past two bays and then along a 0.5-mile stretch of steep, white rock bluff that runs to the northwest. At mile 2,211.6, the bluff cuts back to the southwest. Here you have a choice: You can either paddle to the portage take-out to the left of the dam or paddle about 0.4 mile north to the Holter Lake Lodge ramp (46.99246/-111.99540). There is a good restaurant at the lodge; you can get a cold beverage and a custom-designed cheeseburger at the bar. The bar itself is a real antique. According to the bartender, the structure was originally installed during the steamboat era at a Fort Benton bar and brothel. In the mid-1800s, Fort Benton was a wide-open town at the end of the navigable Missouri. Elbow up to the bar, have a cold one, and imagine the unbuttoned pageantry this bar has silently witnessed.

Just to the east is the Holter Lake Recreation Area (406-235-4314), where you can camp or fill your water jugs. There are some shaded sites for tent folk near the water to the north of the boat ramp. The campground manager here, Rocky Infanger, has assisted paddlers on numerous occasions. I found this to be a great stop; everyone here–the campground hosts and other members of the staff–were very helpful.

Author's kayak at the Dearborn Country Inn pull-out. Paddlers are welcome here; there is a nice floater's camp behind the inn.

If you want to manually portage the Holter Lake Dam, the take-out is on the left (west) side of the dam (mile 2,211.1; 46.98971/-112.00659). As you approach the dam, the take-out will be apparent. From here you'll follow a gravel road down for about 0.4 mile to a ramp and campground. Once you are downhill, the gate across the road may be closed. To your left there is a path that leads you to a smaller gate. Continue on this path to the road leading to the ramp (46.99351/-112.01007). There are nice shaded campsites here, vault toilets, and water. This is a popular campground for anglers; you'll see many drift boats here. The stretch below the dam is blue ribbon fishing for many miles. Special regulations apply, so get a copy of the rules.

If you came ashore at Holter Lake Lodge or the nearby campground, you can probably arrange for a ride down to the campground and ramp at the Wolf Creek Bridge (mile 2,208.4; 47.02109/-112.01330). I visited the bar at the lodge and met Bill and Jean Anderson from Stevensville, Montana. We talked and had a few beers, and they agreed to help me with my portage to the Wolf Creek ramp the following day. If you put in at the Wolf Creek ramp, you will miss the 2.5 miles of the river immediately below the dam and the Wolf Creek Bridge.

◆ Downstream Holter Dam put-in (mile 2,210.7) to Great Falls take-out (mile 2,121.5): 89.2 miles *(Maps 1.A.8–1.A.9)*

The water below Holter Dam is clear and cold. You'll see many large trout as you float along with a good current. About half a mile below the Wolf Creek ramp (mile 2,208), you will be just a shade over 112 degrees west longitude, the farthest west that you can be on the Missouri River. Your latitude is 47 degrees north and will continue to increase. You will not see a sustained drop in latitude until beyond Montana's border with North Dakota.

This is a blue ribbon trout stream, and according to biologists this section supports as many as 3,800 fish per river mile. You'll see enough of them to believe this statistic. You'll also see significant numbers of anglers in waders standing in the shallows or floating the river in drift boats or on mini-catamaran-style rafts. In fact, you have to pay careful attention to successfully thread your way through the congested areas. If you can, give anglers a wide berth. Try to slip by them without paddling if that is possible. Most anglers realize that you are not going to be able to stop your boat for them. If you can, however, pick a course that does not cross the area into which they are casting. If this is not possible, call out to them to let them know that you are coming through, and pass by them with a minimum of paddling so you don't scare the fish. They will appreciate the courtesy.

Along the left shore you will see a railroad line that parallels the river, but you won't see any trains. Several years ago, a section of track was washed away near the town of Ulm, some 50 miles downriver. To date, this washout has not been repaired. Also paralleling the river is Interstate 15. You'll get occasional views of that highway and cross under its bridges six times. This is not a remote area. Pristine, yes; remote, no. On the surrounding hills, pine trees are scattered among striking and colorful rock formations. Even with a nearby interstate, there are many beautiful vistas. You should see many bald eagles, ospreys, and pelicans.

Campsites along this stretch are generally limited to those established on public land, mostly at ramps. Most of the land along the river is privately held. The Craig Fishing Access Site (F.A.S.) ramp and campground is upstream from the bridge on the left at mile 2,203 (47.07394/-111.96223). There is water here and toilets. Farther downstream you'll pass for the first time under I-15. Pay attention in this area because there are some large rocks in the channel that you must avoid. A half mile down from the bridge, on your left, is a railroad tunnel. This is almost exactly at river mile 2,200. I saw many big trout as I paddled through here.

Less than 4 miles downstream from Craig is the Stickney Creek F.A.S. ramp (mile 2,199.3; 47.11679/-111.94531). This is an undeveloped site; there is a vault toilet but no water. I would not recommend camping here. The Spite Hill F.A.S. is 0.7 mile farther downstream on the left. There is no ramp here and no water, but there is a vault toilet. Access from the river is moderately easy, and camping is permitted. About half a mile beyond Spite Hill, the river turns to the northeast. You will see a power line and a number of homes; stay to the right as you work around the next bend. There is a small gravel ramp on the right side (47.12799/-111.91486) before you cross again under an I-15 bridge. The Dearborn River joins the Missouri on your left (~ mile 2197.4).

The Mid Cañon Fishing Access Site is 1.4 miles downriver (mile 2,195.9 left; 47.12356/-111.88434). There is a hand-launch site here for paddlers and drift boats, and a vault toilet, but no water. Less than a mile ahead you will again pass under a section of I-15. Immediately after that, on your left, you will see the Dearborn Country Inn, a must-stop for paddlers. Although primarily catering to fly fishers, you will find good hospitality here. The owner, Marty Williams, welcomes voyagers. He has a small camping area near the river outfitted with a shower and a toilet. Pull out at the landing near the railroad

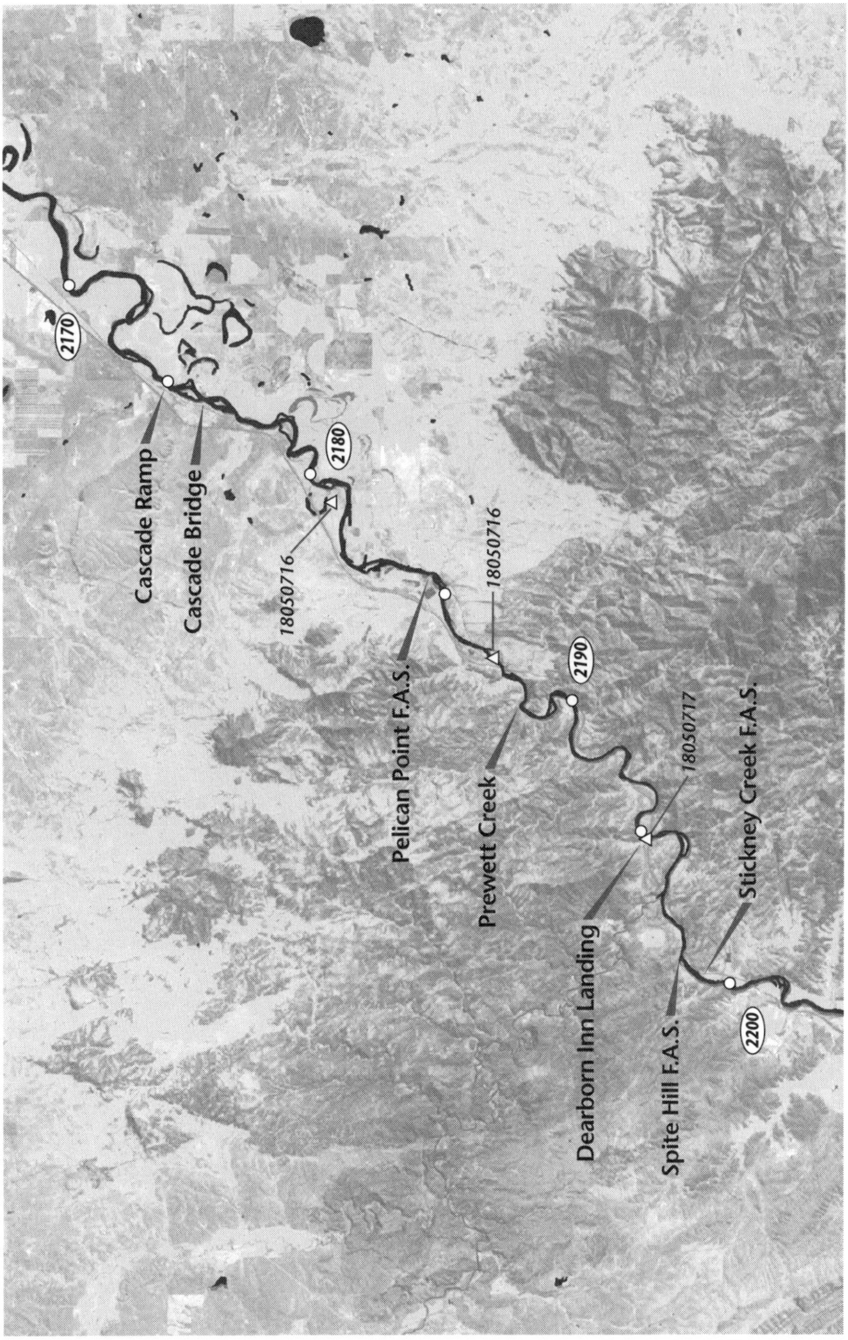

Map 1.A.8: Mile 2,200 to 2,175; some of the best trout fishing water that you will ever paddle.

trestle bridge, walk under it, and follow the path up to the inn. This stop is about 16 miles downriver from Holter Dam.

If you continue on, you'll cross under I-15 twice in the next 2 miles and work through a series of sweeping river bends. By the time things straighten out, you will have floated 6 river miles to make less than 4 as-the-crow-flies miles. Just before the river straightens, you will pass three fishing access sites. The first is at mile 2,190 on the right. About 1.4 miles downstream on the right is the Mountain Palace ramp (47.16140/-111.82293). There is camping here and a vault toilet, but no water. The Hardy Bridge access site is 0.9 mile downstream on the left. Camping is permitted; there is a vault toilet, but no ramp and no water. The Prewett Creek F.A.S. is just before mile 2,188 (47.17086/-111.82696). Here there is a ramp and vault toilet, but no water. Camping is permitted. Across the road is Osterman's Missouri River Inn, a four-minute walk from the campground. At the inn you can get a very good meal.

One mile downstream from the Prewett ramp, you will cross under I-15 for the last time until you arrive at Great Falls. There are rapids here, beginning with a set you will need to negotiate as you pass under the bridge. Once past the bridge, the river forks at a low-lying, car-sized boulder. You should approach this feature with care, and be prepared to make a hard left turn as you get close to it. The fast water continues beyond this obstruction for almost 0.5 mile. This section, known as Halfbreed Rapids (recently renamed Pine Island Rapids), is popular with rafters. A drift boat guide told me that this section provides him with a chance to "dampen" an ungracious client.

Pelican Point Fishing Access Site is 2 miles downstream from the end of the whitewater excitement (mile 2184.4; 47.20114/-111.77270). The river widens and the current slows as you approach the Pelican ramp, where there is camping and a vault toilet, but no water and little shade. I pulled in here for a rest and saw a young girl catch a nearly 2-pound trout while fishing for just a few minutes from the ramp. So maybe you can do without the shade.

Pelican Point is 26.6 miles downstream from Holter Dam. The next ramp where you can take out is 8.5 miles downstream from Pelican Point, below the town of Cascade. I saw few areas along the shore where you might camp as I paddled to Cascade. So once you get to Pelican, you are at a decision point. If you started at Holter Dam and elect to continue on, you may end up paddling nearly 40 miles by the end of the day. However, there is generally a pretty good current until you get past Cascade. If the weather is holding, consider going for it. There is a very good stop at Cascade.

After a brief rest at Pelican Point, I continued on to Cascade. Before I reached the town, I saw several bald eagles and ospreys. About a mile below the ramp, the river widens considerably. This section is the Tintinger Slough. Here there are several large islands and some areas of marsh. You will need to pick your way through the channels here. Stay with the channel with the best flow. As I neared Cascade, after mile 2,177, I stayed left. At the Cascade Bridge, also stay left. The Cascade ramp is a mile downstream from the town, at mile 2,175 (47.28074/-111.68891). There is pretty much nothing at this ramp; it's a dump (literally a "recycling area"), but the town itself is nice. The fishing access site at the bridge (right) is closed.

As I approached the Cascade Bridge, I couldn't decide whether to go left or right. I let the boat decide, and it tended left so I followed that channel. I paddled along a steep shore with homes scattered, and then saw a guy talking on his cell phone on the shore. I hailed him, he asked how far I was going, I told him, and then I asked if there was a place to camp nearby. He said, "You can camp right here. Tie your boat up at my dock." So I did.

My benefactor turned out to be Terry Curnow, who along with his wife, Pam, took me in, watered and fed me, and arranged for my accommodations. It turned out that my hosts have regularly hosted paddlers coming down or going up the river. They own the local motel (badgermotel@mcn.net) and Laundromat, and Terry builds heirloom quality wooden kayaks. So consider a stop at Cascade; it is a nice little town with good friendly people. You can rest and resupply here.

With decent weather, the nearly 50-mile paddle from Cascade to Great Falls is a two-day affair. The current slows down considerably, and your aspect changes frequently as the river snakes all over the river bottoms. So you may periodically have to deal with headwinds. For a better appreciation of just how winding the channel is in this section, consider the fact that you will paddle 2 river miles for every 1 as-the-crow-flies mile between Cascade and Great Falls.

◆ Cascade (mile 2,175) to Great Falls take-out (mile 2,121.5: ~ 53 river miles *(Maps 1.A.8 & 1.A.9)*

If you want to see the big birds of prey–eagles and ospreys–this is a prime section to paddle. Between Cascade and Ulm, almost 25 miles, I saw nine bald eagles and four ospreys. The landscape generally flattens out, and here the river has taken advantage of topography's loosening of the leash. Former traces of the river's paths can be seen almost everywhere you look. There are numerous small oxbow lakes throughout the area. These provide good habitat for waterfowl and a host of other riparian creatures.

If you are looking for a place to camp below Cascade, you can find sites every few miles. About 0.4 mile after the Cascade ramp, there is a possible campsite on the right. A mile farther down you'll see the Wing Dam Fishing Access Site on the left (mile 2,173.7). The wing dam is a large wooden structure that you cannot miss, designed to protect the nearby railroad bed from being washed out by the river. A mile farther downstream, after the channel cuts sharply to the left, you'll see an island with possible campsites.

At the tip of the next bend (mile 2,172), I observed two immature bald eagles, while engaged in what appeared to be aerial combat, tumble to the shore locked talon to talon. Either this was a territorial dispute or what passes for lovemaking among the big birds. In any event the action was rough. I came around the bend just in time to see them hit the ground and bounce. They seemed stunned, and I was curious, so I pulled into shore and got out of my kayak. They were face to face, clutching each other tightly, and they did not disengage until I got within 10 feet of them. One of them flew to the branch of a nearby tree. The other turned to face me and glared. These may have been immature eagles, but they were impressively big when I got close to them. As it was clear that I was interrupting something, I stepped back to my kayak slowly.

The river continues to wind around a series of long bends. Nearly 7 miles farther downriver, as you work around the Nelson Island bend, you'll see a private boat ramp (mile 2,165.3). Beginning at mile 2,163 and continuing for the next 9 miles, there are several potential campsites. Once you round the sharp point at mile 2,159, you'll see homes on the left; on the right you will find a level sandy beach. The downstream side of an inside bend often provides a nice sandy place to pull out.

As you round the next big bend 2 miles farther downstream (mile 2,157), four large grain elevators will come into view. A half mile beyond this you will cross under a power line. From here it is 1.2 miles to the Dunes Fishing Access Site (mile 2,155.2 left; 47.40012/-111.52704). Here there is a carry-in boat ramp and a vault toilet, but no water. There are shaded sites here, but no camping. The Ulm Bridge Fishing Access Site is on the right, less than 4 miles downstream (mile 2151.4; 47.43036/-111.50171). After you cross under the bridge, you'll see the ramp on the right. There is a vault toilet here. The town is about a half mile to the northwest. I stopped here briefly and talked with a local man who was picking up soda cans, beer bottles, and broken glass. I helped him gather up the trash as we talked. He said that families bring children down here and that someone has to clean the place up. It occurred to me as I paddled away from the ramp that I should have asked his name. Somehow, we should honor folks like this; sadly there are few of them.

◆ Ulm (mile 2,151.4) to the Great Falls portage take-out (mile 2,121.5): ~ 29.9 miles *(Map 1.A.9)*

Assuming that you started the day at or near Cascade, you have paddled 25 miles. From Ulm it is about 30 miles to the Great Falls portage take-out. Downstream from Ulm the speed of the current slows considerably. Weather permitting, you should continue on for another hour or two. This will allow you to arrive at Great Falls earlier in the day, and will permit the courtesy shuttle folks more time to get your transportation arranged. It would be helpful to them if you could call from the Ulm area to let them know you are a day out and at about what time you expect to arrive at the take-out.

On the left, as you leave the Ulm ramp, you will see the section of railroad track that the river washed away. You'll continue to make your way downriver on a course that folds back and forth on itself like the center of an accordion. The Smith River joins the Missouri at the bottom of the first bend below Ulm (mile 2,149.6). The Smith River Fishing Access Site is near the mouth in this area, and for a mile or so downstream there appeared to be several possible campsites. I began looking for a campsite as I worked my way around the next bend. I passed some homes on the left, continued for another 1.5 miles, and eventually spotted a deer trail coming down the bank to the water. I put ashore, found an acceptable site, and made my camp (mile 2,146.5). That evening I watched deer cross the river from an island just downstream. In twos and threes, they waded across the shallows to the opposite side. Once across, they worked along the shore, fading in and out behind clumps of willow brush, to a place where they could climb the bank to get to the cornfields above. Looking over my map I could see that I was about 25 river miles from the Great Falls take-out. Looking at the satellite image of the area, I could see that I would be entering an area of greater topographic relief. Here, constrained by the geology, the river's freedom to wander is on a tighter leash.

The river widens as you approach the next point; stay left as you near the bend and then work to the right once you are around the point. The river narrows here, and the current picks up a bit, then the river widens again. At mile

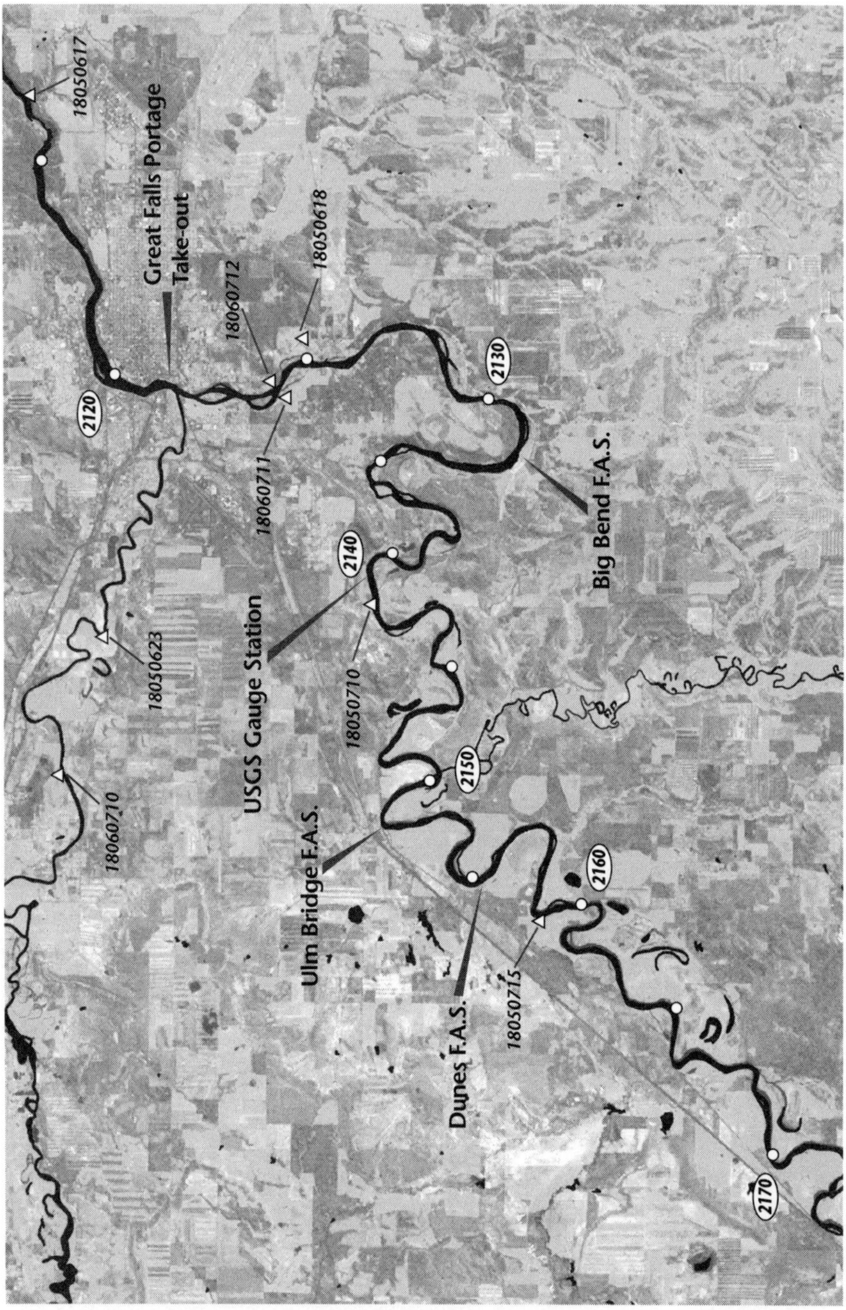

Map 1.A.9: Mile 2,175 to 2,115—You must portage around Great Falls. Phone numbers for a courtesy shuttle are posted at the portage take-out at mile 2,121.5.

2,145, about halfway to the next point, watch for shallows on the right. Once around the bend you will see houses on the left. On the right is a nice level sandy area. For the next several miles, as you work along the shore, you will see several areas where you could camp if the weather closed in on you. However, this section of the river is under the approach lane for aircraft landing at the Great Falls Airport. So any camp along here would be noisy.

As you paddle along this section, you will see Antelope Butte to the northwest. You'll pass under a power line and then by a USGS gauge station on the left at mile 2,140.6. After working a couple miles to the south, the river turns north. As you work closer to the next big bend, you will begin to see trophy homes littering the shoreline. A large home with its own boat ramp is at mile 2,136. A mile downstream, around the point, you will see some castlelike homes above the left bank. As you work your way to the south, you will see some cabins and homes and no trespassing signs on your right, followed by a pump house on the left at river mile 2,134.

As you approach the next bend, you will see a ramp on the right just before mile 2,132. This is not the Big Bend Fishing Access Site. The Big Bend hand-launch site is at a cleared area on the right about a third of the way around the bend (mile 2,131.7; 47.39009/-111.33866).

Just before I reached the access site, I met two paddlers in canoes working their way upriver. We stopped along the shore to talk. The paddlers turned out to be Kay Ruh and Bill Bartlett, from Bozeman, Montana. They had started their adventure at the eastern side of the state and were paddling upstream in stages. Their goal was to reach the headwaters on July 27, 2005, exactly 200 years after Lewis and Clark got there. I explained what I'd done so far, and we compared notes about what was behind each of us. Kay and Bill had paddled from the border with North Dakota, almost 600 miles up the Missouri. And, incredibly, they had paddled and towed their boats up the section of rapids below Marony Dam. They were both in excellent shape, had good equipment, and clearly knew what they were doing. We shared food and experiences. It's not often that you meet fellow travelers on the river. Since most are going downstream, they are either ahead or behind. You hear about those ahead of you, but it's not often that you catch up to them. Anyone coming upstream, however, you'll probably meet. And you want to meet folks like Kay and Bill; this couple is at the far end of the excellent paddler's yardstick.

As you round Big Bend and turn to the north, the left side becomes sandy and very shallow. Work your way over to the right well before the next bend. You'll pass Fisher Island on your right at mile 2,129, and again encounter sandy shallow areas a mile farther downstream. Work over to the right before these shallows. The White Bear Island F.A.S. is at mile 2,127.3; a small access area is on the right. You will see a short section of sand beach sandwiched between riverfront homes, with a willow-choked path leading up to the road. There are no signs that mark this area. As you paddle along the right shore, you should see a stone-lined fire pit and some forked sticks shoved in the sand to hold fishing poles.

From here to the portage take-out ramp is about 6 miles. As a general rule, because of pleasure boat traffic, you'll want to stay to one side. It would be a good idea to put on your spray skirt. At mile 2,124, take the left channel and stay to the right. Once you reach the downstream end of the island, you'll approach another island. Work over to the right and stay along the shore. You'll cross under the Highway 89 bridge, and paddle less than 0.2 mile to reach the portage take-out ramp on the right at mile 2,121.5 (47.49492/-111.30999). You'll see a large sign that says, PORTAGE HERE, which also instructs you to see the sign's backside for shuttle information. Four telephone numbers are provided:

MRCC (Medicine River Canoe Club)	406-452-7379
MRCC	406-727-2762
MRCC	406-452-6946
PPL	406-268-2300

The sign also provides the information that a phone is 0.5 mile downstream. There is a larger and busier boat ramp just downstream on the right (47.50071/-111.30788). If you have a cell phone, call from the portage ramp to arrange for a shuttle. This ramp does not see the heavy use that the downstream ramp enjoys. Along the shore nearby are motels and restaurants. You could, of course, enjoy a night of decadence and shuttle out the morning after.

I had already arranged for a shuttle with some colleagues at the Lewis and Clark Foundation, but I did call the first number on the sign to get more information about the shuttles. I spoke with Linda Payne, who told me that paddlers could get a shuttle to the put-in either below Morony Dam or at Carter Ferry. There are some impressive rapids below Morony Dam; this put-in is for experienced paddlers. If you arrange a shuttle, any of the folks coming to pick you up can give you expert advice with respect to your best option.

Do You Put in below Morony Dam or at Carter Ferry, or at the Third Alternative?

Only experienced paddlers should put in below Morony Dam. Although the passage is less difficult at higher water levels, the first set of rapids below the dam is almost a mile in length, ending near Belt Creek (right; mile 2,104.2). There are dangerous shelves along the canyon sides and many sharp-edged rocks to be avoided. Make a mistake here and you can damage or destroy your boat. A second, shorter set of rapids is 0.5 mile farther downstream at mile 2,103.5, and a final short set is above mile 2,102. Gilbert Payne, a Great Falls ACA-certified canoe instructor, told me that area paddlers say these rapids are "Class II with Class III consequences." Before you put in at Morony, you want to carefully scout the situation and work out the line you will take through the first and longest set of rapids. After looking the Marony situation over, you may decide to put in at Carter Ferry.

According to Wayne Willkomm, who ran the Marony Dam rapids at low water conditions in the summer of 2004, the *reason the rapids below Marony Dam are so dangerous is that they can lull an unsuspecting boater into going down any one of the easy ribbons off the initial ledges. The rapids consist of these 2- to 5-foot-high ledges followed by the boulder fields, immediately below, which have broken away from the ledge above. One can most easily pass over the ledge at any of the smooth ribbons of water, but the boulder fields immediately below are impassable and one can't traverse across the fields to a safe passage. Thus, any boater becomes like a pinball in a pinball machine, ricocheting off rock after rock. My understanding is that, despite all kinds of padding and life preservers, the [two paddlers who drowned in 2004] first lost arm function, then consciousness, and then drowned, before anyone could get to them. The best and, in some cases, the only way through the boulder fields was to start with a poor ledge crossing; it absolutely had to be done that way.*

The put-in below Morony Dam is at mile 2,105.5 (left; 47.58367/-111.06054). The Carter Ferry put-in is 14.4 miles downstream at mile 2,089.1 (left; 47.76072/-110.89707). If you put in at Carter Ferry, you will miss paddling almost half the distance to Fort Benton. The alternative to these launch sites is the Widow Coulee Fishing Access Site, 3.5 miles below the Morony Dam (right; 47.62839/-111.03214). However, if you have looked over the Morony rapids and (wisely) decided to put in elsewhere, do not expect the complimentary shuttle driver to take you to Widow Coulee. Take the Carter Ferry

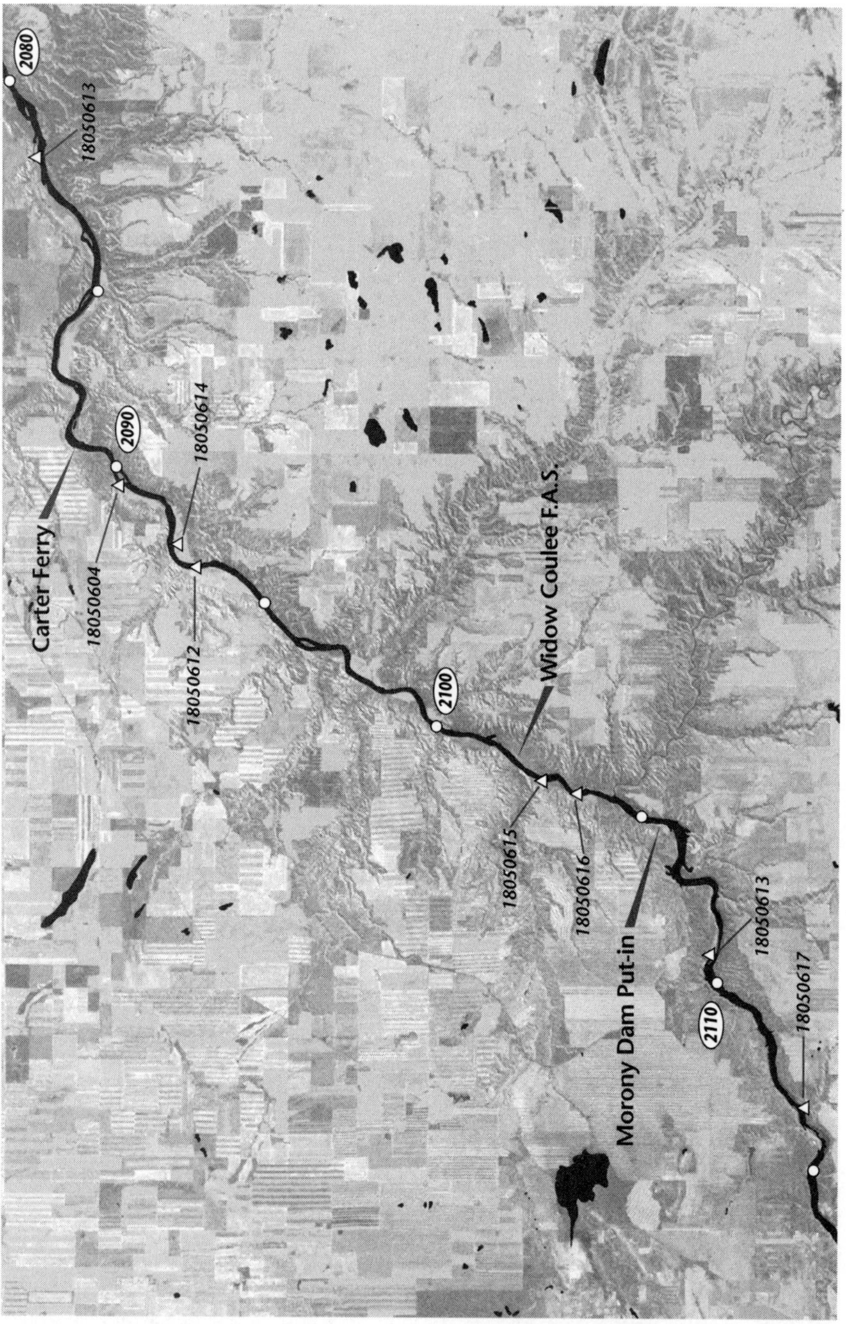

Map 1.A.10: Below Great Falls (~ mile 2,104.2) to near Fort Benton (mile 2,073.9).

put-in with grace. Although the Widow Coulee put-in is just 3.5 miles downriver, it is on the opposite side. To get there you have to drive back to Great Falls, get on the other side of the river, and then drive for more than an hour. Courtesy has limits.

My suggestion is to arrange a shuttle to Widow Coulee if possible. You will avoid the rapids immediately below Morony Dam and still paddle most of the distance to Fort Benton. However, getting to Widow Coulee by road is more difficult than getting to Morony Dam or Carter Ferry. To get to Widow Coulee, you drive east of Great Falls and then come up to the river from the south over a long series of dusty gravel roads. The signage is modest; if you are not familiar with the route, it is easy to get lost. Get a good map. Also, this road becomes slick after just a light rain. As you get near the river, the road descends sharply and there are no guardrails. The drop-off along the side of the road is impressive. Locals will not drive this road unless it is in good condition. Finally, if you are able to arrange a ride to Widow Coulee, persuade your driver to take $10 to get his or her dusty vehicle washed and waxed once safely back to town.

◆ Below Morony Dam (mile 2,105.5) or from Widow Coulee (mile 2,102) to Fort Benton (mile 2,073.9): ~ 32 or 28 miles *(Maps 1.A.10 & 1.B.1–1.B.3)*

From the Morony put-in, it is 3.5 fast-paced and wet miles to Widow Coulee, on the right at mile 2,102. You'll see a vault toilet and a ramp. The camping area is within a barbed wire fence intended to limit cattle traffic. There is little shade and this is not the perfect campsite, but there are limited places to camp downstream. If you arrive at Great Falls by early afternoon, the portage will take some time, and it may be late afternoon before you get to Widow Coulee. So consider camping here. Fort Benton is about 28 miles from here, an easy day's paddle given the good current.

You will have good current and several stretches of fast water on this section. About 2.5 miles downriver you'll see an old cabin on the right. Once you round the next bend, the river will straighten, and you will enter a section of modest rapids at mile 2,098. From here, you'll paddle for 1.5 miles and then work your way beyond two additional short sections of fast water. Beyond this, the river straightens for about 2 miles, and there are areas of level land on your left. As you approach the next bend, you will see trailers on the left. Black Coulee joins the river on your left at mile 2,093. I noted a number of possible campsites as I rounded the bend. Once around this bend, you will come to an area of shallow water and modest rapids (mile 2,091.5). I negotiated this section on the left side. You'll encounter another set of small rapids at mile 2,090 before arriving at the Carter Ferry (47.76072/-110.89707). The Carter Ferry (406-734-5335) is the only river crossing between Great Falls and Fort Benton. From here, you are less than 16 miles from the Fort Benton take-out. There is a house here, with a telephone, a vault toilet, and a ferry.

As you approach the bend downstream from mile 2,080 (see map 1.B.3), you will come to a modest set of rapids. This is the last section of whitewater on the way to Fort Benton. The area along the right shore here is Cottonwood Bottoms. From the neat and tidy gray farmhouse that you see on the right, you have to paddle about 4 miles to get around Roosevelt Island to Fort Benton's Chouteau County Fairgrounds Canoe Camp take-out on the left at mile 2,074.3 (47.80481/-110.67950).

Depending on water levels, you may have to drag your boat over a shallow gravel bar or paddle beyond the camp and work back upstream along the shore to get to the channel leading to the take-out area. The fairgrounds are immediately downstream from the ramp and campground. If you go beyond the fairgrounds, you have gone too far. At the campgrounds there are campsites, vault toilets, and drinking water, and it is just a short walk into town. Stop here; Fort Benton is a great little town.

SEGMENT 1.B: Fort Benton Canoe Camp (mile 2,074.3) to James Kipp State Park (mile 1,921) *(Maps 1.B.1 & 1.B.2)*

- **River miles:** 153.3
- **Difficulty level:** Low
- **Typical time to complete:** 7 to 10 days

In theme parks the profound, subtle, and protracted experience of running a river is reduced to a loud, quick, safe equivalence, a pleasant distraction. People only able to venture into the countryside on annual vacations are, increasingly, schooled in the belief that wild land will, and should, provide thrills and exceptional scenery on a timely basis. If it does not, something is wrong, either with the land itself or possibly with the company outfitting the trip.

Barry Lopez, *About This Life*

This is one of the more remote, most scenic, pristine, and free-running

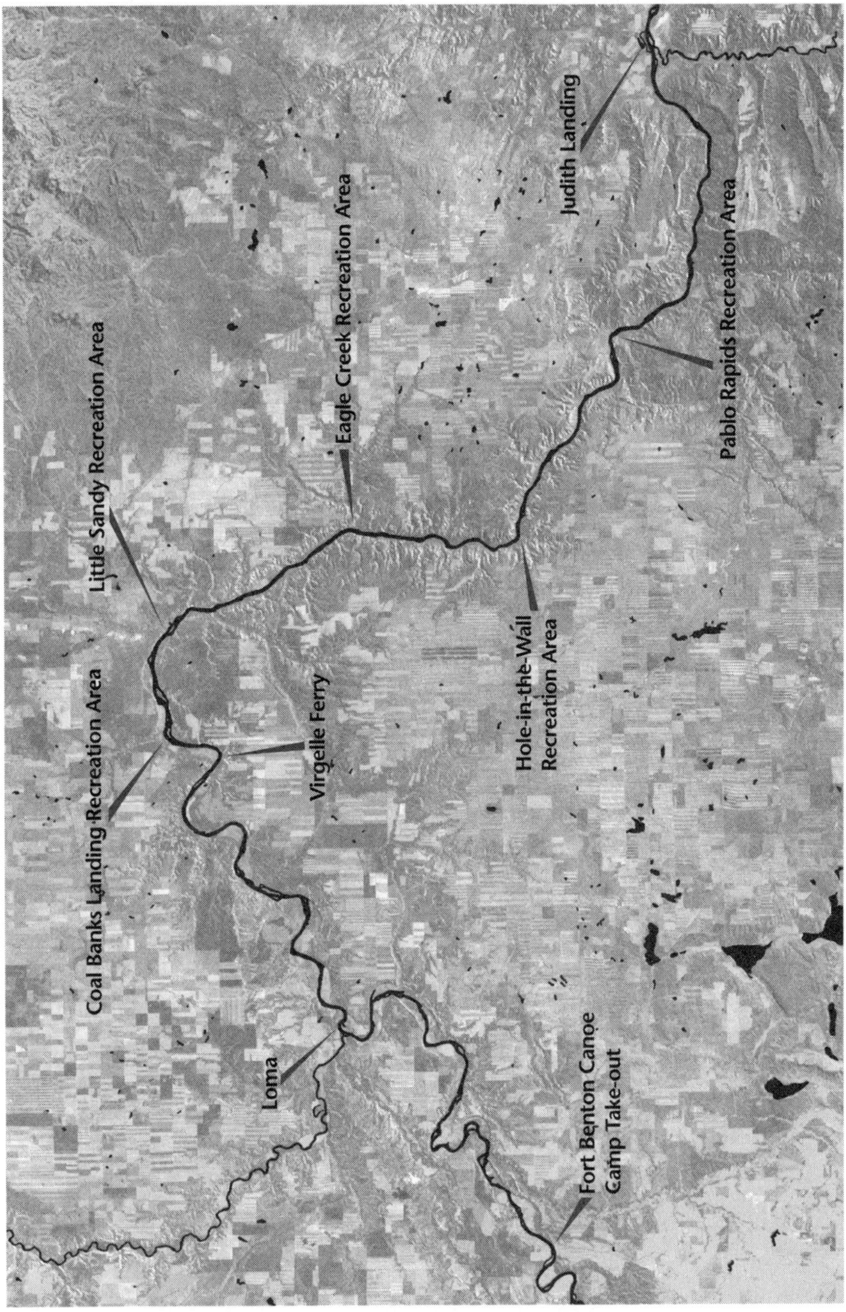

Map 1.B.1: The first 90.9 miles of Segment 1.B (Fort Benton to James Kipp State Park), showing location of the Fort Benton Canoe Camp (mile 2,074.3) to Judith Landing (mile 1,983.1).

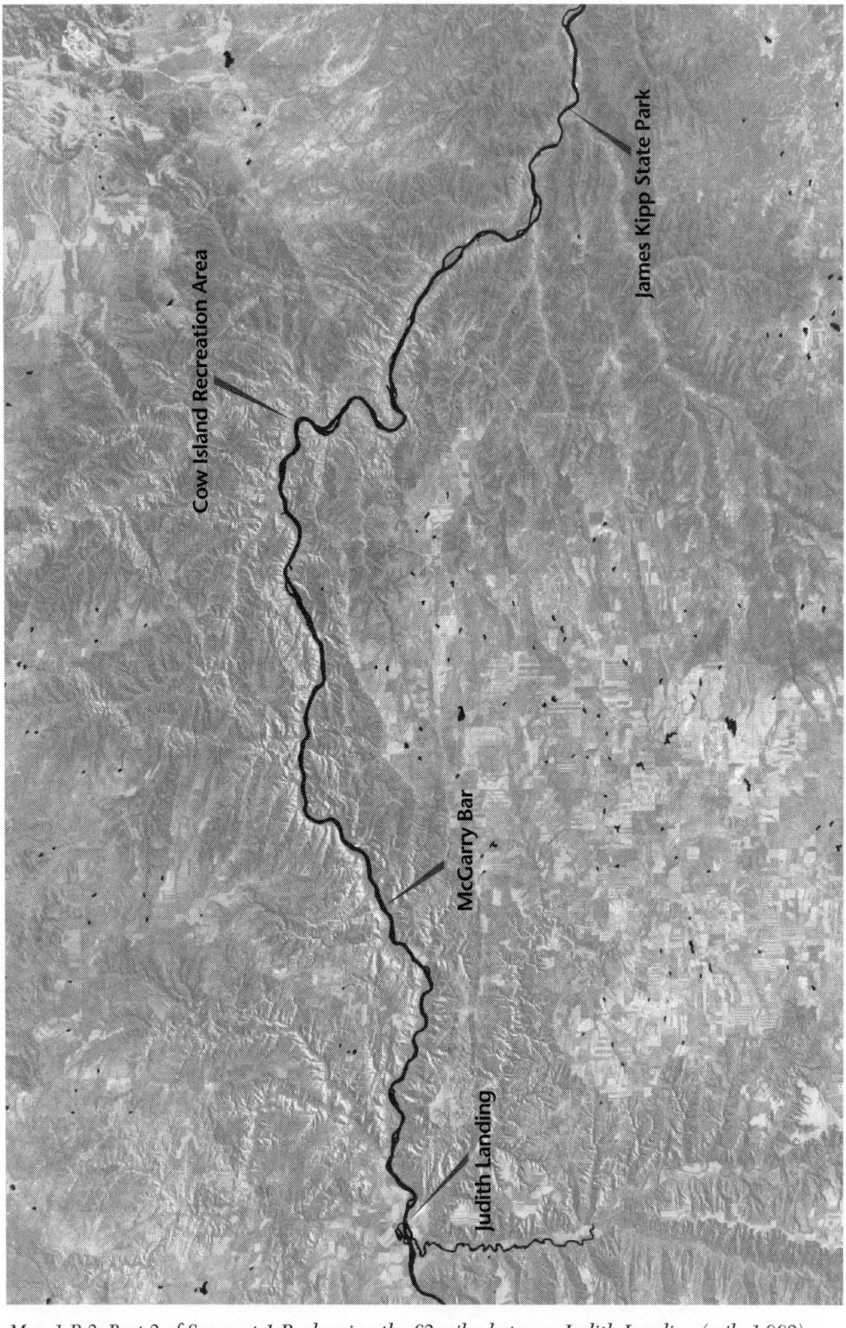

Map 1.B.2: Part 2 of Segment 1.B, showing the 62 miles between Judith Landing (mile 1,983) and James Kipp State Park (mile 1,921).

sections of the river. It is also one of the most heavily floated sections. Every year, thousands of canoers and kayakers start their Missouri downriver float from Fort Benton. From my perspective, this trip is best done in early June, before the river becomes crowded with too many groups of floaters. Although some who start at Fort Benton make the two-day float to Coal Banks (42.6 miles), most are interested in paddling through the White Cliffs area and so continue on, to pull out at Judith Landing (90.8 miles). The trip through the White Cliffs section, the most scenic anywhere along the river, is a three- or four-day float. Individuals wanting to make a shorter trip will typically start at the Coal Banks Landing near Virgelle. There are numerous outfitters headquartered in Fort Benton and one at Virgelle.

The town of Fort Benton, at the historic end of steamboat navigation on the Upper Missouri, is a good place to visit. The first steamboat reached the town in 1860, and when gold was discovered in the Northern Rockies in 1862, this became the principal jumping-off point. From the campground just upstream from the town, it is less than a 15-minute walk. The remains of the original Fort Benton are at the downstream end of town; there is a museum; an impressive sculpture of Lewis, Clark, Sacagawea and her child; a replica keelboat; and a statue of a dog named Shep. The Bureau of Land Management (BLM) maintains the Upper Missouri River Wild and Scenic Visitor Center on Front Street, where you can purchase highly detailed and waterproof maps of the river between Fort Benton and James Kipp State Park (406-622-5185; mid-May to mid-September).

While you are in town, you should visit the immaculately restored Grand Union Hotel and then walk along Front Street, known at one time as the "Bloodiest Block in the West." As the town's historic walking tour brochure relates, this street "was the wildest business district in the West; saloons, dance halls and brothels lined Front Street." Things are more peaceful today, and the town serves as the principal jumping-off point for paddlers starting down the Wild and Scenic section of the river.

Before jumping off I suggest a good meal at Bob's Riverfront Restaurant. I had a couple breakfasts here as I made preparations to start my Missouri River expedition in late May 2002. The food was good, as was the coffee, and the waitress was friendly. Historic photographs, mostly featuring cowboys, graced the walls. The second morning that I had breakfast here, while I was writing in my journal, I looked out the front window and saw an old pickup truck park in front of the restaurant. An older guy got out, dusted himself off, and came in the front door. The waitress, who had been arranging coffee cups on the shelf, glanced up and then said to the man, "You forgot your teeth." The man touched his mouth with his right hand and said, "Shit. I'll be back." He walked out the door, got in the truck, and pulled away. The waitress went right back to arranging cups. When I returned here in early July 2004, the historic photos were still on the walls. Added to the decor, however, were a host of antiques each discreetly sporting a price tag. Here, as elsewhere in town, things are scaling up. But the place remains friendly, and my breakfast was just as good as the one I enjoyed two years earlier.

While you are at Fort Benton, you should also visit the Palace Bar. Here you can enter the front door and turn left for a good haircut or right for a cold beer. If you sit at the bar, look back at the wall to the side of the door that you entered; you will see a head-mount of a huge steer. This is, well was, Ringo, a gentle steer who was considered to be a pet by locals. He liked people, loved to walk in parades, and was, according to one of the most efficient bartenders that I've ever met, "one fence-crawling S.O.B." According to the bartender, Ringo "just liked to get around." If you do stop in at the Palace, enjoy a cold one and toast old Ringo; he clearly was, and remains, a magnificent creature.

The Upper Missouri National Wild and Scenic River

The 149-mile-long Upper Missouri National Wild and Scenic River (UMNWSR) was created in 1976. It is managed by the Bureau of Land Management (BLM) based on three different classifications–wild, scenic, and recreational. As one BLM brochure explains:

Each classification contains several unique characteristics. Wild sections represent vestiges of primitive America and are generally inaccessible; scenic sections are largely primitive and undeveloped, but accessible in places by roads; and recreational sections are readily accessible and may have some development.

The establishment of the UMNWSR was not without controversy. Local landowners feared they might lose rights to land that had been in their families for generations. Ultimately a management program was adopted that attempts to balance the preservation of natural and cultural resources with multiple uses including recreation and livestock grazing. It is important to understand that some 60 percent of the land bordering the river is privately owned; public lands are clearly marked on the BLM's floater's guide. Unless you have explicit permission, you should only camp on public land.

Here, as elsewhere, you should practice "zero-impact" camping. Over the course of the summer, the UMNSWR sees more paddlers than anywhere else on the Missouri River. If the river is to remain "wild and scenic," every paddler must take responsibility to leave things better than they found them. Besides treading lightly, plan on packing out all your garbage and a few extra items that may have been overlooked by previous campsite occupants. Also plan on packing out your toilet waste. You will need to carry a portable toilet, and as the regulations explain, that means:

...either a washable, reusable toilet system or an approved degradable bag system specifically designed for human waste disposal. All portable toilet waste must be carried out of the river corridor and deposited in an authorized disposal facility. The washable, reusable system may be serviced at Kipp Recreation Area. The degradable bag system may be disposed of in dumpsters at the following locations: Coal Banks Landing, Judith Landing and Kipp Recreation Area.

For those of us in small boats, the degradable bag is the way to go. You can purchase bags in Fort Benton at most of the outfitters' shops or at Lehman's True Value on Front Street.

In addition to a waste disposal system, plan on carrying a gallon of water for every day you plan to be on the river. Opportunities to resupply are limited; the two semireliable wells at launch sites (Coal Banks, Kipp) are frequently out of service because of contamination. If water is available at these areas, I suggest that you filter it as a precaution. Locals will tell you not to filter river water, as this does not remove agricultural chemicals and other pollutants such as mine waste runoff. You should contact the BLM office at Fort Benton or Lewistown (406-538-7461) for the latest information.

Information/Maps/Resources

The most up-to-date information on river conditions and regulations can be obtained from the Lewistown BLM's "Upper Missouri River Breaks National Monument" website (www.mt.blm.gov/ldo/um/index.html). Especially useful is the section, "Planning a Trip on the River."

I highly recommend that you purchase a copy of *Montana's Wild and Scenic Upper Missouri River*, by Glenn Monahan and Chandler Biggs. This guidebook is the best source for information for the 149-mile-long Wild and Scenic section between Fort Benton and the Robinson Bridge (Highway 191). This book provides a river-mile referenced digest of historic events, along with information about the area's flora, fauna, and geology. There is no better, more comprehensive source for information on this section of the river. Also providing good information is the BLM booklet, *Highlights of the Upper Missouri National Wild & Scenic River Lewis & Clark National Historic Trail.*

With respect to maps, purchase the BLM's waterproof set, *Upper Missouri National Wild & Scenic River, maps 1 & 2 and maps 3 & 4.* To date, this two-sheet map set, covering the river from Fort Benton to Kipp, is the gold standard for Missouri River paddler's maps. In addition to providing mile-referenced information about the area's history and geology, there are sections on camping considerations, river safety, and comfort. This map can be purchased at the BLM's Fort Benton Visitor Center or ordered from the Lewistown BLM Field Office.

Another useful map is contained in the BLM's brochure, *Floating the Upper Missouri.* This source provides good general information, gives mile-marked information on management classifications of each section, lists 21 recreation areas and their GPS coordinates, and suggests different floating scenarios. This is a very useful document, but the information on where to obtain potable water is probably not accurate. Check about the availability of potable water with the BLM.

Suggested Readings

Some 15 Lewis and Clark campsites are along the river in this section. Several more camps are up the Marias River. Information about what transpired here during the trip west (May 24 to June 12, 1805) can be found in Vol. 4:187–282 (*Journals,* [Moulton, ed.]). Return trip event detail (July 28–30, 1806) can be found in Vol. 8:241–257 of the same source. Context about the events can be found in Stephen Ambrose's *Undaunted Courage* in chapters 18:226–229, 19:230–236, 31:393–394, and 32:395.

At Fort Benton two authors began Missouri River expeditions that resulted in classic accounts. In November 1901, James Willard Schultz floated to the Milk River confluence. His book, *Floating on the Missouri,* relates events of the trip and contains reminiscences of a lifetime of work and adventure along the river. John G. Neihardt launched his 1908 expedition from Fort Benton and eventually made landfall at Sioux City. You will enjoy both of these accounts because, as you float down the river, you will be able to identify many of the areas they describe.

Finally, the Nez Perce Trail crosses the Missouri about a day's paddle above the Kipp take-out. I recommend that you learn about and reflect on the circumstances leading to the flight of the Nez Perce tribe. I found Merrill D. Beal's *I Will Fight No More Forever: Chief Joseph and the Nez Perce War* useful and well written.

Paddler's Notes and Cautions

From a paddler's perspective, the BLM information related to this segment is outstanding. As an agency the BLM takes flack from a host of stakeholders; in this instance at least, they get things right and should be commended for their effort. I've thought hard about what I might add and settled on a review of the more important items that you need to consider, some commentary about my own experiences on this section, and mile marker/GPS information. Because the BLM's maps begin numbering with a Fort Benton start, I provide both Army Corps of Engineers (ACE) "mile mark from the Mississippi" and BLM mileage. Permits are not required to float the river, but be sure to register your float plan at the Fort Benton BLM Visitor Center, with a recreation area campground host, or at the registration box at your launch point. I recommend that you talk with the BLM folks at the visitor center; you will find them very helpful, and they will provide you with the most current information about conditions.

So what do you need to know? First, you will see motorized boat traffic on certain sections of the river. Segments open to traffic all year are the Fort Benton to Pilot Rock section and the Deadman's Rapids to Holmes Council Island section. Segments closed to upstream powerboat traffic on a seasonal basis (Memorial Day through the Sunday after Labor Day) include Pilot Rock to Deadman's Rapids and from Holmes Council Island to the Fred Robinson Bridge at James Kipp Recreation Area. Downstream travel is permitted at no-wake speed. Emergency or law-enforcement boats go upstream whenever necessary.

Camping areas are categorized as developed, minimally developed, or undeveloped. Developed areas are accessible by road and have boat ramps. Minimally developed areas have river-only access, vault toilets, and fire rings. Undeveloped areas have river access and fire rings. During the summer, some of these sites are apt to see hoards of floaters and associated noise. I recommend that you seek camps away from these sites; according to the BLM there are 90,000 acres of public land along the river, so check the map for public land and find better campsites. Islands have special restrictions because of nesting shore birds, so check for restrictions when you register.

According to BLM publications, the average summer current speed is 3.5 miles per hour and most floaters average 20 miles a day. Late May and early

June current speeds are faster depending on upstream snowmelt, rains, and what is being released from the many upstream dams. When I left Fort Benton on May 31, 2002, there was a strong current running, perhaps 4 to 5 mph. My moving average was almost 5.5 mph, and I made the 39 miles to Virgelle after a full day's paddle. With the slower summertime current, this is usually a leisurely two-day paddle. Water temperatures can be frigid during the spring runoff; wear appropriate gear and your life vest.

◆ Fort Benton Canoe Camp (mile 2,073.9) to Coal Banks (mile 2,031.3): 42.6 miles *(Maps 1.B.3 & 1.B.4)*

Note: To assist in the correlation of river mileage information in this section, I provide both ACE and BLM map mile marks for locations. The BLM mile mark is the number after the forward slash, as appears in the mileage information 2,073/1. However, after the first 20 miles or so, the BLM mile-mark locations diverge from the ACE mile-mark locations. I cannot account for this divergence and simply report the BLM mile-mark as I calculate it from the map.

From the Fort Benton (Chouteau County Fairgrounds) Canoe Camp launch (47.80481/-110.67950) at the upstream side of town to the Highway 80 bridge is about 1 mile. If water levels are low, you may have to bump through or walk your boat over gravel bars to get to deeper water. After you cross under the bridge, you pass ACE mile 2,073 and BLM mile 1. The Fort Benton ramp is at mile 2,072.9/1.1 left. You can launch from here, but there can be a fair amount of boat and trailer traffic, and the current can be quite swift because the ramp is on the outside bend.

After the ramp the river proceeds east for almost 4 miles, then angles to the southeast, and then begins a sharp bend to the north after mile 2,068/6. Along the outside bend of this turn is the Evans Bend Recreation Area, an undeveloped site (right; ~ 47.82055/-110.66277); this area stretches for more than 1 mile along the shore. After some 3 miles working to the north, the river cuts back hard to the south. Get used to such contortions. As the crow flies from the Fort Benton floater's launch, it is about 26 miles; to get to Coal Banks you will paddle 41.5 miles. At mile 2,057.5/16.5 right is Senieurs Reach Recreation Area (47.88027/-110.47305), another undeveloped camping site.

You will come to the first set of rapids just before mile 2,055/19. Depending on water levels you may get a bit of spray, but stay straight and there is little to

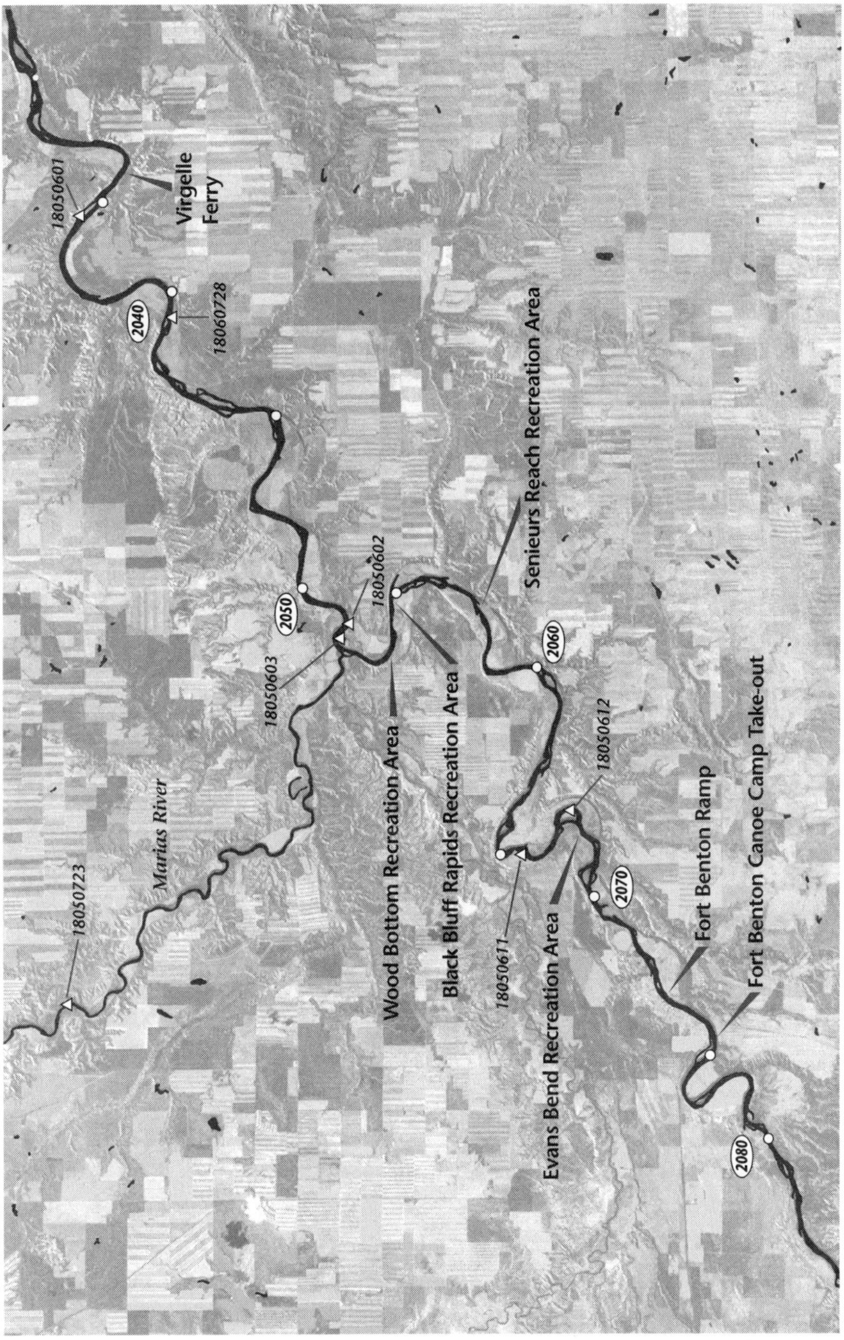

Map 1.B.3: Mile 2,080 above Fort Benton to the Virgelle Ferry at mile 2,034.

worry about. Steamboats had difficulty here; you should get through easily. The Black Bluff Rapids Recreation Area is along the left beginning at mile 2,054.5/19.5. About 0.5 mile below this is the Wood Bottom ramp at mile 2,053.6/20.3 left (47.91155/-110.49283). The Loma Bridge is less than a mile downriver.

The Marias River enters from the left after mile 2,053/21; the river meanders considerably here, so the exact confluence location varies over time. Lewis and Clark aficionados will remember this as "Decision Point," where the expedition paused for ten days to figure out which river was the Missouri. This is, of course, not an issue for downstream paddlers. From here to the Virgelle Ferry (mile 2,034/39.1 left; 48.00178/-110.25309) is 19 miles. Approach the crossing with caution; watch for low cables and stay well away from the ferry. As one author says about barges, "Nothing interesting can be seen from underneath." This is true also for the underside of a ferry.

I recommend a stop at the Virgelle Ferry and a trip to the Virgelle Mercantile (www.paddlemontana.com; 406-378-3110). If the ferry is along the left shore, swing wide around it and land along the shore below. You will find a place there to land and haul your boat out of the water. If you walk to the ferry landing, you will see a bell that you can ring for a lift to the store, which is about a mile up the road. At the Virgelle Merc in the restored ghost town of Virgelle, you will find an antiques store and some of the finest lodging and food anywhere on the entire Missouri River. Owners Don Sorensen and Jim Griffin have restored the original 1912 building and created a B&B that also houses guests in restored homesteader's cabins. Don and Jim also run an outfitting service from their location, the Missouri River Canoe Company, which provides fully guided or just outfitted river trips and shuttle services.

I stopped here because the Merc regularly sponsors a "Touch the Trail of Lewis and Clark Celebration" on June 1, to commemorate the passing of the expedition. A pitchfork fondue (steaks on a pitchfork cooked in a huge kettle) was advertised as well as a rendezvous, primitive cooking demonstration, and Lewis and Clark journal readings. While I was here, I met a group from the Montana Mountain Men Brigade who were planning to boat down the river after the celebration. We shared some meals together in the kitchen, talked about things Lewis and Clark hunting and fishing, and over the course of a few hours decided to float together down the river to their take-out at Judith Landing. The day after the celebration ended, I launched my kayak and paddled to Coal Banks Landing at mile 2,031.3/41.5 left (48.03222/

-110.23444), where I met Bob and Jerek Garritson, Bill Hammer, Nancy Krekeler, and Lyle Schwope, who were floating down the river in period costume in a replica pirogue. Over the next couple of days, we went downriver together. When we camped, I had an opportunity to observe how things were done in the early 1800s. I learned how to start a fire with flint and steel, how to start a fire in a driving rain, and some medicinal uses of local plants. Of course, not everything was exactly as it was back then. Inside wooden chests were coolers containing chilled beverages and elk steaks. Nevertheless, the meals we prepared over the campfire gave me a real taste for the way food was prepared 200 years ago.

◆ Coal Banks (mile 2,031.3) to Judith Landing (mile 1,983.1): 48.2 miles *(Maps 1.B.4 & 1.B.5)*

There is a BLM campground host at Coal Banks, a boat ramp, vault toilet, and campsites with fire rings. The well water is tested monthly, and the results may shut it down. So find out about water availability in advance. Also, it is always a good idea to drop by the campground host's trailer to get a downstream update. Hosts at facilities such as these can often provide helpful information, so bring your map with you to mark in updated information. About 5 miles below Coal Banks is the Little Sandy Recreation Area (mile 2,026.2/46.6 left; 48.02888/-110.13472), a minimally developed area.

Pilot Rock is on the left at mile 2,021.8/51 (~ 47.97330/-110.10664). Just below this at BLM mile 52 is the first of three UMNWSR-designated sections with seasonal motorized boat restrictions (downstream-only travel with no wake). The White Cliffs (also known as White Rocks) area begins near mile 2,020/53; this is perhaps the most spectacular area of the Upper Missouri. If you do not get here early in the season, the place may be overrun with boats. Still, a trip at anytime of the year is worthwhile as the scenery is truly magical. The Eagle Creek Recreation Area is at mile 2,016.7/55.7 left. This is a minimally developed site with a vault toilet and fire rings. There are cattle in the area and fencing generally proves ineffective. Watch your step, and take off your shoes before entering your tent.

You will see a number of landmark rock formations as you work downstream. At BLM mile 56 right is LaBarge Rock, named after a famous steamboat pilot, and at mile 56.9 is Grand Natural Wall. In their guidebook, *Montana's Wild and Scenic Upper Missouri River,* Monahan and Biggs note that Karl Bodmer's 1833 sketch, *View of the Stone Walls,* "is a view upriver from mile

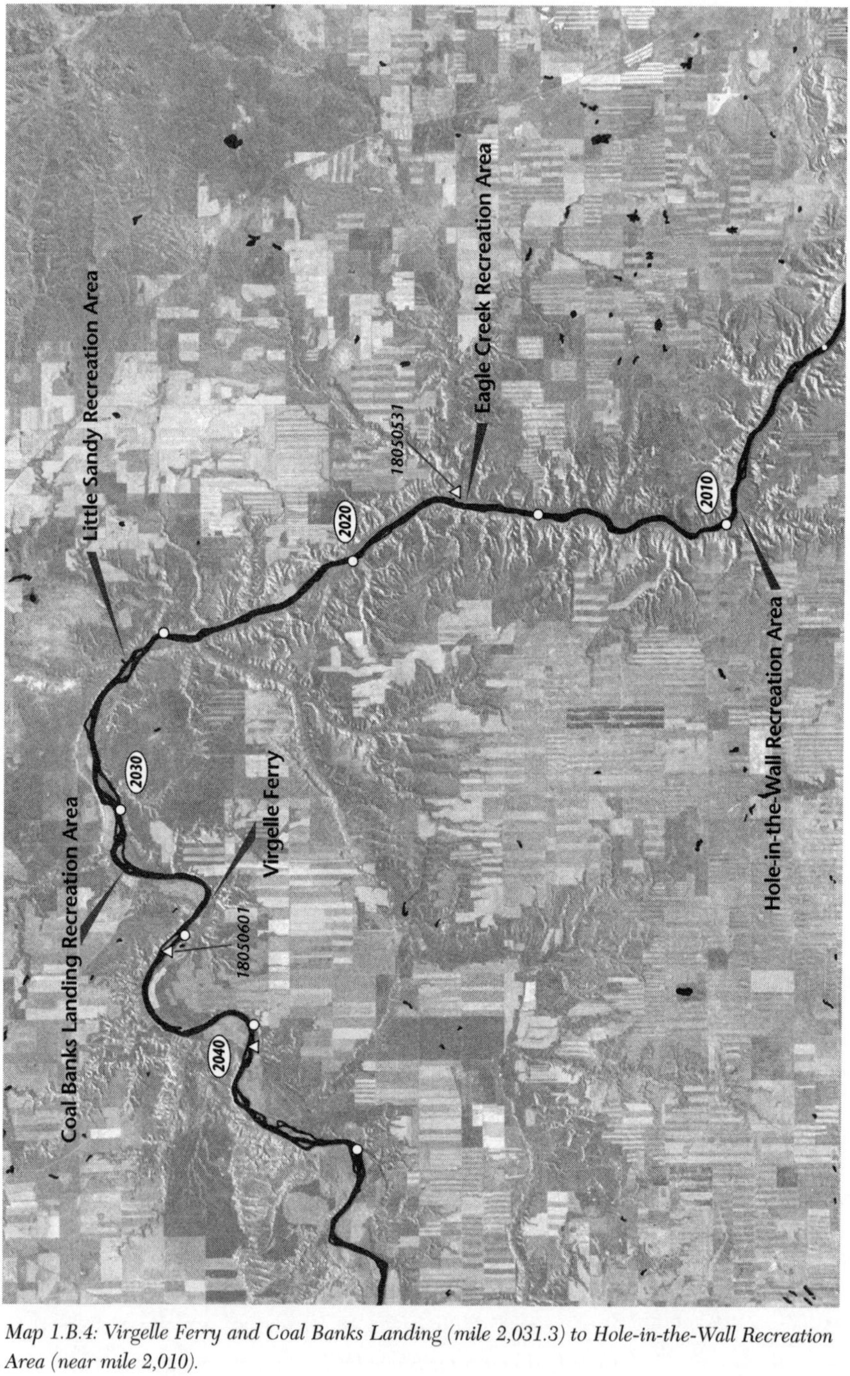

Map 1.B.4: Virgelle Ferry and Coal Banks Landing (mile 2,031.3) to Hole-in-the-Wall Recreation Area (near mile 2,010).

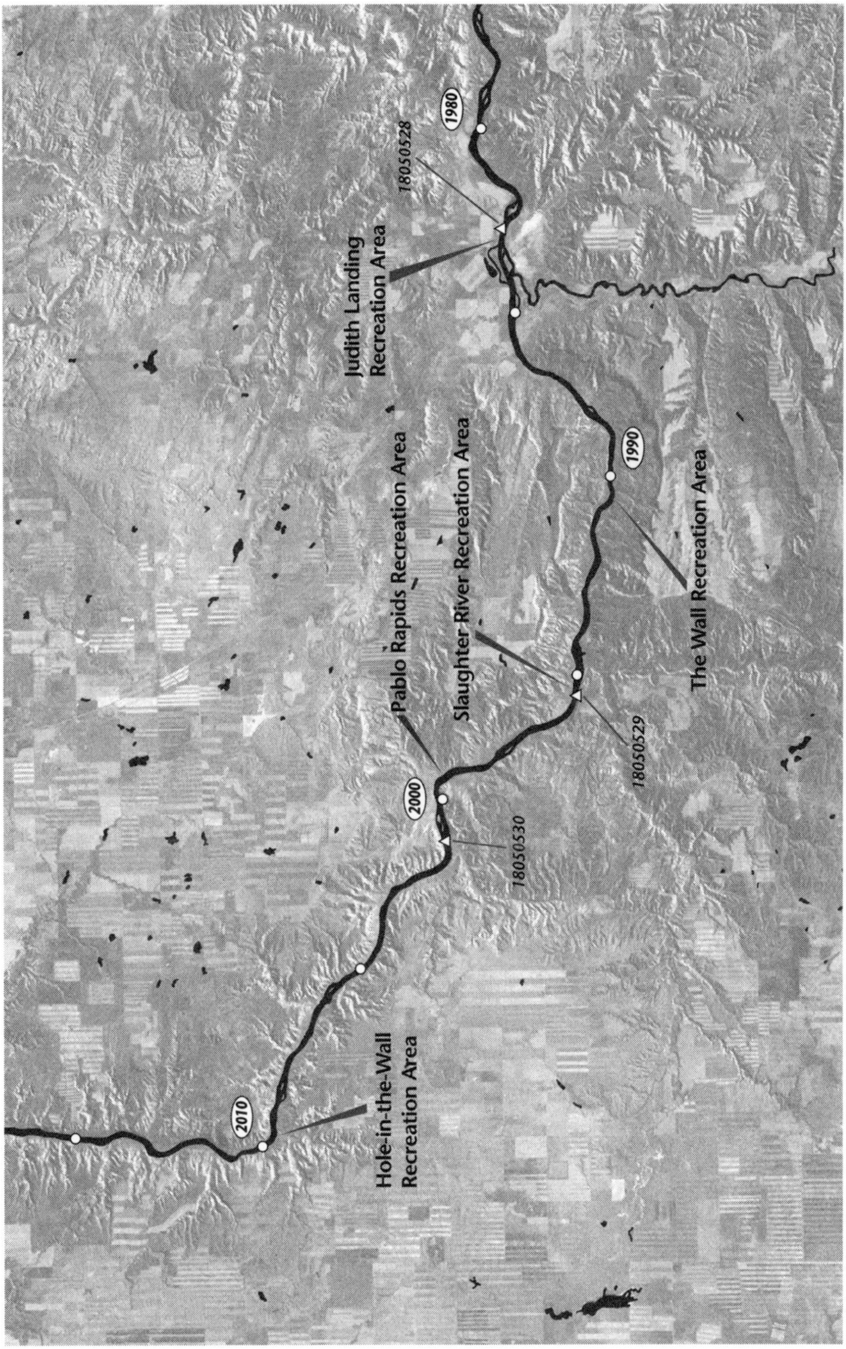

Map 1.B.5: Hole-in-the-Wall (mile 2,009.6) to Judith Landing Recreation Area (mile 1,983.1).

57.2. LaBarge Rock is the dark rock on the left bank, and Grand Natural Wall is on the point on the right bank."

At mile 2,012/59.7 is Kipps Rapids; Eagle Rock is nearby on the left side. About 2 miles downriver from the rapids is Citadel Rock, featured in another well-known Bodmer sketch. The Hole-in-the-Wall Recreation Area is at mile 2,009.6/62.9 right (47.82027/-110.06388), and the formation for which it is named is about a mile down the shore, high up on the right. Five miles below is Steamboat Rock, on the left near mile 2,004/6. On the left just above this feature is Dark Butte Recreation Area (BLM mile 68.8). Dark Butte is on the left before mile 70.

After mile 2,002/70 the river bends sharply to the east; a mile after the turn you will pass Pablo Island, followed by a sharp turn to the southeast. After completing this second turn, the Pablo Rapids Recreation Area (undeveloped) is on your left at mile 1,999.3/76.8. Below this is Pablo Rapids, where you may experience some fast water, depending on upstream dam releases. About 3 miles below the rapids, at mile 1,995.4/76.7 (47.71715/-109.85040), is Slaughter River Recreation Area, which is a minimally developed site with vault toilet and fire rings. Arrow Creek, understood to be Lewis and Clark's "Slaughter River," is about 1 mile downstream on the right. Four miles below this confluence is the Wall Recreation Area at mile 1,990.5/81.3. This is an undeveloped site with a fire ring.

The Deadman Rapids are at mile 1,987/84.5, where the river narrows; expect fast water here. Below Deadman Rapids to mile 92.5, you can expect powerboat traffic. Three miles below the rapids is the Judith River confluence on the right, and a mile after that is the Judith Landing Recreation Area at mile 1,983.1/88.5 left (47.73888/-109.62250). This is a developed site, with vault toilets, fire rings, and picnic tables. A bridge crosses the river at Judith Landing.

◆ Judith Landing (mile 1,983.1) to James Kipp (mile 1,921): 62.1 miles *(Maps 1.B.6–1.B.8)*

The swiftest part of the navigable Missouri is a twenty-six mile stretch east from the Judith; the water is all swift, and there are thirteen rapids in the course. We found well-defined channels of deep water through the Birch, Holmes, McKeevers, Gallatin, Bear and Little Dog rapids, and then drew near the Dauphin Rapids, which I had been worrying about ever since our start from Fort Benton.

JAMES WILLARD SCHULTZ, *FLOATING THE MISSOURI*, [A PASSAGE MADE IN NOVEMBER 1901]

It is some 62 miles from Judith Landing to the pullout at the James Kipp ramp. After floating through the White Cliffs section, many paddlers end their trip at

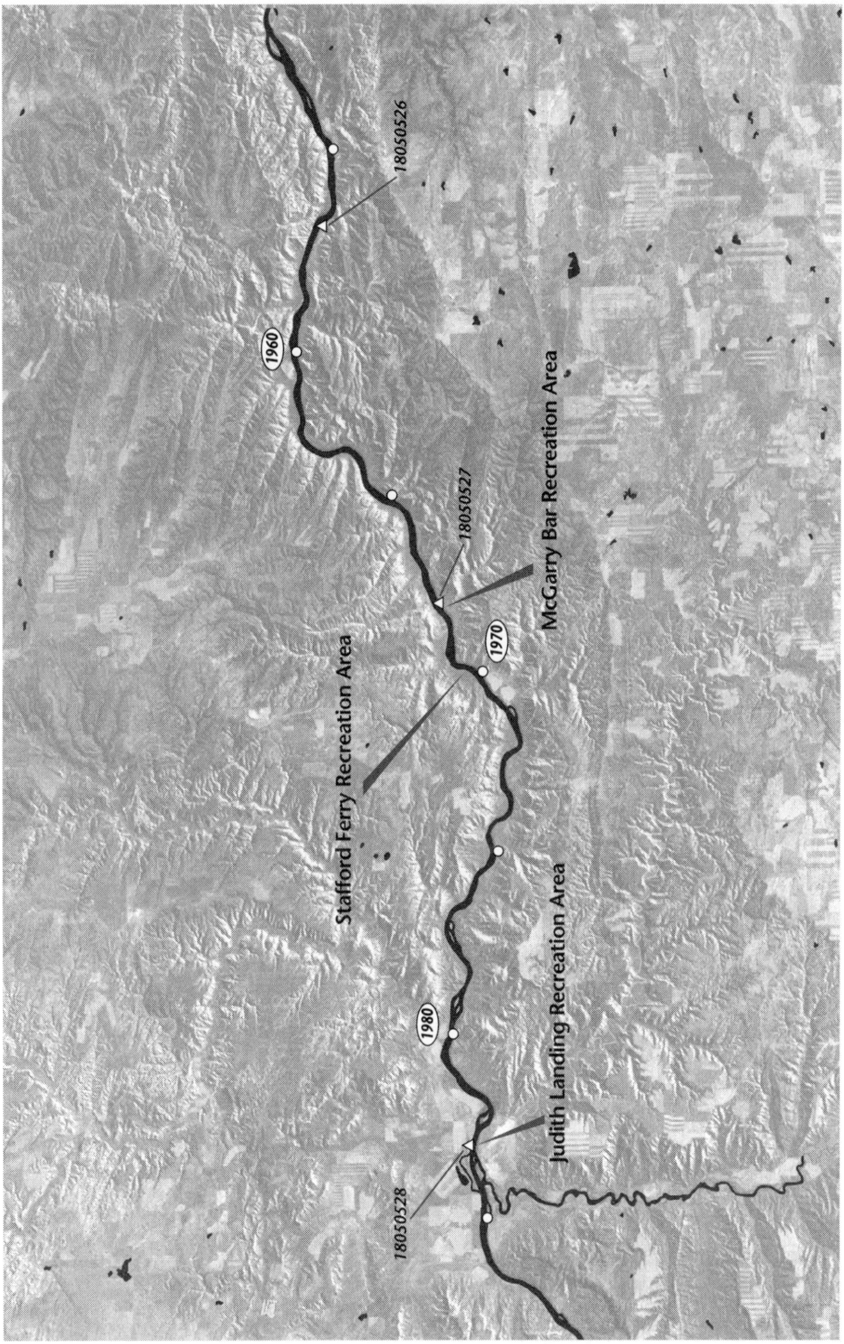

Map 1.B.6: Judith Landing Recreation Area (mile 1,983.1) to mile 1,952.

Judith Landing. So you should see fewer boats as you continue on. If you look at BLM map 3, you will see that below Judith Landing are 13 sets of rapids. Don't get terribly concerned; with the exception of Dauphin Rapids, you need worry little about passing through these features. The water will speed up at most of these locations, and at low water there may be some rocks to avoid, but you can easily pass these sections. This stretch did, however, present steamboats with real issues. On many occasions, particularly during low water years, this was the end of upstream navigation.

At mile 1,979.5/92.5, below Holmes Council Islands, you will pass from recreational into wild river designation. After this there are scattered groves of cottonwoods that offer potential places to camp. I found a nice campsite at mile 1,975.7/96 right. A mile below this is Gallatin Rapids; the river narrows here, the current picks up a bit, and there are rocks to avoid at low water. Pay attention and keep your boat pointed downriver, and you should not have any real difficulty. At mile 1,969.6/101.8 left (47.73788/-109.39074) is the Stafford Recreation Area, an undeveloped site. Less than 2 miles downriver is a campsite with shade, but to get there you have to pass Dauphin Rapids, which is just around the next bend. At normal water levels, there are some shallow boulders to avoid, but these are generally evident.

McGarry Bar is at mile 1,967.7/103.4 right (47.74732/-109.35827). There are nice shaded sites here with fire rings. There is no toilet here; this is one of the undeveloped sites, which should become considerably more attractive as paddlers bag and carry out their own waste. If you have binoculars, watch the hills above the camp in the evening and you may see bighorn sheep. Below McGarry Bar, you enter country with a distinct badlands character; there is little vegetation along the river.

About 20 miles below McGarry Bar is Bullwacker Creek at mile 1,948.3/122.5 left. BLM rangers patrolling the river told me that this was one of their favorite campsites. About 3 miles below this on the left is Cow Island Recreation Area (mile 1,945/125.6; 47.79343/-108.94496). This is an undeveloped site, but there is a long stretch of cottonwoods along the shore that provide afternoon shade. If you do pull out here, look over the BLM map of this area. Notice that the Nez Perce National Historic Trail crosses the river about a mile downstream.

I wanted to camp near the Nez Perce crossing, so I continued downstream and located a campsite at mile 1,943.1/127.8 left (47.77358/-108.94431) with a spectacular view of Cow Island and the hills across the river. Here Chief Joseph

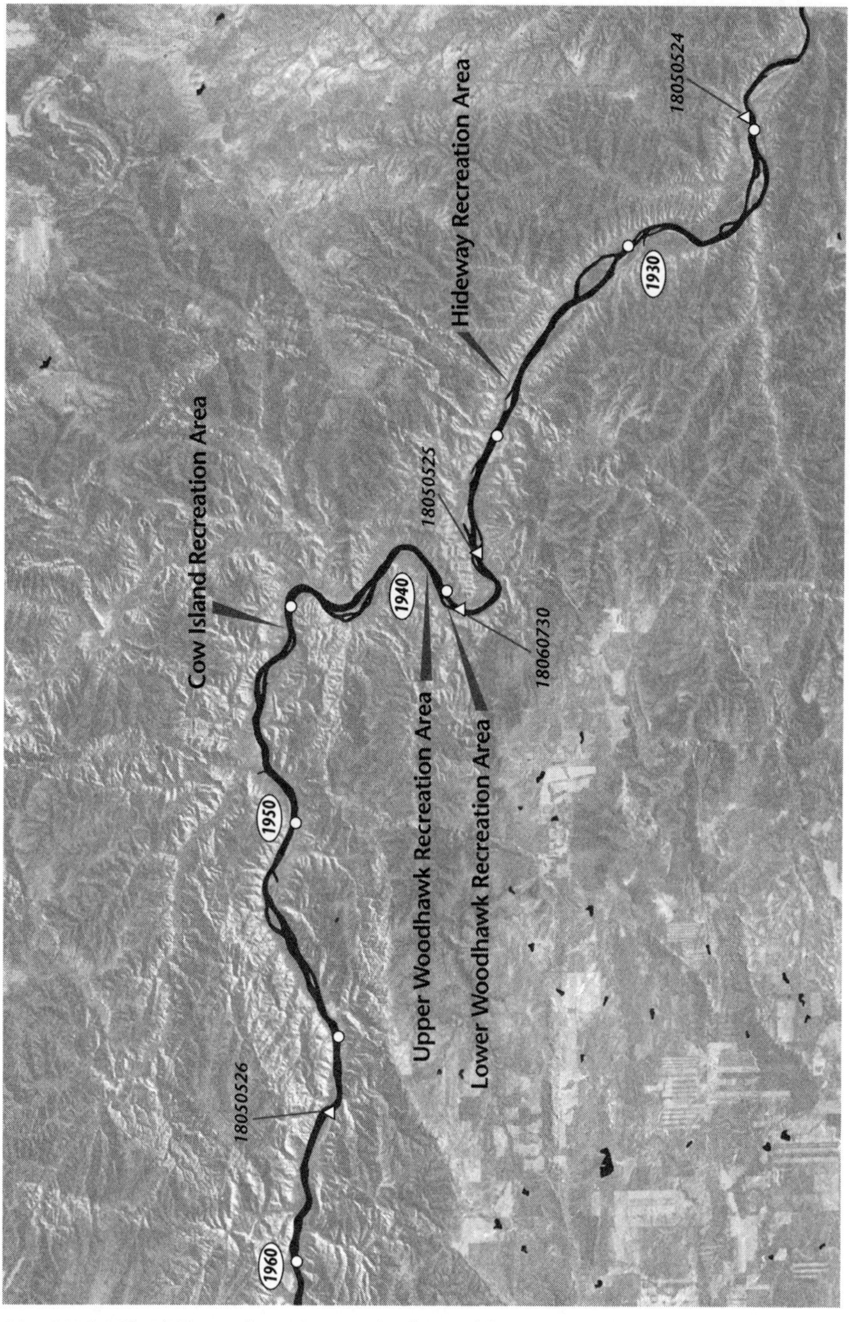

Map 1.B.7: Mile 1,960 to mile 1925. Cow Island, site of the Nez Perce crossing of the Missouri River, is near the top center of the image.

and his band of "nontreaty" Nez Perce crossed the Missouri River on September 23, 1877, in an attempt to reach asylum in Canada. Harried by a pursuing force of some 2,000 soldiers, their flight was stopped 45 miles short of the border. In at least 20 engagements, one here at Cow Island, some 200 Nez Perce braves fought a rear-guard action that defended the fleeing tribe. At the end, more than 300 men, women, and children of the tribe perished.

These were the descendants of the people who provided critical assistance to the Lewis and Clark Expedition. As Stephen Ambrose relates in *Undaunted Courage:*

The Nez Perce had seen the white soldiers hungry and fed them; seen them cold and provided fuel; seen them without horses and put them on mounts; seen them confused and provided good advice; seen them make fools of themselves trying to cross mountains ten feet deep in snow and not snickered; seen them lost and guided them. They had ridden together, eaten together, slept together, played together, and crossed the Lolo Trail together.

Among the Nez Perce fording the river that day, there may well have been descendants of members of the expedition. It bears reflection that 70 years later the Nez Perce would cross Lewis and Clark's Missouri River trail pursued by an army determined to either exterminate them or return them to a reservation.

◆ Cow Island (mile 1,945) to Fred Robinson Bridge and James Kipp State Park (mile 1,921): 24 miles *(Maps 1.B.7 & 1.B.8)*

In low water years like 1863, navigation often ended at Cow Island. This area wasn't necessarily as difficult an obstacle as was Dauphin Rapids or other problem areas further upriver, but Cow Creek provided a good off-loading area with excellent road access out of the Missouri Valley and across the prairie to Fort Benton. Freighting of the goods that were off-loaded from the steamboats was accomplished with wagons, driven by two bullwackers. Oxen were preferred over horses and mules because "they required less food and water, they didn't wander during storms, and the Indians didn't steal them because they couldn't ride them and they were too tough to eat."

The exact amount of freight off-loaded at Cow Island varied from year to year depending on water levels in the Missouri. In 1866 most steamboats were able to navigate as far as Fort Benton into July, so little effort was needed to move goods from Cow Creek. But 1868 was a different story. Joel Overholser reports in the Fort Benton Press, "At year end (1868) the Montana Post reported that 2,500 men, 3,000 teams and 20,000 oxen had been involved in freighting to Fort Benton."

GLENN MONAHAN AND CHANDLER BIGGS, *MONTANA'S WILD AND SCENIC UPPER MISSOURI RIVER*

Cow Island area as viewed from author's campsite at mile 1,943.1 left. In 1877, the "nontreaty" Nez Perce forded the Missouri River near this location.

After Cow Island, you will enter what has been called "the heart of the badlands section of the river." Except for vegetation along the river and where pines grow along valley slopes, the land is barren and hard eroded. This area is remote, wild, and beautiful. With good weather it is an easy day's paddle from a campsite in this area to the James Kipp State Park Floater's Camp. As you round the bend after mile 1,942/129, there are possible campsites on the right. Once you are completely around the bend, the Upper Woodhawk Recreation Area is on the right (mile 1,940.5/129.8; 47.74916/-108.93277). Lower Woodhawk is below, also on the right at mile 1,939.7/131.1 (47.7419/-108.94722).

The term "woodhawk" refers to the men who lived along the bottoms, cut firewood, and stacked it along the riverbank for sale to steamboats, which burned prodigious amounts of wood. On average, a steamboat burned more than a cord of wood an hour. To meet the demand for fuel, woodhawks cut most of the larger trees along the river and eventually had to venture farther inland. The work was hard and dangerous; American Indians frequently attacked the woodcutters.

A mile below Lower Woodhawk, as you round a bend and turn up to the northeast, you pass the former Power Plant ferry crossing. The generators of this plant supplied electrical power to gold mining operations in the Little Rockies, some 20 miles to the northwest. Another 2 miles below is the Hideaway Recreation Area at mile 1,933.9/136.4 left (47.72250/-108.85027), which is an undeveloped site.

You will cross into the Charles M. Russell National Wildlife Refuge near mile 1,932/138.8, and in about half a mile come to Grand Island. The main channel is to the right. In 1901, Schultz camped here and reported "a magnificent grove of tall old cottonwoods" at its upper end. You will see the descendants of some of these trees as you float by the island. As you work around the next bend and approach mile 1,928/142.3, you may see bighorn sheep on the hillside to the right; I was fortunate enough to see a group coming down to water at the river. By remaining motionless and using my rudder to steer, I drifted with the current to within 100 yards of them before they began to move back up the slope.

The Fred Robinson Bridge is at mile 1,921.6/148.8. After you paddle under this bridge, it is 0.5 mile to the James Kipp State Park ramp (mile 1,921/149.2 right; 47.62393/-108.67735). A floater's camp is about 100 yards above the ramp on the left. There is a vault toilet, a water fountain, and several picnic tables with fire rings. The water supply at Kipp is tested monthly during the recreation season. If a test reveals the water is not potable, you will have to filter or boil the water. The regular campground is a short walk up the road, where you will find the campground host.

If you have paddled from Three Forks to Kipp, you have paddled 400 river miles. At this point you have completed the Upper Upper Missouri passage. If you are thinking about paddling to the Mississippi, you are 17 percent of the way there. The Missouri is, as you now more fully appreciate, a very long river. If you intend to continue on, make sure to visit with the campground host and file a float plan. More often than not, the campground host can provide you with the most up-to-date information about facilities ahead, water availability, and any special-use regulations. Below Kipp you enter truly wild and remote country; you also start the Dammed Upper Missouri, which extends nearly 1,189 miles to Sioux City (mile 732) and contains some very demanding sections.

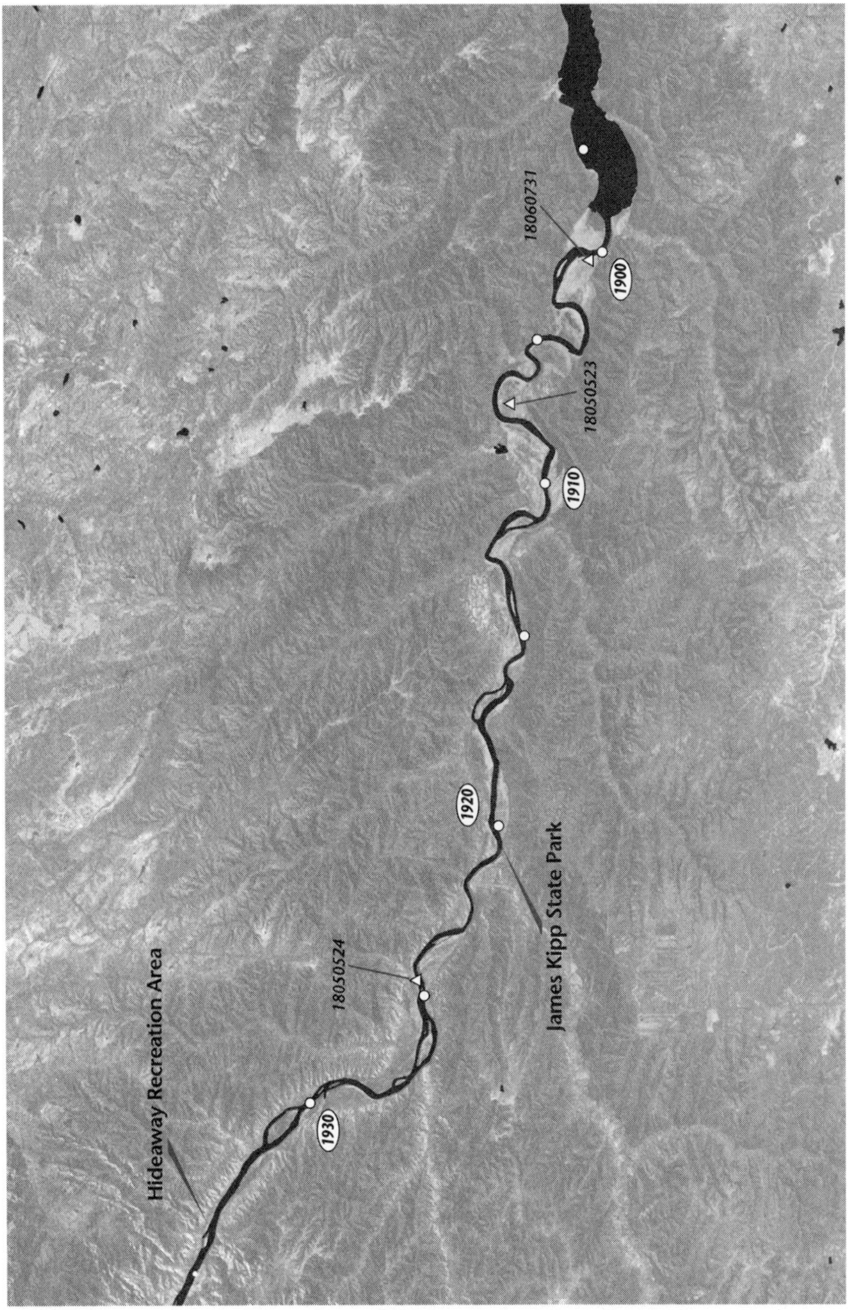

Map 1.B.8: Hideaway Recreation Area (mile 1,933.9) to mile 1,895. The James Kipp State Park ramp and a nearby floater's camp is 0.5 mile after the bridge on the right, at mile 1,921.

SECTION 2: THE DAMMED UPPER MISSOURI (RIVER MILE 1,921 TO 732)

When the Corps built giant dams on the Upper river, one element normally found in such dams was left out. The Fort Peck Dam in Montana, and the dams called Garrison, Oahe, Fort Randall, and Gavin's Point in the Dakotas—these structures had no locks. A pilot could no longer take his vessel past one of these dams, and none wanted to; the age of steamboating on the Upper Missouri had come and gone.

DONALD JACKSON, *VOYAGES OF THE STEAMBOAT YELLOW STONE*

The Dammed Upper begins here, and you are about to enter one of its more difficult segments. The 75 miles between James Kipp State Park and Fourchette Creek Recreation Area passes through one of the most difficult sections of the river. The first 20 miles from the Kipp landing are deceptively easy; then the river channel frays into a 30-mile-long section of loosely braided and relatively shallow channels. At mile 1,876, the river makes a sharp turn to the south, picks up the Musselshell River (mile 1,867) as a tributary, and then angles hard again to the north. This sharp U-turn slows the current dramati-

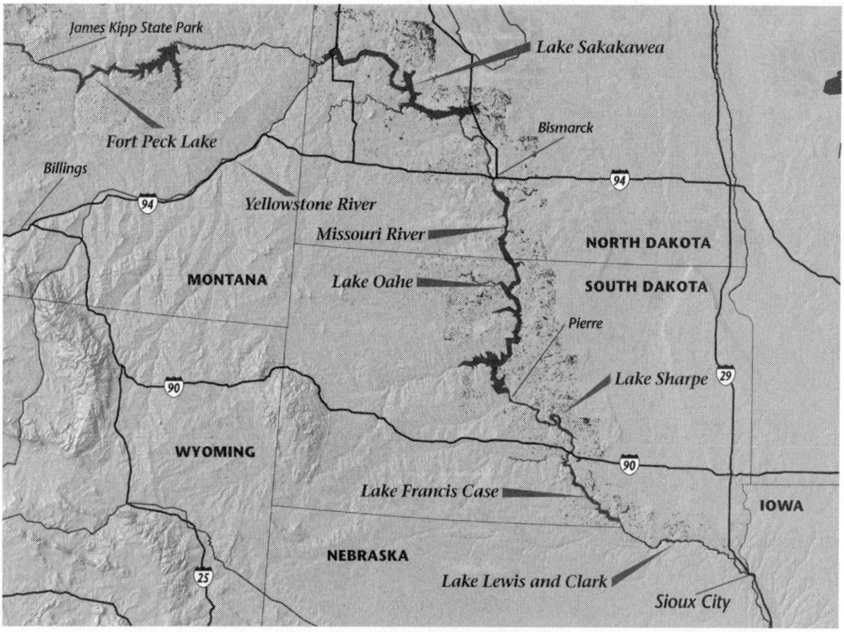

Map 2.0: Section 2—James Kipp State Park (mile 1,921) to Sioux City, Iowa (mile 732).

cally. As a result, much of the river's sediment load is dropped before the river turns back to the north. At low water levels, it can be very difficult to find a channel through this area. Walking along shore is virtually impossible, as the muck is knee- and waist-deep in many areas. Beyond this morass, on the east side of the UL Bend, the river begins to widen out and evidence of current disappears. From a paddler's standpoint, this is the real beginning of Fort Peck Lake, the first of six Army Corps of Engineers (ACE) reservoirs.

This lake is big. It is formed behind the first of six dams on the Upper Missouri. According to a recent ACE publication, the lake is the fifth-largest man-made reservoir in the world and is 134 miles long. It has more miles of shoreline (1,520) than the state of California. With no current to assist progress, you get nowhere if you do not paddle. The wind will come up suddenly and then blow hard throughout the day; making headway can be quite difficult. You might wait on shore for days before the wind blows itself out. Or you can line your boat from shore where conditions permit. With good weather, modest winds, and hard paddling, you might make it to the dam in a week.

So, why bother? When you are paddling this section of the river, it is hard to forget that you are on a huge and long lake. The river bottoms that early explorers paddled, poled, and towed through are submerged. Perhaps the best reason to paddle this section is to experience its stillness. For long stretches, the shore is virtually devoid of all evidence of habitation. Mule deer and elk are abundant. This section has an open and out-there feel that cannot be found anywhere else on the river. This place has held its wildness.

Information/Maps/Resources

The entire reservoir is surrounded by the Charles M. Russell National Wildlife Refuge, managed by the U.S. Fish and Wildlife Service (USFWS). A number of publications are available from the office of the refuge manager in Lewistown, Montana (406-538-8707). One of the most useful maps for paddlers is the USFWS publication *Charles M. Russell National Wildlife Refuge Montana Guide Map and Information* (http://cmr.fws.gov).

The 2004 edition contains two maps–West and East–that depict the lake at a very useful scale (1:200,000 or 1 inch = ~ 3 miles). In addition, a summary of regulations is provided. Of importance to floaters is that camping is permitted within 100 yards of the water, except where designated as closed. Campfires are permitted, as is the collection of dead and down wood. Public recreation facilities are listed, but it would be wise to check on their current status. The section on boating underscores the potential difficulties associated with low water at the west end:

. . . water levels in the river dictate what types of boats may be suitable. Canoes are suitable during all seasons. Boats with outboard motors can be safely used during the spring runoff, but low flows during the remainder of the year may make their use dangerous. The upstream shoreline of the Fort Peck Reservoir also fluctuates according to the amount of water stored. Boaters should be cautious of sand bars and other hazards during periods of low water levels when boating in the reservoir above Fourchette Bay. The delta at the head of the reservoir is generally impassable to all boats. Some boat ramps may not reach the water during low water periods.

Water levels were low in June 2002 when I paddled through this area. Based on what I saw, the advice that "the delta at the head of the reservoir is generally impassable to all boats" is dead right. Only a canoe or kayak could get through. At times I was sliding along the delta's muck in only a few inches of water.

Paddlers should also read carefully the guide map's section "Antlers, Natural Items, Artifacts, Fossils, and Historic Items." Essentially, collection of any of these items is prohibited. It is against the law to search for and remove any natural items or historic objects from the refuge.

Other maps are available. The Bureau of Land Management (BLM) has published a series of 1:100,000 maps as part of their *BLM Special Edition 1987 Recreation Access Guide*. Although out of print, these maps are very useful because they are printed on waterproof material that holds up very well. The Zortman (#16) and Fort Peck Lake West (#17) maps cover the area in this trip segment. The Zortman map provides the names of the river bottoms from Kipp Recreation Area to the west-end beginning of Fort Peck Lake. Information on purchasing these maps can be obtained from the Lewistown BLM office (406-538-7461). The ACE publication *Fort Peck Lake Boating and Recreation* provides very detailed (~ 1:63,360) composite air photos of the entire shoreline from the Fort Peck Dam to the western limit of the refuge. This publication contains a detailed listing of aids to navigation (lights and day beacons) placed on the lake by the Coast Guard, emergency assistance phone numbers, and other useful information. Current information about the lake can be found at the website (www.nwo.usace.army.mil/html/Lake_Proj/index.html).

Suggested Readings

Eight Lewis and Clark campsites are in this segment. Information about what transpired here during the trip west (May 18 to 23, 1805) can be found in Vol. 4:163–187 *(Journals,* [Moulton, ed.]). Return trip event detail (July 31 to August 2, 1806) can be found in Vol. 8:141–146 of the same source. Context about the events can be found in Stephen Ambrose's *Undaunted Courage* in chapters 18:226 and 32:395.

Prince Maximilian's journal and paintings by his companion Carl Bodmer provide an additional source for historical information about this section *(People of the First Man,* Thomas and Ronnefeldt, 1976). Maximilian passed through this area in late July to early August 1833. Of the area's "badlands" landscape he writes:

The mountains here presented a rude wilderness, looking in part like a picture of destruction; large blocks of sand-stone lay scattered about...A few pines and junipers appear here and there, and on the declivities small patches of grass....But the naked, rude character of the Mauvaises Terres seems to be unique in its kind, and the impression is strengthened when you look up and down the river. Only the croaking of the raven was heard in this desolate waste, which even the Indian avoids.

The USFWS publication, *A History* [of the] *Charles M. Russell National Wildlife Refuge Montana,* provides colorful detail about the historic sites in this area.

Good lore and details regarding significant places can be found in James W. Schultz's *Floating on the Missouri 100 Years after Lewis and Clark.* In 1901, Schultz and his American Indian wife, Natahki, floated downstream from Fort Benton to the Milk River, below today's Fort Peck Dam. His intent was to revisit many of the locations along the river where he had worked as a trader in the 1870s. Mixed in with his trip account and stories is good context and useful intelligence for today's paddlers.

For information and context about more recent conditions, there exists no more literate a source than William Least Heat-Moon's travel odyssey, *River-Horse.* Nearly 100 years after Schultz made his last float down the Missouri, Least Heat-Moon powered his boat *Nikawa* across Fort Peck Lake and around the UL Bend as part of a cross-country passage. When he worked his way upstream, water levels were high. He was able to navigate his boat around the UL Bend and make passage for about 10 miles to the north. However, where the river cut back to the west, he encountered a maze of islands, sandbars, and ever more shallow channels. Ultimately, he was forced to continue upstream in a canoe powered by a small outboard.

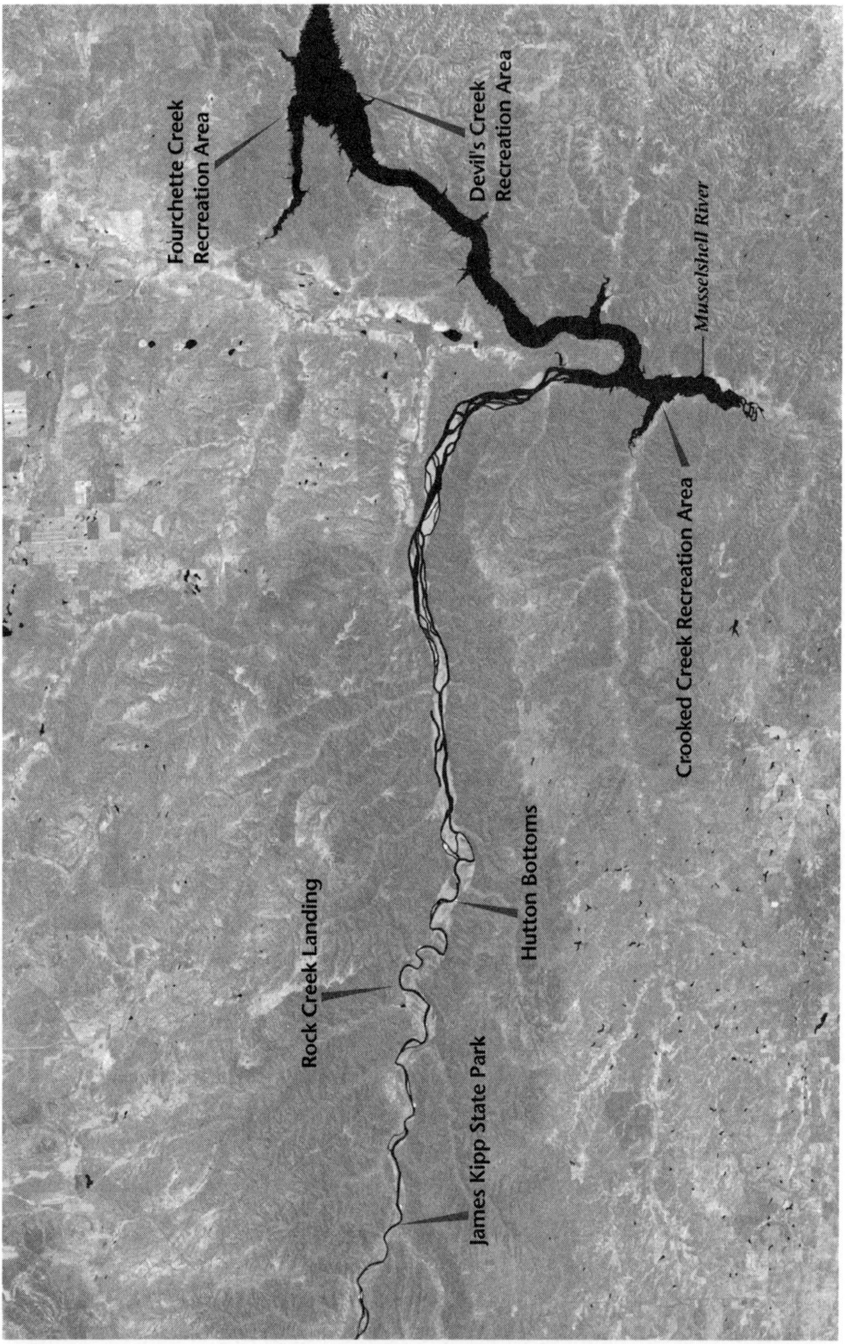

Map 2.A: James Kipp State Park (mile 1,921) to Fourchette Creek Recreation Area (mile 1,846).

SEGMENT 2.A: James Kipp State Park (mile 1,921) to Fourchette Creek Recreation Area (mile 1,846) ***(Map 2.A)***

- **River miles:** 75
- **Difficulty level:** High
- **Typical time to complete:** 5 to 14 days

Paddler's Notes and Cautions

Beyond the drinking water source at the Kipp landing and floater's campground, I am aware of no other reliable sources for drinking water for the next several days. So fill up. It is imperative that an adequate supply be carried. The river carries a heavy sediment load well around the UL Bend, so do not think that you can rely on a filter; it will clog in short order. Also, springs in the area are saline or high in mineral content, so most filtration systems will not produce potable water. Carry at least 6 gallons of water per person. This should get you far enough east on Fort Peck Lake where sediment won't be such an issue for filters. The 6 gallons of water weighs well over 50 pounds, so you must factor this in as you calculate your total load in relation to your craft's carrying capacity.

During the spring, the area near Kipp hosts anglers snagging for paddlefish. Near the Kipp Floater's Camp you are sure to see some of these landed.

Snagging is typically done from the shore with surf-casting–type gear; a large, lead-weighted treble hook is cast well out into the river and then reeled in with yanking motions. Fishing is also done from boats. Stay well away from anyone casting, or playing a hooked fish. A number of primitive campgrounds line the north side of the river, and anglers line the steep banks during the day. Stay as far to the right as you can. Setlines for catfish are run from the shore, and these are sometimes difficult to see. Pay attention. Fortunately the intense shoreline activity dwindles after 2 or 3 miles. With the exception of a few anglers in jet drive powerboats, evidence of human activity diminishes.

- **Kipp Floater's Camp ramp (mile 1,921) to mile 1,884: 37miles** ***(Map 2.A.1)***

Jones Island is at mile 1,917; here the main channel bends to the right. The banks of the river are quite steep, and there is much evidence of recent shoreline collapse. The Rock Creek boat ramp is at mile 1,906.5 left. There are steep banks along stretches of the river, but a mile beyond the ramp I noted a

Fisherman with large paddlefish snagged near the Kipp ramp. Stay well away from anyone casting from the shore or playing a snagged fish.

potential campsite at Kepple Bottoms (mile 1,905.5). An improved, but primitive, campsite is about 4 miles downstream (mile 1902 left). As I paddled by, I noted a picnic table and a vault toilet. Beyond this opportunity, for the next several miles there appeared to be few decent campsites.

The Hutton Bottoms primitive campground is just a bit downstream at mile 1,899.8 right. It also features a vault toilet and campsites. I had planned to camp there but decided to push on because the landing was carved down

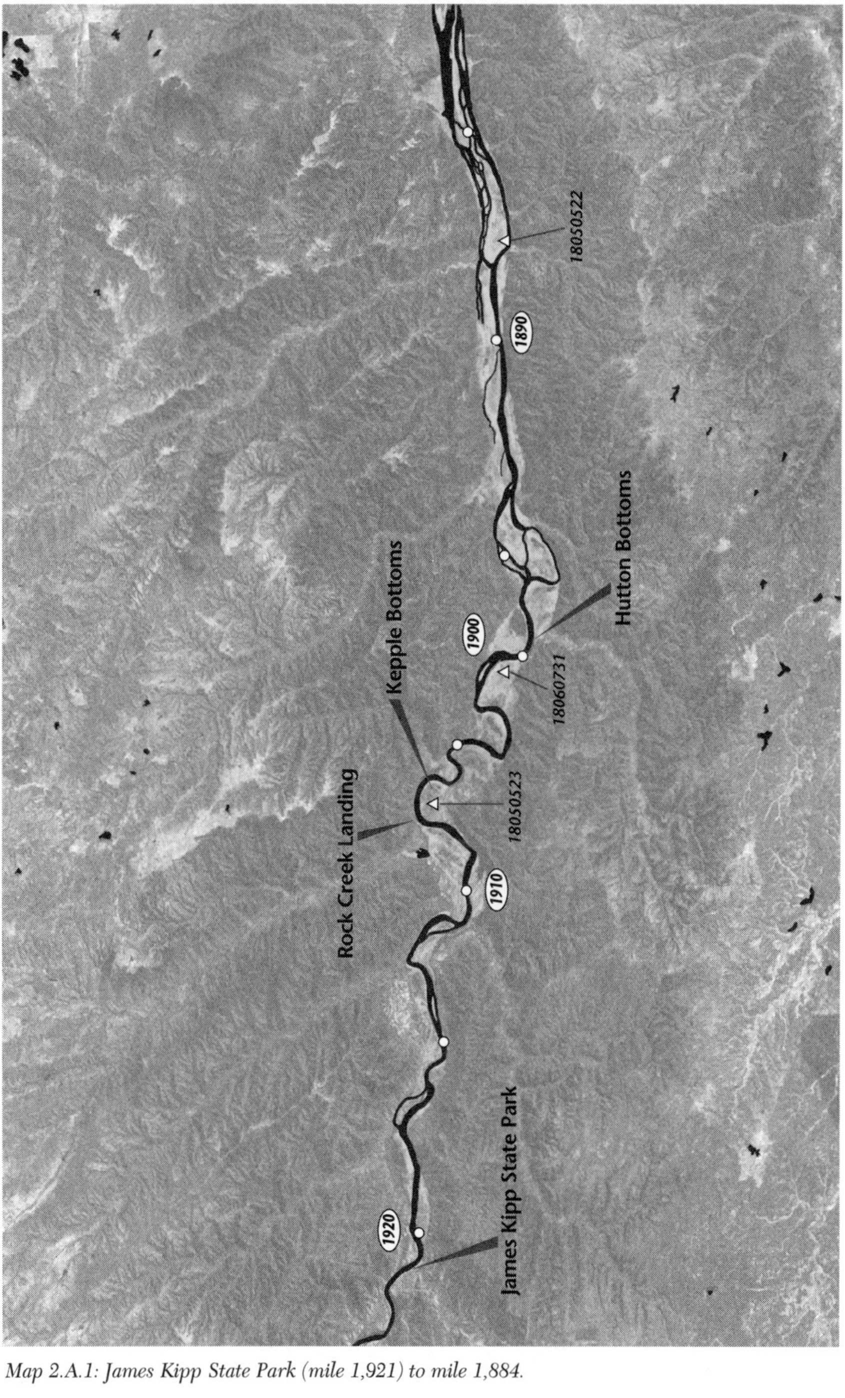

Map 2.A.1: James Kipp State Park (mile 1,921) to mile 1,884.

through a steep riverbank at an impossibly steep angle on the outside bend of the river. With a fast current to contend with, I elected to continue paddling downriver in search of a campsite. As it was raining and getting late, I had to accept a truly marginal, brushy campsite about a mile downstream (mile 1,898.8 left; 47.57921/-108.35555) near–appropriately enough–Miller Bottoms. At this site, I noted a cougar's tracks along the shore; it appeared the cat was feeding on carp stranded in the shallows.

Beyond Hutton Bottoms most maps show the river widening to become Fort Peck Lake. Inspection of the satellite image reveals that this is not the case. The image, taken in the mid-1990s, shows that the river breaks into a shallow maze of braided channels until reaching the west side of the UL Bend. When I worked my way through this area in June 2002, water levels were low. With the exception of a relatively straight 6-mile-long channel beginning at mile 1,893, I found that braided channels continued all the way down to the bottom of the UL Bend. The shoreline was thick with a new growth of thistle. There was little cottonwood but lots of young and bushy willows. On the hillsides, pine trees made their first sustained appearance.

◆ Mile 1,884 to Fourchette Creek Recreation Area (mile 1,846): 38 miles *(Map 2.A.2)*

Paddler's Notes and Cautions

Between mile 1,888 and 1,879, the channel is generally well defined. I stayed to the right until about mile 1,882 then followed the main channel to the north side. The river then widened and the channel angled to the southeast, beginning the UL Bend. The water became very shallow and the channel difficult to follow. The wind picked up, whitecaps formed, and it became very difficult to read the water. I elected to make for shore and found another marginal campsite just below mile 1,874 left (47.54170/-107.91601). The shoreline was muddy and clogged with tumbleweed, and I resorted to using driftwood as rollers to help me pull my kayak through the muck to above the waterline.

The next morning, the wind continued to blow from the northwest. I crossed back to the right (west) and found a shallow channel–2 to 3 feet deep–that I was able to follow until a little after mile 1,868. At this point, it became quite shallow. Although it appeared that Crooked Creek Recreation Area was about 2 miles to the south, I could see that the low water level had stranded

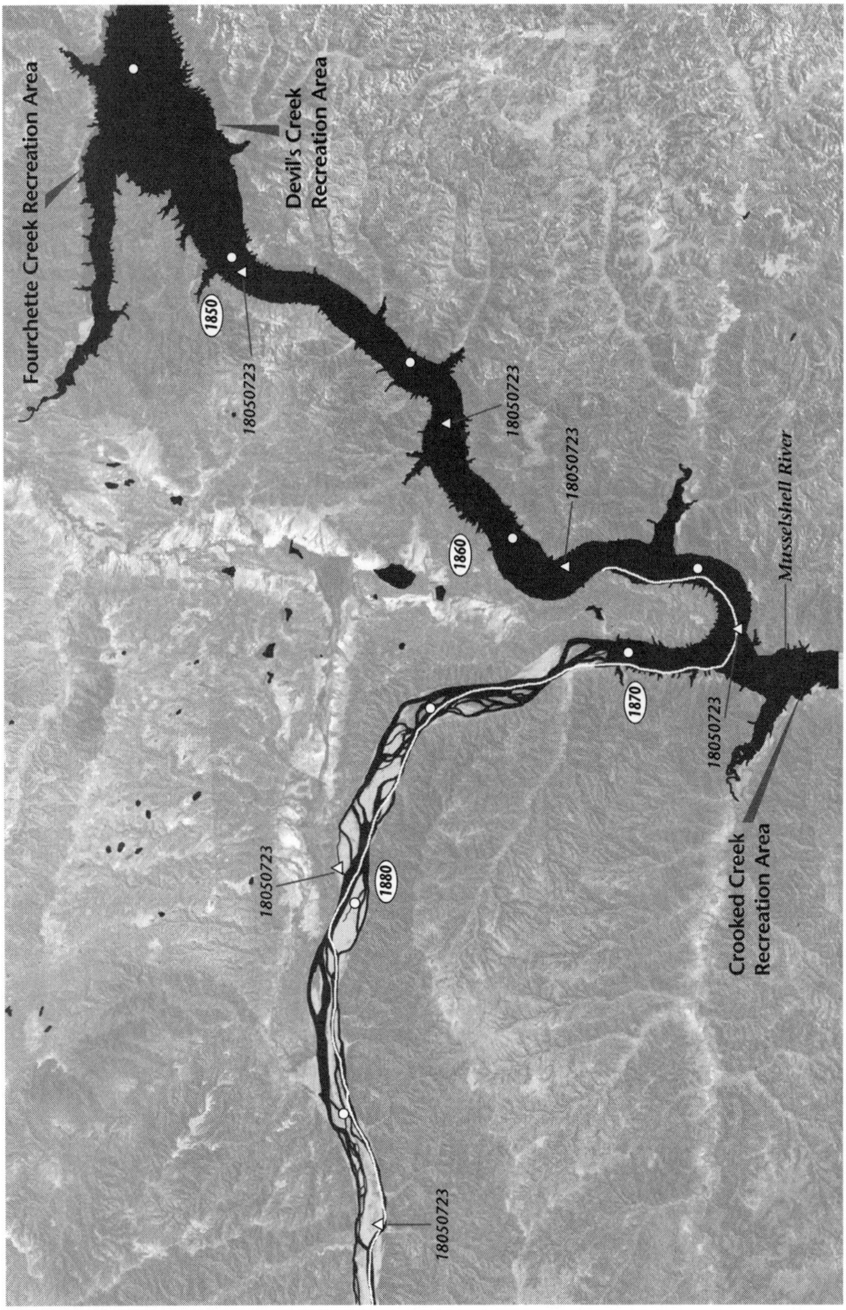

Map 2.A.2: Mile 1,884 to Fourchette Creek Recreation Area (mile 1,846). White line shows my course track in June 2002.

the landing well above the waterline. I elected to continue around the bend. But because of whitecaps driven by the wind, I could see no clear channel. To my right, I could see weedy shallows and tumbleweed hung up on mudflats. I worked my way to midchannel (mile 1,867) until my keel started dragging along the bottom. From this point I paddled, knuckle-pushed, and poled myself for almost a mile to the southeast side of the UL Bend. When I finally reached shore more than an hour later, I was exhausted, and the deck of my boat was a muddy mess.

If I were to do this section again, I would camp a mile or so above the bend (between mile 1,869 and 1,868) and climb a hill to scout the best passage through the area. I noted a couple of possible campsites along the west (right) shore in that area when I paddled through. In any event, this is a very difficult section of the river. The mud is very deep, and like quicksand. You'll need to take your time to work safely through this area.

Once I got to shore, I found a narrow trench of relatively deep water skirting the shore. I beached my kayak, drank water, ate, and rested for about an hour. I then paddled close along the shore for about 4 miles and called it quits for the day at a nice sandy beach (left; 47.49901/-107.86503). After I pitched camp, cleaned my equipment, and ate, I looked over my GPS track for the day. I had made about a dozen miles. Examining my maps, I noted that when I was pushing at the mud and sliding a few inches closer to the shore, I was within a few hundred feet of the Lewis and Clark Expedition's now submerged camp of May 20, 1805. I also realized that just on the other side of the river from my camp was the expedition's campsite of May 19.

I chose to stay on the north (left) side of the river for the passage to Fourchette Creek. Prevailing wind in the area is from the northwest, so it may be better to stay to the lee side (left) as you are rounding the bottom of the bend. Once you get around the bend, you can run parallel, close in to shore. In effect you sneak along in the wind shadow of the shoreline. This is often the most efficient way to progress. Also, if the wind picks up to make it too difficult to paddle, you can efficiently line your boat, as the wind will not push your craft toward shore.

Between my camp at mile 1,862.5 and the entrance to Fourchette Bay (mile 1,846 left), I had to line my kayak because of high winds. The shoreline is ragged but can be walked. As I got closer to the bay, at about mile 1,850, there were a series of inlets that I was able to paddle across. Here, the lake widens considerably. By the time I turned into Fourchette Bay, the northwest wind was really howling, and whitecaps were dancing across the 3- to 4-foot waves in the bay. Because of Fourchette Bay's aspect, which runs almost east-west, the northwest wind had the water really churned up. There was no way to safely cross to the campground. I worked my way around two points at the south bay entrance (about 0.6 mile) and eventually found a nice little inlet where I set up my camp (left; 47.65905/-107.66261). It had been a very hard second day. According to the GPS log, I had made 18 miles in eight hours. I had lined the boat from shore most of the way. In the tent that night, I remember feeling completely spent. And as I made my journal entry for the night, I was truly dispirited. It was the low point of my expedition. I was only two weeks into my effort; I wondered what was ahead and, for the first time, if I could really complete the trip.

I never made it to the Fourchette Creek Recreation Area. The next day, the wind was light and the sky sunny, so I pushed on to the east. But from my camp, I could see a landing, vault toilets, picnic tables, and truck camper rigs. According to refuge publications, no drinking water is available at the facility, but the area sports "improved roads." Almost due south of Fourchette, on the south side of the lake, is Devil's Creek Recreation Area (mile 1,847.5 right). This facility has a vault toilet and camping areas, but the road leading to the area is not listed as "improved." The shoreline in this area is ragged and barren. There is little shelter. With the exception of some anglers working the shoreline for walleye, you probably will not encounter anyone. At the time that I worked my way along the north (left) shore, the water was quite muddy. An attempt to filter water would have quickly clogged my unit's filter.

SEGMENT 2.B: Fourchette Creek Recreation Area (mile 1,846) to Fort Peck Dam (mile 1,771.5) *(Map 2.B)*

- **River miles:** 74.5
- **Difficulty Level:** Medium to high
- **Typical time to complete:** 4 to 8 days

There are 74.5 river miles between Fourchette and the Fort Peck Dam take-out point. However, count on paddling a lot farther when you set out to make this crossing. Beyond Fourchette, the reservoir widens. An examination of the satellite images reveals that this is where the character of the trip truly changes. This is no longer a river float: If you elect to paddle this section of the trail, you will be making passage on big water. The Fort Peck reservoir is a long lake with a

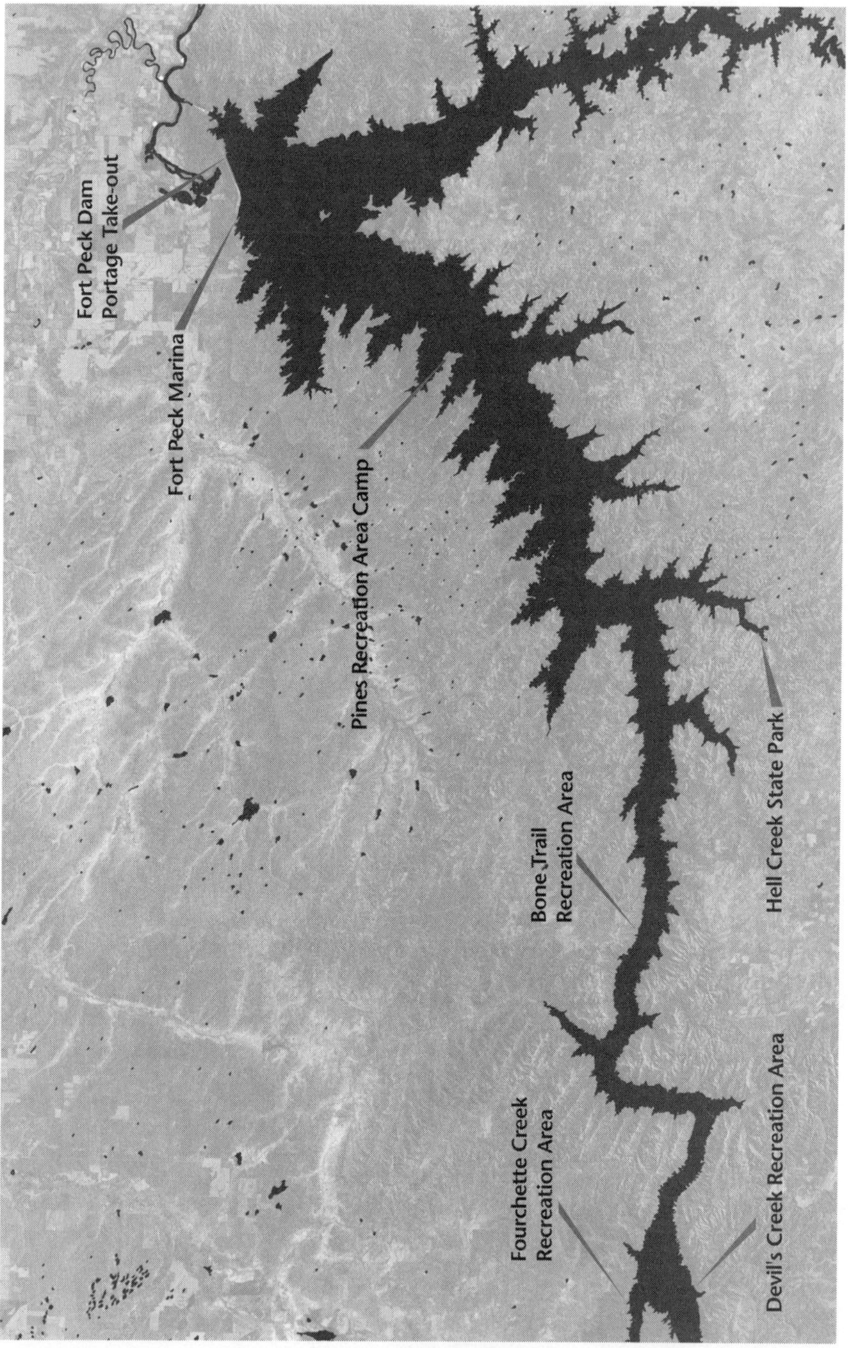

Map 2.B: Fourchette Creek Recreation Area (mile 1,846) to Fort Peck Dam (mile 1,771.5)

very complex shoreline. Long arms of the impoundment extend to the north and south, creating bays more than a mile wide and several miles long. Looking out from the near-zero relative elevation of a kayak seat, it is sometimes difficult to know exactly where you are. The lake seems to present a complex series of wrong course choices. Here you will be glad that you have a compass, your GPS unit, and satellite image–based maps.

Prevailing winds and many storms come from the northwest. It is best to generally hug the north shore as you make your way east. If the weather is good, you can cut some corners and save yourself a bit of paddling. I used this tactic to successfully traverse this section of the lake in five days. However, I enjoyed near-perfect weather and mild breezes; I was lucky. Locals say this lake can blow up very fast and the waves can get enormous. Because you are paddling through long remote stretches, there will be little help if you get into trouble on this lake. You must proceed with caution.

Drinking water becomes less of an issue beyond the Bone Trail landing; the lake water clears up enough so you can purify it without clogging your filter if you allow it to settle out overnight. The impoundment's waters become nearly crystal clear by the time you get halfway down the lake. Paddlers following the north shore will find the only nonlake source for drinking water at the Pines Recreation Area, a day's paddle from the Fort Peck Marina.

For those interested in things Lewis and Clark, the reservoir's waters hide nine expedition campsites in this section, but you can camp along the shore near each of them. The old river channel may lie deep underwater, but this area holds such wild charm that it is not difficult to picture the events that transpired here. And a great deal that was remarkable happened in this section. If the expedition had a "week from hell," this was where it happened. The Corps struggled to make headway in the cold spring meltwater of the current. Riverbanks collapsed, narrowly missing the small boats. A sudden squall nearly capsized the white pirogue, three of the men almost drowned, and gear was lost or damaged. The men had close calls with grizzly bears and rattlesnakes, and sparks from their campfire started a wildfire that nearly deposited a burning tree atop the captains' tepee. This string of events surely had the captains mumbling about what could possibly happen next.

Besides paddling along the expedition's track, there are additional reasons to make this passage. On Fort Peck Lake you will feel a sense of the remoteness experienced by the Corps, and the adrenaline push of a good adventure will sharpen your faculties. From your camps you can hike inland to explore the very same areas walked by the expedition's scouts. On Fort Peck Lake you can still look west, toward the UL Bend at the Musselshell, with sweat and the afternoon sun in your eyes, and see a landscape similar to that seen by early explorers, trappers, and fur traders. And at dusk, you can watch the sunset in the same distant hills.

Fishing on this lake can be exceptionally good. Most small bays have their resident lunker pike, and walleye can be caught fishing from shore. Bring a good medium-weight tackle; these fish are big. I caught and released an 8-pound walleye near the Bone Trail ramp, and watched another fisherman bring in a 20-plus-pound northern. I ate fish every night, sometimes having to release several before I caught one small enough for my needs. Wildlife abounds in the area; if you set up your camp quietly in the late afternoon, you can count on seeing deer or perhaps elk along the shore in the evening.

As you get closer to the east end of the lake, by the last 15 miles or so, you will see numerous anglers and recreational boaters. If you stay close in to the shore, their boat wake should not be an issue. Cold drinks, a very good meal, and gracious hospitality can be found at the Fort Peck Marina.

Information/Maps/Resources

The USFWS "East Map" described in the previous segment is the best resource for paddlers attempting this segment. Besides showing lake access points, the locations of navigation markers are indicated. I used this map in combination with a Garmin GPS unit that I had loaded with base maps from the company's "Roads and Recreation" CD. Because of the low water levels, the shoreline that I viewed appeared sometimes considerably different than what was depicted on the map and GPS screen. In two instances, the GPS screen showed my camp location as being well out in the lake. Nevertheless, by working with the two sources I was able to establish my position.

I found the air photos in the ACE publication *Fort Peck Lake Boating and Recreation* to be only modestly useful. Although I carried this with me, I only referred to it for information about the Coast Guard navigation aids–lights and day beacons–that have been established along the shore. Although this publication also contains a listing of emergency assistance phone numbers and other useful information, I recommend that you go to the ACE Omaha District website at www.nwo.usace.army.mil/html/Lake_Proj/ and navigate to the "Fort Peck Dam/Fort Peck Lake" page for up-to-date information about lake conditions, recreational facilities, and boat ramps. If you have additional questions or concerns, you can e-mail the lake manager via a link on the dam's homepage, or you can contact the ACE Fort Peck Lake project office at (406) 526-3411. The people at this office are very helpful.

Suggested Readings

Nine Lewis and Clark campsites are in this section. Information about what transpired here during the outbound trip (May 9 to 17, 1805) can be found in Vol. 4:130–163 (*Journals,* [Moulton, ed.]. Return trip event detail (August 2 to 4, 1806) can be found in Vol. 8:146–148. Context about events can be found in Stephen Ambrose's *Undaunted Courage* in chapter 18:223–225.

Early explorers and, later, steamboat pilots had a great deal of difficulty navigating this section of the river. Before the dam was built, this section flowed in a narrow canyon with relatively steep sides. Boatmen had to deal with the river's fast current, rapids, shoals, and sharp bends. According to Schultz (*Floating on the Missouri),* who rowed through this section a century ago, this was the "...wildest part of the Upper Missouri." Some 3 miles downstream of Seven Blackfoot Creek, Schultz ran aground at Buffalo shoals:

I stood up and tried to make out the main channel, but here was one place where there was nothing to indicate it; from bank to bank nothing but an undulating ripple of water over the stones. I put on my waders and holding the boat firmly by the bow, dragged it back upstream a short distance, and slowly began to cross to the north side, until I found two feet of water, and then waded slowly down behind the craft, letting it float ahead of me. It ran aground several times, and I found that what channel there was wound like the letter S across the shoal. (Floating on the Missouri).

This section of the river was so problematic to early navigators because it is, geologically speaking, very young. During the last ice age, the bed of the Missouri between Loma and Fort Peck was pushed south. Botkin explains:

The Missouri is an ancient river, for the most of its length it flows through the wide and gently sloping valley that characterizes such a river. But when the ice sheet pushed the Missouri out of its old bed, the river was forced to create a new one. During the height of the ice age, the Missouri was pushed south and forced to flow just south of the ice, where it began to cut a new valley into the countryside. Once that valley was formed, the river was captured by it. (Floating on the Missouri).

Just below the Fort Peck Dam, the Milk River joins the Missouri. The Milk flows in from the north, along part of the Missouri's former bed. I especially like the imagery that Botkin uses to describe the Milk River:

A smaller river it passes through a plain too big for it to have created. It is a young river in an old river's arms.

Schultz's trip account also provides good imagery and colorful accounts. For example, he explains the naming of Kill Woman Creek, Seven Blackfoot Creek, and Hell Creek. The latter *"is named...because a man always has a hell of a time to cross it on horseback, owing to its cut banks and treacherous bottom."*

In his book *River-Horse,* Least Heat-Moon writes of the "White Castle" structure. He recounts identifying the feature as the location of one of Bodmer's paintings:

We coasted to a halt, jubilant as if we had matched a lottery number rather than a painting to a geological formation. For some reason, the 160-year-old watercolor seemed more antique and exotic than the ten-million-year-old bluff, but being in the presence of those two renderings of the remnants of an ancient sea was like discovering a window in the long curtain-wall of time. We might have been standing on the keelboat Flora *herself, with the prince's pen noisily scratching away, the artist laying down his washes, and somewhere beyond the hills roamed bison so thick it seemed that the plains themselves had gained legs, got up, and begun running, and from the high rocks red men watched the little thing-that-walks-on-the-water, part of the vanguard carrying in a new people who would inundate the old ways as the big impoundment one day would the river.*

SEGMENT 2.B.1: Fourchette Creek (mile 1,846) to mile 1,814 on Fort Peck Lake: 32 miles *(Maps 2.B.1 & 2.B.2)*

Paddler's Notes and Cautions

Prevailing winds in this area are from the northwest, but blows from the east and southeast are common. When I paddled through this segment, I had light winds from the south. I chose to stay along the north shore. My rationale was that I could stay close to the shore if the wind shifted to the northwest. I would be able to stay in the "wind shadow" of the shoreline, gaining some shelter from the wind when I needed it. If the wind shifted to the northeast, I would be able to line my boat by working the bow and stern lines to keep the boat from being blown to shore by angling the bow slightly to catch the wind.

My GPS track log shows that I paddled about 9.5 shoreline miles to reach the site of the Lewis and Clark Expedition's May 17, 1805 camp (mile 1,838). From this point the lake begins a sharp turn to the north. You will be paddling a half-dozen miles before you resume travel to the east. I paddled about half this distance (~ mile 1,835), then beached my kayak and ate lunch and rested

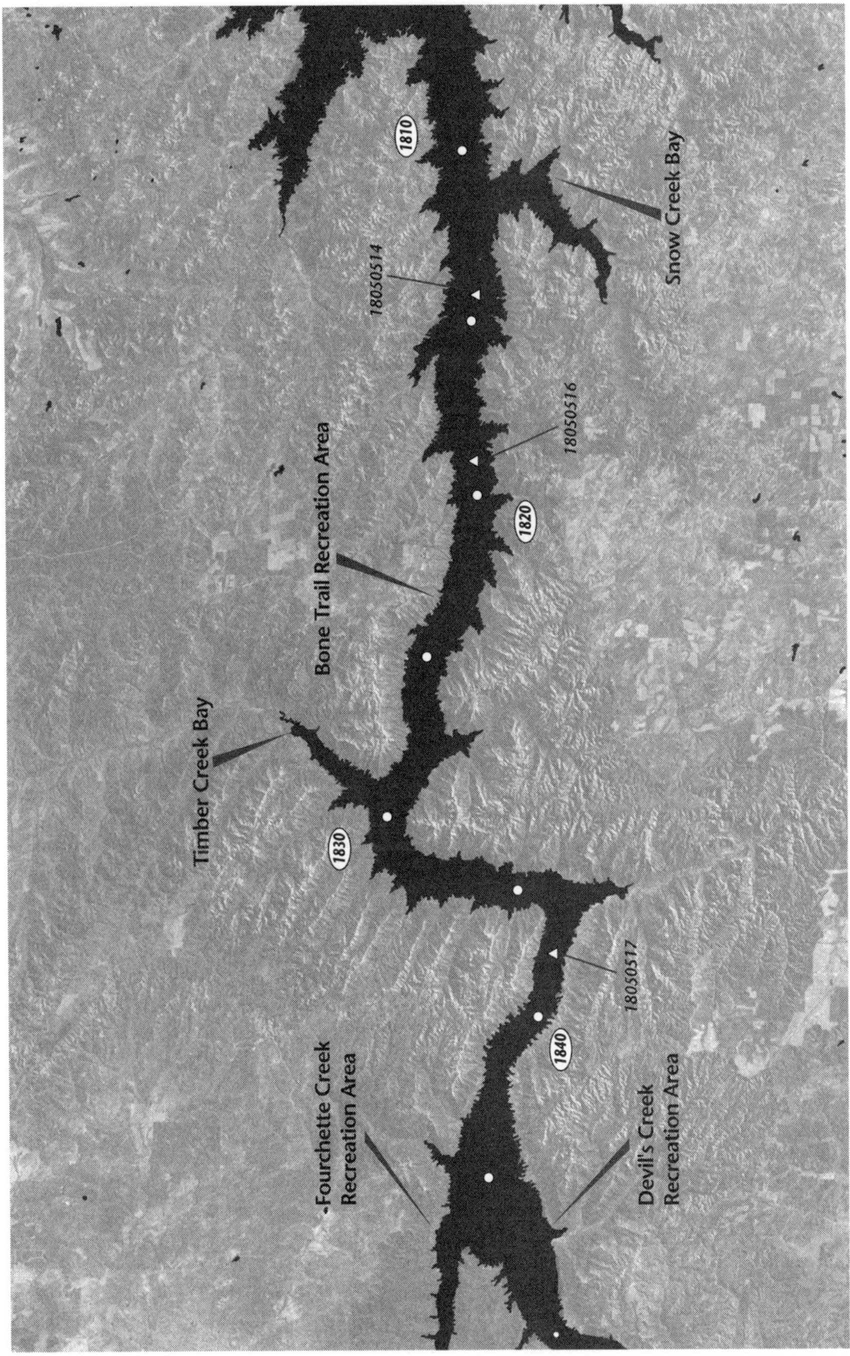

Map 2.B.1: Fourchette Creek (mile 1,846) to mile 1,814 on Fort Peck Lake.

for about an hour. Then I paddled to the opposite (south) shore. There was little wind, so I angled to the northeast. Once across the lake, I hugged the shoreline and worked my way around the bend to the east. By taking this track I saved several miles of paddling. I recommend this strategy, if the weather permits.

Once around the bend I crossed back to the north shore at about mile 1,829 and continued paddling along the shore for about 5 miles until I reached the Bone Trail boat ramp (mile 1,823; 47.67425/-107.24865,) where I spent the night. The Bone Trail Recreation Area has low and high water ramps, a vault toilet, picnic shelters, and a camping area. There are no trash bins, so you'll need to carry your trash for at least two more days until you get to Pines Recreation Area. There is no source for drinking water. The campsites are on an elevated area and are quite exposed to the wind. I decided to camp near the low water ramp.

There were anglers at the landing, most working the lake in pursuit of walleye. I spoke with a local rancher, Don Burke, who earlier had come down to chase one of his bulls out of the area and now was back to repair a downed fence. Don has lived in the area all his life; his ranch is in the hills above the landing. He graciously answered my questions about the area and about his "river rat" childhood in the river bottoms. He told me about cottonwoods so big that you could not reach around them, about the wildlife, and about the fishing. He related that his father had once removed more than 100 pounds of honey from a beehive in a hollow tree. He remembered the river bottoms as a paradise, ruined by rising waters behind Roosevelt's dam.

Later that night, after I finished my journal notes and looked over my maps, I reflected on Don's commentary. The river bottoms were, as he described them, a relative paradise. Now, with the exception of scrub vegetation in the draws, the landscape is barren. Hillside slopes are steep and ragged. The shoreline is a garden of jagged rocks. Because of periodic droughts and the demand for water downstream, water levels fluctuate in the extreme. Shoreline erosion proceeds at an accelerated rate. Material slides into the lake and sediments accumulate at a pace that should make dam engineers blush. I remember thinking that someday, after the lake is slowly choked away by silt and debris, the groves of cottonwoods will return. The river at the bottom of the lake is only sleeping.

From Bone Trail, the lake trends due east for some 18 miles. Again, I recommend staying along the north shore. This is a wild, rugged, and often windy area. The area has historically presented difficulties for travelers. Four miles east of Bone Trail is the expedition's May 16, 1805 camp (mile 1,819), where two men of the party wounded a large panther not far from the camp. This is also where Lewis penned praise for Sacagawea's cool-headed actions two days earlier, during the near capsize of the white pirogue. The incident was probably still on both captains' minds four days later at the Musselshell River camp, where they decided to name a tributary, Sacagawea or "Bird woman's Fork or R[iver]." Five miles to the east of the Panther Camp is the site of the expedition's May 14 and 15 camp (mile 1,814), where the party spent most of the time drying and repacking supplies that were soaked by the near-disastrous pirogue accident. They were unable to sufficiently dry their stores until the weather cleared on May 16. Most of that day was apparently given over to getting things dried out, repacked, and redistributed. It was not until 4 P.M. that they set out. They made only 5 miles before setting up camp for the evening.

SEGMENT 2.B.2: Mile 1,814 on Fort Peck Lake to Fort Peck Dam (mile 1,771.5): ~ 42 miles ***(Maps 2.B.2 & 2.B.3)***

Paddler's Notes and Cautions

After mile 1,809, the lake bends sharply to the north. When the wind is from the northwest, it is best to remain on the left (north) side, hugging the shoreline. On the south side you will pass two large bays. Both Snow Creek Bay (~ mile 1,812) and Hell Creek Bay (~ mile 1806) trend to the southwest. Even a modest southwest wind will drive waves out from these bays. Very rough conditions can result.

At some point, assuming relatively calm conditions, you can cross over to the right (south) side. I crossed at about mile 1,805. Where you cross will determine your open water distance, but count on a crossing of about 2 miles. Before making the crossing you should put in to shore, lunch or snack, drink water, rest, bail your boat, and check all your gear. In addition, you should study the weather signs carefully. It bears repeating that thunderclouds build up suddenly around this lake, and that sudden wind shifts and squalls are common. From this point on, the lake begins to widen out; you must proceed with extra caution.

Once across the lake, hug the shoreline and work your way around the bend. Stop and rest after you are a mile or so around the bend (~ mile 1,801). Examine your maps and images carefully; this is a confusing area to navigate. In front of you, along the left shore, are more than a dozen large bays. From

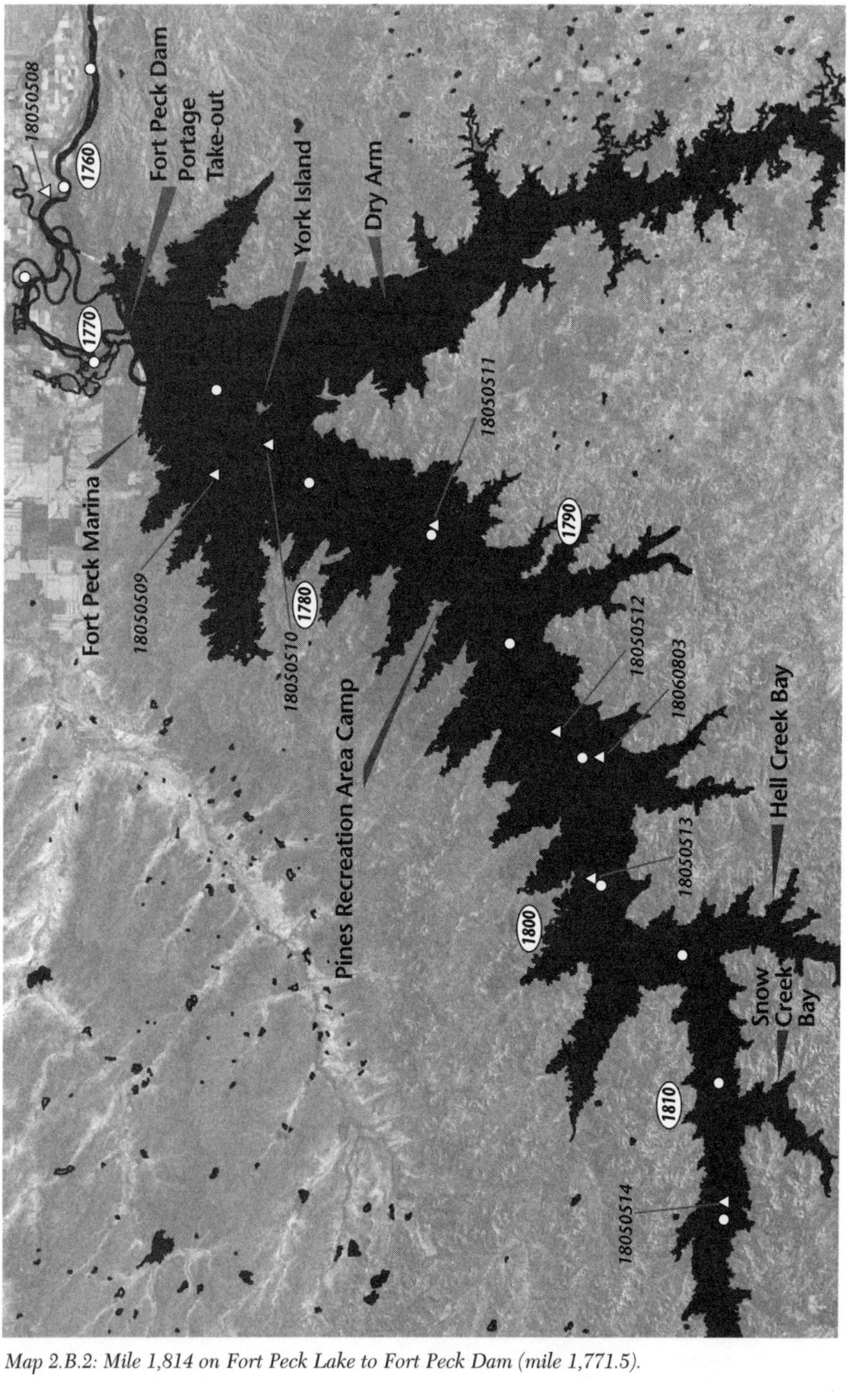

Map 2.B.2: Mile 1,814 on Fort Peck Lake to Fort Peck Dam (mile 1,771.5).

the seat of your craft it is hard to tell where one bay ends and the next begins. If necessary, disembark and climb a hill to get a better perspective. The right shore has fewer bays but progressively widens away from the marina and dam, which are on the left shore. Also, on the right shore, before you get near the dam, you will encounter the lake's huge Dry Arm. This feature extends many miles to the southeast; if the wind is from the east or southeast, the necessary open water crossing to the dam can be problematic. It is possible that you might have to wait on the west side of the Dry Arm for several days before conditions permit a safe crossing.

So here you must make a choice. Do you remain on the south side or cross to the north shore? I decided to follow the north shore route when I made my way through this area because I enjoyed good weather, I wanted to stop in at the Pines Recreation Area (~ mile 1,787), and I planned to take out at the Fort Peck Marina. I crossed back to the north side at about mile 1,800, intending to camp near navigation marker F as shown on the USFWS East Unit map. I could not locate the marker, so I picked a spot just to the northeast of the Lewis and Clark Expedition's May 13 camp. My campsite coordinates were 47.74778/-106.81808. This was the best campsite on the lake; it was in a small pocket bay, well sheltered, and on firm sand. At dusk, a large mule deer sauntered down the hill and watered within 50 yards of my tent. In the water a few feet from shore, a huge pike surfaced, eyed me, and then disappeared with a quick flip of its tail. The evening's sunset was spectacular.

The next morning, shortly after putting in, I found the F navigation marker, one bay to the east of my camp. As I paddled, I frequently looked at my map and the satellite image of the lake. I had counted five bays that I would need to cross before I got to the Pines Recreation Area. The mouth of each of these bays is about 2 miles across, but even in a modest blow you should be able to work across them because of the periodic shelter afforded by their fractal-like geometric complexity. However, conditions at each point will need to be assessed. The shoreline in this area alternates between ragged and mucky, so lining your boat is not always a productive option. If things are too rough, there are many pocket bays that offer shelter, a good rest stop, or a campsite for the night.

As I approached the Pines Recreation Area, I saw tall pine trees, several fishing boats, and the campground. I did not see a place to put in on the west side, so I made my way around the point and its navigation marker (G) and put in at the first bay. I saw people swimming here, and it seemed to offer good access to the campground. I hauled my boat out and walked up to the area where RVs were parked. The sites were nestled among the pines, generally offering good protection from the wind. I talked with some of the campers and got the information that it was quite a popular place. I filled my water jugs, deposited my trash, and walked back to my kayak. After the quiet of the past several days, the campground's noise and bustle was a bit much. I looked over my map. It was 14 or maybe 15 miles to the marina. The next point was about 3 miles distant. I'd done about a dozen miles and was tired, but it was only midafternoon. The weather was holding, so I decided to continue on because I wanted to cut down on the distance remaining to the dam.

By the time I reached the next point, an hour later, thunderclouds were moving in from the west. I paddled around to the east side of the point, pulled in, and made camp under the shelter of a sandy ridge. The coordinates of my camp were 47.85760/-106.57653 (near mile 1,784 left).

Early the next morning I put in and worked my way along the north shore. To the northeast, the dam became visible. At approximately mile 1,779 (47.92261/-106.54455), I began my crossing of Duck Creek Bay. As I got

My camp of June 16, 2002, on Fort Peck Lake, about 10 miles southwest of the marina. This photo was taken in the late afternoon; thunderstorms were moving in from the west. I made a well tucked-in camp on the east side of a point, in the shelter of a low sandy ridge. Note the storm lines solidly anchoring my tent to the ground.

closer, I could make out cabins and homes along the west side, and I could see car and trailer traffic crossing the dam. I angled to the north and east, and eventually reached the shore at the point west of Catfish Bay. The entrance to the marina was not apparent, so I just continued working along the shore until I saw a boat come out from behind the small point that hid the entrance.

The Fort Peck Marina is tucked well back into a small bay and offers good shelter for boats (mile 1,773.3 left; 47.99398/-106.48799). This is often a busy boat ramp, so paddlers should pull out their boats to the side of the ramp. A short hike up the steeply inclined ramp is the marina's bar and restaurant where the food is good, the beer is icy cold, and the hospitality is outstanding. The owners of the marina, Tara and David Waterson, keep a record of paddlers crossing the lake. Be sure to leave a card or information at the bar. And when you finish your journey, drop them a note to give them your update. If you speak with David, you can arrange a portage over the dam. At the time when I arranged transport (boat and gear in the back of a pickup), the fee was $20. You should understand that this marina is a very busy place, and the portage will take place when you can be accommodated.

If you need a break from tent living, the Watersons have "stationary RV rentals" that you can rent for a day or two. They also have spaces for RV camping. If you want to tent, a small primitive campsite (West Campsite) is just around the next point to the north. Continue paddling along the shore. Beyond the marina entrance you will see a picnic area and a cream-colored shelter building. Continue along the shore and you will find a small bay with several campsites. This site offers trees for shelter and shade. There are fire pits, and a bathroom is just up the hill. It is an easy walk from the campsites to the marina, but if you cut across the field to the marina, keep an eye out for snakes. Less than a mile west on Highway 24 is a restaurant with an ATM machine. Across the highway is a small grocery store.

When I arrived at the west end of the lake, I had been on the water for more than two weeks and had paddled more than 300 miles. I was ready for a break. So I stayed at the marina for a couple days to rest, recharge my batteries, and scout the dam for a portage route. Using my cell phone, I set up a meeting with ACE lake manager Roy Snyder. I had previously communicated with him about my mapping project and he had asked me to contact him when I got to the dam.

Roy picked me up in his truck the next day and we drove to his office where we talked about my effort and looked over maps of the area surrounding the

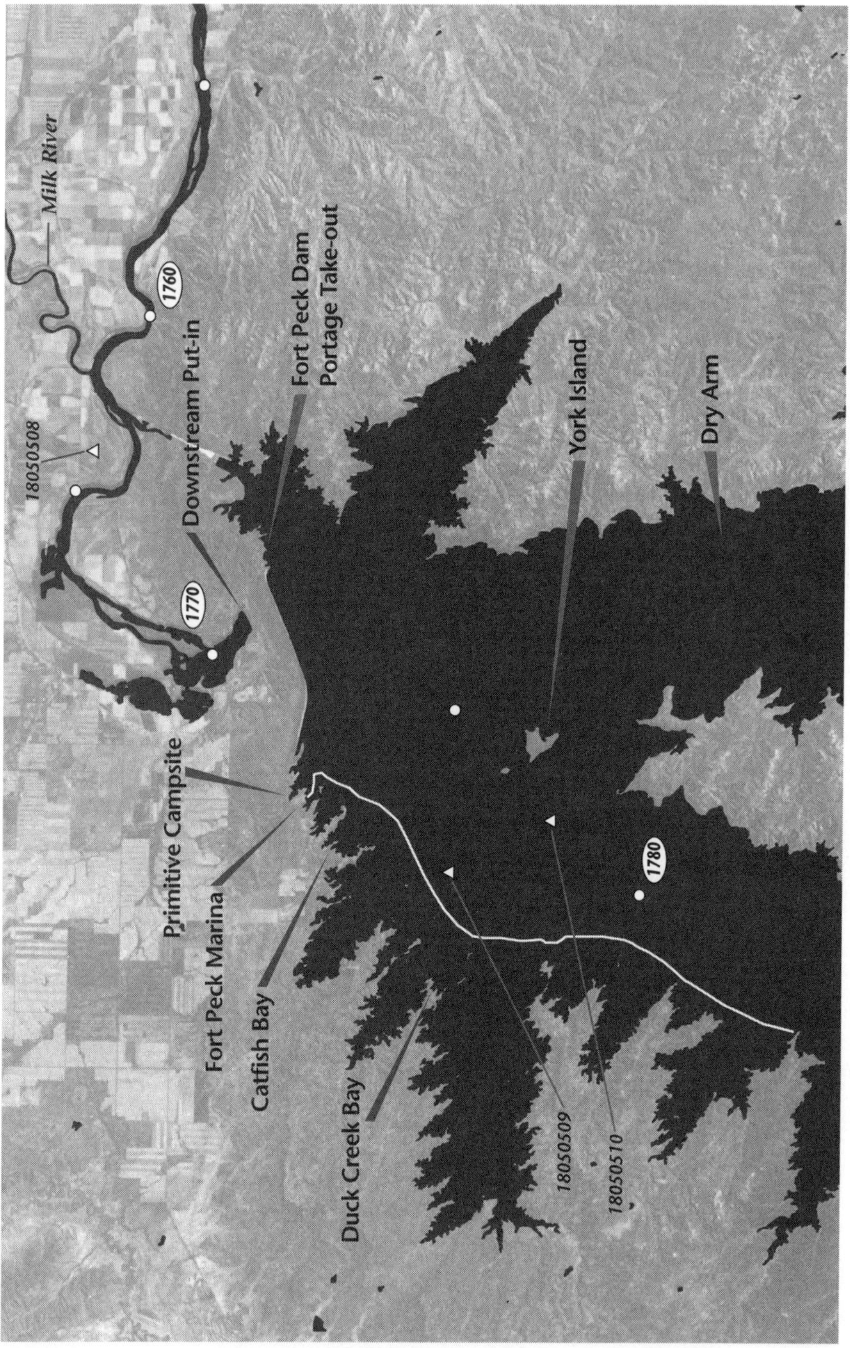

Map 2.B.3: Detail of Fort Peck Dam area. My GPS track is shown as the white line.

dam. We then drove out to the east side of the dam to look over the options for portaging. We walked over the area, looking for the best site for a manual crossover, and decided that the east side of the dam offered the best route.

If you are intent on portaging the dam, you have serious work cut out for you. This is a 1.2-mile portage. Completing this portage will take the better part of a day. The "upstream" take-out is about 4.4 miles east of the marina. The take-out spot (48.00612/-106.39786) is on a sandy point east of the dam's four shaft houses, large concrete structures with orange tile roofs. From the take-out point, cross Highway 24 and take the blacktop road that runs past the powerhouse. Then take the first gravel road on the right. Continue for 0.2 mile. This will get you to a bank that you can get down to reach the put-in (48.01415/-106.42889).

Of the six ACE dams on the Upper Missouri, the Fort Peck Dam is probably the easiest to portage. The remaining dams require considerably longer and more difficult portage routes. If you are carrying a set of transport wheels, this portage can be done in stages. The roads are not steeply inclined, and traffic is not an issue once you have crossed the dam highway. Nevertheless, I recommend that you arrange your transport from the marina. Humping your gear and craft over this distance will be time-consuming work.

SEGMENT 2.C: Fort Peck Dam (mile 1,771) to Williston, North Dakota (mile 1,547) *(Map 2.C)*

- **River miles:** 224
- **Difficulty level:** Low to medium
- **Typical time to complete:** 7 to 12 days

As the crow flies, it is 130 miles from the Fort Peck Dam to Williston, North Dakota. However, on this section of the Missouri you'll have few opportunities to paddle in a straight line. Here the river twists and turns; you will find yourself paddling to the north or south almost as often as you get to paddle toward the east. Officially this stretch is 224 river miles long, making this the longest free-running segment of the Upper Missouri. There is little motorized boat traffic once you are away from the dam and until you get near Williston, perhaps because of the lack of access ramps, fuel stops, and RV campgrounds. These circumstances should recommend the distance to paddlers, but relatively few apparently attempt this section.

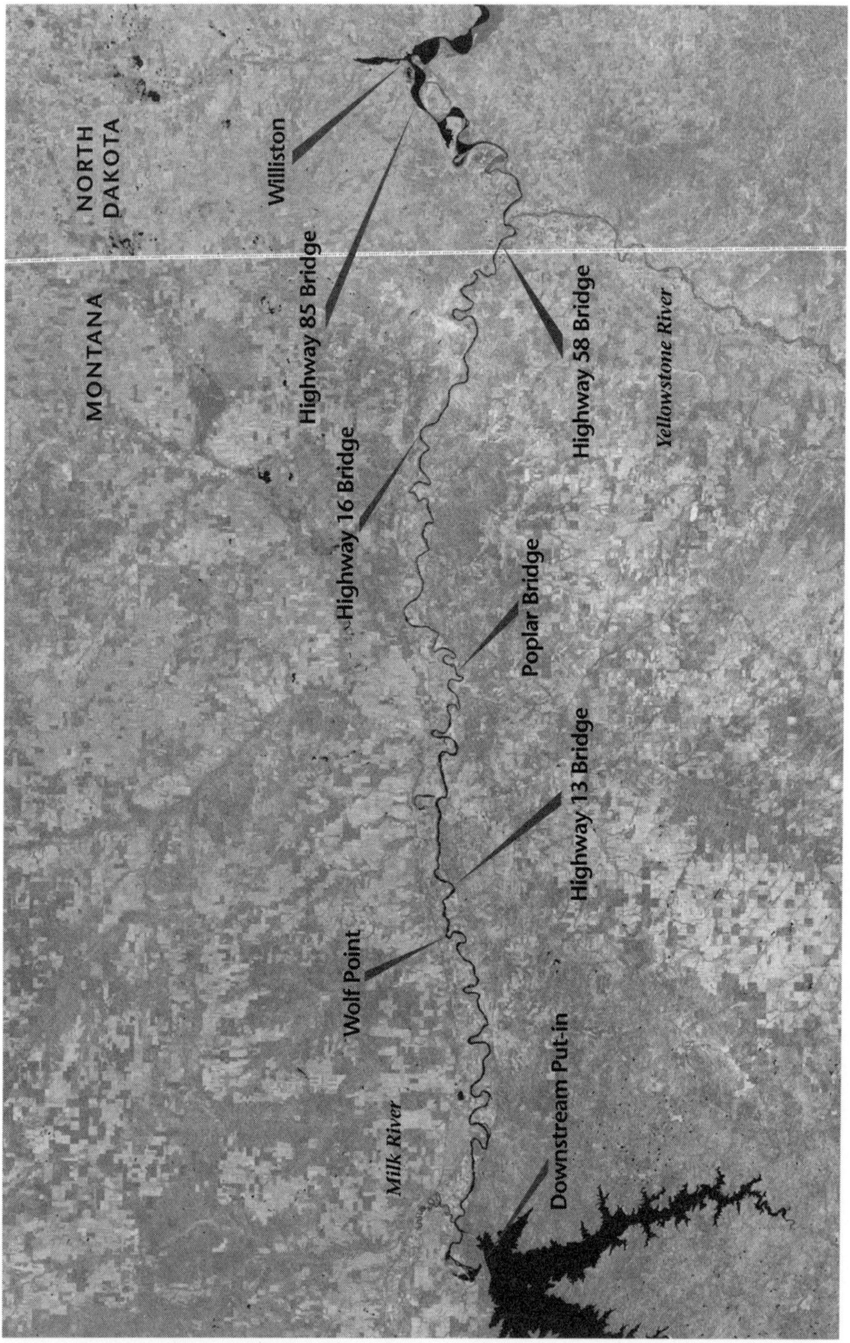

Map 2.C: Fort Peck Dam (mile 1,771) to Williston, North Dakota (mile 1,547).

This stretch is a good one; more paddlers should consider making this trip. If you paddled across Fort Peck Lake before attempting this section, you will welcome the strong current from water released from the dam. Also, with just a few exceptions, the river's path is little influenced by human will. The channel snakes its way to the east for almost 190 miles, where it is joined by the Yellowstone River. Beyond this confluence, the Missouri runs into the far west end of the Lake Sakakawea reservoir. Here the current is slowed and sediment is dumped wholesale, creating a vast area of wetlands. The channel meanders, carving a sometimes-confusing maze of low willow-brush islands, cattail thickets, and extensive mudflats. Nevertheless, the main channel can always be deduced, at least to the Highway 85 bridge, the most convenient pullout when you get near Williston.

The Fort Peck Indian Reservation begins on the north shore at the Milk River and extends east for 130 miles. Paddlers should understand that, for all intents and purposes, reservation lands extend to the water's edge. As an absolute rule, permission should be obtained before camping on reservation property. The Fort Peck Reservation tribal office (Assiniboine and Sioux tribes) phone number is (406) 768-5155. If you have not obtained permission to camp on reservation land, camp along the south shore. Of course, you should always attempt to obtain permission to camp whenever you want to set up.

The river meanders throughout the floodplain in this section. The soil is rich and deep, and steep banks line much of the river. Irrigated-assisted agriculture has expanded over much of the floodplain. Along the riverbank, electric pumps hum, and large irrigation pipes suck water that is sprayed over field crops. Cattle occasionally stand in the water near the shore. Within a day's paddle from the dam, you will hear and then eventually see trains on the Burlington Northern Railroad's tracks. The rails roughly parallel the river for the length of this section–in most instances, along the north edge of the floodplain.

Access is limited to towns along this section, as most are along the railroad line, typically more than a couple miles from the river. There are only a handful of official access points where a boat might be launched. So while there are few opportunities to resupply, you are likely to encounter little in the way of boat traffic. For the most part, when you are in the channel you cannot see much beyond the shoreline banks and vegetation. Thus, it is easy to visualize what it might have been like to paddle through here a century or two ago. Occasionally, you may see inland settlements or spy their grain elevators from the river. Near most towns, cell phone coverage is generally good. So you are not entirely out of communication.

Stands of cottonwood trees line much of the shore. The root systems of many trees have been half-exposed by the relentless undercutting action of the current. Some trees lean out over the water at angles that seem to defy the laws of physics, clinging tenaciously to a bank being undercut by the shifting river. Along these banks, tumbled trees create pockets of snags by capturing drifting trunks and branches. Beavers sometimes exploit these areas, building dens alongside the cut bank amid the flotsam.

It took me eight days to paddle through this section. Afternoon thunderstorms and strong northwest winds slowed me at times. For the most part, however, you can probably count on making at least 25 to 35 current-assisted miles a day in good weather. Compared to Fort Peck Lake, the paddling is relatively easy, although care must be taken as you work around sharp bends and snags. Where the river widens, sandbars are an issue. Occasionally, the channel seems to evaporate, and you must pick your way carefully through the shallows.

Information/Maps/Resources

To the best of my knowledge, there is no good map for paddlers wanting to do this section of the Missouri. I made do with a current Montana Highway Map, printouts of the maps from the MapSource "Roads and Recreation" CD, and printouts from the satellite imagery (N-13-45). The highway map showed me the inland location of the towns, the area road network, and the location of bridges. I printed out the MapSource hard copy at the last minute. Each of these sheets showed a 20-mile-long segment of the river (scale set at 1 inch = 2 miles). In essence, each sheet displayed what I would see on my GPS unit screen as I navigated down the river. With these maps, and my GPS keeping a real-time track of my progress, I knew my position with precision.

The satellite images were an indispensable aid once I passed the Yellowstone confluence. Shortly before this, Lake Sakakawea technically begins. I say "technically" because sediment from both the Missouri and the Yellowstone is being deposited at an advanced rate. This section looks nothing like what you see on the maps. The west end of Lake Sakakawea is a vast silted-in maze of mudflats and scrub-willow-covered islands. However, by referring to the area's satellite image and by taking time to read the river, I was able to stay in the channel. The ACE publication *Lake Sakakawea & Garrison Dam Boating and Recreation* provides dated (1988) but still useful air photo–based maps of the river beginning at the Yellowstone confluence.

Suggested Readings

Twenty-seven Lewis and Clark campsites are in this section. Information about what transpired here during the outbound trip (April 22 to May 9, 1805) can be found in Vol. 4:59–136 (*Journals,* [Moulton, ed.]). Return trip event detail (August 4 to 9, 1806 [Lewis]; August 4 to 5, 1806 [Clark]) can be found in Vol. 8:280–287 and Vol. 8:280–282. Context about events can be found in Stephen Ambrose's *Undaunted Courage,* in chapter 18:217–224 and in chapter 32:395.

The fur trade figures large in this area's history. Hunters, trappers, and traders paddled every mile of the river you will float. The American Fur Company's Upper Missouri River Outfit began construction of Fort Union in the fall of 1829. The steamboat *Yellow Stone* made it up the Missouri to Fort Union in 1832, beginning what ultimately developed into regular steamer navigation on the Upper Missouri. Colorful details about life at the fort and the activities of fur traders and trappers can be found in several sources, but I especially recommend Barton H. Barbour's book, *Fort Union and the Upper Missouri Fur Trade.*

The fort's location, near the Yellowstone's confluence with the Missouri, ultimately facilitated control of the fur trade well out to the Rocky Mountains. According to Barbour, the approximately $40,000 spent on the fort's construction was a very good investment. It soon became the leading producer of buffalo robes, other furs, and skins. Barbour notes that by the third summer of the fort's existence, it held three-fifths of the company's regional inventories. For context, between 1835 and 1837, the Upper Missouri Outfit shipped 95,000 robes. Buffalo robes were the currency of the day. Barbour observes that:

At Fort Union, accounts with Indian as well as white traders were figured in terms of the standard exchange medium, buffalo robes. One robe's value was calculated at "an imaginary value of $3 each in the country." To illustrate, in 1851 a 3-point blanket (a coarse but durable English woolen measuring roughly four by six feet) cost three robes. Two robes bought a two-gallon iron-bound brass kettle, while three inexpensive butcher knives could be had for one robe. A robe also purchased a yard of red or blue woolen stroud cloth or a hundred loads of powder and ball. Good horses might fetch ten or more robes, and guns were similarly expensive. Other fur values were calculated in *proportionate fractions of robes, with so many raccoon, fox, or beaver skins equaling one robe. Robes sold at Saint Louis for about six dollars.*

Fort Union also was an important stopping place for adventurers, scientists, and artists. Famous guests included George Catlin, Prince Maximilian and Karl Bodmer, and John James Audubon. Maximilian's journal entries from June 24 to July 5, 1833, provide good detail about the fort. Because Fort Union was at the head of steamboat navigation at the time, Maximilian and his party took a keelboat upstream to Fort MacKenzie, at the mouth of the Marias River. His journal entries of July 6 to 21, 1833, cover the area between the fort and the area near today's Fort Peck Dam.

I highly recommend reading Maximilian's journals. The stretch between Fort Peck Dam and the Yellowstone retains many of the features that he describes. He has a fine eye for landscape detail and provides good information about the crew's extraordinary efforts to make progress up the shallow Missouri. For example, on the second day out, Maximilian writes that the men towing the boat ("engages") were working very hard:

...the current of the river being very strong; they were sometimes obliged to climb, in a long row, up the hills, where we saw them suspended, like chamois, in dangerous positions....In other places, the engages who were towing were obliged to make a way on the bank by cutting down large poplars and thick bushes, which often cost much time and trouble. Here they often met with rattlesnakes, of which they killed several (Vol. 23: 28).

Progress up the river was slowed as the keelboat had to be worked around snag piles and pushed over shallows. The riverbank frequently collapsed as men tried to haul the towlines along the shore. To tow their boat through one snag field, Maximilian writes that:

The men, in a long row, had to step or jump from one of these snags to another, the sand being too soft to bear their weight; but they frequently missed the snags, and fell between them, up to their arms, into the river, so that many of them, who had never before done such work, trembled all over, and returned to the vessel (Vol. 23: 29–30).

If you paddle this section, you will be lucky if you experience only one thunderstorm accompanied by high winds. If you've read Maximilian's account, you'll have the comfort of knowing that earlier adventurers also had to deal with extreme weather. And that *"the mosquitoes were very troublesome."* Even though you are floating with the current, the river will still test your wits and stamina. Reflecting on the trials and tribulations of those who passed before you can generate small comforts.

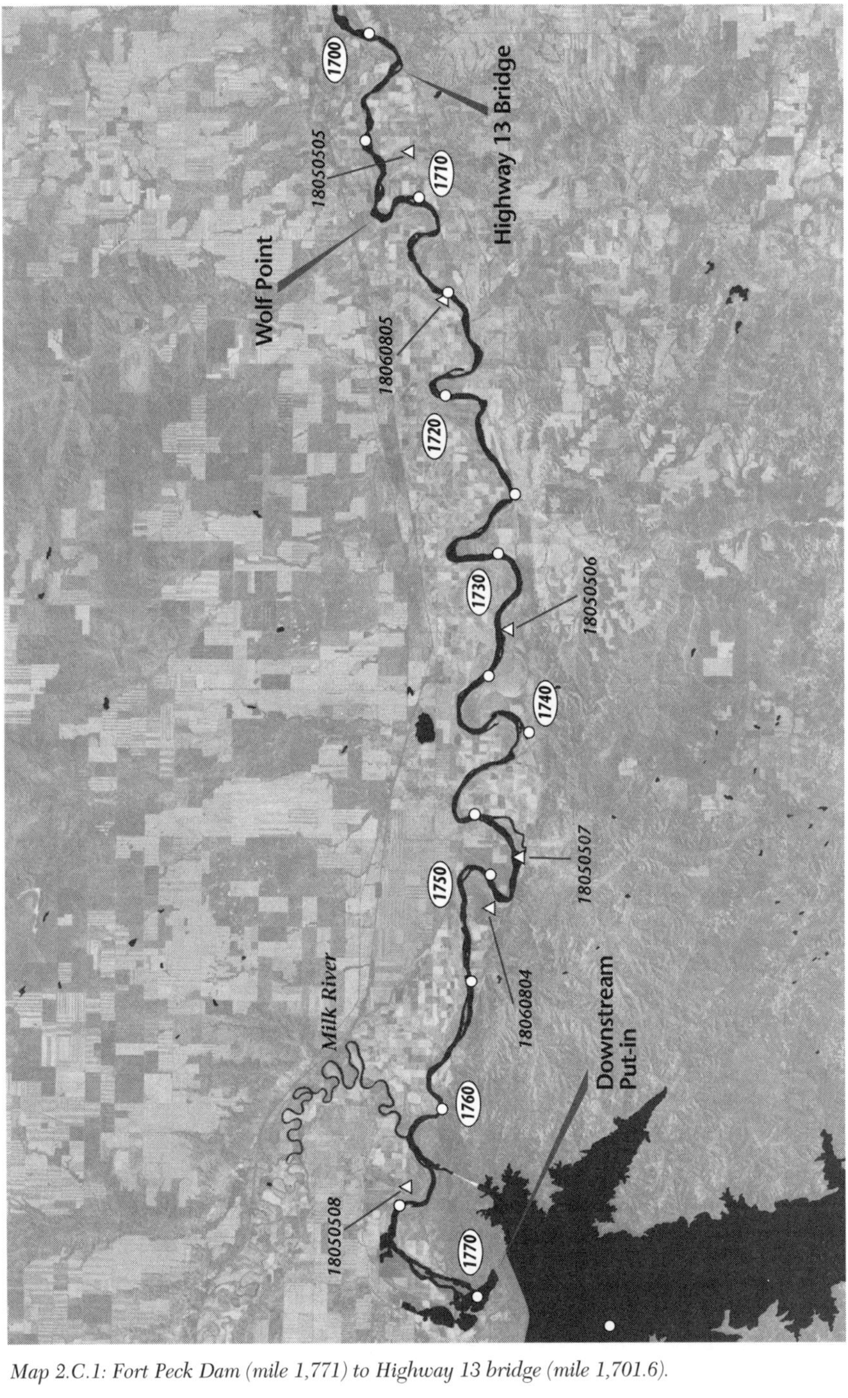

Map 2.C.1: Fort Peck Dam (mile 1,771) to Highway 13 bridge (mile 1,701.6).

◆ Downstream Fort Peck Dam put-in (mile 1,771) to Highway 13 bridge (mile 1,701.5): ~ 70 miles *(Maps 2.C.1 & 2.C.2)*

Paddler's Notes and Cautions

One-half mile downriver (mile 1,770.5) on the left is the recommended take-out point for the Fort Peck Recreation Area's West End Campground (48.01414/ -106.42888). This is a very nice campground with all amenities. Although this very popular campground is typically full during the month of July and on all major holidays, campground staff will make every effort to find paddlers a tent site. Nearby are the Powerhouse Museum, the Fort Peck Hotel, and a new interpretive center (scheduled to open in 2005). About a mile from the campground are the town post office and a grocery store. If you do stay here for a day or two, and I recommend that you do, locate the campground host for more information about the status of things and for assistance in lining up a ride into town. You will find that most RV campers are quite interested in your adventure, and that some will volunteer to assist you before you can ask.

If you have used the portage service offered by the marina, you will probably be put in at a small bay off Highway 117, just before the bridge (48.02382/ -106.44374). If you work around the point, and stay on the left (west) side, you will come to a fishing access structure just before the bridge. Near this structure you can tie up, walk up to the road, and cross the bridge to the Park Grove Cafe and Bar. A convenience store is also across the street. This is, for all intents and purposes, your last chance to stock up on groceries, ice, and gas until you get to Williston, North Dakota, some 224 miles downriver.

Although there is generally a good current below the dam, it is a good idea to check the release schedule with the dam manager. Since the water pushing through the dam's turbines is coming from the deeper part of the lake, the downstream river water is icy cold. Trout fishing is said to be particularly good on this stretch. Consider purchasing a fishing license, if you haven't already, and some bait. The river remains crystal clear for nearly 10 miles until the Milk River adds its heavy sediment load (mile 1,761.5). Beyond this confluence, the Missouri resumes its muddy way.

Before you begin downstream, look over carefully the downstream area satellite image. At the time I paddled away from the dam, the main channel was on the left side of the first island that you will encounter. The channel to the right was not passable. However, this section of the river seems pretty

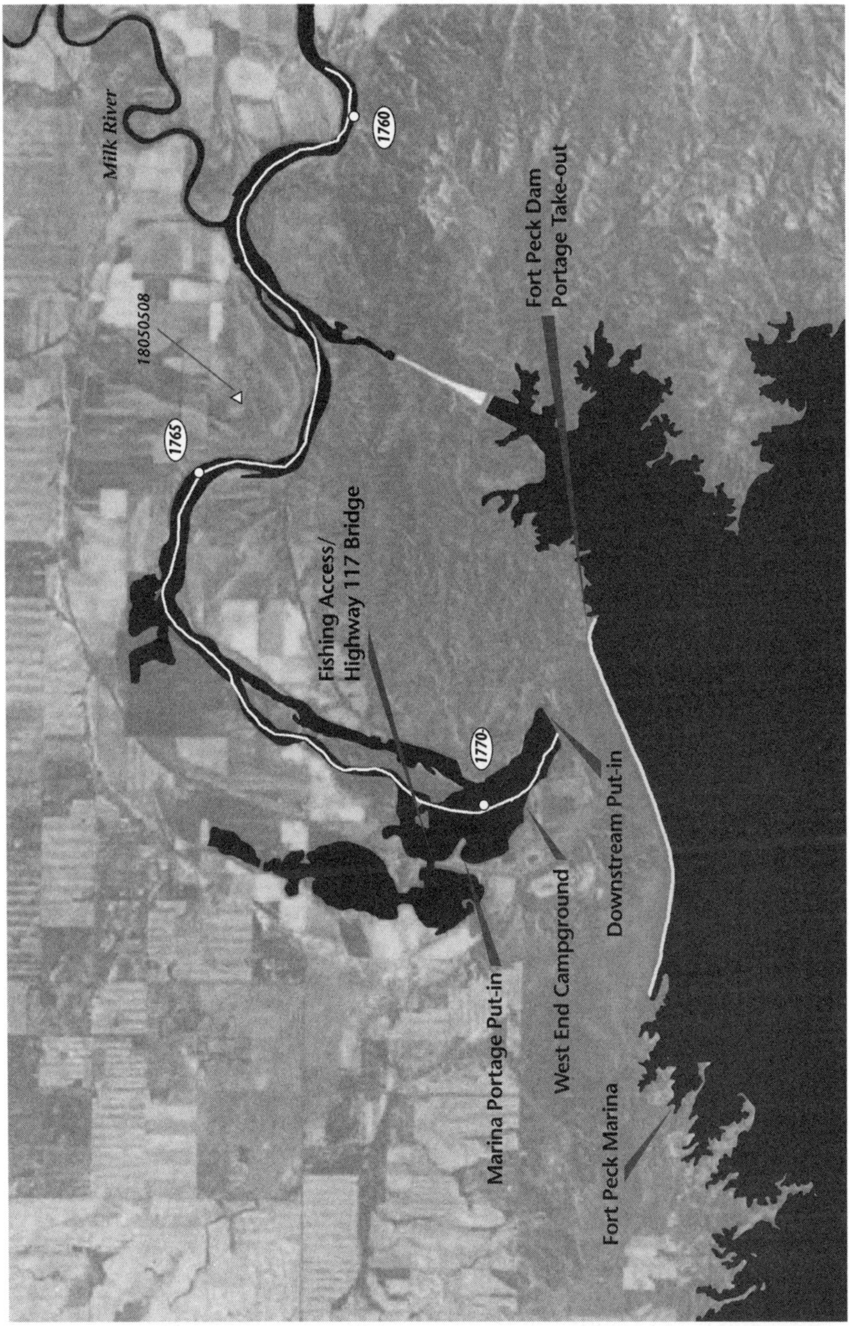

Map 2.C.2 Fort Peck Dam downstream area. White line shows the track from the downstream portage put-in site to beyond the Milk River. River miles are shown as white dots.

dynamic, and circumstances are clearly fluid. Look over the situation and seek information from local boaters or a park ranger.

As you begin your way downstream, look for bald eagles in the cottonwood trees below the dam. In the winter, large numbers of eagles roost in the trees along the shore below the spillway. Beyond Duck Island, at river mile 1,767 right, the river makes a short series of gentle bends to the confluence of the Milk River (mile 1,761.5 left). The sediment from this tributary merges with the clear water from the dam for the next couple miles. Although portions of the Milk River serve as the western boundaries of the Fort Peck Indian Reservation, most of the reservation extends along the left (north) bank of the Missouri until its confluence with the Big Muddy Creek, 140 river miles to the east.

You'll get good assistance from the current in this section. I left the dam at 2:30 in the afternoon and paddled till 7 P.M. Thunderstorms were moving in from the southeast so I made camp on the right bank (mile 1750.5; 48.02367/ -106.12488), just around the bend from the Frazer Pump Station. That night as I completed my field notes, I calculated that I had made 23.5 miles, averaging 4.6 mph. And I remember thinking that after crossing Fort Peck Lake, and working hard for every mile, this section was going to be really enjoyable. The next day was anything but. I only made 14 miles. The weather was iffy when I pushed off. NOAA weather radio called for afternoon winds from the northwest with 50 to 70 mph gusts accompanied by rain.

Downstream (near mile 1,749) the river cuts sharply to the left and, depending on how much water is being released from the dam, you may encounter a short stretch of rapids. I stayed left on my approach to this point, looked things over, then swung out into a fast current at midchannel. There were several snags and some large rocks that I had to avoid. These rapids are not particularly difficult, but this is another place where you have to pay attention. I had thought that I might be able to sneak around the inside of this bend into slack water on the downstream side of the point. However, as I floated up to the point, I could see that I couldn't do this because that area was thick with snags. The current at the outside bend of the turn was really ripping, and the shoreline was ragged. My best advice here is to stay left when approaching the point, and then read the river. If you are among a group of boats, send a more skilled paddler ahead. Watch her. Then follow.

As you approach the bend at mile 1,738, be aware that a series of small wing dams have been constructed along the inside (right) of the turn. When I came to this bend, a storm was blowing in hard from the northwest. I was looking for a place to put in on the right bank. I worked about halfway around the point and pulled in behind one of the wing dams. I hauled my boat up, secured it, and made for the trees as sheets of rain and hail pelted me. Across the river, now churning with whitecaps, was another pump station. A man in a pickup parked by the pump house was looking at me. He had apparently seen me come around the bend and swing into shore. I waved to him, and wondered what he was thinking about the spectacle. I found shelter behind a large cottonwood and determined to wait until the storm passed.

The storm continued all day. The wind blew hard, and the rain let up only occasionally. By midafternoon, I decided to set up camp in the shelter of the trees on the point (mile 1,736.5 right; 48.03256/-106.00627). As I searched for a place to pitch my tent, I noted that the area hosted a thriving colony of young poison ivy plants. It was not until I focused on the issue of where to put my tent that I saw these plants were all around me. And I made a mental note to remind you, my reader, to keep a better eye out for this riverbank hazard.

That night I heard railroad train whistles for the first time. From this point on, the Burlington Northern tracks are a mile or two to the north and generally parallel the river. As you work your way downstream, you may occasionally catch a glimpse of a train.

A second set of rapids lurks 11 miles downstream, just before mile 1,725. Here the river is pinched into a narrow channel, funneled against the base of a steep hill along the right bank, and forced to make a sharp left turn. The river's course changes abruptly from the southeast to the northeast. From this point the river runs due northeast for about 3 miles and then (~ mile 1,722) begins the bend around a half-mile-wide finger of land extending from the right bank 1.5 miles to the north.

As I got around the tip of the finger, I was able to get to the left bank for shelter and good current. I looked on shore and was surprised to see a number of white tepees in a clearing and several pinto horses in a corral. For just an instant, it was as if I had been transported back in time. Then, among the trees, I saw pickup trucks and horse trailers. I reminded myself that I was paddling alongside the Fort Peck Reservation.

Wolf Point, at river mile 1,708, should be approached with caution. When I rounded the bend and the settlement came into view, I was paddling along the right shore. Six shots were fired in my direction. Judging from the report, the shots were fired from a small-caliber handgun. I heard two of the bullets zing by me at the surface of the water. Ahead along the left shore was a green family-style canopy tent and a group of young people. There was some scuffling going on, and it appeared that some of the kids were restraining one of their friends. I continued to paddle, staying as close to the right bank as possible. By the time I got across from them, and took a good look at them, they totally ignored me, acting as if nothing had happened.

I still do not know what to make of this event. When the shots were fired, I was more than a hundred yards from the group. Not an effective range for a handgun, yet I heard two of the bullets zip by uncomfortably close. Obviously I was not welcome here. I have no idea whether these kids were drinking or on drugs, or just bored and trying for some excitement. Or whether some jerk was just trying to impress his buddies or a girlfriend. I continued to paddle at the same pace I was using as I approached and rounded the bend, and left Wolf Point to its own devices. I was angry about the shots being fired. Moving along at just 3 miles an hour, you are a slow-moving target. Stopping here is a bad idea. In the summer of 2004, a paddler that came ashore was badly beaten by a group of young toughs. As you approach Wolf Point, stay river right; don't bother stopping.

The Highway 13 bridge and Lewis and Clark Park (1,701.5 left) are 6.5 river miles downstream. About 40 yards before the boat ramp, on the shore below the shelter, is an area where you can pull out (48.06702/-105.53874). But don't stop here either. Although there are shelters, fire pits, and a camping area, the site is obviously a popular party spot. My gut feeling is that if you pitch a tent here you are asking for trouble.

◆ **Highway 13 bridge (mile 1,701.5) to mile 1,665: ~ 36 miles *(Map 2.C.3)***

Paddler's Notes and Cautions

I continued paddling downstream and began looking for a more suitable camp. Six miles downstream I found one of the most memorable campsites of my trip (mile 1,696 right; 48.08826/-105.45308). I set up my tent on the right bank in an area sheltered by a small cream-colored stone bluff. Beautiful pink wild roses climbed along the rock face. Upstream there was evidence of cattle, but I was able to pitch my tent just east of a barbed wire fence that promised to hold back any four-legged curiosity seekers. My camp was protected from the wind; I had a secure site. Before retiring for the night, I looked at my map. I'd paddled about 37 river miles. For the next dozen miles the river straightened out, and there were no towns until Poplar. After spending so much time paddling north

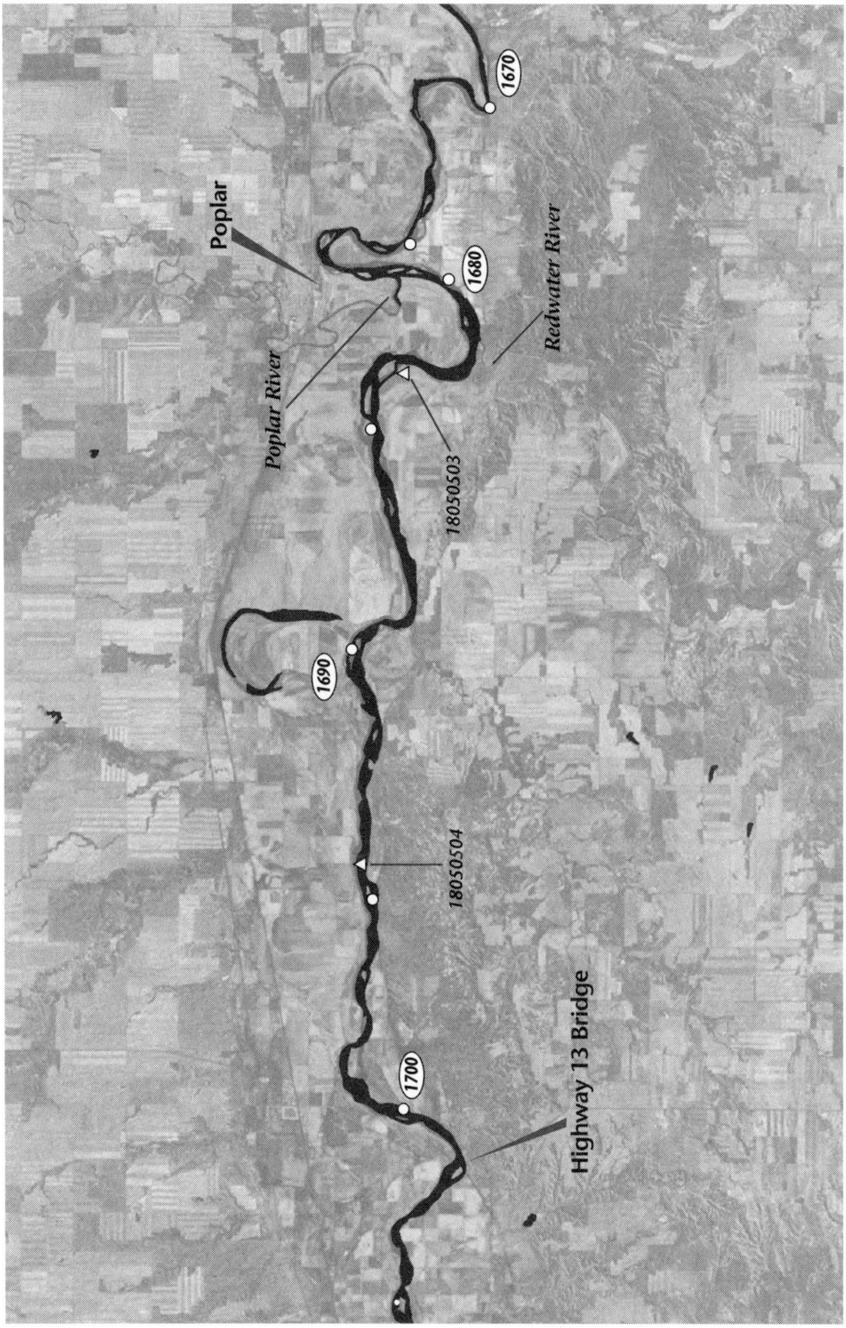

Map 2.C.3: Area between the Highway 13 bridge (mile 1,701.5) and river mile 1,665. This section of river straightens briefly then resumes its contortionist ways.

and south working around long river bends, and having been shot at, I was looking forward to a bit easier time of things.

The next morning started out very well. Seven miles downstream, I rounded the inside of the bend at mile 1,689 and surprised a cougar drinking water from the river. At first glimpse, because of its tan color, I thought it was a deer. Then its long tail bushed out and it sprang back into the brush. I stopped to examine the tracks. They were big cat tracks. It was definitely not a deer.

By the time I had paddled another 6 miles downriver (mile 1,683), a strong southeast wind started to blow, and I had a hard time working my way over to the right side at the bottom of the bend. The area widened out, and the low hills on my right seemed to funnel the wind right at me. A small creek, labeled on one of my maps as the Redwater River, joined the Missouri just after mile 1,681 (right). I stayed along the right bank to keep out of the wind. The river turned north, and I began working my way around another long north-pointing finger. Shortly after I passed the mouth of the Poplar River (mile 1,679 left), I briefly flirted with the idea of portaging across the long bend. It looked to be about 100 yards through the trees to get to the downstream side of the finger. On closer inspection, I could not see a clear path through the vegetation. I reminded myself to not get cute. I continued paddling.

About 1.5 miles to the north, at the top of the bend before the river turns to the south, you'll have a good view of any passing trains and can see the town of Poplar to the northwest. The channel is on the left (north) side of this bend. Three miles downstream, at mile 1,674, is the "400 river miles" from Fort Benton point. If you started at Three Forks, you have almost paddled 650 miles. For additional context, if you intend to paddle all the way to the confluence at the Mississippi, you have completed about one-quarter of the distance. If you are going to pull out at Sioux City, the beginning of the Channelized Lower Missouri, you have 942 miles before you.

◆ Mile 1,665 (west of Poplar Bridge) to Highway 16 bridge (mile 1,620.7): 44.3 miles *(Map 2.C.4)*

Paddler's Notes and Cautions

The Poplar Bridge is at river mile 1,663.3. I could find no easy pullout at this bridge–not that I would consider camping by a bridge in this area. I continued downstream and camped about half a mile above the Lewis and Clark Expedition camp of May 2, 1805. Thunderstorms were moving into the area,

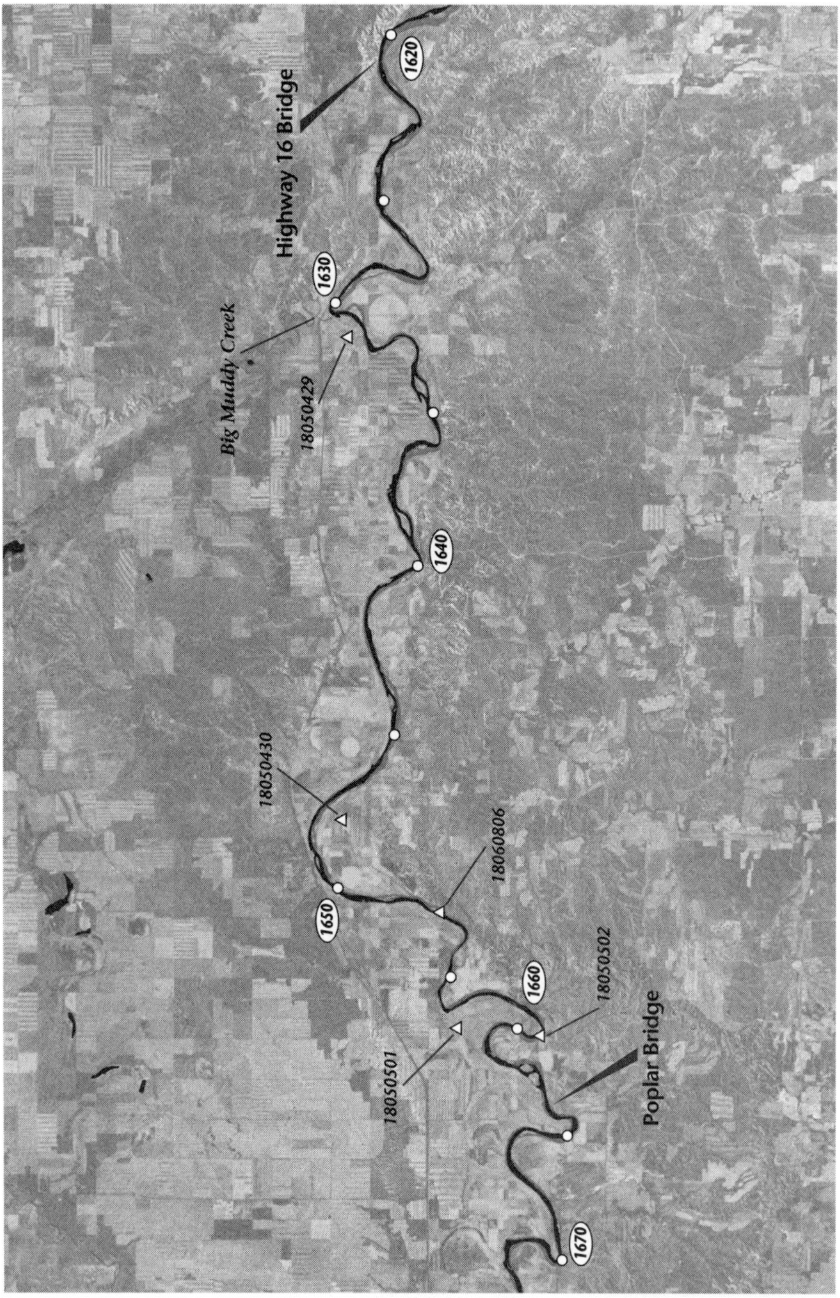

Map 2.C.4: Mile 1,665 (west of Poplar Bridge) to mile 1,621 (Highway 16 bridge). Here you will paddle every-which-way but due west. There are 29 as-the-crow-flies miles and 48 river miles between these points and the Highway 16 bridge.

so I settled for a level but brushy site. I set up my tent back from the bank; it was well hidden. Shortly after I got in the tent, it began to rain. At dusk it let up briefly. Across the river I saw headlights, and a truck pulled up near the bank. A few minutes later I was startled by two very loud rifle shots. I started to wonder about the wisdom of concealing my camp in the brush. Next I saw a large wall tent being set up in an area lighted by the truck's headlights. When this was done, a large fire was started. About this time a bad thunderstorm rolled through, wind-driven rain hosed my tent, and lightning flashed uncomfortably close. I closed my rain fly and went to bed. Shortly afterward, as the storm intensified, I heard a lot of commotion on the other side of the river. The truck was started and doors slammed. I guessed that the wind knocked down their tent and they retreated to their vehicle. I paddled by the camp the next morning. Indeed the tent had been knocked down. It looked like all were still asleep in the truck.

A mile below my camp, the river made a tight U-shaped bend back to the northeast, ran straight for 2 miles, and then flowed around a second U bend. In a 6-mile stretch of the river, you'll find yourself paddling almost every possible compass direction. Here the river would make a contortionist blush. Periodically, you'll paddle alongside a series of starkly beautiful bluffs that contain the river's right bank. This line of hills runs up to the northeast, below

Downstream view from mile 1,641. At the bluffs about a mile ahead, the river cuts sharply to the left (northeast). This bend was known to steamboat pilots as the "Devil's Elbow."

Author's kayak on shore at river mile 1,630, ready to shove off for the next leg of the trip. Freight train moving west in the distance.

Brockton (mile 1,649 left). Half a mile beyond Brockton I stopped for lunch and rested. I also tried my cell phone and got good reception.

Nine miles downstream, at mile 1,640 right, the river butts into a beautiful section of rock bluffs and then turns 90 degrees to the northeast. According to the 1894 Missouri River Commission map of this area (#61), a similarly sharp bend here was known as the Devil's Elbow. The current through here is quick but there are no rapids; I went through in midchannel. The 1894 map also shows the location of Fort Stewart as being about a mile to the northwest. A note on the map states that the fort's chimney remained and that it was established in 1854. A second sharp bend is 4 miles downstream at mile 1,636.

The Big Muddy Creek joins the Missouri just before mile 1,630. As I paddled by, I saw a number of locals fishing near the creek mouth and kids on four-wheelers. I rounded the bend and pulled over to camp on the right bank. It was a marginal camp, brushy with bad mosquitoes (48.14049/-104.60590). But I had done 30 winding miles and I was tired. The railroad line was directly across the river.

As I was hauling my kayak ashore, a passenger train with big upper deck vista windows raced by. I waved, the engineer hit his whistle, and then I pulled my boat back in the weeds. A minute or two afterward, two boys on four-wheelers raced up on a path by the railbed. They slid to a dusty halt directly across from me and looked downstream. I heard one of them say, "Where'd he go?" I stayed in the brush. After a minute, they raced down a trail that paralleled the other side of the river looking for me. I was in stealth mode, not interested in attracting attention to my presence. There was a lane that came down to the river on the opposite shore. Judging from the debris it was another party spot. I slapped mosquitoes, set up camp behind a screen of willow bushes, fixed dinner and ate, then went to bed. I listened to trains rumble throughout the night.

From Blair to the Highway 16 bridge (mile 1,620.7) is less than 10 miles. Once you get to the bridge, it is 25 as-the-crow-flies miles and 39 river miles to the confluence of the Yellowstone. Colorful bluffs line both sides of the river basin; this is a beautiful area to paddle through.

◆ **Highway 16 bridge (mile 1,620.7) to Highway 85 bridge (mile 1,552.6): ~ 68 miles *(Maps 2.C.5 & 2.C.6)***

Paddler's Notes and Cautions

Once you pass under the Highway 16 bridge, the river proceeds southeasterly in a relatively straight track for the next 15 miles. The first 6 miles are named on the 1894 map as the "St. Ange Reach." Rivermen found this stretch

There is outstanding scenery along this section. A colorful bluff is at river mile 1,612 right. Note the coal seam about a third of the way up from the base. Early explorers commented frequently on such features. Dark clouds indicate the approach of a thunderstorm.

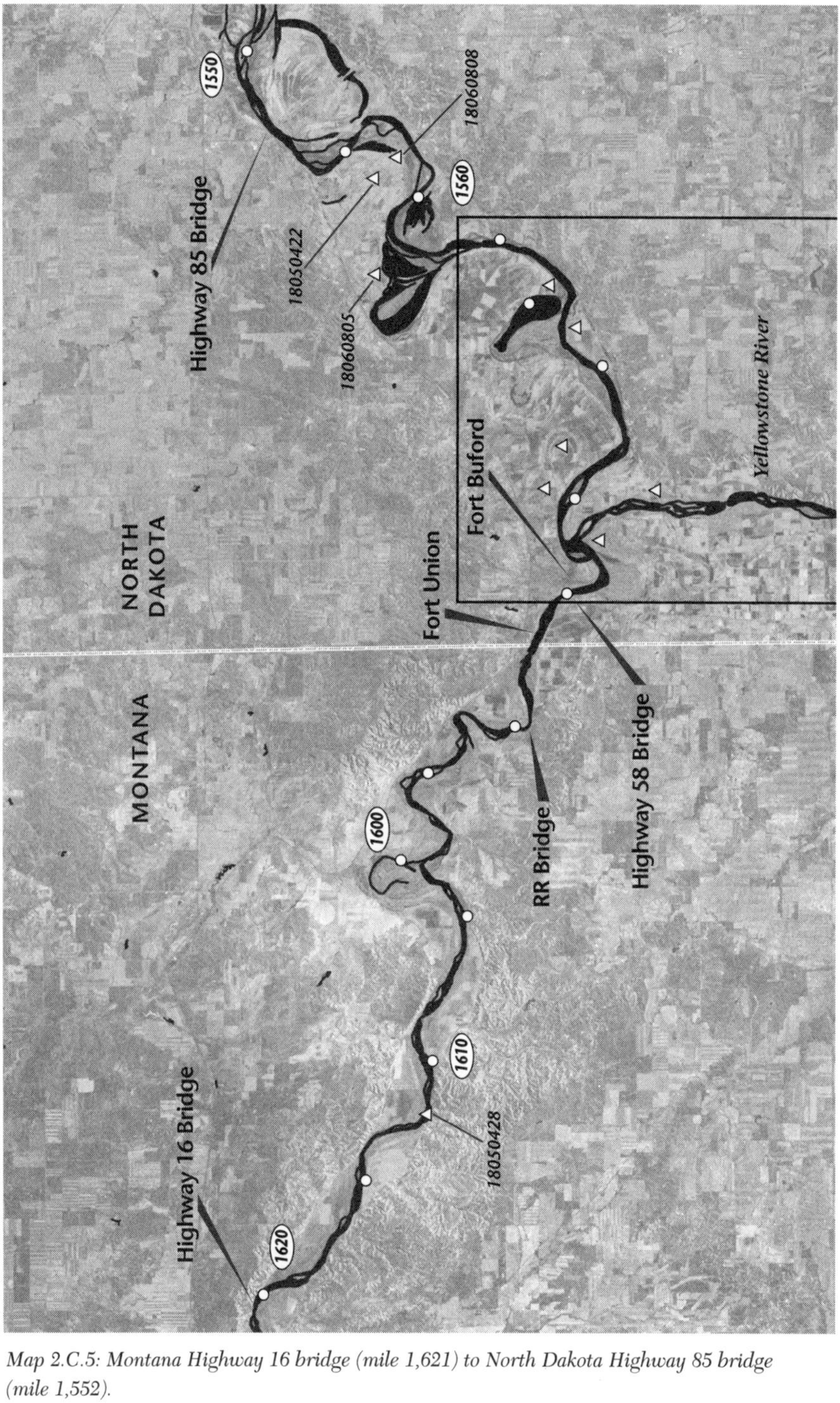

Map 2.C.5: Montana Highway 16 bridge (mile 1,621) to North Dakota Highway 85 bridge (mile 1,552).

particularly difficult to navigate because of its many sandbars. At the south end of the reach, near the bend at mile 1,612 right, there is a pretty bluff with a jet-black coal seam on its face. Steep bluffs line both sides of the river along this section, and there is great scenery.

Because of thunderstorm activity, I stopped paddling twice that afternoon. I put in first at 2 P.M., waited for a half hour, and then pushed off again. I paddled for another hour then had to get off the river again as another storm closed in. I gave it up and set up camp at mile 1,609.5 right (48.04661/ -104.28519). I managed to get my tent up and my gear stowed just before the heavens opened up. I had only made 21 miles for the day. I had wanted to get farther downriver because I wanted to reach Williston in one more day. Now I had nearly 50 river miles ahead of me if I was to get there in just one more day of paddling. But it wasn't to be. The stormy weather continued well into the night. The lightning was fierce. A tree near my camp was struck and the ground shook under my tent.

I learned an important lesson at this site: Do not assume they are all cows. The afternoon before, when I set up my camp, I noticed cattle tracks along the riverbank. But I selected this site quickly because a storm was moving in fast. Early the next morning I was wakened by snorting sounds outside my tent. I zipped my rain fly down a short way and saw a large bull circling my tent, pawing at the ground and tossing up dirt. I decided to be very quiet. I wondered if he would charge the tent. Lying there it occurred to me that my tent's shape, viewed from the right angle, might resemble that of another bull resting on the ground–in Paul Bunyon's blue ox "Babe" sort of way. The thought that I might be trampled by a vision-challenged bull wasn't at all comforting. At least, I remember thinking, my tent was not red. Ultimately, after an hour of snorting and tossing dirt, the bull disappeared into the brush. I made some tea, ate a breakfast bar, and quietly packed up my gear and got out of there. I kept a careful eye out for the bull the whole time.

About 2 miles downriver (~ mile 1,606) I encountered a mile-long section of shallow sandbars. Here I had real trouble following the channel. There seemed to be several possible braids to pick from. Shallow channels crisscrossed each other, detoured around snags, and broke off every which way. I could not find deep water, so I tried to follow where the current was making the freshest cuts alongside the sandbars. I bumped along the shallow bottom, eventually finding deeper water. Nine river miles downstream (miles 1,604 to 1,599 are now part of an oxbow) at mile 1,592 left, you will see the river in the

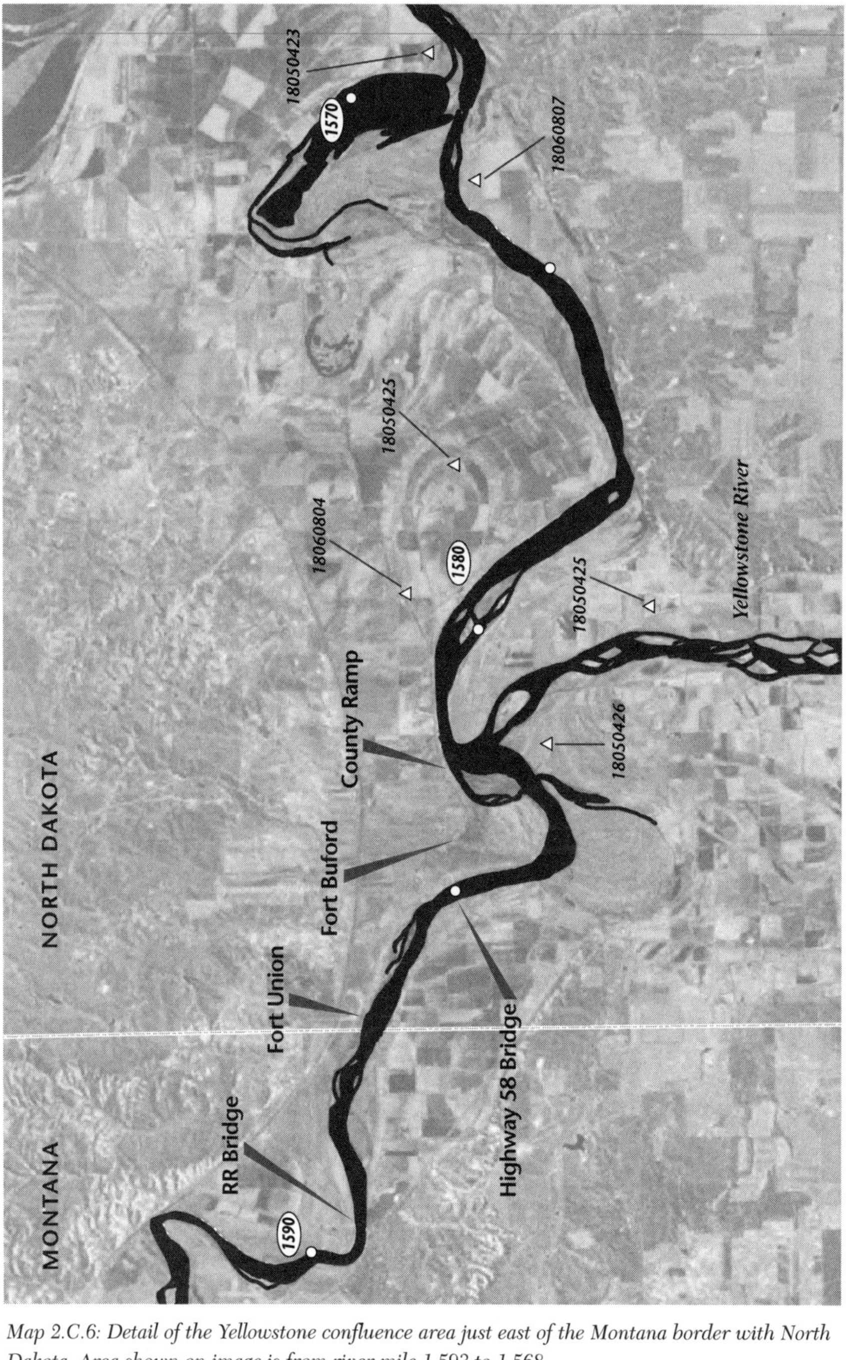

Map 2.C.6: Detail of the Yellowstone confluence area just east of the Montana border with North Dakota. Area shown on image is from river mile 1,593 to 1,568.

process of undercutting the Burlington Northern Railroad bed. Heavy rocks had been dumped along a 100-yard-long section of the shoreline along the outer bend of the river to shore up the railroad bed. This appeared to me to be a losing proposition, as riverbank at both ends of the rock pile was being carved away by the current. To the southeast of this activity is the town of Snowden, where a spur of the rail line cuts to the south.

Continuing downstream for 3 miles, you will reach the railroad lift bridge at mile 1,589. The main channel passes under the section of this bridge that can be reeled up to allow headroom for large boats. As I paddled under this structure, I wondered, "What were they thinking when they specified this bit of engineering?" I later learned that it dates back to a time when the railroad was being built and folks were assuming that steamboats would continue to ply the Upper Missouri.

You will reach the North Dakota border after mile 1,586.8. Almost immediately on your left is Fort Union–or at least the reconstructed version. I tried to find a place where I could pull in to visit, but the bank was steep and the vegetation thick; I could find no good access. I was disappointed that I could not put in; from what I could see, the reconstruction looked nicely done. All along the river it seems that tourist attractions have turned their backsides to the river traveler, just as towns did upon the advent of the railroad.

Two miles beyond Fort Union you will pass under the Highway 58 bridge. The channel then turns south and around a bend to the Yellowstone confluence. The County Park and boat ramp is at mile 1,581.4 left (47.98596/-103.98196). The ramp and dock is on the outside (left) bend of the river below the confluence; the current is very strong in front of the ramp. Besides providing access to the Fort Buford State Historic Site, this is the last sure take-out that you can count on before the Highway 85 take-out, some 25 miles or 4.5 hours downriver. I recommend that you put in here for a rest. It appeared as if you could camp here in a pinch, but the place was a bit of a mess when I visited. There is a vault toilet and picnic shelters, but the fire rings near the shelters have been removed. West of the ramp is a faucet with a hose that provides water, apparently intended for washing down boats. The water from this source has a distinct yellow cast, and I do not know if it is safe to drink. I would filter the water just to be safe if you choose to fill up here.

Working downstream from the County Park, the river makes a sharp bend to the left at mile 1,577.6. After that the channel winds through a series of willow thicket flats, shoreline cottonwoods, and low-lying river bottom. When I

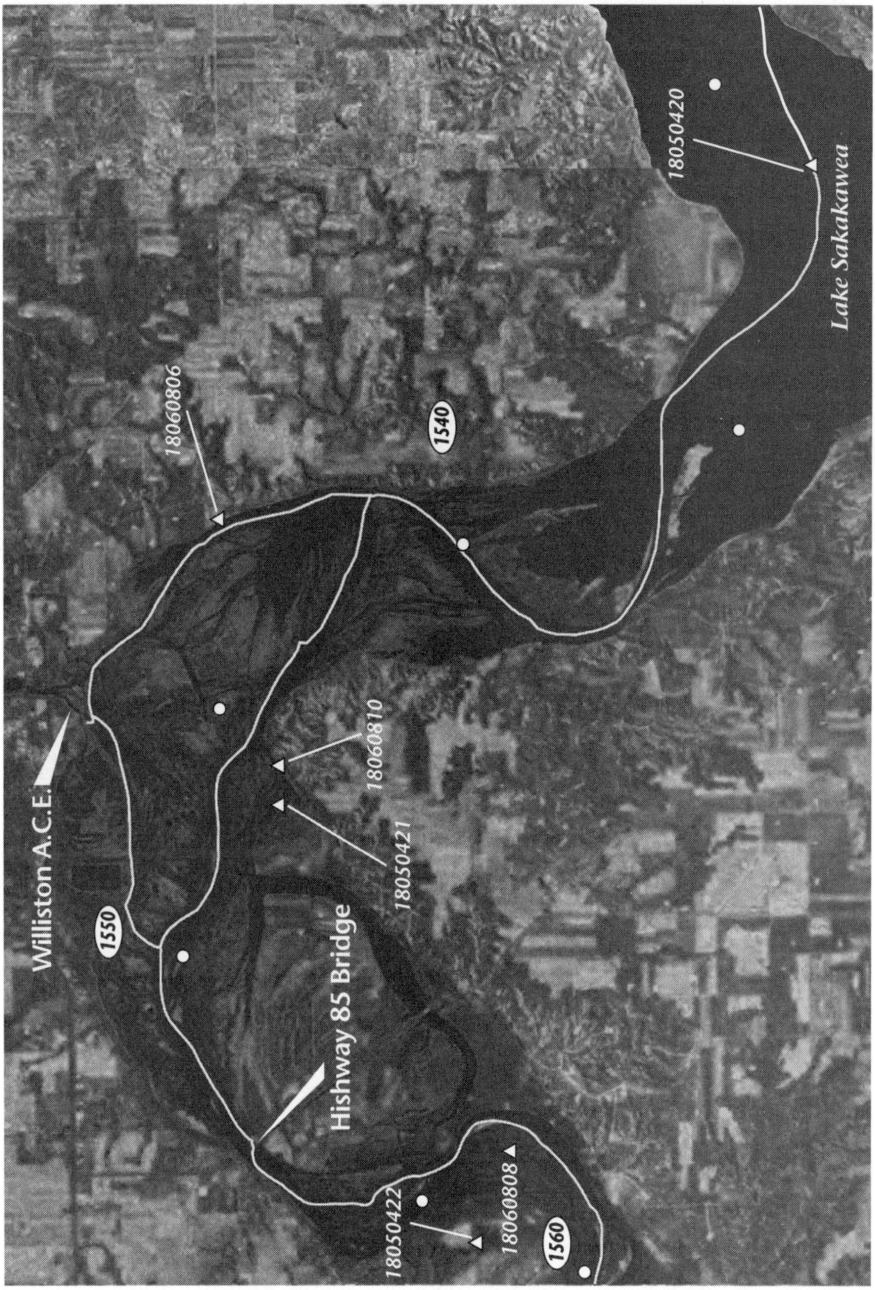

Map 2.C.7: Detail of area below mile 1,570 to the Highway 85 bridge (mile 1,552) and take-out ramp near Williston, North Dakota.

paddled through, there was a good current and the main channel was not hard to follow. There is said to be a narrow channel to the Lake Trenton Recreation Area on the left somewhere after mile 1,562, but I could not find it. The entire area was silted in and thick with vegetation. Examination of the satellite image suggests that a great deal of channel shifting occurs in this area. So my course track should not be relied upon as the set-in-concrete way through.

Shortly after mile 1,556, I hailed two anglers on the bank and asked them about any camping places before Williston. They told me I could camp at a boat ramp on the right just after the Highway 85 bridge. I continued paddling for another 40 minutes, passed under the bridge, found the Highway 85 bridge ramp at mile 1,552.6 right (48.10830/-103.71384), and pulled my kayak to shore. There was a parking area and a vault toilet. I found a nice sandy campsite just down the shore, hauled my boat up, and set up camp. At the parking lot there was a nice billboard commemorating the inauguration of the facility, but the place was a mess. There were thick weeds growing around the toilet, which had not been serviced for quite some time.

I talked with a couple who had brought their son to the landing to catch some catfish; they told me it was a weekend party spot. They gave me a ride across the bridge to a gas station and convenience store a couple miles up the highway. I filled my fuel bottles, got some snacks, two bottles of water, and a six-pack. I made a phone call to Jeff Keller, an ACE ranger, who was my contact person in Williston. Jeff gave me instructions on how to paddle to the station, and I returned to my camp to celebrate my safe passage of more than 500 miles.

SEGMENT 2.D: Williston, North Dakota (mile 1,552.5), to Garrison Dam (mile 1,390) on Lake Sakakawea *(Map 2.D)*

- **River miles:** 162.5
- **Difficulty level:** High
- **Typical time to complete:** 12 to 15 days

From the Highway 85 bridge at Williston to the Garrison Dam at the downstream end of Lake Sakakawea, it is 162 river miles. As the crow flies, the distance is 115 miles. For the most part you'll continue to paddle eastward, but as you get farther down the lake you will finally get the sense that you are starting to turn south. In fact, by the time you arrive at Garrison Dam, you will have dropped about a half degree of latitude from where you started at Williston. If

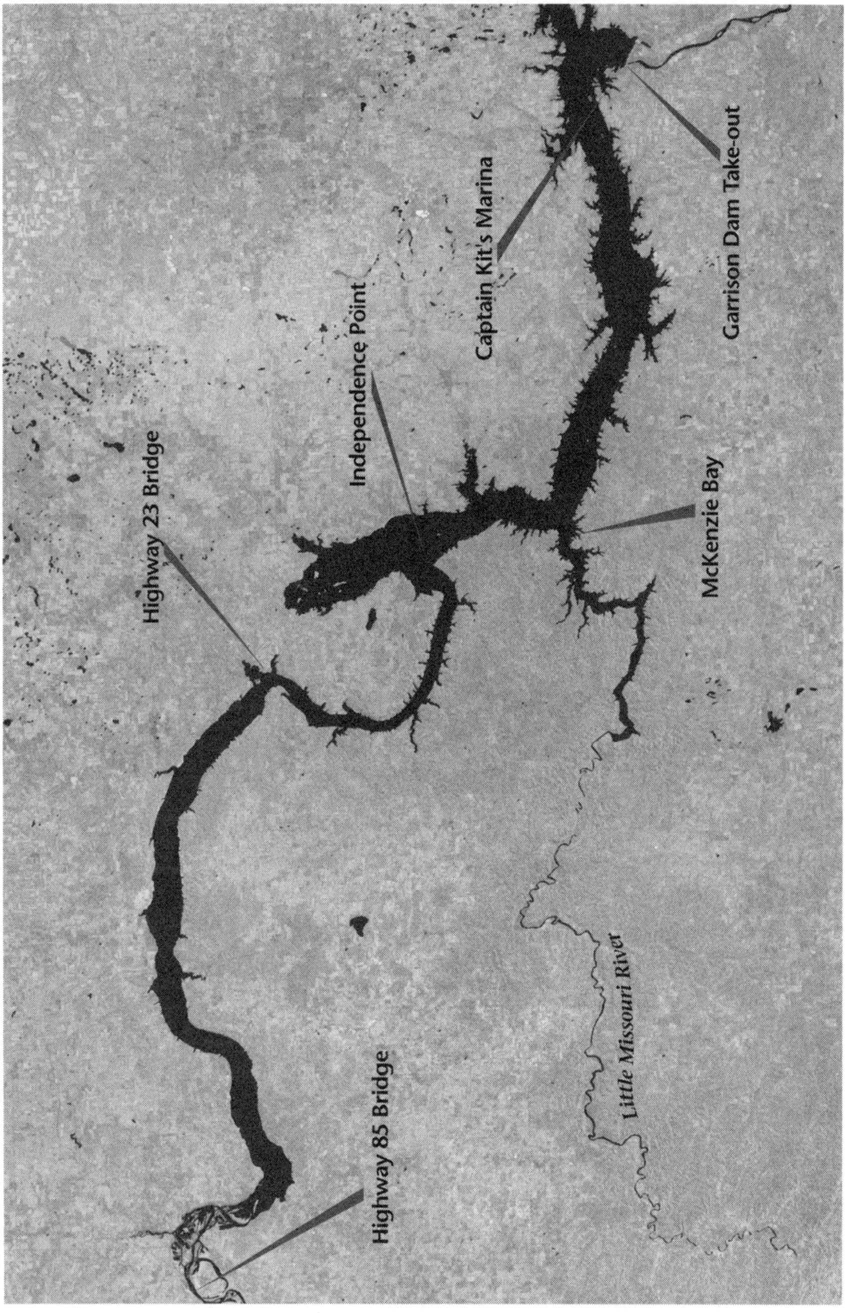

Map 2.D: Lake Sakakawea from the Highway 85 bridge (mile 1,552.5) at Williston, North Dakota, to Garrison Dam (mile 1,390) at the downstream end of the lake.

you started at Fort Benton, here on Lake Sakakawea you finally turn south to begin sustained decreases in latitude after more than 500 miles of paddling.

Compared to Fort Peck Lake, this area is less remote and the shoreline more regular. A day or two of paddling will get you to the beginning of a string of nice campgrounds and the occasional marina. This is a popular fishing lake. The walleye fishing is world class, so you'll see many fishing boats. On the west end of the lake, however, you will encounter a long section of marsh and mudflats that is often very difficult to paddle through. Unless the water is running high and the current has cut a deeper channel, you'll only see a foolhardy powerboater in this area. This lake does have long stretches of shoreline with no road access and many great campsites with incredible vistas from the bluffs above. Lake Sakakawea's sunsets are knock-your-wet-socks-off spectacular.

From a technical standpoint, this is not an easy paddle. This lake is long, with a width varying between 2 and 5 miles. When the North Dakota wind starts blowing, the lake kicks up fast, and conditions get very rough. Your safest course is to stay close to shore. For the most part, pick a side of the lake and stay on it, get on the water early, make whatever mileage you can, and then get off the water as the wind picks up. Here is where a book entitled The Zen Guide for Paddlers will someday be written. You learn to graciously accept what the lake presents: Forget your schedule; you are where you are.

Information/Maps/Resources

Sources of information for paddlers about Lake Sakakawea are scant. The best you can do is to order a copy of the ACE publication (Omaha District), *Lake Sakakawea [&] Garrison Dam Boating and Recreation* (May 1988), which provides useful maps and 24 air photos each covering about a dozen miles. Although the lake's water level may be significantly different than what it was when the air photos were taken, the essential form of the shoreline remains. I found the photos of the area at the west end of the lake to be very useful. You should also obtain a copy of the ACE map, *Lake Sakakawea [&] Garrison Dam, North Dakota*. This map shows the area from the border with Montana to Washburn, North Dakota, at a scale of 1 inch = 7 miles (1:63,360). As with the maps of each of the ACE reservoirs, this map lists public recreation facilities and their features and provides emergency phone numbers. Current information about ACE facilities on Lake Sakakawea can be found at www.nwo.usace.army.mil/html/Lake_Proj/index.html.

An additional source for paddler information is the Discover North Dakota website's "Boating in North Dakota" page at www.state.nd.us/gnf/boating/boatramps.html. This site includes information about Missouri River boating access ramps and their facilities. Each ramp's status (usable, marginal, or unusable due to water level) is noted, and a contact person is listed for more information. Finally, you can download a map that shows the locations of North Dakota's Missouri River boat ramps at this site.

Suggested Readings

Seventeen Lewis and Clark campsites are in this section. Information about what transpired here during the outbound trip (April 9 to 21, 1805) can be found in Vol. 4:14–59 (*Journals,* [Moulton, ed.]). Return trip event detail (August 10 to 13, 1806 [Lewis]; August 6 to 13, 1806 [Clark]) can be found in Vol. 8:153–158 [L] and Vol. 8:282–297 [C]. Context about events can be found in Stephen Ambrose's *Undaunted Courage,* in chapters 18:212–220 and 32:395–398.

In addition to things Lewis and Clark, I suggest you read Charles Larpenteur's *Forty Years a Fur Trader on the Upper Missouri.* Larpenteur's account covers activities in the area between 1833 and 1872, and he is one of the best sources for information about the fur trade in this area.

For information about the area's geology there is no better source than Hoganson and Murphy's *Geology of the Lewis and Clark Trail in North Dakota.*

SEGMENT 2.D.1: Highway 85 bridge (mile 1,552.6) to mile 1,523 (open water Lake Sakakawea): ~ 30 miles (Maps 2.D.1 & 2.D.2)

Paddler's Notes and Cautions

You have two choices for making passage through the marshes and mudflats south of Williston to the "real" beginning of Lake Sakakawea. You can head out from the Highway 85 bridge and stay to the right in the Inside channel (see Map 2.D.1) or, if the water level is high enough, you can take the Outside channel route. The latter begins at a narrow channel at mile 1,550, leads to the ACE station at Williston, and continues along the left bank to the mile 1,541 junction. At low water levels the Outside channel to Williston is not passable.

Before making a decision about which track to take, I recommend that you contact one of the ACE rangers at the Williston office (701-572-6494) for

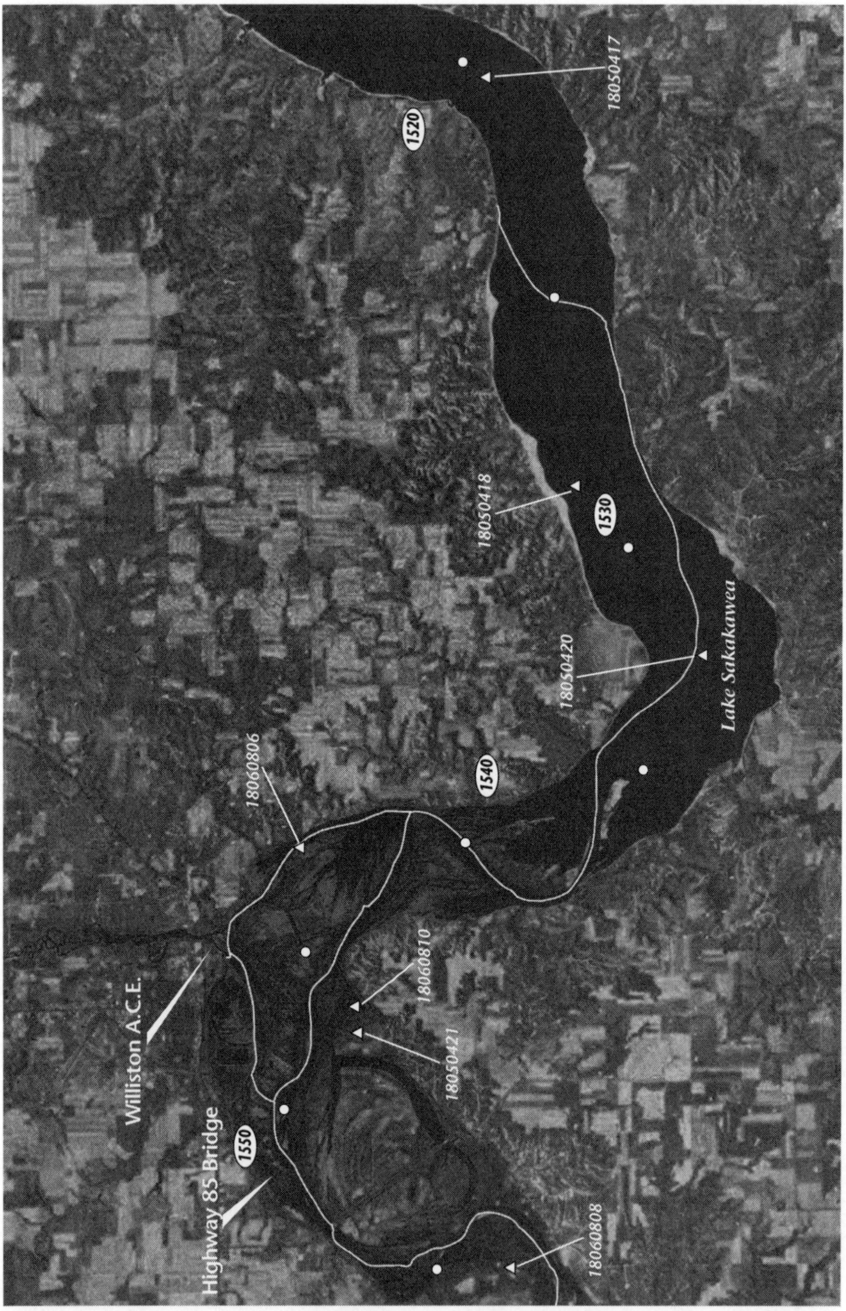

Map 2.D.1: Area downstream from the Highway 85 bridge (mile 1,552.6). Course track options (Inside or Outside) are shown with a white line, as is the track beyond the junction point (~ mile 1,541) to mile 1,523, the approximate beginning of open water.

information about the current situation. Although the channels in Maps 2.D.1 and 2.D.2 look relatively well formed, this is not how the situation appeared to me as I worked my way through this area. Shallow islands thick with willows, sandbars, and mudflats have created a mazelike series of channel options to choose from. This circumstance extends for more than 20 miles to the south. You will need to work your way through this section with care.

Whichever route you elect, start out early in the morning. Do not start out after midday. Beyond the Highway 85 bridge, there are few if any campsites for at least a dozen miles. The river is lined with willow thickets and cattail marsh. There are many low-lying islands flanked by mudflats. As the river turns to the south, the current slows and massive amounts of sediment are deposited. The location of the main channel regularly shifts, and even local river rats are sometimes perplexed by the changes.

- **Highway 85 bridge (mile 1,552.6) to the left (Outside) channel and downriver to mile 1,541: ~ 12 miles** ***(Map 2.D.1 & 2.D.2)***

I chose to take the Outside channel to the Williston ACE station because I wanted to map the way in as a GPS track and I wanted to talk about the area with local officials and rivermen. Also, I needed to pick up a resupply package sent to the Williston post office in care of general delivery, do some laundry, and gather intelligence about getting through the mudflats and marsh at the west end of Lake Sakakawea. I spoke over the phone with ACE park ranger Jeff Keller and got instructions about paddling to the station. Essentially, Jeff told me to stay left and look for a narrow channel on my left after about 2 miles (see Map 2.D.2). The current was moving very fast; I missed the entrance and ended up having to paddle against the current for more than an hour to get back to the channel. This was a painful exercise.

Directions for the Outside (Left) Channel Passage

A word of caution: At low water levels, this channel may be impassable. In April 2004 this channel was nearly dry. Check with the rangers at the ACE station for information on current circumstances. If you have a GPS unit, set waypoints to navigate to the ACE station using the information listed below. Again, examine the route shown on Map 2.D.2. The GPS coordinates for waypoints A through E are as follows:

A	Channel entrance, left (north)	48.12373/-103.66350
B	Rock levee, stay right (east)	48.13008/-103.65251
C	Rock levee remains on left (north)	48.12910/-103.62475
D	Entrance to small bay, left	48.13544/-103.60281
E	Pull out near ACE station	48.13647/-103.60473

From the Highway 85 bridge, paddle about 1.5 miles along the right shore. At mile 1,551, you will need to angle to the left to stay in the main channel. The channel into Williston is on the left, to the northeast of mile 1,550. It is easy to miss the channel's narrow entrance, so look sharp. Once you are in the channel, getting to point E is straightforward. At the ACE station pull-out (E), depending on the water level, you may find a relatively level area where you can pull out. However, you'll need to climb over riprap to get up to the gravel road that runs along the top of the levee.

The Williston ACE station is on the north side of the dike. I found all the people in this office to be especially helpful. If you want to get to town, the business district is a couple miles up the road that runs north in front of the ACE office. A sporting goods store is less than 0.5 mile up the road. Unless you have a support vehicle, you'll need to hitch a ride. If you just start walking up the road, odds are you'll be offered a ride. Understand, however, that ACE personnel cannot pick up hitchhikers when driving ACE vehicles.

The area around the pull-out is not secure–this is another circumstance when having a paddling partner would be an advantage. One of the rangers told me about some paddlers who left their boats and gear here to go into town. When they returned, some of their gear was missing.

Before you head downstream, you should visit the ACE office. If one of the rangers is available, ask about conditions downstream and for information about the best path through the shallows. ACE personnel are on the river on an almost daily basis; they are your best source for information. You should also ask for permission to fill your water bottles since your next opportunity to refill is a couple days down the lake. Finally, you should leave information about your float plan at the office. At the first opportunity after getting through the west end marshes, you should call the office to confirm your safe passage.

Once you shove off, head east. A half-mile down the shore you will reach the confluence of the Little Muddy River. As you paddle by the river's mouth, look upriver and you'll see a rail bridge. Once past the Little Muddy stay along the left shore. The shoreline will angle to the southeast and then to the south

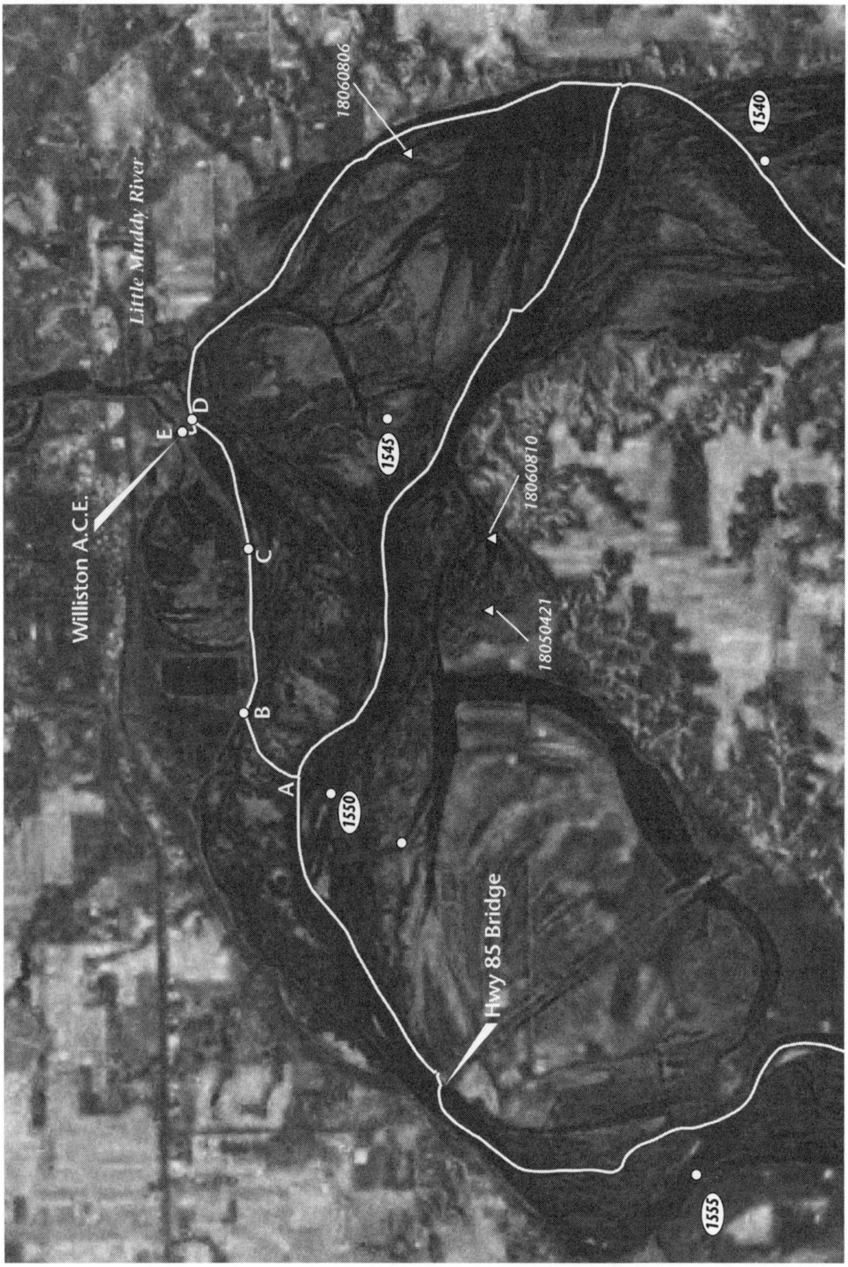

Map 2.D.2: Downstream area from Highway 85 bridge (mile 1,552.6), showing course options as recorded in June 2002. Both track options are shown. GPS waypoint locations (A–E) are for the Outside channel track. Point A is the channel entrance, approximately 2.5 miles from the Highway 85 bridge. This channel is narrow, easy to miss, and not passable at low water levels.

(see Maps 2.D.1 and 2.D.2) for the next 4.5 miles. This will put you in the vicinity of river mile 1,541, where the Inside (right) channel joins your track and the main channel begins a long sweep to the opposite (right) shoreline.

Directions for the Inside (Right) Channel Passage

Before you start, carefully examine the Inside passage GPS-based course track displayed in Maps 2.D.1 and 2.D.2. This is the main channel; most often this is the easiest way to go. To take the Inside route, follow the main channel east for 2.5 miles; continue past the Williston entry channel. From this point, you will paddle 6.5 miles to the southeast, toward the left shore. Do not turn to the south until you have reached the shore. Do not deviate from this course unless you are advised by the ACE rangers that a new channel has developed. Although your route appears clear (see Map 2.D.2), you will need to read the water carefully. Again: **Do not attempt to take any shortcuts;** follow the main channel to the southeast. When I paddled through here, the water was high and the current very fast. I found deeper water along the left side, but this may not be the case when you paddle through. Eventually you will reach the opposite shore, where the two channels join above mile 1,541.

- **Beyond the Outside and Inside passage junction at mile 1,541 to mile 1,523 (open water): 18 miles *(Maps 2.D.1 & 2.D.2)***

Once you arrive at the junction near mile 1,541, following the channel becomes increasingly difficult. Carefully examine Map 2.D.1. Beyond the junction, the main channel turns to the southwest for about 3 miles. The entrance to the American Legion Park, campground, and boat ramp is near mile 1,538.5. However, I was unable to locate any obvious channel to the ramp through the marsh. At mile 1,538, the river begins a wide turn back to the opposite (left) shore. When I talked with Jeff Keller, the ACE ranger, about this section, he told me that once I came around this turn, I would see houses along the left bank and that the channel ran directly to the shore in front of them. When you paddle through here, you will probably see several instances where a good current seems to flow down a side channel on your right. Unless you have good information otherwise, do not be tempted to seek a shortcut. Stay in the channel that heads almost due east, directly for the houses on shore.

The area to the south of mile 1,537 is extremely hazardous. Channels into this area evaporate into quicksand-like mudflats and impenetrable willow thickets. This is approximately where a family spent 48 hours stranded in their canoe on a mudflat. They attempted to cross a mudflat, got stuck, and had to be rescued by an airboat. Stay in the main channel. If you examine my track from mile 1,537 to the left bank (see Map 2.D.1), you'll see this leg runs east for about 2 miles. Once you arrive at the opposite side and are offshore from the houses, the channel begins to slowly angle to the southeast, toward the center of the lake. When you get near the houses, you are at an important decision point. As you work along the shoreline, and until the channel takes you beyond the point (mile 1,533 left), there are only a handful of places where you can pull out in an emergency. Beyond this, the channel moves away from shore, and there are no easy pullouts for the next 10 miles.

From mile 1,533, the channel works its way east for 3.5 miles. Along the right shore, you will see the remains of what must have been a thick stand of cottonwoods that was flooded as the reservoir filled with water. There are standing tree trunks, stumps, and a host of loose, large floating stems and pieces that could become battering rams if the weather kicks up. Since the channel generally follows the edge of this water hazard, prudence dictates that you should attempt this section in good weather. Also, because you are paddling east, you'll have the best light for reading the river later in the morning through the early afternoon.

Eventually you will reach the right bank a little before mile 1,529. For the next 3 miles the channel appears to remain along the shoreline. When I paddled through here, it was early evening, so I looked for a place to camp. I could not find one. Along this shore (south of mile 1,525), the channel seemed to evaporate. Farther ahead, another stand of flooded trees loomed. I followed an anemic current that cut back to the opposite shore, working my way around stumps and mudflats. Because it was late, the light was not good; I had difficulty reading the water. As I worked my way north to the center of the "lake," I found a bit more current and deeper water. Still, it was difficult going. At one point I avoided a mudflat only because there were gulls standing along its margins. Out in the middle, almost exactly at mile mark 1,525, I located a better current and followed it to the northeast toward the left shore. After about 2 miles of paddling, I finally reached the shore as darkness settled in. I found a place to camp and stopped for the night (mile 1,523 left; 48.05727/-103.30214).

That night I reflected on the day's effort. I'd made some 25 river miles. And

I'd made mistakes. I started too late in the morning. I expected that there would be places to camp all along the way. I assumed that the marsh and mudflats would end before they did. The last series of mudflats did not show on the maps or air photos; it was a complete surprise. Still, I'd gotten safely through a very difficult maze of mudflats, willow thickets, islands, flooded woods, stumps, and floating logs. Without the help of the ACE rangers at Williston, I doubt I would have navigated these hazards successfully. Having the satellite image of the area on deck was very helpful. Looking east from my camp, I could see that I'd reached open water, the real beginning of Lake Sakakawea.

SEGMENT 2.D.2: Open water Lake Sakakawea (mile 1,523) to Highway 23 bridge/Four Bears/New Town area (mile 1,481): 42 miles *(Maps 2.D.3 & 2.D.4)*

Paddler's Notes and Cautions

There are 43 river miles between the start of open lake at the west end (~ mile 1,523) to the Highway 23 bridge. Before attempting this section you have to decide which side of the lake–left or right–you want to stay on. The wind can come up with extreme quickness on Sakakawea; attempting to cross over to the other shore, even in the best weather, is a gamble that you should not take. There is a casino near the Four Bears Campground; take your chances there.

I chose to stay along the right shore. I initially had anticipated northwest winds for most of my passage and thought I would be able to skirt the left shoreline in the shadow of the wind. Also figuring into my thinking was the fact that there are several parks along this side, with hot showers and drinking water. I reasoned that this approach should make my effort a piece of cake. Not so. A southeast wind was freshening the next morning when I put in. Ultimately, I decided to cross over to the right shore at about mile 1,520.

My decision turned out to be a good one; I had stiff southeast winds for most of my passage. Locals say southeast winds are common at this time of year, although really big storm winds come from the northwest. In retrospect, I recommend the right side. By staying close along the right shore, I was often able to stay in the wind shadow. Had I been on the left, I would have had to deal with large swells, built up by the wind blowing across the lake. Also, a storm wind from the northwest would have blown me out to the center of the lake. On the right side, this wind would have pushed me to shore.

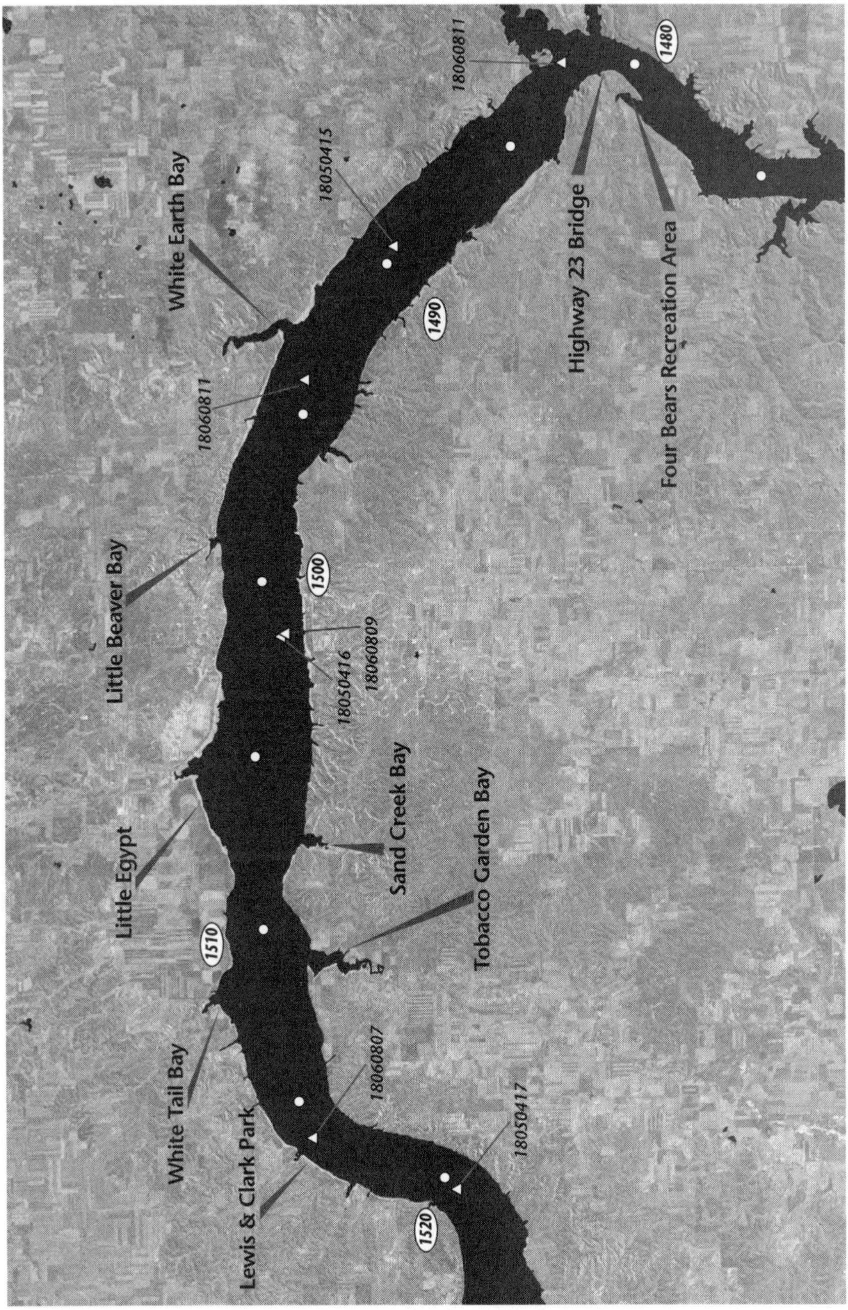

Map 2.D.3: West end of Lake Sakakawea (mile 1,523) to Highway 23 bridge/Four Bears/New Town (mile 1,481).

Before making the final decision to cross over, I paddled around the point (~ mile 1,521 left) to better gauge conditions. I paddled another mile, passed several good-looking campsites, and came to a nice sheltered bay in front of a church camp. From this point I made my crossing, taking a diagonal track to the northeast for a distance of 4 miles. I made landfall along the right shore at about mile 1,518 (48.08845/-103.21760). By the time I got across, the wind had picked up substantially. I was glad to be paddling out of the wind. Along this shoreline there appeared to be numerous campsites.

Ten miles to the east is Tobacco Garden Bay. The bay entrance is at mile 1,511 right (~ 48.12088/-103.11333). It is a 2-mile paddle into the campground, but worth every stroke. The Tobacco Garden Campground is neat and well run. The owners, Bruce and Debby Erickson, are exactly the kind of folks you hope to meet. They loaded my kayak and gear in their truck and took me to a sheltered and shady campsite. There are good hot showers at their bathhouse, and their restaurant has outstanding fare. I recommend the cheeseburger with everything and fries, or a steak. There is always a good crowd of locals here. I spent a couple days here, resting up for the very long push ahead. While I was here, I assisted Bruce and Debby with the catering of a family reunion. In addition to helping with the set-up and take-down, I served as "Chef David," carving up a pig that Bruce had roasted in his mother-of-all-gas-fired-smoker-grills.

While I was camped at Tobacco Garden, I also experienced a mother-of-all-windstorms. While having breakfast in the restaurant, I learned of an approaching storm with wind speeds forecasted to exceed 70 mph. I went out to check my tent's storm lines and returned to the shelter of the restaurant. Looking out the window, I watched the northwest sky take on a foul look and a huge, yellow dust cloud race across the lake, toward the campground. When the storm hit, the building literally shook. Trees were bent over, limbs snapped, and the air was filled with debris. I watched the wind rip awnings off RVs, saw a beer cooler overturned, and watched full beer cans bounce like tennis balls along the ground. This was a truly sobering experience. Because this wind came up so fast, I am convinced that if I had been on the water, even near shore, the situation would have been extremely dangerous.

When I spoke with Bruce about the windstorm, he related that such winds are called "straight winds," and that they occur a couple times a summer. Every year a handful of boaters get caught in such storms, with dire consequences. Local anglers and sailors listen to NOAA weather radio, and get to shelter if high winds are forecast. Later that day I saw a large sailboat that had been caught out on the water during the storm. Its sails were shredded, its mast was snapped, and the rudder was broken.

When you leave Tobacco Garden Bay, if you look to the north across the lake, you should be able to see White Tail Bay (also known as Lund's Landing). This camp and boat ramp is about 4.5 miles to the north. As you work your way along the right shore, you will paddle to the northeast for about 2 miles to round the first point. On the bluff at the tip of this point is the Tobacco Garden Light (~ mile 1,509). If for some reason you want to paddle to the opposite (left) shore, this would be where you should cross over. The distance for the crossing at this point is less than 1.5 miles. Beyond this, the distance between shores does not similarly narrow for almost 25 miles. My recommendation is that you stay along the right shore.

If the wind is blowing from the southeast or east, the water may be quite rough once you round the point. However, 1.5 miles down the shore is Sand Creek Bay. You can pull in here if you need to seek shelter. From here, the shore runs almost due east for 10 miles; if you have a southeast wind, stay as close to the shore as you can for easier paddling. I had a northwest wind when I paddled this shore. This created a following sea that eventually changed to a quartering sea. By early afternoon, the waves had built up to the point that I had to find a place to put ashore. I found a campsite near Maybell Flats, at mile 1,502.5 (48.11788/-102.92831). Just west of my camp was a gravel road and a house. The roads in this section provide access to a number of oil wells in the surrounding hills. You will also see active oil rigs along the shore and in the nearby hills. I was warned to never camp by these oil rigs because they can emit hydrogen sulfide, a relatively odorless gas that can asphyxiate you.

Slightly more than 5 miles from Maybell Flats, you round a long point and the shore finally bends to the southeast. From this point on, you begin to earn some serious drop in latitude. But you'll work hard to get south if the wind is blowing. I got up early the next day to beat the wind, but by the time that I pushed off whitecaps were forming. I again had a northwest wind and a following sea. By 10 A.M., I was running with 4- to 5-foot swells, and the wind was continuing to pick up speed. By noon I had made almost 14 miles and was pretty well spent. I worked my way along the shore and put in to search for a place to camp. Because of the low water level, I walked almost 100 yards through muck to get to relatively firm ground where I could pitch my tent. There were no trees for another 200 yards in from my campsite. I set up my tent among

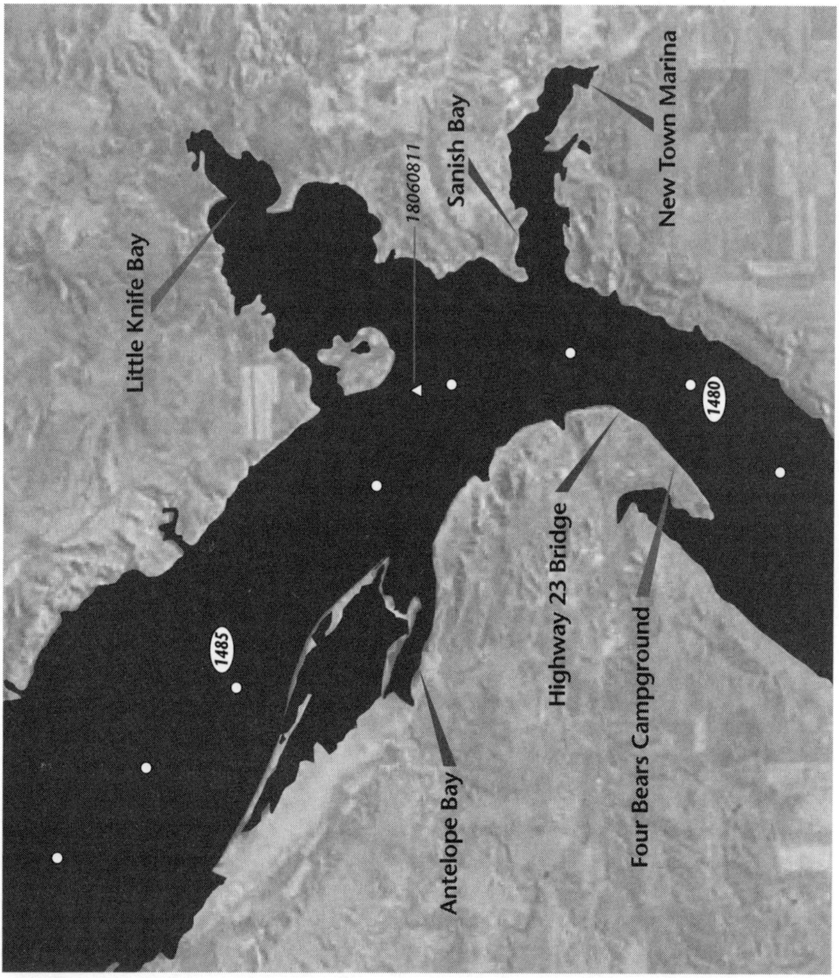

Map 2.D.4: Antelope Bay (mile 1,487) to Four Bears Campground (mile 1,479). I have altered the image to show the "dead-end" pocket bay that I paddled into. A series of shoals run along the outside of this bay, separating it from open water to the north and from Antelope Bay to the south. Paddlers should stay to the outside (left) of these shoals until about mile 1,483.

the weeds at about mile 1,486 (48.02195/-102.64096). This was a poor site; I had no shade or shelter. I set up here only because I was not ready to hump my gear any additional distance.

Once I'd rested a bit, I hiked inland and up the side of a hill to get a better view of what lay before me. Looking out at the water I could see that I was just inside a long shoal that gradually hooked back to the shore. This was one instance where the satellite image was misleading. The photo (see Map 2.D.4) shows dry land immediately above Antelope Bay, so it was taken when water levels were lower than I encountered. Looking out from a hilltop I could see that I had paddled just inside a 2-mile-long basin with no apparent exit on the downriver end. As I approached this area in my kayak, it appeared that there was an inside passage. This was not the case. In effect, I had paddled into a dead-end pocket.

When you approach this area, beginning roughly at mile 1,486, my advice is to stay well to the outside. If water levels are very high, it might be possible to work through on the inside, but you will want to get ashore and climb a hill to look things over. In retrospect, if I were to do this section again, I would try to stage my previous day's stop so that I could get beyond this area by mid-morning, before the wind picked up. Then I could camp at Four Bears Campground about 5 miles downriver, or continue farther down the lake.

At mile 1,482 you will begin to round the bend; Little Knife Bay is on the left. Also on the left, a mile farther down, is Sanish Bay. The New Town Marina is about a mile inside this bay on the right. I did not visit this marina, but several people that I talked with told me that it was well run. I stayed along the right side of the bend, paddled under the Highway 23 bridge (~ mile 1,480.6; 47.98064/-102.56968), and then paddled along the shore in front of the Four Bears Recreation Area (mile 1,480). The campground looked neat, mostly occupied by RVs, but there were some tent sites along the shore where you could easily pull your boat out. This is not a full-service campground, but there is drinking water, a vault toilet, and a place to pitch your tent. A casino is just up the road. I was told on more than one occasion that if you put in here, someone should always remain at the camp to watch over your gear.

◆ Highway 23 bridge/Four Bears/New Town area (mile 1,480.6) to Independence Point (mile 1,453): 28 miles *(Map 2.D.5)*

Five miles down the lake is the "600 miles from Fort Benton, Montana" point where by way of reference you are 847 miles from the eadwaters at Three Forks. If you intend to end your odyssey at Sioux City, 742 miles of paddling remain; you are more than halfway. But to keep things in perspective, if you are going to St. Louis you still have more miles ahead of you than you have behind. You will not get to the halfway point until you pass mile 1,160.5. My advice is not to dwell too long on this circumstance. You are more than halfway

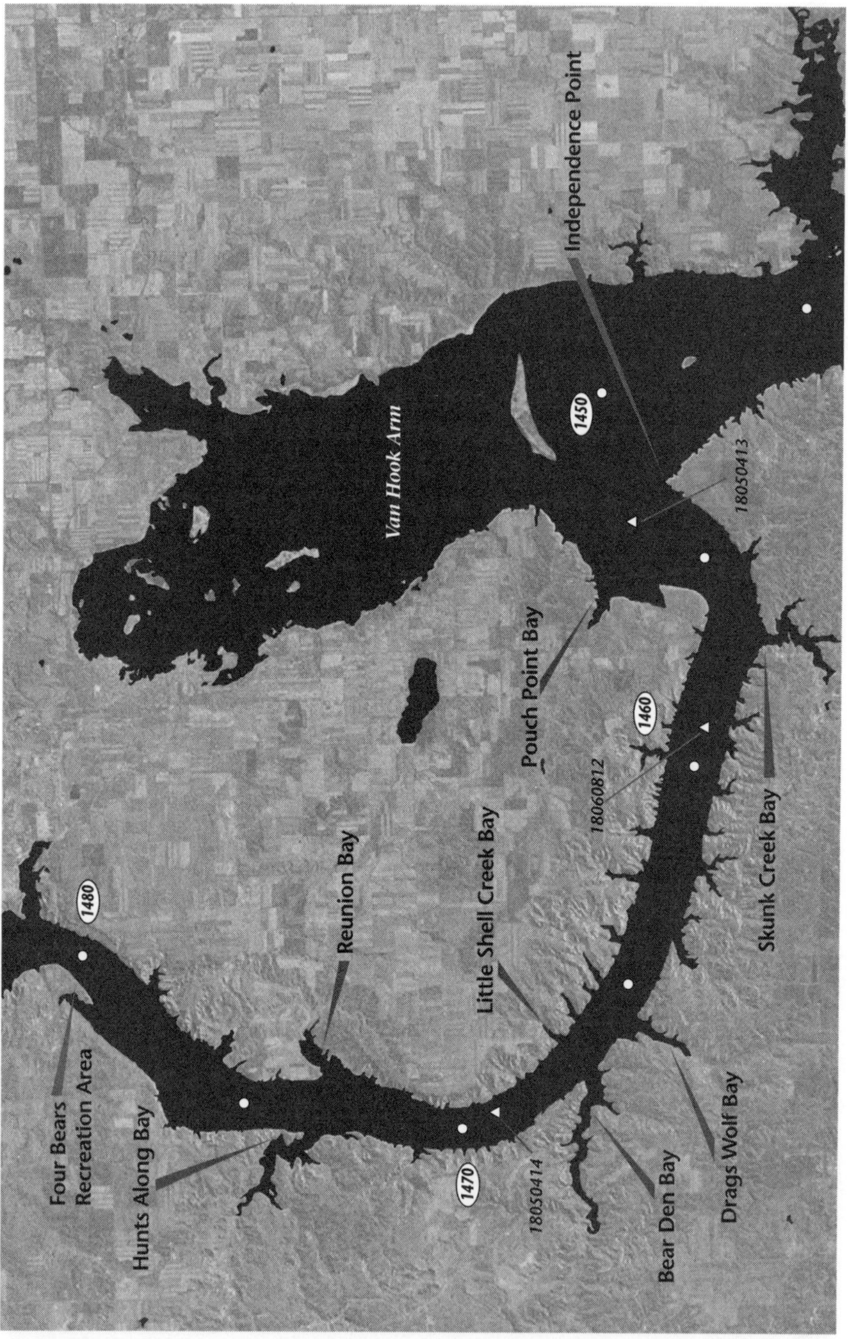

Map 2.D.5: Four Bears Recreation Area (mile 1,480) to Independence Point (mile 1,453).

down Lake Sakakawea. From this point, it is only 84 river miles to the Garrison Dam. Focus on what's in front of you.

This next stretch is a very nice area to paddle through. The distance between the shores is not much of an issue. If the wind shifts, you can easily cross over; there are many places where the lake constricts and the distance to the opposite shore is less than 1.5 miles. Also, there are long bays that offer good shelter on both sides of the lake. There are two very pretty bays at mile 1,473: Hunts Along Bay on the right and Reunion Bay on the left. When I paddled through this section, I stayed right until mile 1,471 and then cut across to the opposite shore as the wind began to blow from the southeast.

Thunderclouds were starting to stack up on the horizon, so I paddled 4 more miles and then put in at Little Shell Creek Bay (mile 1,467 left) to search for a campsite. The area along the shore was deeply incised by runoff coming from the hills above my camp. If I read the signs right, there had been quite a storm several days before. I set my tent up on higher ground on a small level area about 30 yards from the shore, in the shelter of a low ridge (47.81699/ -102.61038). From the doorway of my tent, looking across the lake, I could see the green flashing navigation light at the north end of Bear Den Bay.

It stormed that night, with lightning and strong wind gusts, but little rain. When I awoke the next morning, the wind was blowing so hard from the southeast that it would have been pointless to try to paddle any distance. I spent the morning cleaning gear, and then went hiking. I climbed the bluff above my camp to get a good view of what lay ahead and to see if I could get cell phone reception. I could get no reception, but the view was outstanding. Just below the ridge, I could see a small pocket bay with what looked like an outstanding campsite. I followed a well-traveled deer trail down to the bay and looked the site over. Had I paddled just a bit farther, around the next point, I would have had a much better site.

The wind was still blowing hard at midday, effectively pinning me ashore. It was brutally hot, probably well over 100 degrees, and I had no shade. I sat, sweated, and then got in the water to cool off. I repeated this exercise several times. Around 4 P.M., a pickup truck drove slowly up along the shore, past my camp to the point. A middle-aged man and an older woman got out of the truck cab and grabbed fishing poles, a tackle box, and folding chairs out of the truck bed. After they arranged their equipment at the shore and began fishing, I walked over and visited with them. The man had brought his mother fishing, the point was a good place to catch walleye, and they were using minnows for bait. They lived on the reservation. A road had been cut to the upstream end of the bay, and when it was dry it was possible to drive a truck to the point. There were lots of deer in the area, and one wild horse that limps. The man had thought about building a sweat lodge on the property. I observed that I already had one in my tent. We laughed about that. We talked about the weather forecast, and he said that it looked like we would have another day of wind from the southwest, or maybe the southeast.

By late afternoon the wind seemed to die a bit, and I decided to move to the other side. I packed up and began my crossing. The wind picked up as I was about halfway across and whitecaps began to form, so I paddled toward Drags Wolf Bay. I found a good camp above the shoreline on the downstream side of the bay entrance (mile 1,465.5 right; 47.79087/-102.60390). Here I had shelter and a breeze, and I was better positioned for the next day's paddle. For the next several miles of the next morning's effort, the lake angled to the southeast; on the right side I would have the best chance to find shelter from a southeast wind.

From Drags Wolf Bay to Skunk Creek Bay (mile 1,457 right), it is about 9 miles. There are several small bays along this stretch; most offer good campsites. There is a particularly good-looking site at mile 1,460.5. I did not stop at the Skunk Creek Recreation Area; there is no water there, and there were personal watercraft zipping around the mouth of the bay. I did talk with some anglers who told me that I might be able to get water from one of the houses about a mile up the road. I continued to paddle on and approached Independence Point (mile 1,453; 47.77791/-102.35319). On the left shore, to the north, is Pouch Point (47.80010/-102.39810). I could see the gleam of white RVs, and several boats working the water offshore. According to anglers that I talked with, this is a well-run, full-service campground.

At this point the thought of a hot shower may be tempting, but to get to Pouch Point you will have to paddle several miles out of your way. Also, to continue on from there you will have to make a 4-mile open water crossing to Independence Point. If the wind picks up and blows hard from the southeast, you might be forced to wait at Pouch for days.

I was fortunate not to have a wind at the time that I approached and worked my way around Independence Point. With a good southeast wind, the water at the point would surely be quite rough. The shoreline is low lying and just irregular enough to provide an occasional opportunity to seek shelter from the wind. The beach is mostly gravel and small rocks, so finding a place to pull

Sunset on Lake Sakakawea. Looking west from my campsite of July 5, 2002, at mile 1,439.3, about 3 miles north of McKenzie Bay.

out is not an issue. But there are cattle here that typically occupy the limited places where trees might provide shade for your tent.

Once around Independence Point (mile 1,453), you are at another decision point with respect to which side of the lake to be on. If the wind is from the northwest, you may be tempted to cross over to the left shore as you get closer to McKenzie Bay. This would allow you to paddle along the north shore in the shadow of the wind. This crossing would be a bit more than 2 miles, less at lower water levels. Indian Hills Resort (mile 1,428 left) is reported to be one of the best stops on the lake. It has a small restaurant, showers, and good, sheltered campsites. If you elect to paddle the north shore, however, you will have to make another couple-mile open water crossing to get to the Garrison Dam pull-out. I suggest that you do this near mile 1,421 left, before you get to Nishu Bay.

My recommendation is that you stay right, along the south shore, to the dam. If the wind is from the northwest, you'll have shelter until you reach the upper end of McKenzie Bay. If you are on the north shore, you may have to wait several days until conditions are right to make the open water crossing necessary to get to the Garrison Dam take-out ramp.

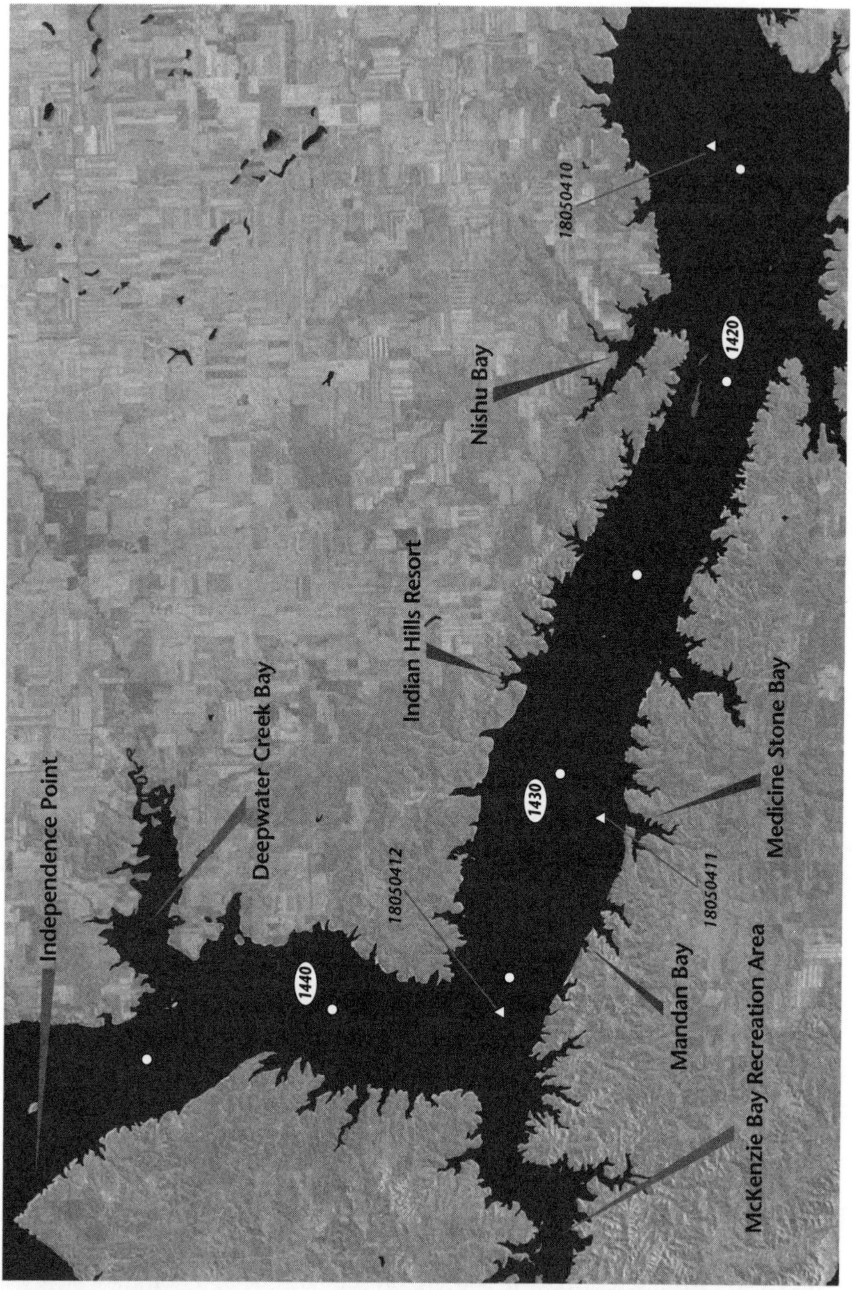

Map 2.D.6: Independence Point (mile 1,453) to mile 1,412. This stretch can be hard paddling if the wind is from the southeast, but I recommend that you stay right, working your way along the south shore.

◆ Independence Point (mile 1,453) to mile 1,412: 41 miles *(Map 2.D.6)*

Once you are around Independence Point, the shoreline angles to the southeast for 8 miles. Between miles 1,445 and 1,441, the shoreline is rugged and there are few places to put ashore. Be sure that good weather will hold before paddling this section. Once you round the long point at mile 1,441, you will cross the mouth of a large bay. A northwest wind will make this a rough crossing. After you cross the front of this bay, however, the shoreline angles to the south and you will pass several bays that you can paddle into for more shelter. There are numerous good campsites from this point on. I camped along a small inlet just above Saddle Butte Bay (~ mile 1,439.3; 47.661960/-102.29476). To the west of my camp, I could see Saddle Butte in the distance; the sunset that night was spectacular.

Along the next 3 miles, to the north side of the McKenzie Bay entrance (mile 1436.5), there are numerous places to pull out and good campsites. McKenzie Bay Recreation Area is 5.5 miles up the bay. Anglers that I spoke with along the way told me that this is another well-run facility. However, by this point of my lake expedition I had zero inclination to add any extra mileage to what I would have to paddle to get to the dam. Most of the miles that I paddled on Sakakawea were hard won. Still, this detour might be worth the extra 11 miles of paddling if the weather has turned bad and you need to pull off the lake for a couple days.

McKenzie Bay is actually the confluence of the Little Missouri River. The shortest distance across the entrance to this bay is 2.25 miles. Along the north side, there are a series of small pocket bays where you can put in to prepare for the crossing, or camp and wait for better conditions. When I shoved off, I headed almost due southeast, angling toward the closest point of the opposite shore (mile 1,436 right). The GPS coordinates of my landfall were 47.59792/-102.27867. This crossing should only be made when conditions are favorable.

The shoreline from this point is relatively steep and rugged, but populated with numerous small bays with good campsites. As I made my way along this shore, the wind freshened from the east. I paddled into whitecaps for about 3 miles and then pulled out for a shore lunch a mile east of Mandan Bay (~ mile 1,433). A mile up this bay is a graveled road, County Highway 8. If for some reason you need to end your lake crossing, this would be a good place to pull out. After an hour's rest I pushed off again, but had to pull out after another hour of hard paddling into the wind. I found a nice little bay with trees for shade and waited for more than five hours for the wind to ease. To pass the time, I hiked up the bluff above the bay. Looking to the east, I could see that

View of Lake Sakakawea shoreline looking east from the bluff above my camp of July 6, 2002. This unnamed bay is about 2 miles east of Mandan Bay, at mile 1,432.3.

the lake widened considerably and the ragged shoreline extended for as far as I could see. In addition to an outstanding view, I was able to get cell phone reception at this higher elevation.

The wind never let up that afternoon. So I gave up my notion of making any more mileage that day and set up my tent (mile 1,432.3; 47.56433/ -102.18860). When the wind picks up on this section of Sakakawea, paddling is difficult. Every mile you make can feel like a supreme accomplishment. This sentiment is, of course, one that experienced paddlers will fully appreciate. Others can, however, savor partially the pain-to-progress purchase of heading into this lake's waves and whitecaps by reflecting on the statement of a fisherman that I talked with when I reached Dakota Waters Resort (mile 1,414) the next day. After he helped me tie off my kayak at the dock, he said, "You must be the poor bastard that I saw paddling into the wind yesterday." Yep.

From this point east, the shoreline consists of one bay after another, most separated by high hills that end in steep cut bluffs at the water's edge. You will paddle by three large bays, each bigger than the previous: Medicine Stone Bay (mile 1,431), Red Butte Bay (mile 1,426; navigation marker F), and Beaver Creek Bay (mile 1,418). When I paddled by the front of Beaver Creek Bay, there were many walleye anglers trolling offshore and casting toward the shore.

I had to thread my way through them, working around them so as not to disturb the fish. It goes without saying that you want to stay well back from a boat trolling lines astern. Sometimes you will have to paddle in place to allow angler's lines to pass in front of you. Technically, as a paddler you have right-of-way. By long-standing custom, however, you are expected to yield to anglers with lines in the water. This is more than just a courtesy; it is the prudent thing to do.

There are many good-looking bays where you can pull out along this shore. Most offer sheltered campsites. Between mile 1,424 and mile 1,419, there were occasional herds of cattle, mostly cows and calves, but I did note several bulls. For about half a mile before the entrance to Beaver Creek Bay, there are few places to pull out and many cattle along the shore. It is 1 mile across the front of Beaver Creek Bay. If the wind is from the southeast, you may have to angle to the south (inside the bay) for more sheltered paddling. Before making your way across, take a couple minutes to study the situation. If there are whitecaps, you might see an area of somewhat calmer water along the bay's opposite shore. Under certain conditions, this may extend a good distance out from the other side of the bay. This is a wind shadow, the area that you should work toward to save yourself some effort.

As you look up Beaver Creek Bay, the left fork takes you to a boat ramp and primitive campground about 2 miles "up" the arm on the right. Once you are across the bay, there are 2.8 miles of shoreline before you round a final point and the shore turns to the south (~ mile 1,415.5). Before I made this crossing, I paddled up to some fishermen to ask about camping. They told me they were staying at the Dakota Waters Resort, that it was a good place, and that the 1806 Steakhouse is by the resort's campground. I asked for a sight bearing to the resort, and they pointed me toward a cluster of trees almost due east. I said that the distance looked to be about 3 miles and they said that was about right.

After talking with the fishermen I examined the ACE lake map. What the fishermen told me didn't appear correct. On the map, Lake Shore Park and Dakota Waters were shown as being well around a point north of the bearing that the fishermen had directed me to take. I paddled a bit farther along the shore and asked fishermen in another boat about the location of Dakota Waters. They pointed to the same cluster of trees. So I decided to make the crossing and asked them to keep an eye out for me. Ultimately, I learned that my version of the Sakakawea map displayed incorrectly the location of Lake

Shore Park and Dakota Waters. This error has been corrected on a newer version of the map. The lesson here is to seek local knowledge. If I had followed my map, I would have missed entirely the good steak and cold beer that I enjoyed at the 1806 Steakhouse later that night.

◆ Mile 1,412 to mile 1,389 (put-in below Garrison Dam): 23 miles *(Maps 2.D.7 & 2.D.8)*

About three-quarters of the way across, the sky darkened and the wind picked up hard from the east. I had a very difficult last mile to the bay entrance where the resort was located. But the vision of a sizzling steak and a cold beer motivated me so I gutted it out. By the time I got near the entrance to the bay, the wind was blowing so hard that I could make no headway. I had to angle to the south, put ashore, and line my kayak for 0.25 mile along the shore to get inside the bay. Once I got inside the bay, I was able to get back in my kayak and paddle to the Dakota Waters ramp.

The owners of the resort, Kevin and Laura Heinsen (701-873-5800), were very helpful. They directed me to a campsite with a bit of shelter, hauled my gear to my site, and showed me where I could pull my boat ashore to keep it safe. I had just set up my tent and was pounding down stakes for my rain fly's storm lines when a sailboat came into the bay and pulled into its slip in the inlet just below my camp. A short while later a stocky bearded man who turned out to be the boat's captain came up the bank, looked over my camp, and said, "You're the kayaker." The man turned out to be "Judge" Mike Quinn, captain of the 34-foot S2 sailboat. Mike explained that he runs the Sail Sakakawea charter service (701-748-6111) and that he had "adopted" another kayaker a year before. Mike invited me to visit with him, his wife Sissy, and daughter Erin aboard his sailboat. Mike mixed gin and tonics and we talked about the lake, looked over maps, and told our stories. By the time I headed out, I was invited to dinner the next day at their home in Hazen, and was in the process of being provided with a list of folks downriver that I should call in the event of any difficulty. Mike and Sissy officially enlisted me in the region's "Kayakers Safety Net." Mike also told me about an upcoming bluegrass festival at Cross Ranch State Park, a one-day paddle below Garrison Dam.

I spent two days at the Dakota Waters Resort. This is another well-run campground, and the folks are paddler-friendly. I recommend that you stop here. I had my first shower in eight days, did laundry, and emptied out my

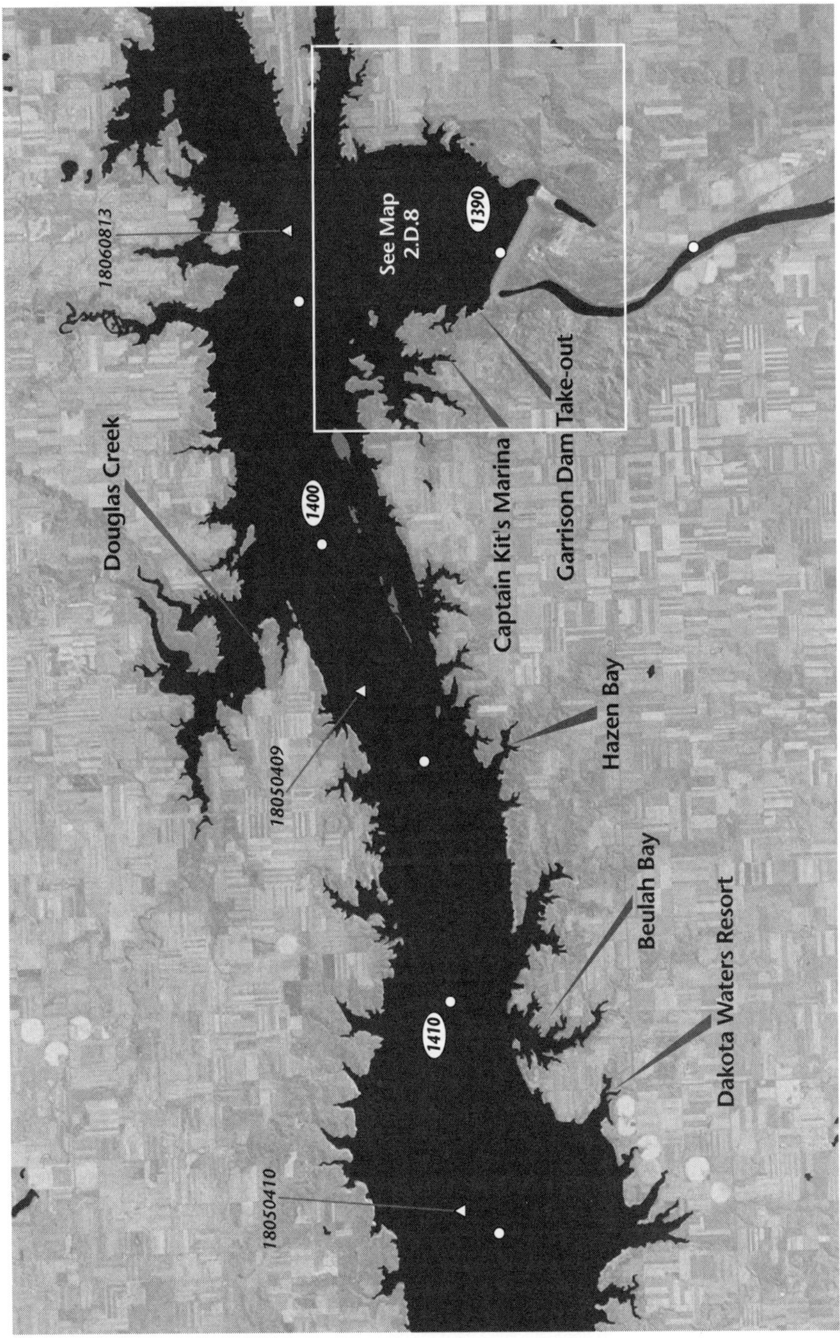

Map 2.D.7: Dakota Waters Resort (mile 1,414) to south of Garrison Dam (mile 1,384).

kayak for a good cleaning. When I mentioned to Kevin that I needed to send some of my GPS tracking hardware to San Diego for repairs, he arranged for his son Corey to drive me to a nearby town to send it out by UPS. The nearby 1806 Steakhouse turned out to be every bit as good as the fishermen had promised. It is a popular local restaurant, has very good meals, and offers an outstanding selection of beverages. The "Dakota hunting lodge" decor is particularly well done.

When I departed from Dakota Waters, a stiff northwest wind was blowing. The first 3 miles, until I reached the entrance to Beulah Bay (mile 1,411), were very difficult paddling. I cut inside the bay to paddle in more sheltered waters. The campground here is well inside the bay. Some of the tent sites are sheltered. This is not a full-service campground. Once around the point at the east side of the bay, you'll have decent shelter from a northwest wind.

There are several potential campsites along the next 1.5 miles, before you come to the next large bay (Expansion Bay; ~ mile 1,409). After you cross to the far side, you will begin a nearly due east paddle that continues for about 3 miles. Along this stretch there are several sites where you could pull out and camp if the weather suddenly turned nasty. Hazen Bay is at mile 1,405.5. The campground here is another that is well inside the bay and offers some amenities. According to Captain Mike Quinn, a young couple has purchased the cabins along the bay and will be living there. They will have small A-frame cottages to rent and will be glad to help paddlers.

After you cross the front of Hazen Bay, the shoreline angles up to the northeast. As I paddled by here, I had a strong northwest wind that pushed up large swells that broke hard along the shore. A following sea built up and conditions started getting a bit dicey, so I put in to a small bay at mile 1,405 right. I pulled my kayak ashore and waited for the wind to diminish. The wind never stopped. At midafternoon I set up my tent in a nice sheltered spot (47.51622/ -101.63050), and took a long nap. This lake teaches you to accept what progress it permits.

At mile 1,405, given good weather, you are within a day's paddle of Garrison Dam. The shoreline continues to angle to the northeast for the next 8 miles. There are numerous small bays with sheltered campsites along the way. You'll see an occasional cabin and a few homes along the shore beginning at about mile 1,401. If you paddle 11 more miles, you'll reach the Garrison Dam take-out (mile 1,390 right; 47.50905/-101.43950). However, just beyond mile 1,397 is a good shortcut to Captain Kit's Marina (701-487-3600) and Lake

Sakakawea State Park (701-487-3315), upstream from the dam (see Map 2.D.8). If the wind is blowing hard from the southeast, this shortcut will save a couple miles of very difficult paddling. The shortcut may involve a short (~ 20-yard) portage if water levels are low.

Prior to approaching the point at mile 1,397, create the following GPS waypoints, naming them as indicated:

F	Bay entrance to shortcut	47.54969/-101.46385
G	Narrows or short portage	47.54443/-101.46651
H	Marina entrance	47.52904/-101.45899

Set your GPS to route you to these points.

To get to the shortcut to Captain Kit's Marina, you will have to paddle around the point at mile 1,397 (see Map 2.D.8). Immediately after you round the point, bear right into the bay (GPS point F). Stay to the right side and work yourself to the back of the bay (G). You will see a relatively narrow cut that you can paddle through to enter the bay to the south. If the water level is low, you will have to drag your boat across at least a 20-yard-long saddle of sand. I found several pieces of driftwood to use as rollers under my kayak. This made the effort easier.

Once you get to the inner bay, you will see that it has three arms and that houses line the shore. Paddle toward the bay that is almost due south (H). The marina is on the left side about a mile inside this arm. This is a well-sheltered marina that harbors some very large vessels. As you paddle to the south, away from the shortcut, the entrance to the marina will not be visible. Just keep paddling to the south. There is often a fair amount of boat traffic into and out of the marina, so the entrance to the marina should quickly be apparent. You will need to navigate around a series of floating wave barriers to get into the marina. There is space alongside the boat ramp where you can pull out.

The owners of the marina, Kit and Fay Henegar, run a first-rate operation. Although they were busy, they proved to be extremely helpful. Kit helped me pull my boat up near the ramp, and then we retired to his office to talk about the lake while looking over my maps and satellite images. I was particularly interested in talking with Kit about local wind and weather patterns as they relate to the question of which side of the lake to make passage along. Kit agreed that a passage along the right (south) shore seemed to make the most

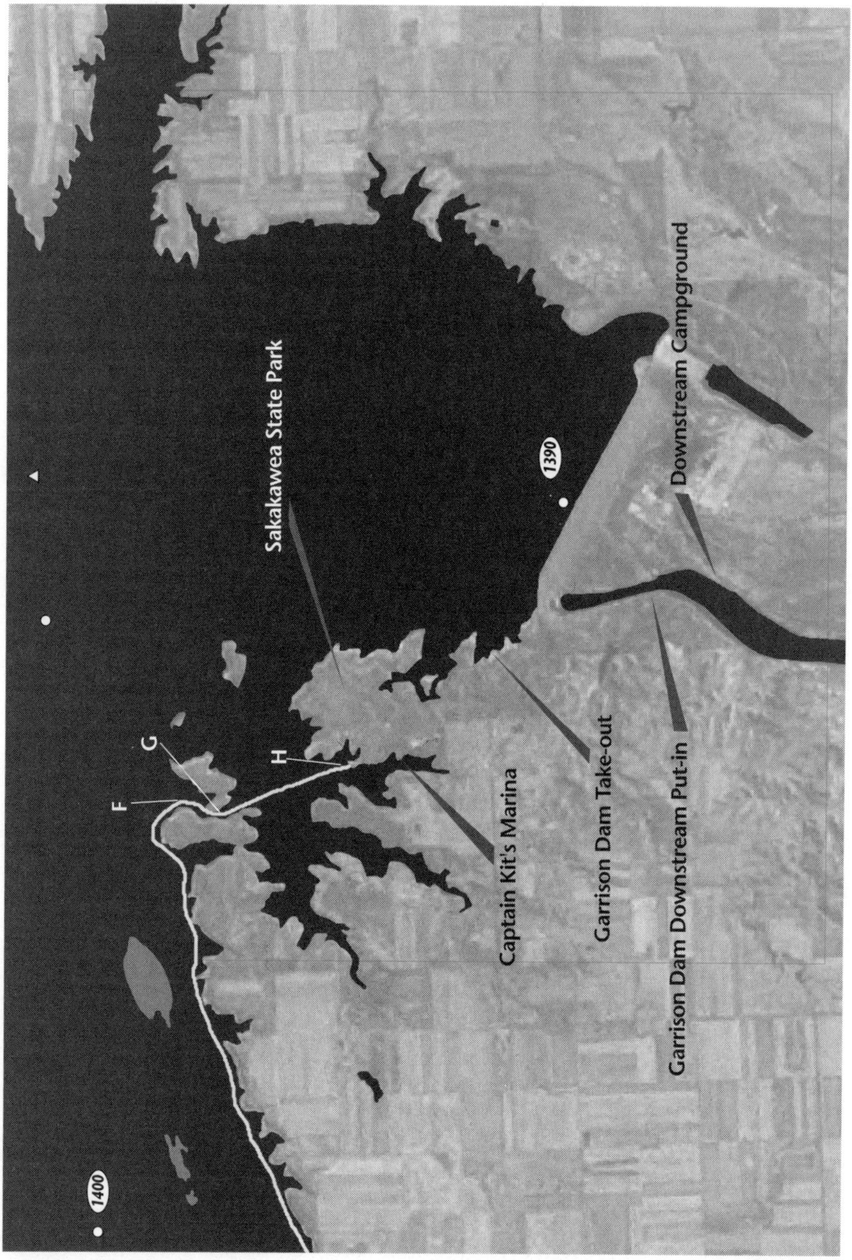

Map 2.D.8: Garrison Dam area, showing an optional shortcut that can be taken to Captain Kit's Marina. When a southeast wind is blowing, the last 4 miles to the dam can be a very difficult paddle. Waypoints F–H will take you through a protected passage to the marina. If water levels are low, you will have a short portage at point G.

sense. He emphasized that the lake can blow up very quickly, and that even large vessels can get into trouble if they do not seek shelter in time.

Captain Kit's Marina or Bayside Marine (701-654-7446) provide portage service to either the nearby Lake Sakakawea State Park or the downstream campground (701-654-7440 or 1-877-444-6777). Because these are busy operations, you should call ahead to let them know when you will arrive. Also, as is the case with all portage service providers, expect that they will need to work the haul of your equipment into their schedule. At the boat ramp near Captain Kit's, you should find some shade, drink a cold one, and just relax. You have successfully paddled nearly 180 miles on a reservoir that has more than 1,880 miles of shoreline. In places, this lake is more than 6 miles across; you have made safe passage down the entire length of the largest ACE reservoir in the nation. Rest and reflect. Consider the ACE factoid that there is enough water held behind this dam to cover the entire state of North Dakota with half a foot of water–more than enough to float your boat.

Captain Kit's Marina is within Lake Sakakawea State Park. The campground office is a short hike to the east. Although primarily set up for RVs, there is some shade, and the folks at the main desk will make a good attempt to get you in a sheltered spot. Because the campground is on a point, there is usually a good breeze and few mosquitoes. I visited here with the park manager, John Tunge. John is a member of a multiagency safety task force that focuses on encouraging safe boating practices on the lake. He provided several anecdotes about bad weather kicking up fast on the lake and small craft operators getting into serious trouble. He emphasized the need for paddlers to stay near the shore and keep up with NOAA weather reports, and for everyone to wear life vests at all times. Like many officials that I talked with, John was clearly worried about "Lewis and Clark adventure boaters" who might get in over their heads on the lake–figuratively and literally. After having made passage on this big lake, I understand clearly why he has good reason to worry. You cannot push the safety envelope on this lake.

The Garrison Dam downstream put-in is at the boat ramp (mile 1,389.1 left; 47.49106/-101.42869) below the powerhouse tailrace area, 2.2 blacktop road miles from the take-out. This is a long manual portage. If you do stay a day or two at the state park above the dam, you'll certainly meet folks that will be willing to haul your gear to the downstream put-in or campground. It is a good idea to offer to pay for such assistance, although every time that I made such an offer it was declined.

The downstream campground has both developed and primitive campsites. This is a very nice campground, but because you are back in the river bottoms the mosquitoes can be bothersome. Virtually all sites are shaded by large cottonwood trees, and many developed (e.g., RV pull-in sites) sites are near the river. The primitive campground is some distance from the river, so if you want to camp here, I suggest you explain to the campground host that you are a paddler and ask to be assigned a site near the river if one is available. Besides making it easer to launch, you will have easier access to a hot shower. At the time I visited this campground, the nightly fee for a primitive campsite was $10. The fee for a regular campsite was $14 per night. In my book, the hot shower is worth the additional $4. While you are here, you can tour the dam power plant, visit the fish hatchery, and fish in a pond where you can catch a mess of nice trout for dinner. The town of Riverdale is 4 or 5 miles by road from the campground. The ACE office is in Riverdale (701-654-7411); there is a post office and a library where you can get Internet access. If you ask around, you should be able to arrange a ride into town.

SEGMENT 2.E: Downstream Garrison Dam put-in (mile 1,389) to Bismarck, North Dakota, and the official start of Lake Oahe (mile 1,312.5) *(Map 2.E)*

- **River miles:** 76.5
- **Difficulty level:** Low to moderate
- **Typical time to complete:** 2 to 4 days

Between the Garrison Dam put-in and Bismarck are 76 river miles of easy paddling. If you have traversed Sakakawea, this section should be a totally enjoyable float. Dam releases provide good current in the river, and there is some shade along the shore. There are many nice places to camp along the shore and a really outstanding state park where you can camp among old-growth cottonwoods. You'll paddle by the Knife River, near the Indian Village National Historic Site, and by Washburn, where you can visit Lewis and Clark–related exhibits. When you get to Bismarck, you can tie up to the dock at a great little riverside bar and grill. Just downstream, on the opposite side of the river, you can put in at a truly paddler-friendly marina.

Before you head south from the Garrison Dam Tailrace ramp or the campground, you should contact the Garrison Powerhouse for information about

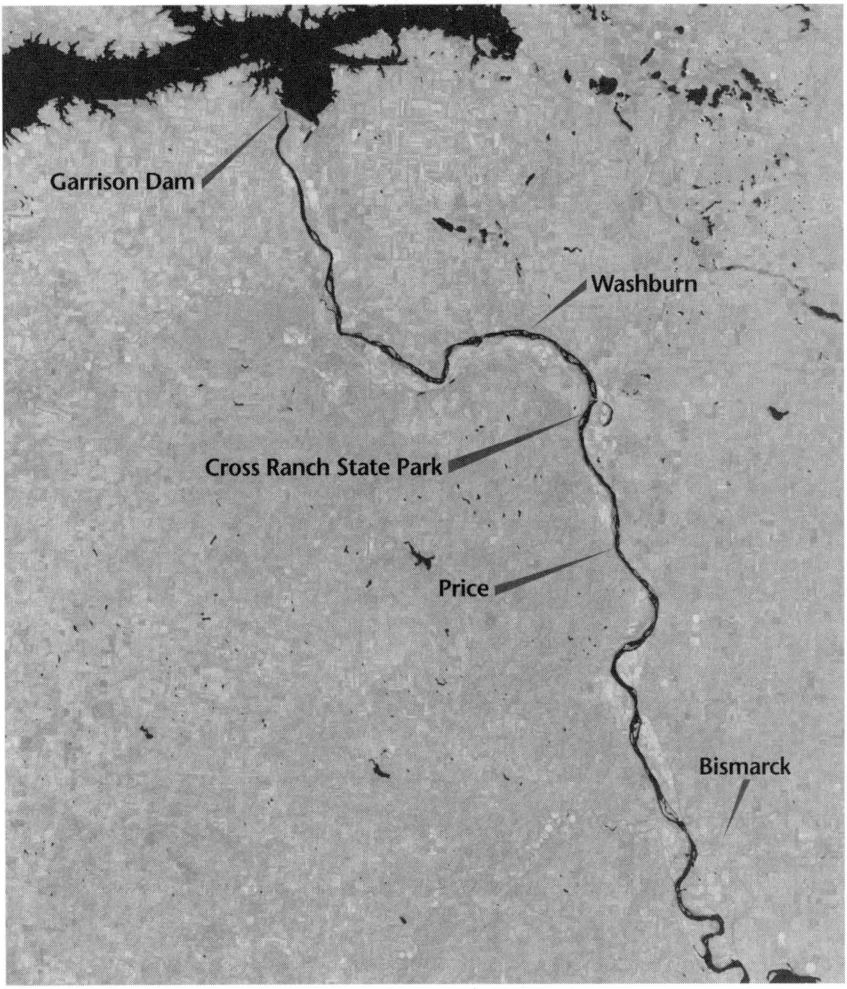

Map 2.E: Area between Garrison Dam (mile 1,389) and Bismarck, North Dakota (mile 1,312.5).

their projected releases (701-654-7441 ext. 3200). With this information you can time your departure to take advantage of the current. And you'll have a better idea of when you will experience the best flows and changes in water level, as you work your way downstream. You must pay attention to releases, as they relate to water level variations. During my stay at the campground, I was fortunate to have the opportunity to speak with ACE head ranger Linda Phelps and her husband Chuck, the dam's outside maintenance foreman. Over lunch in Riverdale we talked about safety issues related to paddlers. They both stressed that dam releases change water levels substantially and cautioned against camping on a low-lying shoreline or low island. They also told me to urge paddlers to always pull their boat well ashore and tie it up securely. Chuck related that at least one group of paddlers had upset downstream landowners by camping on private land without permission. Apparently the paddlers had quite the bonfire and left a mess behind them. Because of the unfortunate actions of these slob paddlers, a long stretch of shoreline above Washburn has been posted.

Information/Maps/Resources

To my knowledge no good paddler's map exists for the river between Garrison Dam and Bismarck. Nevertheless, this is a very nice float. The countryside is scenic, and the channel is generally easy to follow. I worked my way through this section using a North Dakota highway map and Landsat imagery to assist my progress. Since I made passage in 2002, the USGS Columbia Environmental Research Center has posted high-resolution air photos of the river from Garrison Dam to Bismarck (http://infolink.cr.usgs.gov/index.htm). If you go to this site and follow the links to the "Garrison Dam to Bismarck, North Dakota" imagery, you can view these photos. Where appropriate, I have used this imagery as a base for my maps. The size of the files associated with these images is gargantuan. Rather than downloading them, you can copy lower resolution versions by right-clicking on the individual images and saving them as JPEG images ranging between 60–130 KB. Prints made from these images will still provide adequate detail.

The "Boating in North Dakota" www.state.nd.us/gnf/boating/boat ramps.html provides a current list of boat ramp locations and facilities descriptions. The map accompanying this information is of poor resolution. During the boating season this website is said to be updated every Thursday. The site can be consulted for information about each ramp's status (usable, marginal, or unusable) due to water level and for the name of the agency that maintains the facility. General information about parks, including good maps of facilities, is available from North Dakota's tourism website (www.ndtourism.com) by clicking on the "Outdoor Adventure" tab. Also linked to this site is information about canoeing in North Dakota, and downloadable guides for fish identification and bird watching. You might also look over the interactive mapping utility at www.state.nd.us/gis. This site allows you to design a custom map for any area in the state.

Currently there are two area outfitters providing canoe rental and guide service on the river between Garrison Dam and the Bismarck area. Matah Adventures, operated by Peder and Tone-Lise Stenslie (701-663-0054; matah@btinet.net), and Lewis and Clark Canoe and Kayak Rentals (701-462-3668/701-462-8635). The Cross Ranch State Park also provides canoe rental and transportation services (701-794-3731).

Suggested Readings

There are more than a dozen Lewis and Clark campsites in this segment including Fort Mandan where the expedition wintered for some four months. Infor-mation about what transpired here during the outbound trip (October 20, 1804 to April 8, 1805) can be found in Vol. 3:186–332 and Vol. 4:7–14 (*Journals,* [Moulton, ed.]). Return trip event detail for area camps (August 14 to 18, 1806) is found in Vol. 8: 298-309. Context about events can be found in Stephen Ambrose's *Undaunted Courage,* beginning in chapter 15, page 177 through chapter 18, page 213.

To these sources I also suggest that you read Daniel Botkin's descriptions of the area, "Fort Mandan Park, North Dakota: Winter on the Plains" and "Knife River Indian Villages: Choosing a Place to live Within Nature's Constraints and Opportunities" in *Passage of Discovery* (pp. 144–154.) Botkin provides good food for thought, as in the following passage:

Today we often romanticize about nature. Most of us see nature on television, in the comfort of central heating and air conditioning. Or we go to the ski slopes or snowmobiling with the best of modern gear. It is cold, but relatively few of us test ourselves against winter as did Lewis and Clark and their men, arriving at a place strange to them, maintaining good terms with the Mandans, building shelter for the winter, and finding food. In the spring, they would move forward into an area completely unknown to the mapmakers who'd come to St. Louis. It is well to remember the difficult winter Lewis and Clark spent with the Mandans when we romanticize about nature and believe that what we may conserve will always be benign for us to visit. It is just as likely to be like Clark's hunting trip, with falls through the ice, buffalo too lean to eat, and the constant danger of frostbite.

◆ **Garrison Dam put-in (mile 1,389) to Cross Ranch State Park (mile 1,348): 41 miles *(Map 2.E.1)***

Paddler's Notes and Cautions

There are 34 river miles from the Garrison Dam put-in (mile 1,389 left) to the

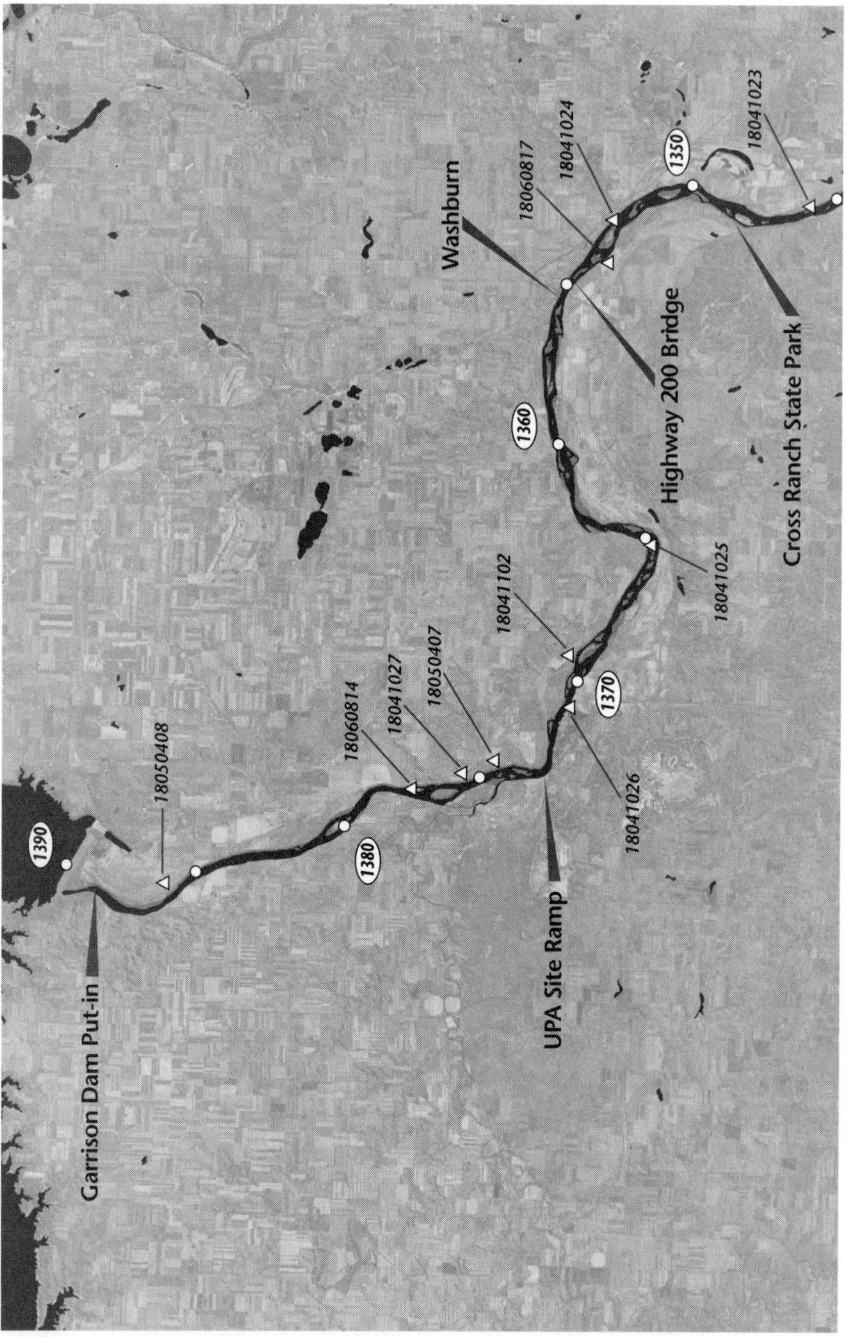

Map 2.E.1: Garrison Dam (mile 1,389) to Cross Ranch State Park (~ mile 1,348).

Highway 20 bridge at Washburn (mile 1,355). If you camped at the downstream campground, you'll need to scout for trails leading down to the river where you can launch your boat. Make sure to lather up with bug repellent before humping your gear to the water's edge. Also, there's poison ivy here; stay on the trail and watch where you put your feet. Remember that water levels vary considerably because of dam releases, so keep your gear on high ground until you are actually ready to pack and launch. If you take your boat to the water's edge, secure it. The water level can rise so quickly that an unsecured boat may take off without you.

By midmorning, water released from the dam creates a 5 to 7 mph current that will carry you along nicely. For the first couple miles beyond the downstream campground, beginning around mile 1,387, the left shoreline consists of high sandy banks interspersed with occasional low areas that would make nice pull-out sites. Also near mile 1,387, on the right, you will see a floating boat dock extending out from a sandy beach. This is the Missouri River Lodge's private dock (877-480-3498; www.moriverlodge.com). At the lodge you will find friendly folks and nice accommodations with good meals. If you call ahead and there are vacancies, I suggest that you spend a day or two here. There is excellent fishing along this stretch of the river; the resort's website notes that the state record Chinook salmon and brown, rainbow, and cutthroat trout were caught within 20 miles downstream of the dam. The Missouri River Lodge is part of a ranch that has some 3 miles of river frontage. There is a nice trail system for hikers and lots of wildlife, including both bald and golden eagles and ospreys. No camping is allowed on the ranch because there have been three wildfires started by careless campers.

I moved over to the right side of the river by mile 1,384, finding deeper water along that side. At mile 1,381, the river widened somewhat and became shallow. I had to work my way around a series of sandbars, first going to the left shore and then back to the right at mile 1,379. You'll need to pay attention here, as conditions can change considerably from year to year. Essentially you are threading your way around a series of flats and sandbars. I continued along the shore until the upstream end of Knife River Island (~ mile 1,377), where I followed a channel that led me along the island's left shore. I was told that paddlers camp on this island; it is wooded and there appeared to be many potential campsites.

Just below the island, on the right, is the Knife River confluence. A half-mile below is mile mark 1,374; there are sandbars and shallows in this area so pay close attention. For context at this point, as you thread your way through the shallows, you are 700 river miles from Fort Benton and 947 miles from the headwaters confluence at Three Forks. If you are going the entire way to St. Louis, you are not yet halfway there. The river begins a sharp bend to the east at mile 1,373. Around this bend on the right is a boat ramp just before the UPA power plant (mile 1,372.5; 47.28731/-101.33958). At the parking area there are vault toilets, but there is no water. The city of Stanton is nearby.

This stretch of the river has very good fishing, so you can expect to see many boats. Most of the anglers work the areas downstream from the many wing dams along the right shore. Beginning at about mile 1,372, there are numerous places where you could pull out on both sides of the river. Along the right shore, beginning at about mile 1,370, there are several wing dams with nice sandy areas on their downstream sides. Some of these areas have trees that provide good shade and shelter. Along the left shore, the area near mile 1,370 is thought to be the actual location of the expedition's Fort Mandan. Here the Corps wintered from early November 1804 to early April 1805.

Beyond the power plant, the river angles to the southeast for a half-dozen miles, and then bends sharply to the north just after mile 1,366. Fort Clark was established near this bend in 1830. This site can be visited and contains foundations of fort structures (701-328-2666). When I paddled around this bend, there were cattle lounging along the sandy shore, some standing in the shallow water on the downstream side of the point. I saw a cabin and a dock on the opposite shore, so I paddled over to see if I could get some water. I hailed a man who was repairing an outboard motor and asked if I could fill my drinking water bottles. He said to come ashore; I did and introduced myself. His name was Al, and we talked for a while as he finished working on an old Mercury outboard. His wife drove up on a four-wheeler and took my water bottles away to fill. Al described the river ahead as getting shallow and full of mudflats. Al's wife returned with my bottles. The water had a distinct yellow tint; she told me not to worry, that it was "from an artesian well, and it may taste a bit funny but it's good to drink." I was just happy to have my bottles refilled; the day was brutally hot, it was only noon, and I had polished off both bottles. I thanked them, returned to my kayak, added some sports drink powder to one of the bottles, and then pushed off.

Between miles 1,362 and 1,361 right, there are several places where you might pull out; beyond that the river widens and becomes shallow. I encountered a series of mudflats and had considerable difficulty threading my way through narrow channels with an anemic current. Eventually, I worked my way to the left side and stayed there for the last 5 or 6 miles until I reached the Highway 200 bridge at Washburn. This can be a difficult area to navigate at low water. You'll need to proceed carefully to avoid getting hung up in the shallows.

Just after the bridge, on the left, is the Washburn ramp, fish-cleaning station, picnic area, and primitive campsite (mile 1,355 left; ~ 47.28929/-101.03841). Water is available. I did not stop here as I wanted to make a bluegrass festival at Cross Ranch State Park, another 7 miles downriver. However, if you are interested in things Lewis and Clark, this is a must-stop. This is near the area where the expedition wintered in 1804. The Lewis and Clark Interpretive Center is just up the highway (701-462-8535), and the Fort Mandan reconstructed site is 1.5 miles to the north. As I approached the Washburn area, I kept my eyes open for riverside access to Fort Mandan, but I could find none.

As you work your way below Washburn, you will get an occasional glimpse of the "other" Lewis and Clark trail–Highways 1804 (east side) and 1806 (west side). These roads run roughly parallel to the Missouri River for much of the length of the Dakotas. More often than not, however, these highways are a couple miles away from the river. Here, you are winding your way downstream at 3 miles an hour, while families in air-conditioned RVs charge up and down their trail at 60 miles an hour. Ghandi's statement, "There is more to life than increasing its speed," comes to mind. Whether you are following the trail of earlier explorers, or seeking respite from the pressure of stuff, or simply wanting time to reflect on the river of your own life, floating the Missouri can provide the mental equivalent of downshifting. As your speed is reduced, there is more time for undirected thought. Time slows, then mates with the pace of the current. You feel the fold and warp of the land and sense a relationship with the flow of the river. You are at a boundary layer, at the interface of solid and liquid. At the best moments of reflection, eddies form, fluid and temporal, and you perceive surface patterns that you never noticed. You begin to sense underlying features, and you begin to truly read the river.

From the Highway 200 bridge at Washburn to Cross Ranch State Park (701-794-3731), it is almost 7 miles. In my opinion, the best place for paddlers to camp is at the park's group tent camping area at mile 1,348.3 right (47.21460/-100.99378). Before I stopped here, I called ahead and talked with Dennis Clark, the park's manager. Dennis told me that there was a ramp and primitive camping area about 2 miles farther downriver (Sanger Campground and ramp ~ mile 1,346 right), but he suggested that I pull out at the group campground because I would have better access to the Missouri River Bluegrass and Old Time Music Festival and the park's other amenities. The Ma ak oti hiking trail connects the Sanger unit with Cross Ranch. If you choose to camp at one of these locations, call ahead for the most current information and to alert the rangers that you will be coming in from the river.

Cross Ranch State Park is adjacent to a preserve run by The Nature Conservancy. As you approach the park you'll see very tall cottonwoods. This is one of the last remaining mature cottonwood floodplain forests in North Dakota. A Nature Conservancy brochure, *Cross Ranch Nature Preserve, Self-guided Nature Trail,* provides the information that cottonwoods are pioneer species; their seeds only germinate at areas freshly disturbed by the river's meandering. Since the dams went in, disturbance associated with flooding has been contained, and conditions required for germination are all but absent. As the brochure puts it, "The successional cycle has been broken and the existing cottonwoods are destined to be the last of their kind to reign over the Missouri River floodplain."

There is no ramp or designated pullout site below the group tent camp area at Cross Ranch State Park. The take-out area may be marked with a pole and windsock, and you should see signage associated with a shoreline walking trail as you approach the location of the group campground. Call ahead to find out how the take-out site for the group camp area is marked. You'll have to scout carefully for a decent place to make your landing as the bank is steep and lined with riprap. If a good current is running, it may be best to float just beyond the area where you make your take-out, turn back upstream, and make your approach. Take your time and try to locate a couple rocks that you can slide your bow between. Also take extra care in getting out of your boat; the rocks will be slippery and there is deep water just offshore. Immediately up the bank is one of the best places to camp on the entire river. Huge cottonwoods provide shade and shelter, a water faucet is nearby, and a short walk will take you to the park headquarters where you can register, get an exquisitely hot shower, and find out more about the area's flora and fauna.

Ranger Dennis Clark's recommendation to stay at the main park turned out to be very good advice. The music festival was put on by the Bluegrass and Ol' Time Music Association of North Dakota, a.k.a. "BOTMAND." It was a wonderful affair, with folks sitting in a shady glen around a band shell listening to some of the sweetest sounding music I've ever heard. The campground was packed with day visitors and RV campers, and there were food vendors and merchandise retailers. Besides a couple of big-name groups, there was a lot of very skilled local talent. Dennis introduced me to the folks running the festival, and got me signed up as a volunteer to assist with parking, ticket sales, and cleanup. This got me a free admission to the concert for just a couple hours of work each day.

The festival is typically held annually on the second weekend in July. If you can time your arrival for this event, you will have a wonderful opportunity to listen to some outstandingly mellow music and meet folks who truly appreciate the great harmonies of traditional music. All-in-all, this was an outrageously mellow experience.

Late Sunday afternoon, after I assisted with the cleanup, I returned to my tent and began preparation for heading out the next day. Two couples on heavily loaded Harleys pulled into the group camp area looking for a site to pitch their tents. I walked over to talk with them. I told them it was a good location, so they decided to make camp. I learned they were from Glidden, Iowa. The two women were semiprofessional bowlers; they carried their bowling balls and shoes, and were stopping at tournaments along the way. One couple owned a bowling alley and the other worked in a modular home factory. As they were leaving for town to get dinner, they asked if they could get me anything. I asked them to pick me up some beer and gave them a few dollars to cover the cost. They returned later with a case of Budweiser and a quart of Bloody Mary mix.

That night, around a small campfire, we drank "red beer"–a can of beer poured into a tall plastic cup with a good splash of Bloody Mary mix. I listened to their stories and learned that they were making a big loop through Minnesota, across South Dakota to Sturgis, out to the Rocky Mountains, and then back to Iowa. They talked about their kids, learned lessons, tough love, and dealing with strong prairie winds and semis on a bike. I talked a bit about my trip and some of my own difficulties with the elements. We drank more red beer, and before retiring for the night we settled on the time-tested wisdom that the journey, not the destination or distance, was the reason we were "on the road." In the morning, I fixed them coffee; we packed up and said good-byes, and they rumbled off on their Harleys.

Ranger Dennis Clark came by to take me in to town for lunch. We talked about paddling on the river. He told me that there was a canoe outfitter in

Washburn, Matah Adventures (701-663-0054). This outfitter rents canoes and provides guide service. Dennis also told me an instructive story about a group of canoeists who camped on an island near Cross Ranch State Park. Apparently they set up camp at low water; at some point in the night the water level, and flooded their camp. They had very little time to abandon their camp and make it to higher ground. They were fortunate to have only lost some gear in the incident.

- **Cross Ranch State Park (mile 1,348.3) to Bismarck (mile 1,313): ~ 35.3 miles** ***(Maps 2.E.2 & 2.E.3)***

Paddler's Notes and Cautions

From Cross Ranch State Park to the outskirts of Bismarck is less than 32 river miles. With a good current running, and because the river's path is relatively straight, you can make Bismarck with a full day's effort. Two miles south of the main park is the Sanger Campground and ramp (~ mile 1,346 right). There are primitive camping sites along the shore, and 15 RV and vehicle-based tent camping sites with electric service are just inland from the ramp. Water, vault toilets, and a recycle bin are just before the boat trailer parking area. Up the road, there is a self-registration station, where you'll need to fill out a form and pay a modest fee for your tent site. If you want a modern bathroom and hot shower, you'll need to walk the trail to the visitor center, 2 miles to the north. This should be done in daylight.

Between Cross Ranch State Park and Sanger Campground, there are a series of mudflats. If the water level is low, you'll need to work your way carefully through this section. I started out along the right shore, then crossed over a shallow flat to get on the left side and paddled along a steep bank following the channel. It ended up being about 2.5 actual miles to get to the Sanger ramp. From the opposite side of the river, it looked like a nice camp with an easy pullout and some shade. Less than 5 miles farther is the Steckel Boat Landing (mile 1,342 left; ~ 47.13129/-100.94525). The town of Price is about 3 miles downriver from Steckel. You'll see a few houses inland from the river and the town's name spelled in white rocks on a neighboring hillside. Price is right (mile 1,339).

Beyond Price, the river angles to the southeast for about 4 miles. On the right, you'll also see a section of Burlington Northern Railroad track that parallels the river too closely. If you look to the southwest, when you get a good view, you'll see Horseshoe Butte and Stonehouse Butte, each over 2,000 feet in elevation and less than three-quarters of a mile from the river. Farther in the

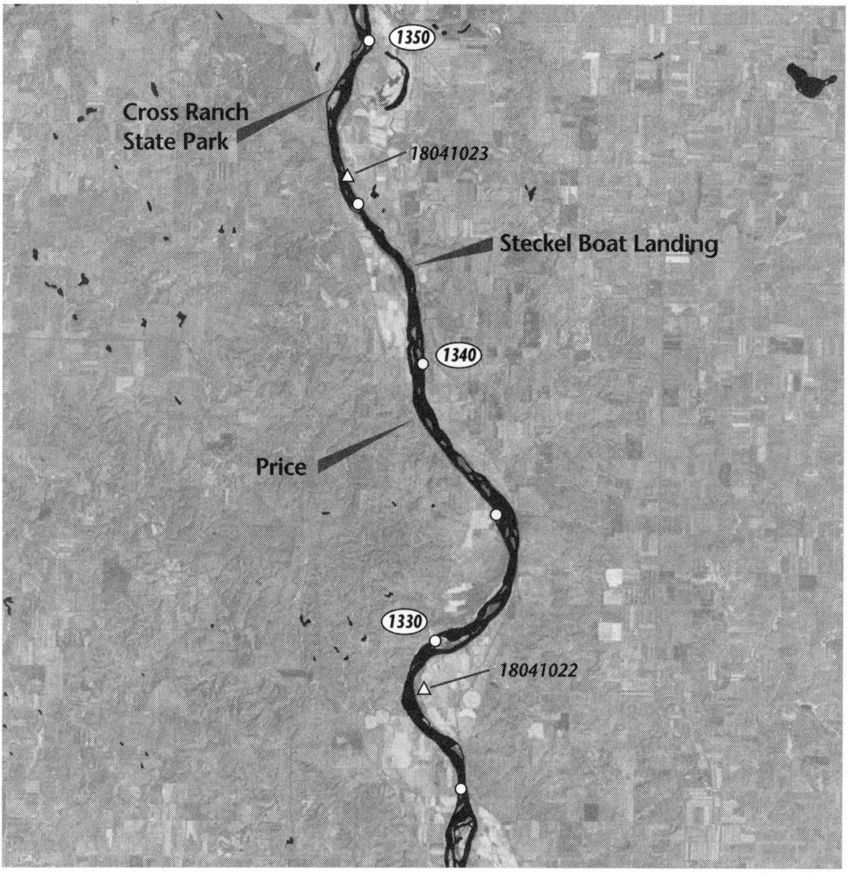

Map 2.E.2: Cross Ranch State Park (mile 1,348) to mile 1320.

distance, you may see Square Buttes; the highest of the three at 2,053 feet in elevation.

At river mile 1,335, the river begins a long sweeping turn to the southwest. On the left, at mile 1,334, is Highway 1804 and the town of Wogansport. As the river turns back to the southwest, at mile 1,331, there are a series of islands with sand beaches, vegetation enough for shade, and possible campsites. If the weather went sour and you camped here, the next day's distance to Bismarck would be about 15 miles. Another area of possible emergency campsites is on the left shore between miles 1,328 and 1,326. Of course, you should attempt to get permission before you set up camp.

When you get a couple miles farther downriver, you will begin to see some cabins and the first of a series of substantial homes with shorelines littered with riprap to slow erosion. Riprap lines both shores as you get close to Bismarck. As I approached this section, I assumed that the channel was on the left side near the docks of the homes. However, the water got increasingly shallow, and I had to work my way over to the right side. I stayed on the right, in a good channel all the way through most of Bismarck (see Map 2.E.3).

This is not a place you want to paddle through on a summer weekend. Recreational boat traffic is thick, so boat wake can be a real issue. If your timing is wrong and you have to press on, it would be best to work through the area early in the morning and stay to the far right, out of the main channel. I worked through here on a weekday in the late afternoon. There was a good deal of traffic, including pontoon boats, water-skiers, and personal watercraft, but I had no incidents.

As you approach Bismarck, you will first see the I-94 bridge (mile 1,315.3; 46.82193/-100.83389). Just upstream from the bridge and on the left shore, you will see a modest-sized paddle wheeler. I later learned that this ship is having a difficult time plying the local waters profitably. Clearly, at lower water levels this replica steamboat is constrained to just several miles of the river. There are three additional bridges to pass under; they are the Burlington Northern Rail-road bridge (46.81728/-100.82803), the I-94 Business Route bridge (46.80897/-100.81561), and finally the Highway 810 bridge (46.79660/-100.81725). Immediately on the right after passing under this last bridge is the dock for the Broken Oar Bar and Grill (46.79916/-100.82132). This is a popular riverside bar; the drinks are ice cold and the food is good. I recommend a visit; the people are friendly, you'll meet local water folk, and it provides a good opportunity to get local intelligence about conditions downriver.

◆ **Bismarck area (mile 1,319 to mile 1,310): 9 miles *(Map 2.E.3)***

Paddler's Notes and Cautions

If you plan to stop in Bismarck, I recommend that you put in at the Southport Marina (701-258-0158). The marina is on the left side of the river, less than a mile downstream from the Highway 810 bridge. Before I put in here, I had spoken with the marina's developer, Kevin Turnbow. He instructed me to cut over to the left shore immediately after the bridge because of a series of shallow downstream mudflats and sandbars. When I worked my way across, the water level was low–2 to 5 inches over one of the sandbars that I skirted. As you

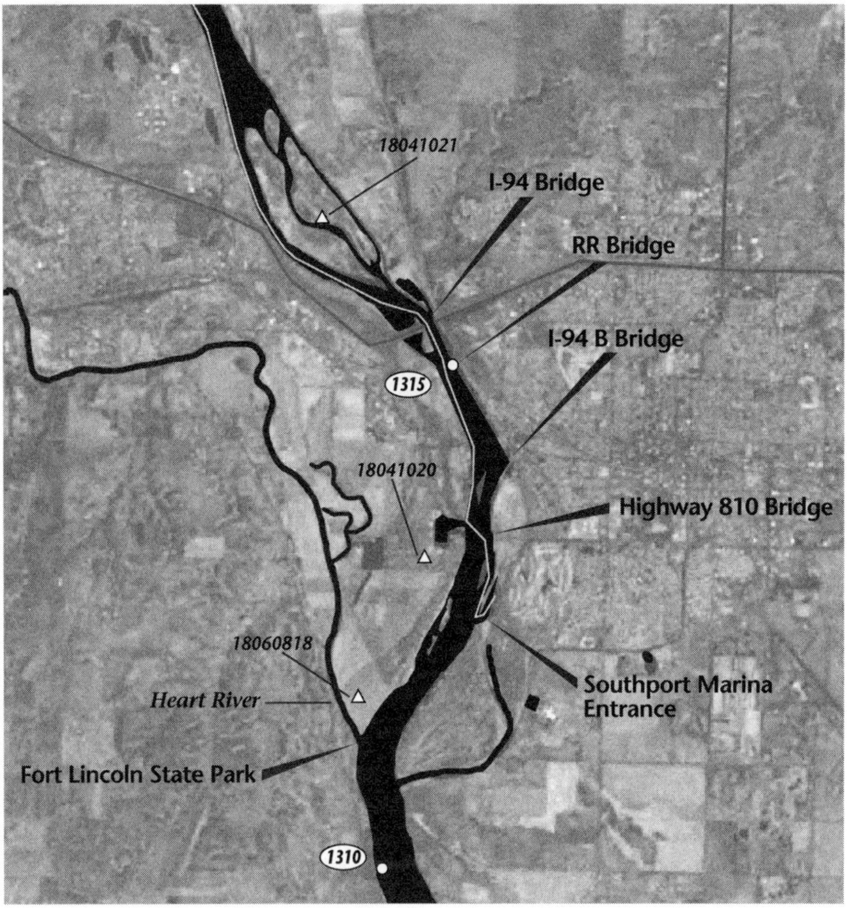

Map 2.E.3: Detail of Bismarck area showing my July 2002 course track to Southport Marina. Weekend recreational boat traffic is quite heavy here; it is best to paddle this segment early in the morning or on a weekday.

work your way down the shore, you will pass a series of riverfront condominiums that are part of the Southport Development. The entrance to the marina is at mile 1,312.6 left (46.78408/-100.82013). Paddle into this channel and then turn left (north). Keep paddling until you pass under an antique steel bridge; the marina office and convenience store is on your right.

Kevin's marina manager, Dee DeBell, welcomed me in and showed me where I could tie up. After I cleaned up, Dee escorted me to Kevin's office. Kevin turned out to be extremely gracious and we hit it off instantly. We talked about the river, his efforts to develop the waterfront, court battles to get and defend construction permits, and his wetland mitigation effort at the north end of the marina. Judging from what I saw, it is clear that a great deal of careful thought has gone into this project. Kevin related that he was willing to assist paddlers with a shuttle to a motel or to a grocery store for supplies, and that there was a small area at the north of the marina where paddlers might camp with permission.

Later that afternoon Kevin and his gracious wife, Leeann, took me to the Broken Oar, where we had beers and shook dice for "clamdiggers." These drinks were served up by handsome waitresses with nautical names like "Topside" and so forth. A number of locals joined us. One of the people at the table was David Castillo, the chef at Huff Bar and Grill, a day's paddle downriver. He invited me to visit with him when I got down that way. In every respect, the Broken Oar had a good feel to it; the folks on the outside deck were clearly enjoying themselves. At this latitude, winters are long and summers are short; you make the most of the hot July weather.

Later that evening I made contact with Bill and Dina Butcher, sailing companions of Mike Quinn of Lake Sakakawea. Bill and Dina are also members of the Sakakawea Dam Yacht Club and self-confessed members of the "Missouri River Kayakers Underground Railroad"–an unofficial support group of water people who sometimes provide assistance to paddlers. I stayed with them for a few days while waiting for a shipment of my repaired electronic gear. Bill and Dina were great hosts, had many good stories related to sailing on the reservoir, and are exactly the kind of people you hope to meet.

The area around Bismarck is rich in history; there were large Mandan and Hidatsa villages here, and the Heart River and Fort Lincoln are just to the south. Seven miles south of Mandan on Highway 1806 is the 400-year-old "On-A-Slant Indian Village." Most Lewis and Clark–related guidebooks have information about this site and other area attractions.

SEGMENT 2.F: Bismarck, North Dakota (mile 1,312.6), to Oahe Dam, South Dakota (mile 1,072.7) *(Map 2.F)*

- **River miles:** 239.9
- **Difficulty level:** High
- **Typical time to complete:** 17 to 22 days

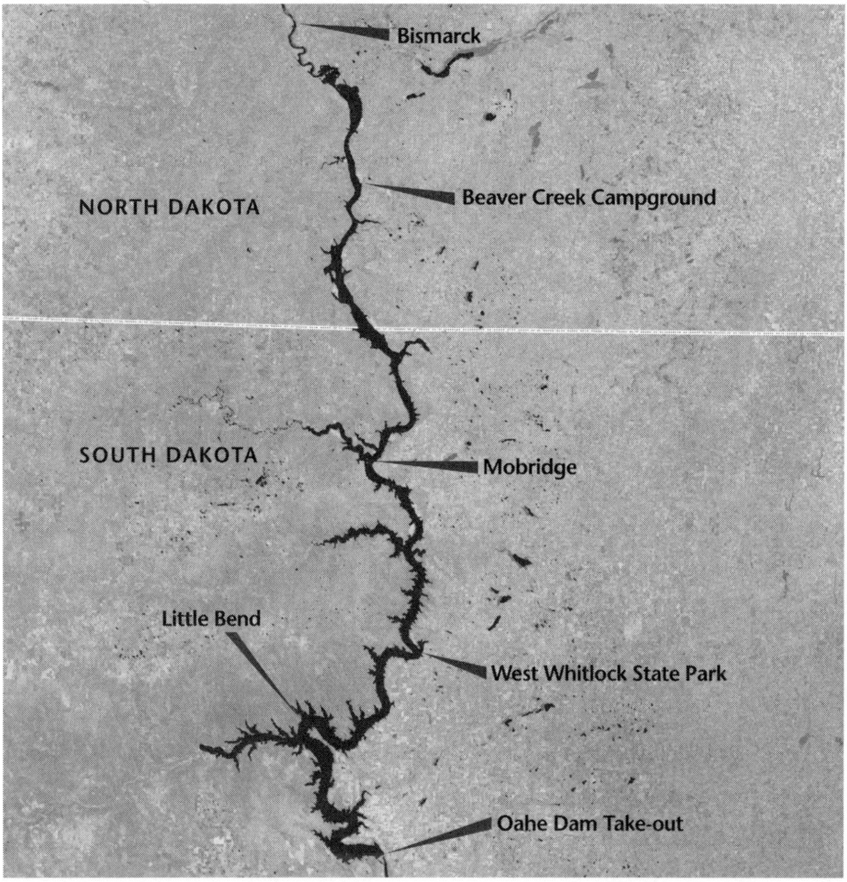

Map 2.F: Bismarck, North Dakota, at mile 1,312.6 to Oahe Dam at mile 1,072.7 above Pierre, South Dakota. Paddling on Lake Oahe is potentially hazardous under the best of conditions.

> *Someone must have told me about the Missouri River at Bismarck, North Dakota, or I must have read about it. In either case, I hadn't paid attention. I came on it in amazement. Here is where the map should fold. Here is the boundary between east and west. On the Bismarck side, it is eastern landscape, eastern grass, with the look and smell of eastern America. Across the Missouri on the Mandan side, it is pure west, with brown grass and water scourings and small outcrops. The two sides of the river might as well be a thousand miles apart.*
>
> JOHN STEINBECK, *TRAVELS WITH CHARLEY*

Lake Oahe technically begins at Bismarck, North Dakota, and ends at the Oahe Dam, just north of Pierre, South Dakota. About two-thirds of the lake is in South Dakota. Oahe Dam is close to the geographic center of the state. ACE claims Lake Oahe as being 231 miles long with 2,250 miles of shoreline. When I left Bismarck, however, I did not see what I would consider open water until I approached Beaver Creek, some 57 miles downstream. After you reach open water, Lake Oahe ranges between 1 and 4 miles wide.

A day or two south of Bismarck–depending on current and weather–you'll find a bar and grill with truly gourmet cuisine. I recommend that you stop there and enjoy a "last supper." A few miles beyond this stop, the real Lake Oahe begins. This lake has a well-deserved reputation for being the most dangerous for small craft of all the Upper Missouri's reservoirs. The lake trends north to south and is relatively narrow, and winds from the northwest or southeast can come up quickly and blow hard for days at a time. Local anglers have a healthy respect for the lake's ability to quickly generate big waves. Many fish from deep-V hull Lund boats designed for big water. Fishermen that I talked with told me that this lake is no place for small craft. And that they have learned to head for shelter at the first sign of deteriorating weather. For those in canoes or kayaks, heading to shelter means getting to shore. This is an often muddy exercise whenever the lake levels are low. You may have to negotiate through knee-deep mud for several yards to get to firm ground.

So why recommend a passage on this lake to experienced paddlers? Perhaps because it presents such a magnum-caliber challenge. This lake will test your skills, conditioning, judgment, and patience like no other body of water that I've paddled upon. Besides frequent stiff headwinds and rough seas, there is little vegetation on long stretches of the lake; shelter is limited. The terrain is mostly barren and rugged. Long stretches of shoreline are virtually uninhabited. During the summer, you can expect midafternoon temperatures in excess of 100 degrees Fahrenheit. When you ultimately pull out at the landing just above Oahe Dam, you will be physically–and probably emotionally–spent. But you will have the satisfaction of knowing that you have successfully negotiated the most difficult obstacle to making a complete passage down the Missouri River.

Information/Maps/Resources

The "Boating in North Dakota" page at www.state.nd.us/gnf/boating/boatramps.html provides a current list of boat ramp locations and facilities descriptions. During the boating season this website is updated every

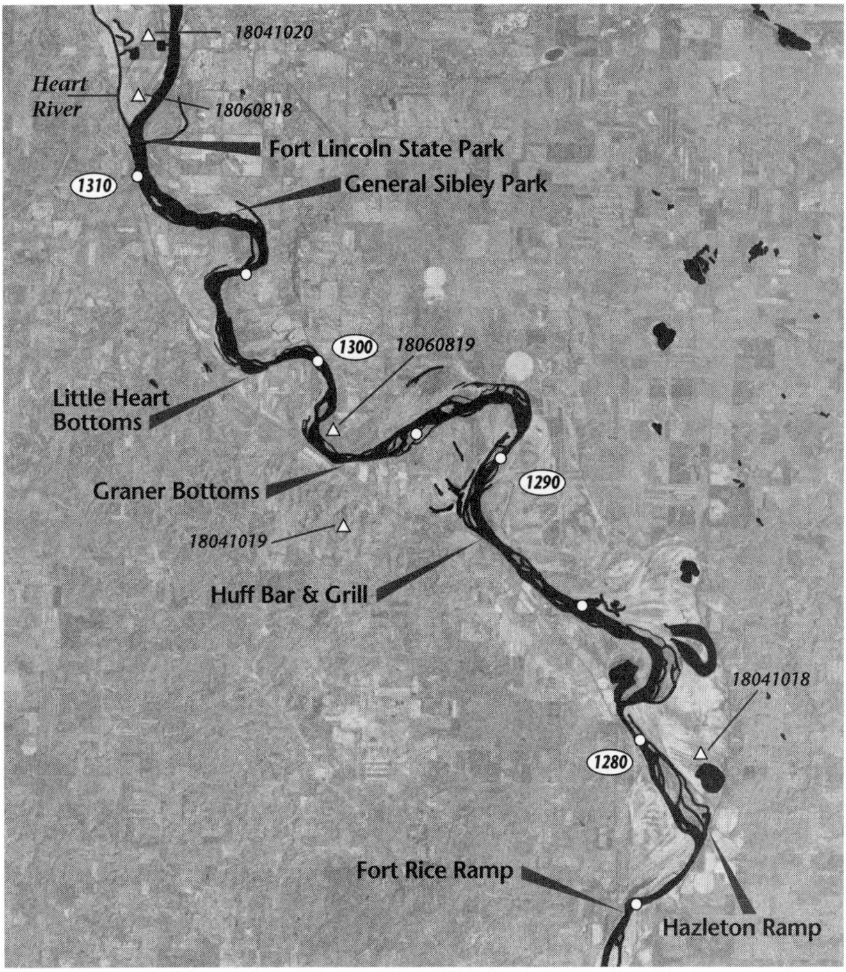

Map 2.F.1: Lake Oahe: Bismarck (mile 1,312.6) to Fort Rice ramp (mile 1,275).

Thursday. Consult this site for information about each ramp's status (usable, marginal, or unusable) due to water level and for the name of the agency that maintains the facility.

The ACE publication, *Lake Oahe [Oahe Dam] Boating and Recreation,* contains 4 small-scale maps and 30 large-scale, air photo–based maps. Each air photo shows some 8 to 10 river miles; most photos were taken in June 1987. Although dated, these air photos show still useful shoreline detail and the pre-reservoir main river channel location. I used this source along with the ACE map, *Oahe Dam and Lake; South Dakota/North Dakota.* My version of this map was published in March 2001; it provides an adequate representation of the lake's shoreline and relatively current information about recreation areas and their facilities. I used this map in my waterproof map sack, folded to display the section of the lake that I was negotiating. Current information about ACE facilities on Lake Oahe can be found at www.nwo.usace.army.mil/html/Lake_Proj/index.html.

General information about parks, including good maps of facilities, can be obtained at North Dakota's tourism website (www.ndtourism.com) by clicking on the "Outdoor Adventure" tab. Also linked to this site is information about canoeing in North Dakota, and downloadable guides for fish identification and bird watching.

Suggested Readings

There are seven Lewis and Clark campsites in this section. Information about what transpired here during the outbound trip (October 16 to 20, 1804) is in Vol. 3:175–189 *(Journals,* [Moulton, ed.]). Return trip event detail (August 18 to 19, 1806) can be found in Vol. 8:307–310. Context about events in this section is found in Stephen Ambrose's *Undaunted Courage,* in chapter 15.

I particularly recommend that you read Prince Maximilian's account of his June 1833 steamboat trip on the Missouri River from Fort Pierre to Fort Clark, Vol. XXII, Part I of *Maximilian, Prince of Wied's, Travels in the Interior of North America, 1832–1834* in Thwaites, Early Western Travels 1748-1846. Maximilian provides good descriptions of the area's natural and cultural landscapes.

- **Lake Oahe: Bismarck, North Dakota (mile 1,312.6), to Beaver Creek Campground (mile 1,255.6)**

- **River miles:** 57
- **Difficulty level:** Low to moderate
- **Typical time to complete:** 3 to 4 days

LAKE OAHE: Bismarck to Fort Rice ramp: ~ 37 miles *(Map 2.F.1)*

Paddler's Notes and Cautions

The Heart River joins the Missouri on the right 1.5 miles below the Southport

Marina. I was told that there is a privately run campground just up the river on the west shore. Just beyond this confluence, also on the right (mile 1311) is Fort Lincoln State Park (701-663-9571). If you are going to camp at Bismarck, Fort Lincoln has all the amenities and offers relatively good access to the city. As you work your way farther downstream from here, you will have to carefully watch for shallow water and sandbars. General Sibley Park is on the left at mile 1,307.3. There is camping here, but the approach to the ramp is up a channel that I could not locate as I paddled by. Little Heart Bottoms (a.k.a. Schmidt Bottom) is at mile 1,302.5 (right). There is camping here, but if you have come this far I recommend that you continue on. Across the river is Kimball Bottoms, a popular area for four-wheeling and dirt bike racing. To get away from the noise, continue on for another 6 miles to Graner Bottoms (a.k.a. Sugarloaf, at mile 1,297.8; 46.65542/-100.71485). There is a good ramp here, shade, a vault toilet, water, and helpful campground hosts.

The Graner Bottoms Campground is 8 miles upstream from Huff. However, Huff is just 4 miles down the road from Graner. The campground hosts assisted me with transportation to the Huff Bar and Grill, where I was graciously received by David Castillo, the chef that I had met at the Broken Oar Bar in Bismarck. David took a few minutes to sit down and talk with me. He noted that he had been a chef in New York City, and that he was in the process of introducing some "nontypical" dishes to the local menu: stromboli, sushi-grade salmon, and fresh seafood. For Mother's Day he had a barrel of Maine lobsters flown in. He said that the folks told him they could not believe how good the seafood was, that it was so much better than what they got at Red Lobster. But since most of his patrons come in expecting steak, the process of expanding the menu was proceeding slowly.

We talked about the restaurant business and then went over the night's specials. David suggested either the shrimp scampi or the chicken breast stuffed with blue crabmeat. I was having a hard time deciding, so David volunteered to fix me a plate with both entrees. Before he returned to the kitchen, I asked about the bowling machine in the corner. I had not seen one like it for 20 years. David laughed and said, "It's a classic, but we repair that thing every week. They throw the balls too hard."

Before the food arrived I sat at the table writing up my field notes for the day. A man came in the door and saddled up on a barstool. He ordered a drink from the bartender, an attractive woman with a bright smile. After taking his first drink, he asked her, "What's your name, dear?" She replied "Julie." This exchange was repeated several times before she went back into the kitchen to retrieve my food. I concluded that the man had obviously had a few drinks before showing up here. With my meal delivered, she returned to the bar. The man again asked her, "What's your name, dear?" This time she answered, "Cindy." For some reason unknown to me this seemed to finally satisfy him, as he did not repeat the question. When she delivered another cold lemonade to my table with compliments from the chef, I said, "Thanks, Cindy." We both got a laugh out of that. Later, when David was able to return to my table, we talked about having a good person to work the bar. I related what I'd overheard; he laughed and said he was very lucky to have "Cindy" working there. As I worked my way downriver, I heard from a number of people about the good food at the Huff Bar. I recommend that you put in here; the food and the atmosphere are both excellent.

To get from the Graner Campground to the pull-out near the Huff Bar, you have to paddle 8 miles around a bend. On your right, you will see evidence of a recent forest fire among what was a nice stand of cottonwood trees. Watch for sandbars; you'll find it challenging to stay in what passes for the channel. Halfway around this bend on the left (~ mile 1,292), you will see a ramp and a vault toilet. This site was not on any of my maps, but it may be Maclean Bottoms (a.k.a. the Gun Range), where there is primitive camping, a picnic shelter, and a vault toilet. When you finally get around the bend, the river turns to the southeast. The Huff Bar pullout is on the right at mile 1,287.8 (46.62937/-100.65740). You will see the bar, a white building, from the river after you round the bend and begin to turn southeast. Look for a set of old wooden stairs coming partway down the bank. Pull over on the level area below these stairs and tie your boat off. Climb the stairs, and cross the field and the highway to the bar. Enjoy some of the best cuisine that North Dakota has to offer.

There are only a handful of possible campsites between Huff and Fort Rice, a distance of nearly 14 river miles. You'll paddle a relatively straight section to the southeast; the river will widen and then bend back to the southwest. At mile 1,281 the river narrows, cuts back sharply to the southeast, and then considerably widens. This area is shallow, and there are many sandbars to avoid. The shoreline is low and brushy, and there are many dead trees above the shoreline. If the wind is strong from the southeast, this will be a difficult section to paddle. The Hazleton Ramp, at the old ferry crossing, is on the left, just above mile 1,277 (46.52740/-100.54305). The Fort Rice high water ramp is 2 miles downriver on the right (46.50569/-100.58363). A mile up the road to the north is a gas station. A half mile downstream is the Fort Rice low water ramp, with primitive camping, a vault toilet, picnic tables, and fire rings. There is limited shade here. There are some houses within walking distance, so you may be able to get your water jugs filled. You'll really know that the gods are smiling in your direction if, while you are walking up the road to get some water, you encounter a Schwan's truck and score a half gallon of ice cream and a big stick of beef summer sausage. I did.

LAKE OAHE: Fort Rice ramp to Beaver Creek: ~ 20 miles *(Map 2.F.2)*

The Lake Oahe ACE map shows a facility named Badger Bay across the river from the Fort Rice ramps. I saw no evidence of this facility. From Fort Rice to Beaver Creek Campground is about 20 miles. There are few places to camp along the way, so unless it is still early in the day I recommend you camp at Fort Rice. You will paddle under a power line near mile 1,272. The Cannonball River joins the Missouri on the right at mile 1,270.5. Below this, at low water levels the channel meanders and you will need good light to follow the braided channel through a 10-mile-long series of mudflats. As I neared the end of this morass, I made the mistake of thinking I saw a shortcut that would cut a mile or so from my effort to get to open water. The smaller channel I took initially looked like it would get me to the downstream end of the mudflats. It did not. It took me two hours of work through knee-deep mud to get back into the main channel.

After I extricated myself from the mudflat at mile 1,260, I worked my way over to the left side, which appeared to be deeper water. As I approached the shore I could see a point ahead. And I could see a cloud of dust was blowing fast toward me, so I got close in to shore. The wind picked up quickly to 30 or 40 mph, and I was enveloped in a dust storm that lasted for half an hour. I could barely see the shoreline 20 feet in front of me. I came to a ramp (mile 1,259; 46.29311/-100.56731) and pulled in to wait out the storm. This turned out to be the Beaver Creek low-water ramp. After the wind subsided I continued on.

The river narrows one last time at mile 1,258, and then becomes progressively wider. At this point, Lake Oahe finally shows itself. Walker Bottom and the Prairie Knights (Casino) Marina (701-854-7777) are near mile 1,256. This is a developed campground, with showers in the bathrooms, RV hookups, and a telephone. When I paddled by the marina in 2003, the one ramp that I saw was well out of the water, and the facility appeared marginal. However, when

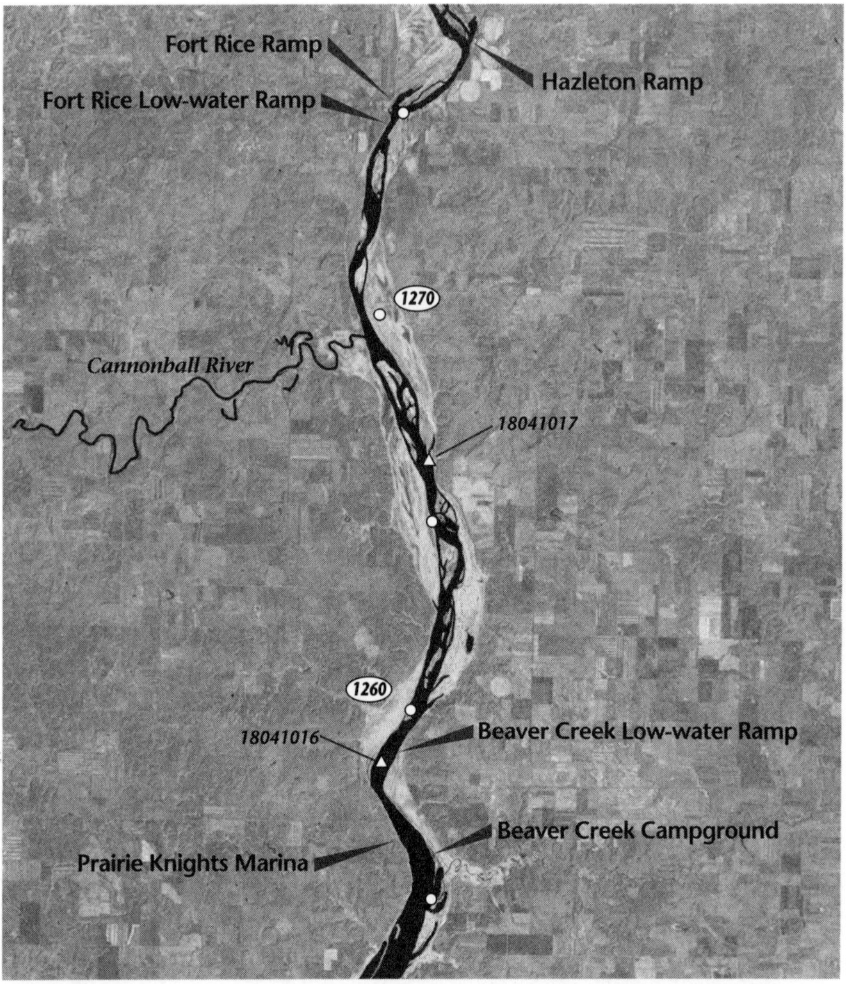

Map 2.F.2: Lake Oahe: Fort Rice (mile 1,275) to Beaver Creek Campground and ramp (mile 1,255.6). Below the Cannonball River is an extensive area of mudflats and braided channels.

I spoke with personnel at the marina in August 2004, I was told that they were operational and would welcome paddlers.

Almost directly across the river is Beaver Bay and the Beaver Creek Campground. This is a well-run campground with shaded campsites. There is a bathroom with great hot showers. To get into the Beaver Creek Campground you will have to paddle 0.5 mile farther to the south to find the entrance to Beaver Creek (mile 1255.6 left; 46.25065/-100.53946). Once you locate the

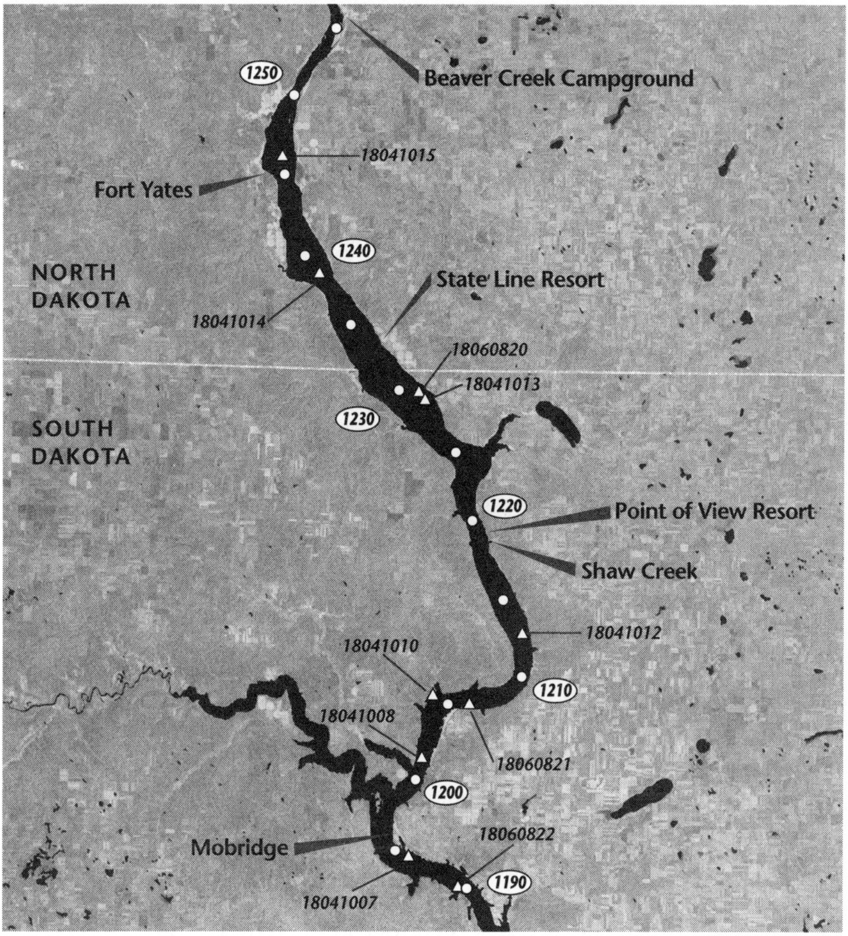

Map 2.F.3: Lake Oahe: Beaver Creek Campground (mile 1,255.6) to Mobridge (~ mile 1,195).

entrance, you will paddle more than a mile upstream to the ramp. At low water, the end of the ramp will be more than 20 yards from the creek. Nevertheless, this is a very good stop. At the time I was here the campground host was Don Hatfield, an ACE park ranger. Don brought his truck down to the ramp to help me get my gear to a campsite. We hit it off immediately.

Don turned out to be an articulate, straight-talking, Redman-tobacco-chewing cowboy. We spent a good bit of time together talking about Lake Oahe, going over the maps I had, and talking about water safety issues in general. Don asked good questions about my effort and my equipment. Over the course of our discussion, I also got to know a bit about his remarkable background. In his earlier incarnations Don was a rancher and elk hunt outfitter. As a young man, he was a member of an Army Airborne unit and had parachuted into Europe in World War II. We talked about the Lewis and Clark Expedition, and it was clear that he had read the journals. Also, we talked about Ambrose's book, *Undaunted Courage*. We agreed that we liked the book because Ambrose had been "out there"; he had traveled and camped along the trail. As Don put it to me, when speaking of another of Ambrose's books, *Band of Brothers,* "he got it right." There is no question in my mind that Don would know.

That night as I recorded the day's events in my journal, I wrote about Don, noting how much I appreciated his help. An outdoorsman, with a profound respect for the forces of nature based on a lifetime of outdoor work and adventure, he clearly has a low threshold for foolishness. If you were to spend some time with him, I am sure you'd get his message: "You go out there prepared, you look after yourself and take care of your gear, and you don't put others at risk." Before I left the next day, Don drove me up to the overlook above the campground. We looked out at the maze of mudflats and shallows that I had threaded through, and then down at the lake. There was a long stand of submerged trees along the left shore. We talked about the best way through, which side of the lake I should go down, and how much different this would be at higher water levels. Before I shoved off, I asked him to use my camera to take a couple pictures of me. I had virtually no pictures of me with my boat along the river. He took a couple of excellent photographs.

- **Lake Oahe: Beaver Creek Campground (mile 1,255.6) to Mobridge (~ mile 1,195)** ***(Map 2.F.3)***

- **River miles:** 60.6
- **Difficulty level:** High
- **Typical time to complete:** 3 to 6 days

It is poison—rank poison to knuckle down to care and hardships. They must come to us all, albeit in different shapes—and we may not escape them—it is not possible—but we may swindle them out of half of their puissance with a stiff upper lip.

MARK TWAIN'S *LETTERS TO WILL BOWEN*

This is where you get on the real Lake Oahe. High winds, large waves, and submerged trees form a triple threat of hazards that have caused many to reconsider their vow to paddle the entire Missouri River. I heard many stories about paddlers that made it just a little ways up or down this section, and either came to understand their peril and turned around, or were beaten back by brutal winds and high waves. Included among the paddlers that decided to get a ride around the lake are some highly experienced folks, and their numbers include some that had paddled upstream from St. Louis. The decision to bail under these circumstances is understandable and prudent.

Under the best of Lake Oahe conditions, you will be going into a stiff wind perhaps half the time, sometimes only making a mile or two an hour. If you decide to make passage on this lake, you had better understand that this lake kicks up fast and you need to be near the shore so you can get off quickly. Forget your schedule. Between Beaver Creek and Mobridge, South Dakota, there are extensive groves of submerged trees. These are particularly hazardous obstacles. They can prevent your access to the shore. Large branches and tree trunks break free and have the potential to become wave-driven battering rams. If you do decide to make this passage, I guarantee that you will be surprised on at least one occasion by a stealth tree trunk, branch, or log lurking just below the surface. You can decide to bypass these upper Lake Oahe water hazards. If you want to get back on the lake below most of the submerged trees, you might be able to arrange a portage from Beaver Creek to Mobridge.

In my opinion, you should only attempt this passage if you are an experienced paddler, if the weather forecast is good, and–maybe–if you're feeling lucky. In any event, you'll need to proceed with caution. In talking with paddlers who have successfully navigated this lake, all made the point that you must be very patient on Oahe. There will be days when you will pull off the lake after only an hour or two of paddling because the wind suddenly blows up, and some early mornings when the wind is blowing so hard that you will decide not to leave the tent. Many Lake Oahe boaters that I talked with in 2002 suggested that paddlers should stay close along the east (left descending) shore, relating that the weather had settled in a pattern of predominantly southeast winds. However, they also noted that most of the really bad winds, and thunderstorms came out of the northwest. Because this lake trends mostly along a north-south axis, if you stay along the east shore you gain relatively consistent protection during sustained periods of southeast winds. When a really hard wind comes fast out of the northwest, it will blow you to shore, not across the lake. I generally followed the east shore as I made my way down the lake.

Finally, make sure to listen to NOAA weather radio at least two or three times during the day. Reception can be problematic, so when you come ashore at midday you may need to hike to some elevation to get the forecast. Watch for snakes. Also, ask any anglers that you meet about the weather forecast; they may be able to update your information.

Information/Maps/Resources

Information sources for the North Dakota section of Lake Oahe are listed in the previous section. Information on South Dakota's Lake Oahe boat ramps, parks, and recreation areas can be found by following the links at www.sdgfp.info/parks. Navigate to the "Publications" section of this site to download campground maps, a pamphlet titled *Canoeing and Kayaking in South Dakota,* and a booklet, *Birding in SD State Parks*. Current information about ACE facilities on Lake Oahe can be found at www.nwo.usace.army.mil/html/Lake_Proj/index.html.

Suggested Readings

Twenty-two Lewis and Clark campsites are in this section. Information about what transpired here during the outbound trip (September 28 to October 15, 1804) can be found in Vol. 3:123–175 (*Journals,* [Moulton, ed.]). Return trip event detail (August 20–25, 1806 can be found in Vol. 8:310–323. Additional context is found in Stephen Ambrose's *Undaunted Courage,* in chapter 14:174–182.

In addition, my favorite source for ruminations about Lake Oahe's cultural and natural landscapes is William Least Heat-Moon's *River-Horse,* pages 271–288.

Paddler's Notes and Cautions

At normal water levels, Lake Oahe nearly triples in width about 5 miles below Beaver Creek, near mile 1,250. At low water levels, many ramps and camping areas are 0.25 mile or more from the water. To get a suitable campsite, you may have to slog through several hundred yards of mud before you get to firm ground. It is critical that you contact appropriate agencies for up-to-date information.

As you approach Fort Yates in the Standing Rock Sioux Indian Reservation (~ mile 1,244 right), extensive areas of submerged trees begin off the east shore. A ramp, primitive campground, and picnic shelter is at the north edge of Fort Yates (46.10447/-100.63279). Across from Fort Yates is the Cattail Bay

(Winona) ramp. I could not find a way into this area because of low water and submerged trees. I estimated that the ramp might be about a quarter mile inland. As I worked south from here along the east shore, I threaded my way along areas of submerged trees until I reached Langelier Bay at mile 1,235 left. There is primitive camping here, and water at the fish cleaning station. The State Line Resort (701-336-7765) is less than 2 miles down the shore. There is a ramp (45.95845/-100.48038), and on the bluff above, a nice restaurant along with camping, a hot shower, and a Laundromat. The owners, Ken and Dana Moser, are friendly and flexible; they allowed me to pitch my tent in the windbreak by the restaurant, where I was able to enjoy some shade.

The border between North and South Dakota is not marked, but it is just below the resort near mile 1,232. You will know that you have arrived in South Dakota when you paddle below the north end of State Line Bay on the west (right) shore. Six miles downriver, the lake briefly narrows to less than 1.5 miles across and then widens again. On the left near mile 1,224 is Pollock Bay. At low water the ramps up this bay are unusable. Three miles to the south on the left is the Point of View Resort (mile 1,221; 45.82698/ -100.36805) at Ritter Bay. This is a good stop. The owner, Bob Shadwell (605-889-2326), has hosted many paddlers. Although low water has made the resort's dock unusable, you can pull out along the shore and walk up to the resort. The take-out may be muddy so locate the firmest ground that you can find. At the Point of View Resort, there is a bar and restaurant, cabins with hot showers, and campsites.

When I pulled in here, I did not know exactly where the resort was. There were a number of homes and cabins along the shore. I was fortunate enough to meet Dean Ulmer, a stockman and rancher, who was chasing his cattle back over a section of fence that they had knocked down. I helped him direct the herd back to where they belonged, and he gave me a ride up to the resort, introduced me to Bob, and bought me lunch. We talked for a while, and Bob suggested that I stay the night. Although I had made only 14 miles so far that day, I could not turn down Bob's hospitality or the chance to learn more about the lake. Besides running the resort, Bob is a professional fishing guide, so he knew the lake well. Before Dean departed for Mobridge, he gave me his phone number and told me to call him when I got to Mobridge, a day's paddle to the south.

Later that afternoon I walked down to my kayak to get a few things and make sure my boat was secure. As I was starting back to the resort, a man drove up in a John Deere four-wheeler. He turned out to be Don Barr, a local fishing guide who works for Whitlock's Resort in Pollack. We talked for a while about the lake, and he offered to drive me back to Point of View. On the way back we stopped at his cabins, and he showed me an old collection of framed arrowheads. We talked about the problem of relic hunters working the shorelines of the lake for "archaeological materials," including bones and skulls. With low water levels, more sites are exposed. We shared the opinion that it would be very bad karma to disturb any of this material. Don, a former Green Beret and Vietnam veteran, is one of a number of locals keeping an eye out for looters. If you do see any cultural material, leave it where it remains. It is against the law to destroy, excavate, or remove any archaeological materials. If you discover materials, you should note the location (GPS the coordinates) and relay the information to the local authorities.

My chance encounter with Don got me thinking about the inappropriateness of this area for "geocaching," the practice of GPS-directed prospecting for caches left at published coordinates. Besides appearing as suspicious behavior, the process of hunting around for a hidden item could be easily mistaken as a search for antiquities. Locals have zero tolerance for grave robbers. As one area resident related to me, "if you are in the wrong place at the wrong time, you might well get the shit kicked out of you before you can protest your innocence."

While visiting with Bob at Point of View, I learned that he had only owned the resort for a couple years. He had always dreamed of owning his own fishing resort and was now in the process of making his dream a reality. Before he took over the property, the resort had been the object of some neglect. He was clearly making progress toward revitalizing the place, even though the lake's low water level had caused the waterline to retreat more than 100 yards from the resort dock. Bob and his clients have to put in at the Shaw Creek ramp, about 2 river miles to the south. Over dinner that night we talked about walleye fishing, water level issues, and restoring classic pickup trucks. The next morning, after breakfast, I resumed my expedition down the lake.

After the Point of View Resort you will pass the Shaw Creek ramp at mile 1,218.6 right (45.7974/-100.34380). Along this shore, to the south, are some trees and a couple potential campsites. The west shore becomes steep and barren. Along the east side you will once again encounter submerged trees and see tree trunks standing in the water. At about mile 1,215, on the left, you will see a road leading to Hanson Bay. Three miles farther down, the lake begins a 6-mile-long bend to the west. Rorgo Bay is near the start of this bend. My map shows a gravel road leading to this bay, but I did not see a road when I passed.

The lake then begins a 7-mile run to the south. I stayed along the east shore for both these sections. As you get closer to Mobridge, the water will become shallow, and there are patches of submerged trees and stumps along your approach to the railroad bridge. There are few opportunities to pull out anywhere along this section until you get near the bridge. There is a level and firm area of shoreline just after you pass Water Plant Bay (mile 1,198.6 left).

Your choices for camping in the immediate Mobridge area are limited. The Country Camping RV Park is about a quarter mile inland from the area just before the Highway 12 bridge (~ mile 1,197.7). Unfortunately there is no easy way to get your boat and gear up a steep ravine and across the railroad tracks between this campground and the river. The Indian Memorial Campground is on the west side of the lake. To get there you'll have to paddle more than 1 mile across the lake, and then 1 mile back to the north to the ramp. Because the wind can pick up quickly in this area, I recommend that you stay on the east side. Four miles below the bridge, you will see the town of Mobridge. However, at low water levels, nearly a mile of mudflats separates the town from the river's edge. I suggest that you continue on for about 3 miles, past the ramp at Revheim Bay, and put in at the Bridge City Marina (mile 1191.4; 45.51594/-100.38811). The marina is adjacent to the Indian Creek Campground, about 3 miles from town. The park ramp is a mile farther down, inside Indian Creek Bay.

The owners of the marina (605-845-9129) are Jerry and Janice Frailing. Over the years, Jerry has assisted paddlers in countless ways, including arranging transportation into town for supplies and helping paddlers connect with people to arrange shuttles to West Whitlock or Oahe Dam for those who decide to quit the lake. Ask for permission to tie your boat up at the dock. It will be safe here. There is a "convenience" store at the office, and if you are inclined, you can rent a cabin. Jerry is a reliable source for current information about the lake. The Indian Creek Campground is right next to the marina. This campground has all the amenities, everyone on the staff is friendly, and the place is one of the best run campgrounds that I visited.

Mobridge is worth a visit. There are grocery stores in town, and a very good meat market where you can get some excellent buffalo jerky. A Burger King is next door. There is a downtown with a good selection of bars, a public library where you check your e-mails, and a nice local history museum at the north end of town. The stock auction barn is worth a visit if it is open. Dean Ulmer, whom I met at Point of View, invited me to visit and observe the proceedings of a cattle sale. I was able to sit in the bleachers above the sale corral and watch the bidding action for cattle sold singly or in groups. I was lucky to sit next to a bidder who graciously answered my questions about what was happening. Many of the cattle were being sold off because of the drought; ranchers could not afford to truck in hay or to ship their cattle to greener pastures farther south.

At the campground I met Lynnard and Catherine Spiry. Lynnard introduced himself by walking over to my tent and saying, "You're not from around here, are you?" I said, "No, sir." He suggested that I face the door of my tent in the opposite direction. I had aligned it with the door facing to the northwest. He explained that we would be getting a storm that night, and that it would probably come from the northwest. I thanked him for the information, turned my tent entrance to the southeast, and put out my storm lines. A little while later he called out from his camper across the lane, "Young fella, you look like you could use a meal. Come on over and have some pork chops." I walked over, met his wife, kids, and grandkids, and had a great meal. Later on, after I had explained that I was a geographer working on a guidebook, I learned that Lynnard had grown up on a farm near the park and worked in fields now under Lake Oahe waters. Lynnard contacted his brother Jim, a former sheriff, who brought over old river survey maps and photographs. We spent a couple hours talking about Mobridge before the dam changed the river into a lake. Before I departed the next day, Jim took me to see the local sights, including the museum and the Sitting Bull Memorial, on the west side of the lake.

◆ Lake Oahe: Mobridge (~ mile 1,195) to Bush's Landing (mile 1,125) *(Map 2.F.4)*

- **River miles:** 70
- **Difficulty level:** High
- **Typical time to complete:** 5 to 10 days

There are times when the Missouri seems so long, you wonder how it ever manages to flow up and over the curvature of the earth.

WILLIAM LEAST HEAT-MOON, *RIVER-HORSE*

On the left as you paddle downstream from the Indian Creek Campground, you first pass Blue Blanket Bay and then come to Thomas Bay at mile 1,185.6, where there is a ramp, a vault toilet, and drinking water. Less than 4 miles

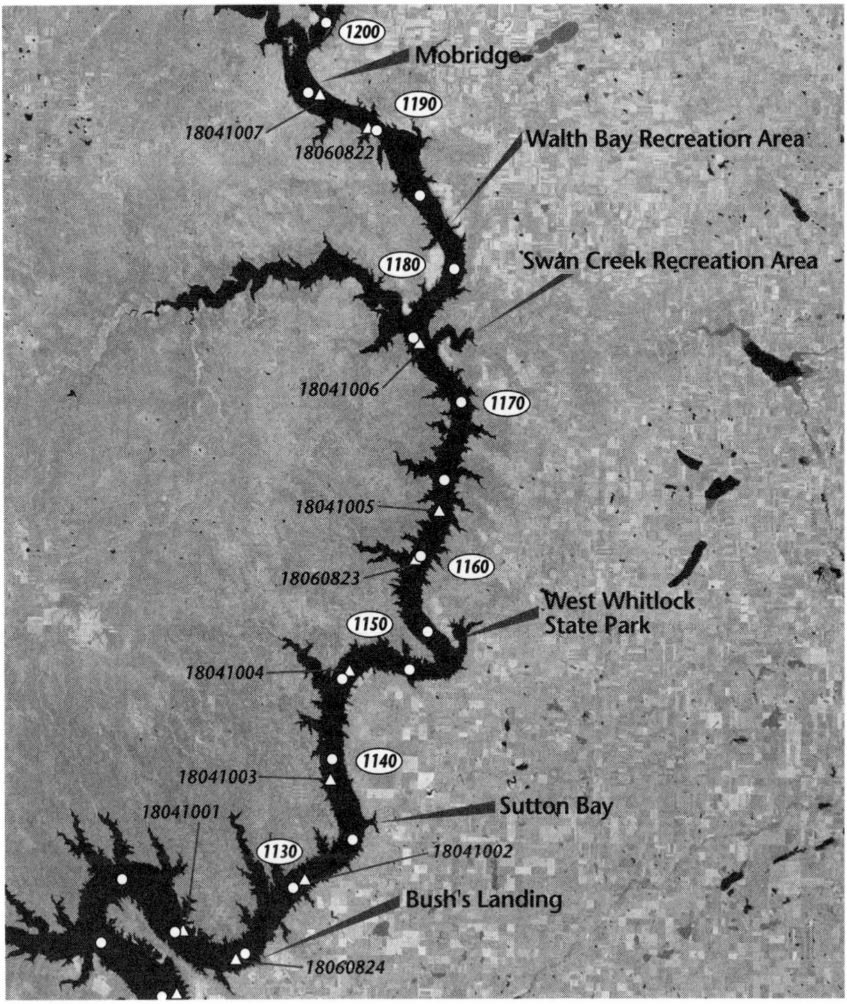

Map 2.F.4: Lake Oahe from mile 1,200 above Mobridge to Bush's Landing at mile 1,125.

farther down is Walth Bay (left; 45.41117/-100.27203), where there is a ramp, camping, a vault toilet, and drinking water. This area is occupied by locals for most of the summer. Their RVs were all attached by hoses to the one water source at the campground. I had to ask one RV owner to detach his hose so I could get water. Between the music, four-wheelers, and fireworks, everyone seemed to be having a good time. It was pretty wild and noisy the night I camped here.

I recommend that you continue along the east shore beyond Walth Bay. At mile 1,181, the lake turns to the southwest. After 5 miles, the lake will again turn to the south. When you get beyond mile 1,175, you will see the entrance to Swan Creek. The Swan Creek Recreation Area is 2.7 miles up this bay; there is a ramp, developed campsites, toilets, and showers. I did not visit this area because I was not interested in paddling the extra miles to get in from and then back out on the lake. Although it was brutally hot, it was only midmorning, and I still had a good supply of water in my jugs.

The Le Beau ramp is 3 miles down the left shore (mile 1,172; 45.27466/ -100.26398). There are some trees for shade here and a vault toilet. In an emergency this would make a decent camp, although there is no source for drinking water. After paddling by a series of bays for the next 7 miles, you will arrive at a small bay leading to the Dodge Draw ramp (mile 1,164.3 left; 45.17525/ -100.26600). There is a vault toilet here, some shade to rest under, and a sheltered area where you might pitch a tent if the weather turns nasty. I camped here; this is a good place to stay to prepare for an early morning departure to West Whitlock Bay, about a dozen miles down the shore on the left, where there is a very nice state park.

The last 6 miles to Whitlock's Bay can be absolutely brutal if there is a southeast wind. Although I left Dodge Draw very early in the morning, I ran into a strong headwind about halfway to Whitlock's. I struggled to make 2 miles an hour against a strong headwind that seemed to funnel right up the lake. When I finally turned into Whitlock's Bay at mile 1,153, I was pretty well spent. Once I got inside the bay and around the point, I had to contend with a following sea with 3- to 4-foot waves. It was not easy going. I pulled in at the swimming beach (45.04158/-100.25587), which seemed to offer the best chance for a soft landing. You will find this beach if you look for a brown bathhouse above a big sandy beach. It turned out that this was a good choice since the shore gets a bit rocky as you work around the next point to the boat ramp. This is also a good place to pull out because there are nice shady tent sites just across the road from the swimming area. If you want free camping, you will find primitive campsites, water, and vault toilets at East Whitlock, on the east side of the bay.

The West Whitlock State Park has all the amenities and shade. You'll need to walk up to the park entrance booth to arrange the necessary paperwork and pay for a campsite. There is a full-size earth lodge here that you should visit. Within easy walking distance is the West Whitlock Resort (605-765-9174). The owners, Monty and Nancy Cronin, are friendly and helpful. At the resort there is a bar, a convenience store, and a place to do your laundry. This is the early morning and lunchtime hangout for local residents and park staff. It is a good place to meet good folks, get local color, hear some great fish stories, try a "red beer," and crunch down on a meal of deep-fried chicken gizzards dipped in ranch dressing. If you have or are able to arrange transportation, there are two very good steak houses nearby. Get information about these restaurants at the bar.

Make sure that you have good weather before you get back on the lake. When the wind starts blowing, as it does almost every afternoon, the area between Whitlock's Bay and the Highway 212 bridge gets very rough. An early morning departure is a good idea. If there is no wind when you depart from the swim beach, you can cut across to the point on the west side, paddle under the bridge, and then angle across the lake to get back to the left (east) side. Or you can push off from the beach and head due east to get along the left descending shore. In either event, you want to go down the bulk of this lake on the left side because this provides better shelter from the very frequent southeast winds. If you do get northwest winds, this shoreline is jagged enough to provide frequent shelter as you work your way around points and by bays. There is virtually no cell phone service until you get near the dam, some 80 river miles down the lake.

There are three ramps on the left shore before the Highway 212 bridge. The first is the South Whitlock's ramp at about mile 1,152; the second is the Bob's Resort ramp, and the third is Highway 212 bridge access, just before the bridge at mile 1,151.4. After you pass under the bridge, the first large bay on the east shore is Swede's Draw (mile 1,150). From this bay you will paddle a couple more miles to a point where the lake cuts sharply to the south. As you work your way down this relatively barren shore you will probably see cattle at the water's edge. There are few decent campsites. If the wind picks up, and most days it will, a good destination for the day is Sutton Bay at mile 1,137, where there is a ramp (44.88150/-100.36082) and a vault toilet. But there is no source for water, and you are out of range of NOAA weather radio.

If the weather holds, you might consider going on to Bush's Landing, at mile 1,125. Assuming that you left from Whitlock, this would make for a 28-mile day, which is a very good day's paddle on this lake. Do not expect to get this kind of mileage consistently. If there is any question about the weather, stay at Sutton. There is little vegetation along the shore between Sutton and Bush's Landing, and at low water levels you will have to traverse a long area of mud-flats to get to shore.

At Bush's there is a ramp (44.75495/-100.51527) and a vault toilet. You can find a campsite off to the side of the ramp, but keep an eye out for snakes as you work through the brush. The Sunset Lodge (605-264-5480) is about half a mile up the road. Most of the anglers pulling their boats out at the ramp will be happy to give you a lift to the lodge. At the lodge there is a telephone, convenience store, a bar, restaurant, and motel. This is another "paddler-friendly" stop. Take your towel with you and a change of clothes. You can get a shower here and a great meal. The bartender will help arrange a ride back to the ramp. If you spend some time at the bar, you should be able to get an accurate weather forecast, up-to-date information about conditions downstream, and good local color. If the weather report is good, get to bed early. The next 20 miles ahead can be some of the most difficult water you will ever paddle.

- **Lake Oahe: Bush's Landing (mile 1,125) and Little Bend to Oahe Dam take-out (mile 1,072.7)** ***(Map 2.F.5)***

- **River miles:** 52.3
- **Difficulty level:** High
- **Typical time to complete:** 3 to 7 days

Just beyond Bush's Landing you will begin to work your way around Little Bend, an 8-mile-long projection of land that creates a tight U-shaped bend. Here some cautions are in order. Every fisherman that I talked with told me that the waters at and around the "bottom" of this bend can be very rough. The Cheyenne River flows into the lake on the downstream right side, and a southeast wind will generate large waves and confused seas near the confluence. There are few places along the shore where there is any shelter if a storm blows up and you have to pitch a tent. Further compounding the difficulty is the fact that you cannot see the horizon to the south and west as you work your way along the upstream side of the point. Your view is blocked by a string of hills, and you do not get your first look at weather that might be moving in until you round the point. Once you round the bend and get halfway along the downstream side, you will reach the Little Bend ramp and primitive campground. Here also there is little shelter. So navigating safely around Little Bend is a challenge best attempted during fair weather.

If a period of bad weather has settled in, for example, several days of strong

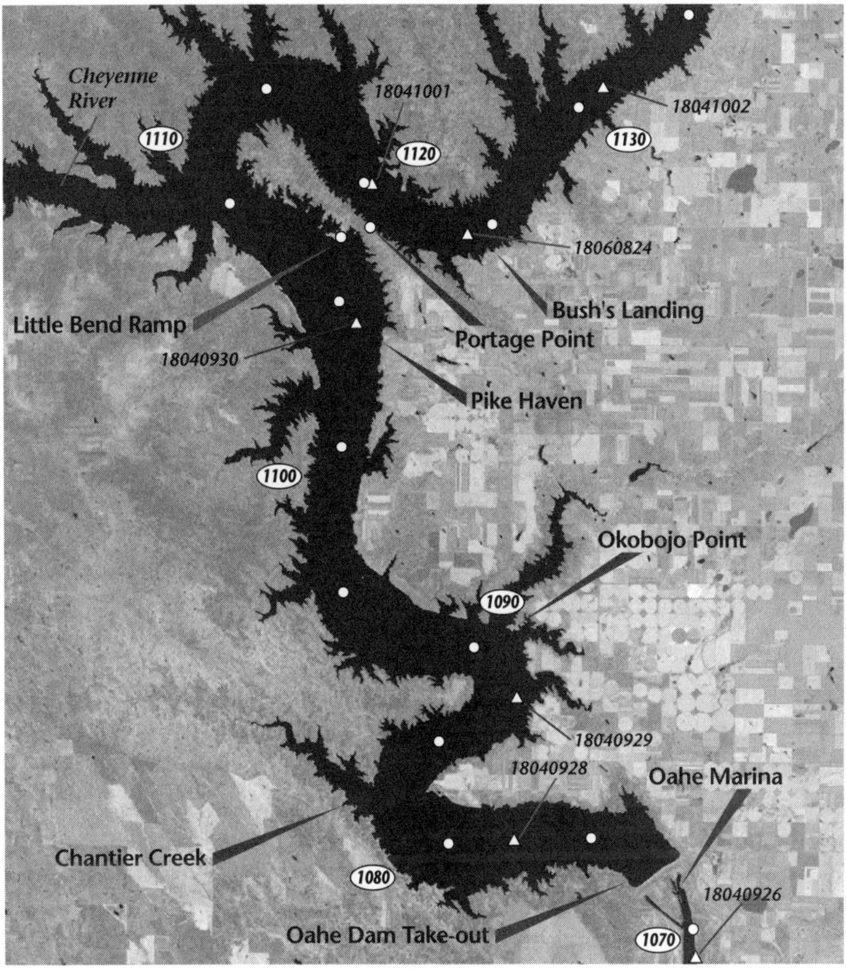

Map 2.F.5: Lake Oahe: Bush's Landing (mile 1,125) and Little Bend to Oahe Dam take-out (mile 1,072.7). Map shows a possible portage route near mile 1,121. A portage across the neck of the peninsula to the Little Bend ramp at mile 1,106 would be difficult but not impossible. If a period of bad weather sets in, conditions around the tip of Little Bend can become extremely rough, and nasty conditions can last for days; when this occurs a portage may be the only way to get below this feature.

winds or the weather report calls for severe late afternoon thunderstorms, you should not attempt this passage. Also, because of Little Bend's northwest to southeast aspect and because prevailing winds are from either of those directions, you probably will have to work against headwinds for half the distance around the bend. So you have three choices: You can try to arrange a portage to Pike Haven Resort on the other side of the bend, you can "manually" portage the bend, or you can wait at Bush's for good weather.

A manual portage across Little Bend is very difficult, but not impossible. As the crow flies, the distance is about ½ mile. You will have to get your gear and boat through weeds and brush, up a steep hill, across the road, and down to the water on the other side. You must watch where you put your feet. There is a healthy population of rattlesnakes on Little Bend. The portage route begins at the head of a small bay at mile 1,121 (44.76235/-100.61417). Scout to the southwest to find the best route up the bank and low hills. Within a quarter mile you will come to a road that leads to the boat ramp. From here, you can either take the road to the ramp (~ 1 mile, you will see it) or work your way down to the head of the bay lying about a quarter mile below. If you are lucky, you'll get your boat and gear to the road and someone in a truck will stop to help you finish your portage. I scouted this route in July 2003; at that time water levels were low, but the shoreline was relatively firm. Do not attempt this portage if it has recently rained, as the hillsides and ravines will be impossible to climb because of slick mud. And again, this will be a difficult portage, and you must keep an eye out for rattlesnakes.

The paddle from Bush's Landing along the upstream side of Little Bend to the point (mile 1,114) is about 11 miles. The shoreline is rugged but picturesque. There are numerous small bays, and in good weather this is a delightful stretch. It is about 3.5 miles around the tip of the peninsula. As you finish rounding the point, you will get your first good look at the sky to the west and south. Across the lake you will see the confluence of the Cheyenne River. If you have been living right, the sky will be clear, the wind will be calm, and the waves will be less than 4 feet.

If you have not been living right, like the rest of us, my Little Bend storm experience should be illuminating. When I rounded the point in July 2003, there was a very black sky to the southwest. A line of thunderstorms was advancing toward Little Bend and the Cheyenne River. I could see the repeated flashing of lightning. I immediately started looking for a campsite with some shelter. I ended up paddling for more than 2 miles before a strong headwind forced me to come ashore at mile 1,110. By this time it was clear that I was in the storm track, so I secured my boat and searched for a campsite with some shelter. The wind velocity continued to increase; I could find no shelter, so I set up my tent in the best place I could find. I put out long storm lines and piled heavy rocks over each tent stake. I went back to my boat and got my sleeping bag, pad, water jug, and food bag. It started to rain hard and I ran back to the tent.

Within minutes of securing my tent and crawling into my sleeping bag I was caught in a supremely violent thunderstorm. Windblown rain slammed my tent like someone turned a fire hose on it. Hail hammered the rain fly. Lightning struck nearby, shaking the ground under me. About the time I was thinking that conditions couldn't possibly get worse, sustained wind gusts literally flattened my tent to the ground, and held it there for more than 15 minutes. I was completely pancaked; the wind pressed the tent fabric down on me so tightly that I could scarcely breathe. But my tent held. After the wind died, it returned to near its original shape.

I was feeling pretty good about my survival, when I noticed something moving between the tent and the rain fly. A large rattlesnake had taken shelter with me during the storm. He coiled and began rattling. I froze. To my considerable relief, he eventually calmed down and slipped away into the brush.

So take it from me–even without the snake issue–this Little Bend area can be a very difficult feature to successfully navigate. Powerful summer storms, and the "straight winds" that accompany them, are not uncommon. They come up fast, and blow like hell. Velocities of 80 to 100 mph are not uncommon. If you elect to paddle around Little Bend, do so during good weather. Get off the lake quickly if conditions start to sour. Secure your boat, find the best campsite you can, get your tent up quickly, and set out storm lines. Set big rocks over your tent stakes, crawl in, and hunker down.

If you are fortunate enough to experience continued good weather and light winds after you round the point, continue to make your way along the left shoreline. The Little Bend ramp is inside the bay at mile 1,106. There is camping along the shore nearby; you will see it as you approach. At the campsites there are vault toilets, picnic tables, and fire rings. There is no source for drinking water. I was told by several locals to watch out for rattlesnakes if I camped here. The Little Bend ramp is 19 miles from Bush's Landing. If you can, I suggest you continue along the shore for another 4.5 miles to the Pike Haven Resort (605-264-5465). This resort is just up the hill from the ramp at mile 1,104.6 (44.70816/-100.60119). You can camp here; there is a nice bathroom and shower house. This is an angler's resort, but you will be welcomed here. The people are friendly and helpful, and there is an excellent steak house. The restaurant advertises that it has "the best steak on the river." They got that right–I was served one of the best steaks that I have ever tasted. Order the rib eye.

From Pike Haven to Oahe Dam is about 32 miles. With good weather and a solid effort, you can make the dam in a full day's paddle. Stay along the east shore. After you paddle by mile 1,102, keep an eye out for a large herd of horses. I was fortunate enough to watch a herd come down to the shore to water. Mixed in with the solid-color horses, the blacks and red-browns, were several pintos. For all intents they looked just like a wild herd. I was quite intrigued because until now, after more than 1,000 miles of paddling, I'd seen only herds of cattle and buffalo.

Below mile 1,100 you will pass a large bay known as Mail Shack Creek. According to the folks at Pike Haven Resort, this bay provides excellent shelter during really bad storms. The ruins of Fort Sully are along the shore somewhere to the northeast as you paddle by mile 1,095. From here the lake turns to the east, and then turns sharply back to the west. If the weather is good, you can cut across to the point on the west shore. Depending on the angle that you take, this can be a 2- to 3-mile crossing. Along the tip of this point, there are several nice small bays and what looked to be decent campsites. To cut corners and save some paddling, I cut back to the east shore at about mile 1,087. Then I worked my way around the point, and pulled in to Peoria Flats (mile 1,079) to set up for a 4-mile open water crossing to the opposite side. I almost got stuck at Peoria Flats. The wind picked up, and I had to wait until almost 6 P.M. before it got calm enough to cross over to the ramp on the right (west) shore near the dam. If I were to do this section again, I would stay on that side all the way to the dam, once I crossed over to the point on the west side below Fort Sully.

The Lake Oahe take-out is on the west side at mile 1,072.7 (44.44528/ -100.42200). You will not see the take-out as you work your way along the west shore until you round the final point. A manual portage to the downstream side of the dam, either to the marina below the dam or to Campground 3 below the stilling basin, is more than 2 miles. Get a ride. Many of the folks staying at the Oahe Downstream Campground use this ramp (West Side) to put their boats in when they fish Lake Oahe. After they pull their boat out, you might ask for assistance in portaging your boat and gear. If no one is around, you can get cell phone reception if you climb one of the small hills above the parking lot. The Oahe Marina and Resort (605-223-2627) will portage you for a modest fee, but expect some delay, as they will need to work you into the schedule. Down's Marina in Pierre (605-224-5533) also provides portage service, but they typically haul larger watercraft, and because they have to come from Pierre, their fee may be prohibitive.

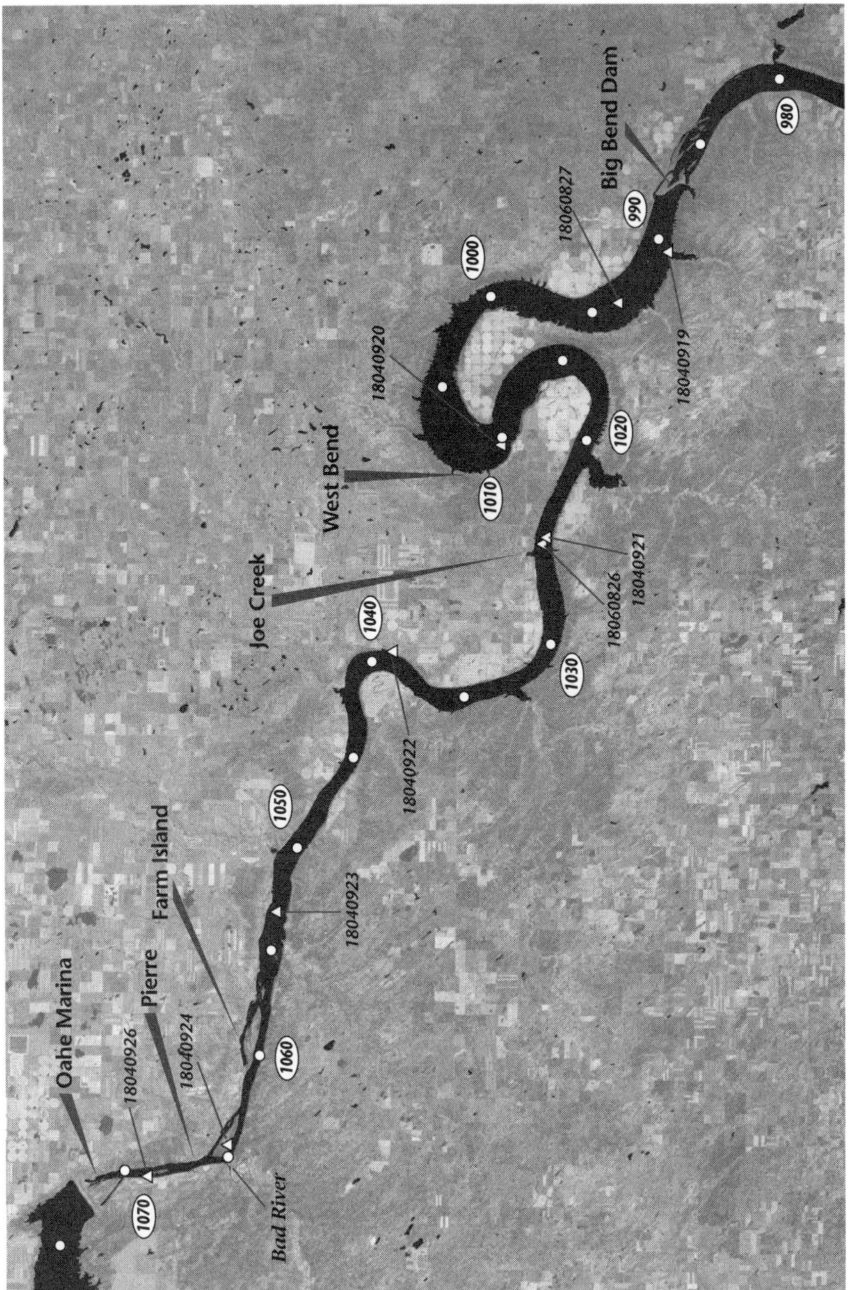

Map 2.G.1: Lake Sharpe from mile 1,071 to Big Bend Dam at mile 987. The central feature of this section is the river's 25-mile-long loop that returns to within 1.5 miles of its starting place.

If you are unable to connect with either of these possibilities, you can call the office at the Oahe Downstream Campground (605-223-7722) and explain that you are a paddler needing help to get from the West Side ramp to the campground. Park officials cannot give you a ride in state vehicles, but they may be able to arrange for a pickup by the campground host. When I spoke with the park supervisor, Pat Busher, he told me that they would "not leave anyone stranded on the ramp." As a paddler you truly appreciate folks with this kind of attitude.

The Oahe Downstream Campground is a very nice stop. There are three campgrounds to choose from, and each has many sites shaded by large cottonwood trees. I recommend getting a campsite close to the water at Campground 2. Sites here will cost more than a tent site because they have electricity, but they allow you access to the marina and bathrooms with showers. The marina has a nice restaurant, bar, convenience store, and rental cabins. Doug Mahowald, the owner, has assisted numerous paddlers, and you should visit with him. Depending on the volume and timing of water releases from the dam, the character of conditions downstream can vary tremendously; Doug or one of his fishing guides will have current information. If you are not concerned about amenities, you can settle for less at Campground 3.

SEGMENT 2.G: Lake Sharpe–Downstream Oahe Campground (mile 1,071) to Big Bend Dam (mile 987) *(Map 2.G.1)*

- **River miles:** 84
- **Difficulty level:** Low to moderate
- **Typical time to complete:** 5 to 7 days

Seven miles above [Big Bend Dam], the Missouri strikes against a hard peninsula that forces it nearly ten miles north before it again reaches a more tractable terrain and turns to resume its southeasterly run to the sea. The Big Bend is, to my mind, more accurately a loop in the shape of a turkey's head, the long neck to the south, the beak to the west. From Lewis and Clark on into steamboat days, passengers sometimes went ashore at the narrow base to take a constitutional over the open but uneven ground to the other side, less than a mile distant today, but three times that before the dam. William Clark reported doing it and so did Prince Maximilian, both of them watching their boats labor around the bulgy spit, land now intensively plowed, a piece one would walk these days only to recapitulate a historical circumstance.

William Least Heat-Moon, *River-Horse*

Introduction to the Segment

When you launch from the campground below Oahe Dam, you begin an 85-river-mile passage on Lake Sharpe, to the take-out at Big Bend Dam. The central feature of this lake is Big Bend, where the river makes a 25-mile-long loop before returning to within 1.5 miles of its starting place. Prairie grasslands surround the lake, and cottonwoods, cedar, ash, and oak grow along streams and in the ravines. As you paddle along the shoreline, you will see extensive areas of irrigated agriculture, fed by Lake Sharpe's water. The lake passes through the Crow Creek Sioux and the Lower Brule Sioux reservations. Permission is necessary to camp on tribal lands.

Information/Maps/Resources

As related in the previous section, information on South Dakota's boat ramps, parks, and recreation areas can be found by following the links at www.sdgfp.info/Parks/Regions/LocatorMap.htm.

I recommend that you get the ACE map, *Lake Sharpe and Big Bend Dam.* Make sure you obtain the July 2000 (or later) edition. This version is particularly well done; the shoreline features are accurately drawn and the Big Bend Dam inset is very useful. This map also provides up-to-date information about recreation areas, emergency phone numbers, and phone numbers to the Crow Creek and the Lower Brule tribal headquarters. Current information about ACE facilities on Lake Sharpe can be found at www.nwo.usace.army.mil/html/Lake_Proj/index.html.

Suggested Readings

There are nine Lewis and Clark campsites in this section. Information about what transpired here during the outbound trip (September 19 to 27, 1804) can be found in Vol. 3:88–123 (*Journals,* [Moulton, ed.]). Return trip event detail (August 26 to 27, 1806) can be found in Vol. 8:323–326. Context about events can be found in Stephen Ambrose's *Undaunted Courage,* in chapter 14:168–174 and in chapter 32:400.

Paddler's Notes and Cautions

Water levels immediately downstream from Oahe Dam vary considerably. During the summer, water releases increase as demand rises for electricity to power air conditioning. So on a hot summer day, the current will be flowing fast by late morning. If you want to make good mileage, time your departure to take advantage of this flow. Pierre, the capital of South Dakota, is less than 6 miles downstream. As you approach Pierre, stay left. At mile 1,067.5 you are about a mile east of the location of Fort Pierre Chouteau, said to be the first military fort in the northwest operating from 1831 to 1859. There is a monument at the fort's former location. After passing under a railroad bridge followed by the Highway 14 bridge, you will come to Steamboat Park. There is a boat ramp at mile 1,065.8 left (44.364350/100.36277) on the causeway connecting to Framboise Island.

Here you have two choices. You can pull out and portage over the causeway to get to Griffin Park (0.6 mile down on the left), where you can camp, or you can continue around Framboise Island and on to Farm Island State Park, 5 miles downstream. Griffin Park offers free camping and good access to the city. Down's Marina is also here (605-224-5533). In any event, this would be a good day stop. A canoe and kayak outfitter, Dakota Adventures (605-224-6572) is in town. If the wind is blowing from the southeast, it would be a good idea to make the portage over the causeway to Griffin Park. There are high bluffs along the right shore that funnel the wind upriver.

I did not make the portage across the causeway; instead I continued downstream, staying left along the Framboise Island shoreline. I wanted to see the Bad River, which joins the Missouri on the right at mile 1,065.2. Here, Lewis and Clark first met the Teton Sioux, and this is where a firefight nearly erupted that surely would have ended the expedition. Lilly Park is at the mouth of the river. There are camping sites and a picnic shelter here.

There are buoys at the entrance to the channel leading in to Griffin Park just below mile 1,063. Powerboats and personal watercraft speed in and out of this channel, so watch for traffic as you pass this entrance. The upstream ramp at Farm Island Recreation Area is 2 miles farther down on the left (mile 1,061). The narrow channel leading to the ramp is not marked and is difficult to locate. Here is where a GPS unit is very helpful. The ramp coordinates are 44.33993/-100.28623. Set your unit to navigate to this position. Stay along the left shore until your unit indicates that you have passed the ramp and that it is behind you and to the northwest. Continue paddling, but look back to the northwest frequently; within a tenth of a mile you should see a narrow channel. Follow this channel in for about 250 yards to the ramp. As you get close to the ramp you may see anglers sitting beside the ramp. This is a favorite fishing hole for catfish.

I doubt that I would have found the entrance to the Farm Island ramp without help from my GPS unit. If you miss the upstream entrance and still want to get to Farm Island, you will have to paddle 3.5 miles to the downstream entrance and then another 2.5 miles up Hipple Bay to get to the campground. When you get to the ramp, use your cell phone to call the office of the Farm Island Campground (605-224-5605). You know the drill from here. There are nice waterfront sites at the main campground and bathrooms with showers. The East Campground is where locals tent-camp. There is shade and water, but it is a 15-minute walk to a shower and flush toilet. On the weekend this is a busy and noisy campground. There is a swimming beach, and just offshore, personal watercraft operators speed at each other with insane velocity. Stay at the main campground if there is space. A 4-mile-long nature walk trail connects the campground to Pierre.

The shoreline below Farm Island is shallow and marshy, probably heavily fertilized by nutrients from the city above. There are few if any campsites, much less areas to pull out, for several miles. If you depart from the Farm Island Campground, work south along the right side of Hipple Bay for about 2.5 miles. You will come to buoys that mark the channel to open water. Below Farm Island, continue along the left shore but watch for shallow areas. Eight miles down the lake on the left is Rousseau (mile 1,050.7). You will see the railroad bridge and the Highway 34 bridge that cross Medicine Knoll Creek Bay. On the left, immediately after the highway bridge, is a place to come ashore and a level area with one tree for shade.

On the left, about 2.5 miles below Rousseau, is Mac's Landing (left; 44.29580/-100.03516). This is a private dock, but it has a series of signs giving river mileage to a variety of destinations, including St. Louis. I would be willing to bet that the owners are good river rats and welcome distance paddlers. Just down from here is the Fort George ramp (mile 1,045.7 left; 44.29578/-100.035515). There is shade here but little else. Along the opposite shore there are submerged trees, so you should continue to stay left.

At mile 1,046 you will cross to the east of the 100th meridian. It is perhaps time for some geographic reckoning. If you began your odyssey at the headwaters, you have so far traversed 1,275 river miles; your net longitude reduction is 11.5 degrees. For context, the Missouri's confluence with the Mississippi occurs at about the 90th meridian. The good news is that from the dual standpoints of longitude and total river-mile distance, you are more than halfway to St. Louis. The immediate news with respect to latitude, however, is not good.

For the next 25 miles things go south–the water gets shallow and there are extensive areas of submerged trees.

The De Gray Recreation Area is at mile 1,041.9 left. Watch for shallows and mudflats as you approach the facility. Also, watch for irrigation pump pipes that stretch quite a way out from the shore and some junked agricultural machinery that lurks just under the surface. There is a ramp at De Gray (44.27675/-99.92535), a vault toilet, and modest shade. I suggest you camp here, get a good night's rest, and leave early in the morning if the weather is good.

Below De Gray, the river bends to the southwest and then back to the southeast. The outside of this bend is shallow and contains many submerged trees. Avoid this area by crossing to the opposite (right descending) shore. The lake here is less than a mile across, so this should not be difficult. Once you make the crossing, continue around this inside bend, staying close to shore because there are submerged trees farther offshore. When you are almost completely around the bend (after ~ mile 1,039), you can safely cross back to the left shore. If conditions permit, you can angle across to the point at mile 1,037. But you must complete your crossing before this point, since below here there are submerged trees at the center of the lake. As you continue along you will see irrigation pumps along the shore. Most of these have access roads to the machinery. If bad weather were to move in quickly, you could pull out at one of these pump sites. By about mile 1,030, the shore is mostly gravel. If you encounter really bad headwinds, you can line your boat for most of the next 5 miles.

The Joe Creek Lakeside Use Area is at mile 1,025.7. The ramp is inside a sheltered bay (44.14537/-99.79507). Stop here; this is a beautiful oasis with a vault toilet, picnic shelters, campsites, and fire rings. Contrary to what the ACE map indicates, however, there is no drinking water. There are some trailers up the road, and if someone is home you might ask if you can fill your water jugs. You could also work your way above the beaver dam on Joe Creek to get good water to filter. This area is within the Crow Creek Reservation, and locals come down to swim, picnic, and party at this facility. If the facilities are occupied, you might camp at a small cove that you will see on the left before you come to the ramp. This will give you some separation from the festivities.

Once you leave Joe Creek, you are on the approach to Big Bend. For about 7 miles you will paddle along the left shore, which angles to the southeast. At mile 1,018, you will start your way around the bend. Once you begin, you are committed. There is virtually nowhere to pull out for the next 7 miles. The lake widens here, and you should not attempt a crossing until conditions are good. At mile 1,011, there is a nice sandy area where you could camp (44.15175/-99.60701). Among the trees here, I found a small fire ring, probably the evidence of a stop by another paddler. From here, a crossing to the point on the opposite shore is less than 1.4 miles. This would be a good staging point for an early morning crossing. The alternative is to continue down the left shore to the West Bend Recreation Area, another 2.7 miles. This is a nice campground with all the amenities and shade. There have been some problems with well contamination here, so filter your drinking water. Come ashore before the ramp, where the RVs occupy the campsites near the shore (44.17008/-99.71415). The wooden bridge along the waterfront is a sweet spot for cell phone reception.

The crossing to the point should be attempted only during good weather. There are submerged trees at midchannel. Powerboats have lost their lower units out here. Your best bet may be to leave early in the morning before the wind picks up. Southeast winds predominate during the summer, and by late afternoon the lake gets very rough in front of West Bend. As you work your way around Big Bend, you are making a 25-mile-long loop that returns you to within 1.5 miles of its starting place. Depending on water levels, the neck of the

RV campers enjoying a "bean bag toss" game along the shore at West Bend Recreation Area (~ mile 1,013.7).

bend can be less than 0.7 mile wide. The Narrows Recreation Area is at the neck of the bend, roughly between miles 1,015 and 1,016. I looked this area over carefully with the idea of scouting a portage route. However, the terrain is quite rugged here, and a portage would be extremely difficult.

With good weather you can make the 22 miles from West Bend to the dam in one day. When you cross to the point, you will be on the right shore. There are only occasional emergency camps along this shore; I counted four possible sites between mile 1,005 and mile 1,001. Since this land is part of the Lower Brule Indian Reservation, you should have permission before you camp here (605-473-5666). Once you round the point and begin heading south, you will pass river mile 1,000. From this point on, the "river miles from the Mississippi odometer" begins counting backward from 999. You will know this has started as you paddle by a mile-long section of thick marsh. You should continue along the right shore. At mile 993.5, you will pass Lower Brule and see the town's water tower on your approach.

At West Bend, I was told that this place was "not always friendly to outsiders" and told not to stop here. However, as I paddled by Lower Brule, a young couple along the shore hailed me. We talked briefly; they were friendly, asked numerous questions about my trip, and wished me well as I paddled away. Three miles farther down you will see Counselor Creek. Between here and the Good Soldier Creek ramp, there are big pines along the shore and a series of small bays with good campsites.

The Good Soldier ramp (mile 987; 44.03463/-99.45022) is in a bay that you cannot see as you approach the dam. It is there; trust me. Continue to paddle along the shore toward the dam. When you are 0.3 mile from the dam, you will round a last point and see a small bay with a ramp. This portage is about 0.6 mile. Follow the road out of the parking lot, cross Highway 47, and follow the signs to the Right Tail Race boat ramp and campground. If it is late in the afternoon or if you want to camp in the area, I recommend getting a ride to the Left Tail Race Campground (605-245-2255). If you call the campground and let them know that you would like a campsite for a night, they may be able to arrange transportation. This is a well-run campground; there are shower houses, and the staff is friendly and helpful. Most sites have decent shade, and the showers are long and hot. Because this campground is on a point, there is often a good breeze on even the hottest day. According to ACE, there are two Fort Thompson businesses that may provide portage service for boats: North Shore Bait and Tackle (605-245-2707) and Rank's Service (605-245-2531).

Cockpit view of the approach to the Good Soldier Creek ramp. The ramp is located up a small bay about 0.3 mile before the dam.

SEGMENT 2.H: Lake Francis Case–Tail Race Campground below Big Bend Dam (mile 987.2) to Fort Randall Dam (mile 880) *(Maps 2.H.1 & 2.H.2)*

- **River miles:** 107.2
- **Difficulty level:** Moderate
- **Typical time to complete:** 6 to 7 days

This lake is 107 miles long. With good weather and light winds, you should be able to make this passage in six or seven days. However, you should plan on a couple more days because you will probably experience headwinds at some point. From the standpoint of facilities, this is a paddler-friendly lake; 11 of the 22 recreation use areas have drinking water. At the completion of your passage, you will arrive at Fort Randall Dam near the south end of the state, close to where the Missouri River forms South Dakota's border with Nebraska. You will have earned a full degree of drop in latitude and be within a week's paddle of Sioux City, Iowa.

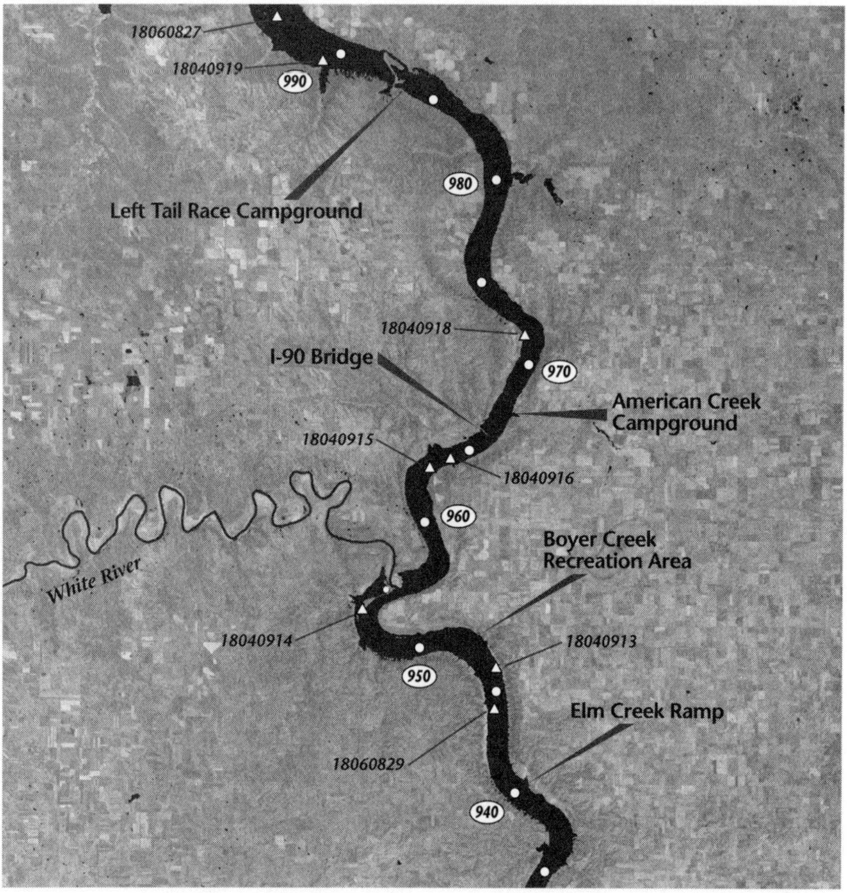

Map 2.H.1: Lake Francis Case: from the Tail Race Campground (mile 987.2) below Big Bend Dam to the Elm Creek ramp at mile 940.

Information/Maps/Resources

I recommend you get the ACE map, *Lake Francis Case*. This map was printed in 1996, but is adequate. Also useful is the ACE (Omaha District) publication *Lake Francis Case [&] Fort Randall Dam: Boating and Recreation Guide*. This large format (11x17) source provides nicely executed maps, each covering about 6 to 7 river miles. This source was apparently published in 1997; I provide updated information where necessary. Current information about ACE facilities on Lake Francis Case can be found at www.nwo.usace.army.mil/html/Lake_Proj/index.html.

Information on South Dakota's Lake Francis Case boat ramps, parks, and recreation areas can be found by following the links at www.sdgfp.info/Parks and clicking on the "Park Locator" link. As related in the previous section, if you navigate to the "Publications" section of this site, you can download campground maps and pamphlets on canoeing and birding.

Suggested Readings

Thirteen Lewis and Clark campsites are in this section. Information about what transpired here during the outbound trip (September 8 to 18, 1804) can be found in Vol. 3:54–88 (*Journals,* [Moulton, ed.]). Return trip event detail (August 28 to 30, 1806) can be found in Vol. 8:326-332. Context about events can be found in Stephen Ambrose's *Undaunted Courage,* in chapter 14:166–168 and in chapter 32:400.

Paddler's Notes and Cautions

Chamberlain is a day's paddle downriver. As you set out from below Big Bend Dam, you will have good current for several miles if you stay in the channel. Start on the right for a couple miles then angle to the center of the lake and work your way around the first bend. After you pass the area of submerged trees just offshore of the outside of this bend, you will see the Crow Creek confluence on your left. By this point (~ mile 980), you can safely begin angling for the left shore. The Crow Creek Massacre site is inland from the left shore; this is sacred ground, and you should not land along this shore except in a dire emergency. There are possible campsites in another 5 miles, as you round a bend and turn to the southeast. Do not camp on the west (right descending) shore without permission. This is in the area of the Lower Brule Reservation, and visits here are actively discouraged.

After you have turned to the southeast, continue on the left for a couple miles. If conditions permit, you can then angle across to the point near mile 972. Continue around the point for a mile and then angle back downriver to the left shore. The American Creek Campground ramp (605-734-5151) is just below mile 968 (43.81972/-99.32944). I recommend that you put in here. There are nicely shaded tent sites on the upstream side of the ramp, and this campground has all the amenities. The staff is friendly, there is a convenience store near the campground entrance, and it is just a short walk into town where you can get almost anything you need. I found this to be one of the most paddler-friendly stops on the entire Missouri River.

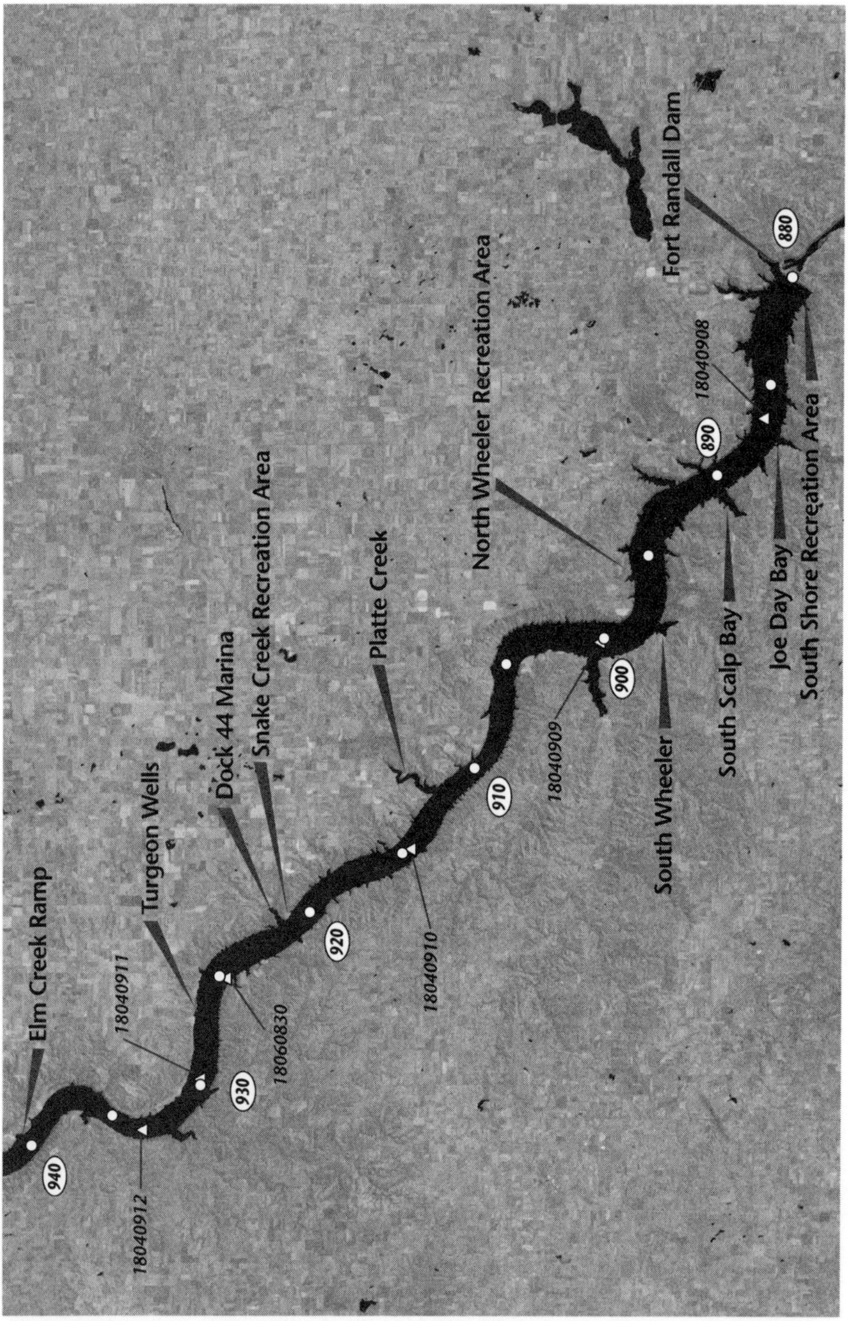

Map 2.H.2: Lake Francis Case: from the Elm Creek ramp (mile 940) to the Fort Randall Dam (mile 880).

The Cedar Shore Resort is just across the lake from American Creek. This is a new development with a hotel, restaurant, conference center, marina, and campground (605-734-6376). Campground sites here have full electrical, water, sewer, and even cable TV hookups. There are restrooms and showers, a coin-operated Laundromat, and camping supplies, beer, pop, snacks, ice, and firewood. I did not stop in here, but as I paddled by I noted that trees have been planted to develop shaded sites.

Stay left as you work your way downriver along the riprap levee that protects Chamberlain. Just below the American Creek ramp is a small bay leading up the creek to the American Creek Marina (605-734-5692). As you continue by Chamberlain, you will pass under two highway bridges (the second is I-90) and then a railroad bridge. In the next 4 miles, before you turn sharply to the south, there are places along the left shore where you might camp. Once you are around the bend at mile 962, you can either stay along the left shore or cross to the right to "cut the corner" by paddling to the inside of the next bend. I marked a possible campsite along this inside bend at mile 958.5. It is 7 to 8 miles before another possible campsite. Once you are around this point, cross back to the left shore before mile 956. You should be left because the White River joins the Missouri from the right (west), and the area above the confluence is low and marshy.

Below the White River, the lake makes a U-turn. As you enter the turn, move out to midchannel. There are extensive mudflats on the left, below the inside bend. By mile 952 you can start working over to the right shore. If the dam has been releasing water, you should find good current here. Because the wind picked up, I started searching for a campsite along the shore. I found a marginal site just above mile 951 (43.64984/-99.44519). There was good evidence of cattle where I camped, so I arranged a driftwood barrier to protect my tent. Early the next morning as I was pushing off, the herd was straggling back to reclaim the beach.

From my camp at mile 951 right, it is about 3 miles before the lake turns back to the southeast. Boyer Creek Recreation Area is along the outside of this bend at mile 947. There is a vault toilet at Boyer. If a southeast wind is blowing, you should work your way around the bend and then cross over to the left shore. The Elm Creek ramp is at mile 940 left (43.56550/-99.31268). You can stop here, but it is probably better to continue on for another mile to the Elm Creek camping area. Here the pullout is not marked, but you will see a vault toilet, a picnic shelter, and a gravel road near the shore. This is a good stop

Site of author's campsite at mile 951 below the White River. Located on the shore along the outside of a sharp bend, a strong current runs just offshore.

because just up the road is Keiner's RV Kampground (605-734-6826), where you can fill up your water jugs. There is no other place to get water as you paddle the 30 miles from Chamberlain until just before the Highway 44 bridge, and filtering the lake water is not a good option since it gets very muddy when the wind blows. As a courtesy, I suggest you leave a few dollars for the water. If no one is around, put the money in one of the site rental envelopes and drop it, along with a thank-you note, in the slot at the office building.

I had to sit an extra day here when a strong southeast wind effectively pinned me to the shore. The wind picked up during the night, and by daybreak the lake was too rough to make the crossing to the opposite shore where I might find sheltered paddling. The wind continued to blow, and by late afternoon I gave up all hope of getting back on the lake that day. The following morning, the wind had blown itself out and I was able to continue. On the Missouri, you go with the flow as the wind permits.

The lake below Elm Creek bends to the southwest for about 5 miles. The water is very shallow along the outside of this bend, so it is a good idea to cross to the point on the opposite (right) shore. From here, work around the point until you pass a bay. The lake narrows briefly here, so cut back across to the east (left) side of the lake. As you paddle along the shore, you will see large herds of cattle, including bulls. After about 8 miles you will reach Turgeon Wells (mile 826.5; 43.44753/-99.20082). There is only a road here, but it is one of the few places where you might camp in an emergency. Buryanek Recreation Area (43.41555/-99.16861) is on the opposite shore 3 miles downriver. This campground now has showers and drinking water. But if you cross over to Buryanek, you will lose shelter from a southeast wind. I recommend you continue on to the Snake Creek Recreation Area at mile 921 left.

As you approach Snake Creek, you will see the Highway 44 bridge. The Dock 44 Marina (605-337-3005) is just up the small bay on the left before the bridge. There is a good restaurant, bar, and convenience store here. Owners Ken and Jackie Dooley helped me arrange a campsite at the park. When I spoke to Ken later, he related that they see a couple kayaks and canoes coming down the lake every year. Ken also told me that once he gave two kayakers a portage to the Fort Randall Dam when they "had just too much of the lake." He explained that windstorms can come up suddenly here and that because this section of the lake angles to the southeast, a northwest wind will blow right down the lake. This forms big waves in the shallow areas, creates very confused wave patterns near the bridge, and produces big rollers along the east shore below the bridge.

The Snake Creek State Park pull-out is about 0.4 mile after the bridge. Pull your boat out on the beach where you see a stairs coming down to the shore. You should see tents and RVs at the campground above the stairs. There is good shade here and all the amenities. After you secure your boat, walk up to the campground and ask for directions to the office or campground host. This is one of the most popular campgrounds in the state, but campground manager David Enke told me that they will make room for paddlers. You can walk or get a ride to the marina for a good meal. Everyone I met was friendly. So this is a recommended stop for voyagers. When I paddled through here in 2003, cell phone reception was nonexistent, but a tower was going up for a marine band repeater. Most area boaters and the folks at the Dock 44 Marina monitor channel 16.

When I left Snake Creek the next morning, a northwest wind was blowing. At first I worked along the left shore, but within a mile the waves began breaking near the shore and the rollers started getting larger. I worked farther offshore and ran with the waves for about 4 miles. Things were starting to get dicey until I rounded the slight bend just below mile 916. Here, I found calm water along the shore and was able to continue on without any issues. The Platte Creek Campground is at mile 912 left (43.30010/-99.00113). You will see the campground ahead on the left as you paddle into the bay. There is a busy boat ramp on the right, so stay left. There are some shaded sites here and hot showers. You can walk to the ranger's station at the park entrance to arrange for a site.

After I had arranged for a campsite, I got my gear from my boat and began to set up camp. It was midafternoon and brutally hot. As I was assembling the poles for my tent, a couple in a pickup drove by. A few minutes later the truck returned and a man called out, "You look like you could use a beer." I looked up and said, "You got that right!" I walked over to the truck and introduced myself to Dan and Nita Foster from Sioux Falls. They handed me a couple ice-cold Bud Lights, and I told them briefly about my expedition. A while later they returned with an invitation to join them for dinner. We agreed that they would pick me up at 5 P.M. That night I enjoyed a great meal and a couple hours of good conversation with Dan and Nita. Both had seen some hard times, were thankful for what they had, and made a practice of helping those stopped along the road. There was an elemental kindness about them. I will always treasure the memory of this chance encounter. Whoever said, "It's not about the destination," got it right. It's about the friends that you make along the way.

From Platte Creek you are about 30 miles from the dam. If you have good weather, this should take about two days. If you have wind, it may take longer. Over the course of this distance, the lake turns to the south, then east, then southeast, and finally back to the east. If you are dealing with a wind, these aspect changes mean that the sheltered side of the lake will change as you work your way south. You will have to decide which side of the lake will provide you with the best shelter as you begin each of these aspect changes. If conditions permit, you may be able to make crossings to minimize your exposure to wind-related issues, since the lake in this section averages less than 1.5 miles across.

When I left Platte Creek early the following morning, a light wind was blowing from the east and southeast. My plan was to get to the North Wheeler Campground at mile 896 left (43.16472/-98.8211) and then see if conditions would permit a run for the dam. I was assuming that the wind would pick up by midday. I continued along the left shore for 4 miles then angled across the lake to the point near mile 905. I worked around this point for a mile and then crossed back to the east (left) side. If you examine Map 2.H.2., you will see that this course positioned me along the sheltered side of the lake for almost the entire remaining distance to North Wheeler. The last mile was difficult because of a headwind, as I had expected.

North Wheeler has vault toilets, drinking water, some shaded campsites, and a few sites with electricity. There is a nice protected bay, with some good tent sites away from the developed area. This is a good place to stop and rest before the final 15-mile run to the dam. If the wind is blowing, spend the night here and make an early morning crossing to the opposite shore. South Wheeler is along the opposite shore (right) at mile 895 (43.14155/-98.80244). There is camping here some sites have electricity, but there is no source for drinking water. A security light burns during the night near the boat ramp.

There are many bays along the right (west) shore, so you will have some sheltered water in the event of a headwind as you paddle toward the dam. The entrance to South Scalp Bay is at mile 890.5. A campground, with drinking water, is on the north shore about 0.5 mile inside this bay (43.10055/-98.76222). Three miles farther along the shore is Joe Day Bay (43.06270/-98.70101). There is a ramp here, camping and a vault toilet, but no water.

The Fort Randall Dam take-out is at the South Shore Recreation Area (mile 880.5 right; 43.05049/-98.58372). I suggest that you do not land at this ramp. Instead, continue on to the beach and picnic area at the south end of the dam (43.04717/-98.57345). If it is a nice day, you may see many people enjoying the beach. Most boaters put their boat in at the ramp, send someone in the boat to this beach, and then drive their truck and trailer to the parking lot of this area. I walked up to a man who was just pulling into the lot with an empty trailer, introduced myself, and asked if he could help me get to the downstream campground. He said, "Sure, no problem." He and his family were camping there also. We loaded my equipment in his truck and he took me to the downstream campground.

There is a campground near the beach, but no drinking water, so I recommend staying at the Randall Creek Campground (605-487-7046), below the dam. A manual portage to the closest downstream ramp and the campground is about 1.5 miles. After you exit the parking area, cross Highway 281 and look for the signs to the campground. Continue along this road to the northeast for about 0.7 of a mile, past the Fort Randall Historic Site on your right. When you come to a T, turn right. Continue for about 0.3 mile to an intersection. Take a left here to get to the boat ramp or go right and follow the signs to the campground office. The Randall Creek Campground has all the amenities and good shade from big cottonwood trees. Getting down to the river from the campground is not easy. The bank is steep and lined with riprap. If you plan to camp here, try to get a campsite with some workable access to the water. I camped near some concrete stairs down to the river. It's a bit awkward, but you can get your boat and gear down these stairs.

The folks that portaged me were the Wolkens from Madison, Nebraska. They were part of a reunion of sorts, and they invited me to dinner that night with several other members of their clan. That night I enjoyed a T-bone steak, fresh corn on the cob, and a Dutch oven–cooked dish of potatoes, onions, and mushrooms. I talked briefly about my trip, and told them about my recent Little Bend storm and rattlesnake experience. Mostly though, I listened to the buzz of conversation and good humor that flowed up and down the dinner table. These were folks that clearly enjoyed being together.

SEGMENT 2.I.: Randall Creek Campground (~ mile 880) to Running Water (mile 840.3) *(Map 2.I)*

- **River miles:** 39.7
- **Difficulty level:** Low
- **Typical time to complete:** 1.5 to 2 days

This 39-mile section of the Missouri is river. It is one of two South Dakota segments listed on the National Register of Wild and Scenic Rivers. It is a delightful section to paddle; the scenery is truly spectacular where you paddle along the base of steep, 250-foot limestone cliffs and loess bluffs. And, if you have paddled down Lake Francis Case, you will be floating along with the first sustained current that you have seen for a hundred miles. Although not as popular as the other free-running segment (Gavins Point Dam to Ponca; 59 miles long), you may see other paddlers enjoying the river.

There are some issues to be concerned about on this section: Dam releases can quickly change the river level, and there are sandbars and occasional snags. Endangered species–piping plovers and interior least terns–nest along the shore and must not be disturbed. The last few miles of this section pass through areas of marsh, and staying in the channel requires good attention. Finally, there are limited pullout sites along this section of the river. This becomes a significant problem because the weather can change quite rapidly. Thunderstorms with high winds and hail, and the occasional tornado, can ruin

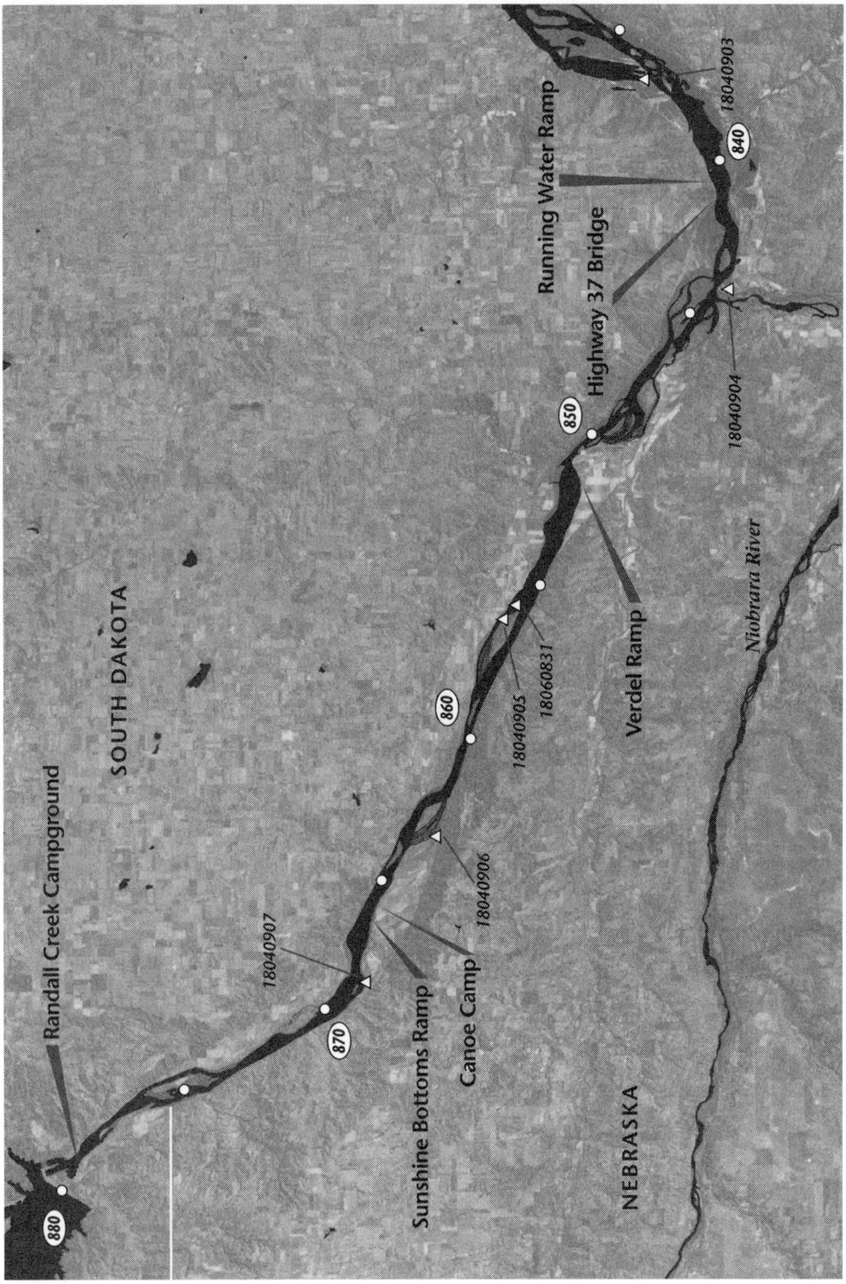

Map 2.1: Randall Creek Campground near mile 880 to Running Water ramp at mile 840.3. Paddlers should stop at the Running Water ramp before continuing on through the 8 miles of thick marsh before the Springfield Boat Basin at mile 831.8.

your day if you cannot get to shelter before the bad weather finds you. I almost had my day ruined when I paddled this section.

South Dakota's river border with Nebraska starts at latitude 43 degrees north, which translates to about the 875-mile mark. Below this point, the Missouri River serves as the boundary. On the Nebraska side, landowners own all the land to the middle of the channel, including sandbars and the river bottom. This has considerable significance for paddlers since there is little public land along the river. You should always get permission before using private land; if you do camp on an island or sandbar, it's a better idea to do it on the South Dakota side. Of course, if a weather emergency forces you ashore, get out wherever you can safely. And wherever you camp, leave it in better condition than you found it.

Information/Maps/Resources

Both South Dakota (www.sdgfp.info/parks) and Nebraska (www.ngpc.state.ne.us) have websites that provide useful material for Missouri River paddlers. At these sites you can get information about parks and campgrounds along the river, and download information focusing on river paddling in general: *Canoeing & Kayaking in South Dakota,* and *General Canoeing Introduction–Nebraska's Canoe Trails*. Both sites also provide information including maps for this section that you can download: *SD Missouri River Canoe/Kayak Map–Pickstown to Running Water* by the South Dakota Department of Game, Fish and Parks, and *Upper Missouri River Canoe Trail: Ft. Randall Dam to Niobrara* by the Nebraska Game and Parks Commission.

High-resolution air photos of the area below the Fort Randall Dam to Springfield, South Dakota, have been posted by the USGS Columbia Environmental Research Center at http://aa179.cr.usgs.gov/1999_Photos/ftrandall_spg/reach.htm. The digital files containing these images are extremely large, and should not be downloaded unless you have a high-speed connection.

Suggested Readings

Five Lewis and Clark campsites are in this section. Information about what transpired here during the outbound trip (September 4 to 7, 1804) can be found in Vol. 3:46–54 (*Journals,* [Moulton, ed.]). Return trip event detail (August 31, 1806) can be found in Vol. 8:332–333. Context about events can be found in Stephen Ambrose's *Undaunted Courage,* in chapters 14:165 and 32:400.

Paddler's Notes and Cautions

This section starts with a 10-mile segment that angles sharply to the southeast. I found good current along the right. The Karl E. Mundt Wildlife Refuge, which is a winter refuge for bald eagles, is immediately below the Randall Creek Campground. Between mile 875 and 870 there are occasional places on the right where you might pull out. The Sunshine Bottoms ramp is on the right at mile 866.1 (42.92189/-98.40782). About 0.5 mile downstream from this, also on the right, is a sign that says, CANOE CAMP. This is a primitive campsite for floaters. There are trailers and cabins just beyond this camp.

After I got back on the river, I could see that a thunderstorm was moving in quickly from the northwest. I paddled along the shore looking for a site where I could put up my tent for shelter. I ended up having to paddle for 2 miles before I found a low sandy beach where I could get ashore (~ mile 863). I was on the water longer than I wanted to be. The sky got very dark and lightning began striking much too close for comfort. I barely got my tent up before it started to hail. Once inside my tent I listened to my NOAA weather radio. As flashes of lightning lighted up my tent, and my rain fly was buffeted by high wind, rain, and hail, I learned that I was in a "severe thunderstorm watch area."

The next morning the river level was down at least 2 feet. Before the storm struck the evening before, I had pulled my boat well out of the water. Now the water's edge was twice the original distance. This served as a good reminder to me to always make sure my boat is well up the bank and securely tied to a tree or stake. If the water can go down 2 feet, it can surely come up that much. If you camp on a sandbar, remember that you might be pulling ashore at low water. Camp well above high water level and secure your boat.

The river becomes quite scenic below the power line at mile 861. Steep bluffs line the right shore. This area has a surprisingly wild and remote character. I had not expected such beauty. As you approach Verdel (~ mile 854 right), the bluffs angle away from the river and the land near the shore levels out. You will see docks and cabins. The Verdel ramp is at the downstream end of the settlement, at mile 851.5 (42.83104/-98.15223), about half a mile before the river narrows as it works around a point. At the ramp there is a vault toilet and a well with a pump. There is little shade here. There is not supposed to be any camping here, but I believe in a pinch you might get permission to set up your tent off to one side or at neighboring property.

Once you are beyond the point at mile 851, the river widens considerably and the area gets quite swampy. After 7 miles you will come to the Niobrara River confluence on the right. The Niobrara State Park is on the bluffs above the river. You will see a former railroad bridge along the shore spanning the river; silt-laden water from the Niobrara will muddy the Missouri flow, and you will paddle along an area of thick marshland. There are supposed to be two wide channels here; the second leads to the village of Niobrara ramp. This channel must be somewhere before mile 843, but I was unable to locate the entrance. From the cockpit of my kayak, the area in front of the town looked like a solid wall of high marsh. A mile farther down on the right, just before the Highway 37 (Standing Bear) bridge, is a ferry landing. However, I recommend that you get over to the left, well before the bridge, and continue on for another 3 miles to the Running Water ramp.

Follow these next instructions carefully. As you approach the bridge (mile 840.9), get to the left. The main channel passes under the first and second spans from the left shore. Once you are past the bridge, stay close to the left shore. The Running Water ramp is 0.5 mile from the bridge, on the South Dakota side, at mile 840.3 (42.77060/-97.97893). The current runs fast here; if you are not careful you can miss this ramp. There is a vault toilet here. You may be able to get permission to camp at one of the neighboring properties. If it is late afternoon or the weather is not good, you should definitely stop here for the night. The area ahead is potentially one of the more difficult sections of the Missouri River.

SEGMENT 2.J: Lake Lewis and Clark–Running Water (mile 840.3) to Gavins Point Dam (mile 812) *(Maps 2.J.1 & 2.J.2)*

- **River miles:** 28.3
- **Difficulty level:** Moderate to high
- **Typical time to complete:** 1.5 to 2 days

The Missouri became progressively shallower until the depth finder was useless, and I looked to our guide, and he said, 'I can't believe how much this end has filled in. It all looks so different.' His directions at first proved sound, and we moved through expeditiously until the reeds became heavy and the strands of water numerous; then we had to slow and guess. Because that section was more swamp than water, the current was again imperceptible. Our charts, older than the reed beds, proved nearly worthless, and the winding channel turned compass bearings to nonsense....

WILLIAM LEAST HEAT-MOON, *RIVER-HORSE*

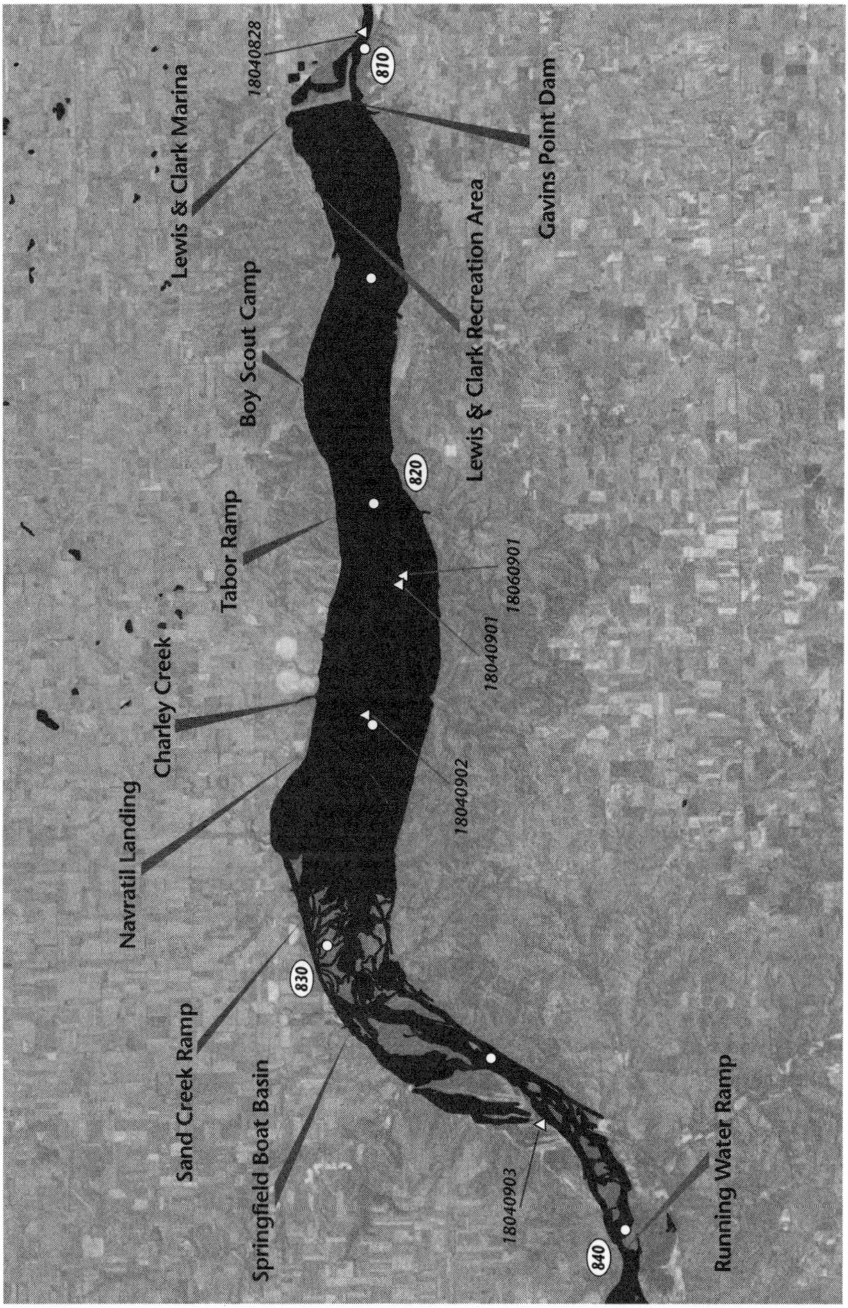

Map 2.J.1: Lake Lewis and Clark from the Running Water ramp at mile 840.3 to Gavins Point Dam and mile 810. See Map 2.J.2 for a zoomed-in image of the area between mile 840 and mile 830, a complex series of channels through marsh.

The area immediately downstream from Running Water degenerates into deep marsh with braided channels for 8 or 9 miles. You will need to find a good channel to the Springfield Boat Basin Campground. I suggest you plan on a half day to successfully navigate through the morass ahead. Because the current runs strong and because there are few if any places where you can pull out along the way, once you start this section you are committed.

When you get below the vast area of marsh in front of Springfield, you arrive at open water on Lewis and Clark Lake. This is the last of the dammed upper lakes; it is small, only 25 miles long, and ranges from 1.5 to 3 miles in width. With good weather and flat water, you should easily complete a passage in a day and a half. There are some areas of good current along the north (left) shore, but the speed depends on how much water is being released at the Gavins Point Dam.

As you work to the dam, I recommend you stay along the north shore, where you get an assist from the current and paddle along a very impressive shoreline. You'll pass a series of golden chalkstone bluffs separated by woody draws of oak and cedar. If you have paddled any of the other lakes of the Dammed Upper, you will have paddled along vast sections of barren wasteland. Here, you find vegetation so lush that it appears as a riot of green. About halfway down the lake, at the Tabor Ramp Primitive Campground, you can camp protected by the huge canopy of any one of a number of enormous oak trees. This shore has what Steinbeck characterized as "the look and smell of eastern America."

Information/Maps/Resources

In 2003, ACE began distributing the newest version of its *Lewis and Clark Lake [&] Gavins Point Dam Boating and Recreation Guide*. Although the air photos used as a base for the maps are more than a decade old, I found the images to be very helpful, particularly for navigating through the maze of marsh at the west end of the lake. There are nine large-format images each showing about a 4- to 5-mile section of the river. Each map shows good detail, is accurately labeled, and provides boat ramp coordinates. In addition, the guide includes a brief section of Lewis and Clark historical information. To obtain a copy of this publication, contact the Missouri River Information Center at Yankton, South Dakota (1-866-285-3219).

Suggested Readings

Four Lewis and Clark campsites are in this section. Information about what transpired here during the outbound trip (September 1 to 3, 1804) can be found in Vol. 3:37–46 (*Journals,* [Moulton, ed.]). Return trip event detail (September 1, 1806) can be found in Vol. 8:337–344. Context about events can be found in Stephen Ambrose's *Undaunted Courage,* in chapters 14:165 and 32:400–401.

The vast area of marsh at the west end of Lewis and Clark Lake has presented real difficulties for other Missouri River adventurers. I recommend you read William Least Heat-Moon's *River-Horse* (pages 257–262) for an account of his 1995 passage through this area. Another account of the difficulties associated with this marsh barrier is found in Chris Bechtold's *A Current Adventure* (pages 71–73). These accounts are instructive.

Paddler's Notes and Cautions

The area between Running Water and Springfield is difficult to navigate. Sediment from the Niobrara River is filling in the western third of the lake. From the seat of your boat, you will see what appears to be an endless succession of mudflats, sandbars, thick islands of marsh, and countless small channels threading through the morass.

I spoke with a number of locals about this area before I paddled through here. David Beckler, the ACE operations manager at the Gavis Point Dam, told me that he duck hunts in this area. He gave me the instruction to stay left for a while after leaving Running Water, and then to follow the main channel as it angles over to the bluffs on the right side near mile 836. Then he said to work along the bluffs until I could see a channel leading to Springfield, which he described as homes and buildings along a high bluff. When I talked with anglers at the Running Water ramp, they provided similar directions.

When I pushed off from Running Water, a 5- to 6-mph current was running. I had no difficulty making the 4 miles to the start of the bluffs. As I worked for about a mile along the bluffs, I noted only one or two places where you might pull out in an emergency. Neither of these spots would make a good campsite, but at least they offered a last-ditch place to get off the water if a bad storm moved in quickly. At mile 835 (42.81112/-97.89641), I began to angle my way toward the opposite shore. I could see Springfield to the north, and found a channel with swift-moving water that seemed to head in the right direction. I

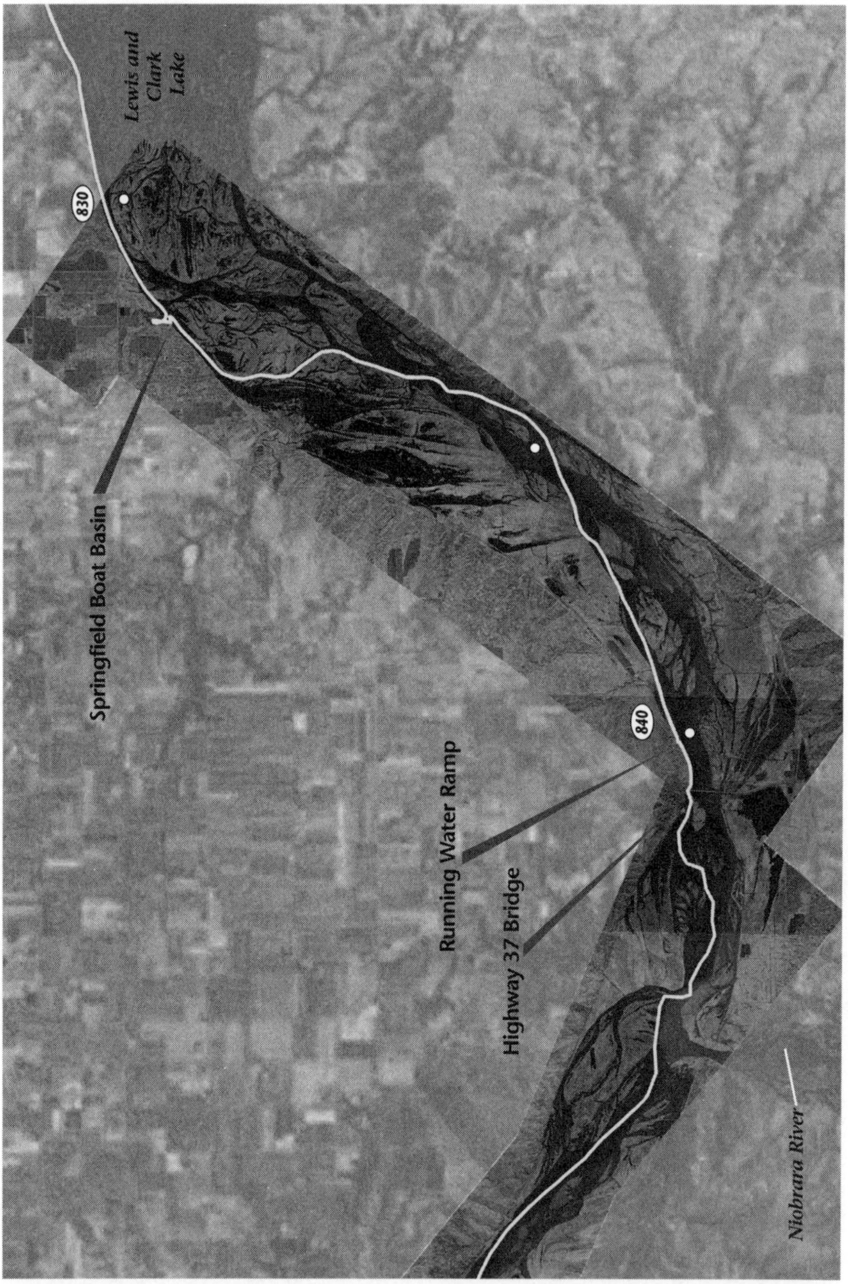

Map 2.J.2: Running Water ramp at mile 840.3 to mile 825, the marsh section at the west end of Lewis and Clark Lake. Newer satellite imagery is superimposed over an older image. My 2003 course track is shown as a white line. Making passage through this section of marsh can be difficult, as paddlers face a myriad of channels.

frequently consulted the image of the area that I had in my clear plastic map case. My satellite photo showed several possible routes including one large channel that would bring me out just below the Springfield Boat Basin, where I wanted to land.

The channel that I elected brought me to the shore just upstream from the town (see Map 2.J.2 for my course track). I worked my way along the base of a steep bluff for about a mile and came to the Springfield Boat Basin, a small bay where the ramp and campground are located. If you paddle back into the bay, you will see several nice shaded sites on the right. This campground has nice hot showers and friendly campground hosts. The town is within walking distance, and there is a nice main street with local establishments for supplies, a good meal, and cold beverages. I camped here on a weekday and pretty much had the area to myself.

That night, as I worked on my field notes for the day, I reflected on my passage through the marsh. The intelligence that I had gathered about the area had been accurate and very helpful. Although the situation is clearly dynamic with respect to new channels forming and old channels disappearing, the general instruction to "get over to the right at the bluffs and look for a channel" was adequate. Although there were moments when I had to study the water carefully to determine where the better current was running, I was able to remain in a good channel all the way across. At different water levels, however, the passage might not be so obvious. In any event, you should cross over to the Springfield side to avoid getting into the marshy area along the right shore. An attempt to make passage on the right gets you into a section of marsh where even locals can get lost. Here the channels branch into ever-smaller segments in a way that produces a pattern with fractal-like complexity.

Once you get below the Springfield Boat Basin, the rest of the lake is relatively easy. Stay along the left shore. At mile 829, you will pass the Sand Creek ramp (42.87224/-97.82710). There is primitive camping here, a vault toilet, and drinking water. At mile 827.8, you will paddle by the Twin Bridges area. There's a level area where you can pull out but nothing else besides the ghoulishly named Deadman and Snatch Creeks. The marsh ends near mile 827, almost a full mile beyond what is shown on the air photo taken almost ten years ago. Within a quarter mile, you will see buoys that mark the entrance to channel along the shore. One mile down from here, as you round a point, you will see the Navratil Landing ramp (42.87011/-97.76801). I saw a pole-mounted security light and a trash barrel when I paddled by.

The Charley Creek access is at the small bay at mile 824.5. There are no facilities here, but there are possible campsites. From an "accuracy in mapping" perspective, Charley Creek is actually another 0.5 mile down the shore. At mile 823, you will see buildings of the Bon Homme Colony. From the shore at least, the scale of their agricultural operation is impressive. I spoke briefly with two young men who were working along the shore. As I departed they wished me well on my journey. About 3 miles farther down the left shore is the Tabor ramp and campground (mile 819.8; 42.85937/-97.65439). The lake narrows to about 1.5 miles across here. On the opposite side of the lake is the Bloomfield ramp.

The Tabor campground is just above the ramp, and there is good shade here provided by large oak trees. According to both the South Dakota Game, Fish and Parks and ACE brochures, there is supposed to be drinking water here. However, when I stopped here in late July 2003, a large wooden box had been placed over the well with a sign that read, SORRY, OUT OF ORDER. It was an extremely hot day, I had paddled for 3.5 hours, I was tired, I had consumed most of my water, and I was probably on the edge of heat exhaustion. I was counting on refilling my water jugs here. Judging from the condition of the box and the sign on it, this well had been out of service for a long time. I remember thinking that I'd like to get my hands on the jerk that made the decision not to repair this well. I found some shade under one of the big oaks where I could cool down and think through my situation. It was too hot to continue on without water, and I could see that thunderstorms were moving in. I decided to set up my tent in a sheltered site and then filter some lake water, risking the chance of clogging my filter with sediment.

As I was setting up my tent, a man drove up to the ramp, got out of his car, pulled an inner tube out of the trunk, and walked out into the water. He floated just offshore for about a half hour until storm clouds began moving in. I walked down to my kayak beside the ramp to get some gear as he got out of the water. We talked for a while; I mentioned that I had come in here expecting to find drinking water, and he told me that the pump had not been working for a couple years. He also told me there are almost always biting flies near the ramp, but that they won't bother you if you get a little ways offshore. He then tossed his inner tube in his trunk and drove away. About an hour later, he returned with a gallon jug of water for me. I thanked him; this was a totally unexpected act of kindness.

One mile beyond Tabor (~ mile 819), there is a nice looking area that might serve as a campsite. A half mile beyond this you will see a gray pump house, and at mile 817.3 you will see the waterfront area of a Boy Scout camp. As you continue to work along the left shore, you will come to a point just beyond mile 815. In the bay immediately around this point is the Gavins Point boat ramp (42.85873/-97.54948). The Lewis and Clark State Park (605-668-2985) begins here, and stretches along the shore for about 2 miles. As you paddle along the shoreline, you will see the campground with RVs and campers. At mile 813 you will see a small bay and the Midway boat ramp (42.86148/ -97.52917).

As I paddled by this park, one of the workers hailed me and asked me how far I was going. We talked briefly, and he said if I needed a ride to the downstream campground, they could help. I continued on because I wanted to get a look at the marina. To get to the marina, you paddle almost to the dam along a breakwater and then take a left. Once you are inside the breakwater, there is a boat ramp on the right (mile 811.5; 42.87300/-97.49068). The location of the marina, restaurant, and resort is along the west side of the harbor. I pulled my boat out over the riprap at the northwest corner. The Lewis and Clark Marina (605-665-3111) offers a portage service.

As I was unloading my boat, two men walked up and asked where I'd come from. I filled them in on my expedition they had a small cooler with them and provided me with a cold beer. It turned out they were Dan Hemphill and Rick Faber, both from Omaha. They were staying at the cabins in the park with their families. They volunteered to help me get my gear to the campground below the dam. Within a few minutes everything was arranged. We loaded my kayak on their pontoon boat trailer and put my gear in their SUV. They took me across the dam to the Tailwaters Campground on the Nebraska side, where I got a tent site near the entrance, close to the ramp. Dan and Rick helped me unload my gear and then invited me to have dinner with them that night. I told them that I'd be happy to tell a couple of trip stories for my dinner. That night I enjoyed a really good meal, great desserts, and many funny stories with several families from the Omaha area who have made a tradition of meeting every summer for a short vacation.

When I got back to my tent that night, I reflected on my good fortune. The portage, the dinner invitation, the good food, and the fellowship–all of this spun out of a chance encounter. And I reflected on the character of my expedition. I'd met so many good people along the way. I was a complete stranger, coming off several days on the water, looking worn on the edges, needing a serious cleanup–admittedly a novelty of sorts–but still a stranger. Yet I had been consistently welcomed and assisted by so many along the way. This trip so far had been a reaffirmation of hope at many levels. And now I was finally done with the lakes of the Dammed Upper. I would have sustained current all the way to the confluence with the Mississippi, and down to St. Louis.

SEGMENT 2.K: Gavins Point Dam (mile 812) to Sioux City, Iowa (~ mile 732) *(Map 2.K)*

- **River miles:** 80
- **Difficulty level:** Low
- **Typical time to complete:** 3 to 4 days

Missouri National Recreational River consists of two reaches. Our 39-mile section stretches from Fort Randall Dam to Running Water, South Dakota. Our 59-mile section stretches from a mile below Gavins Point Dam to Ponca State Park, Nebraska. Both reaches show the Missouri River in its relative natural state, a condition that Lewis and Clark would, to a large extent, recognize today.

George D. Berndt, National Park Service Ranger at the Lewis and Clark Visitor Center at Gavins Point Dam

This 59-mile-long segment of the Missouri River is listed on the National Register of Wild and Scenic Rivers. Here you will have good current, sandbars, and several large islands. The landscape–landform and vegetation–pretty much completes the transition from the West to the Midwest. As you paddle down the river, you clearly see that ranching has given way to large-scale farming. The crops are well-watered, and the fields are bordered by large woodlots. With increasing frequency, you will see towns along or near the river and paddle past many cabins and year-round homes. Recreational use of the river is more evident. Besides powerboats and personal watercraft, you will probably see other paddlers. Yet, with all the traffic, there are long sections of the river that still hold elements of their native wildness.

This is the unchannelized Missouri River. There are extensive areas of shallows and backwaters that you can navigate. Here you will see many species of waterfowl, along with bald eagles and ospreys. There are many nice campsites along this section where you can find solitude and gain an appreciation for what the river was like some 200 years ago. And perhaps, as sections of the Channelized Lower Missouri are modified to increase habitat

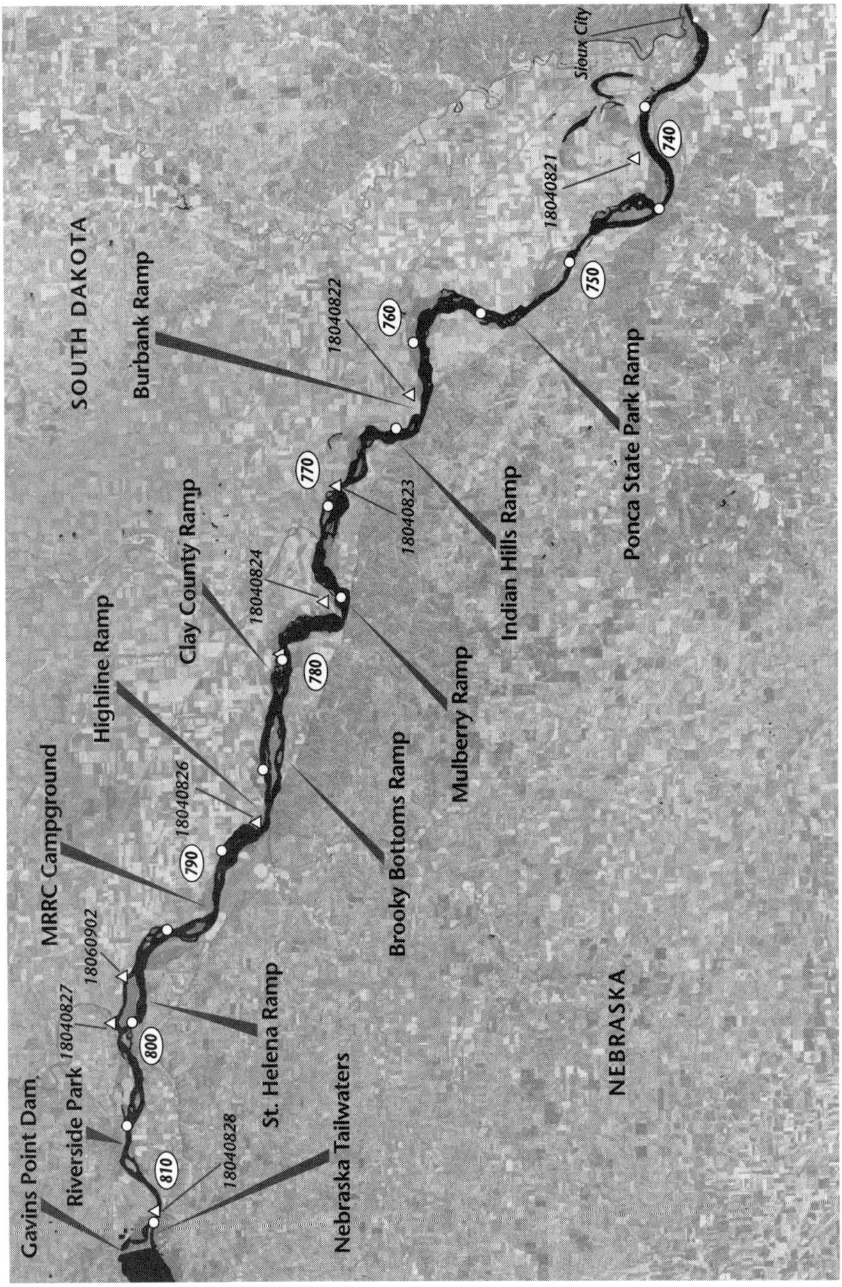

Map 2.K.: Gavins Point Dam (mile 812) to Sioux City, Iowa (mile 732). The first 59 miles of this segment (from Gavins Point Dam to Ponca State Park) is part of the Missouri National Recreational River.

and spawning areas, this is what they will look like 200 years from now. Finally, because the river is relatively free to shift its channel, vegetation along the shore exhibits different stages of succession. Where there has been recent flooding, or where the current has cut away at the bank, there are many disturbed areas. Opportunist plants and weedy species, including poison ivy, successfully colonize these places. When you come ashore, pay attention.

Information/Maps/Resources

As mentioned in a previous section, both South Dakota (www.sdgfp.info/parks) and Nebraska (www.ngpc.state.ne.us) have websites that provide useful material for Missouri river paddlers. At these sites, you can get information about parks, campgrounds, and ramps along the river, and download information focusing on river paddling in general: *Canoeing & Kayaking in South Dakota,* and *General Canoeing Introduction–Nebraska's Canoe Trails*. The Nebraska site also provides a very good, downloadable brochure and map for this section: *Lower Missouri River Canoe Trail: Gavins Point Dam to Ponca State Park*.

Suggested Readings

Eleven Lewis and Clark campsites are in this section. Information about what transpired here during the outbound trip (August 20 to 31, 1804) can be found in Vol. 2:494–508 and Vol. 3:7–37 (*Journals,* [Moulton, ed.]). Return trip event detail (September 2 to 3, 1806) can be found in Vol. 8:344–348. Context about events can be found in Stephen Ambrose's *Undaunted Courage,* in chapters 13:160–164 and 32:400–401.

Sergeant Charles Floyd, the only member of the Lewis and Clark Expedition to perish on the trip, died on August 20, 1804, near Sioux City, Iowa. Dr. David Peck's book, *Or Perish in the Attempt,* provides a well-written analysis of this episode from the standpoint of current-day medical practice.

Paddler's Notes and Cautions

There are three nice campgrounds immediately below the dam in addition to the Tailwaters Campground on the Nebraska side: Pierson Ranch, Cottonwood, and Chief White Crane. These are shaded campgrounds with all the amenities. But they are frequently crowded and do not offer the best access to the river for paddlers without a vehicle. Mosquitoes can be bad at all of these campgrounds, particularly at Chief White Crane. I suggest you stay at the Tailwaters Campground, either at one of the tent-camping sites near the entrance or at the downstream end. There is a bathroom with showers at the center of the campground, a short walk from the tent site area. From this campground you can walk up to the Lewis and Clark Visitor Center, a bit of a hike but worth a visit. Ask the campground host for directions.

The Tailwaters ramp is on the right at mile 810.4 (42.84900/-97.46967). This can be a busy ramp; if you get a site at the downstream tent area, you can easily put in from the shore. Along the opposite shore, known as the Training Dike, there is another ramp. About 1.5 miles down from the Tailwaters ramp, on the inside bend (left shore) where the river turns up to the northeast, there is a small marina (~ mile 809). Once you are around this bend, the town of Yankton is about 3.5 miles farther downriver. Stay left paddle under the Highway 81 bridge, and you will come to Riverside Park and the Yankton boat ramp (mile 805.3; 42.86623/-97.38443). There are nice shelters and a clean bathroom here. This is also a place with good cell phone reception and where you can top off your water jugs.

When I pushed off from the Yankton ramp, I had to quickly get over to the right shore to find the channel. It was quite shallow on the left. From this point on, you will have to read the river; the channel generally is on the right, but you may have to occasionally swing out to midriver to stay in good water. At mile 804 you will see Antelope Creek on your right; this area of the river is known as the Yankton Reach. Near mile 800.5 you will come to the upstream tip of James River Island; here you should stay right. Also known as Jacques Island, this island is well over 2 miles long and heavily wooded. The James River confluence is on the north side of this island at mile 800. According to one South Dakota publication, the James, "a typical prairie stream, has been noted as the longest unnavigable river in the world." As you work along the south side of this island, you will see the Cedar County Park and St. Helena public boat ramp on the Nebraska side (right) at mile 798.7 (42.85109/-97.26878).

Stay right as you pass the downstream end of the island. A mile farther you will start to work your way to the south around Jacques Bend. A local outfitter's base camp (Missouri River Expeditions; 605-360-2646) is at mile 796.5 left. The river in this area can be shallow, and the channel to the camp can be difficult to locate. You should call ahead for up-to-date information on the situation. MRE offers kayak rentals, shuttle service, and custom tours featuring gourmet meals. The owner, Chad Cadwell, is something of a local legend. I've paddled with this outfit; staff members are experienced paddlers, good souls, and true river rats.

At mile 795 the river narrows, and you may experience some fast water. After the shore pinches in, the river widens. It gets shallow here, and there are sandbars, so you will need to pay attention as you work to the left shore. The river again narrows at mile 793 as you work around St. Helena Bend. Just around this bend, on the left, is the Missouri River Rafting Company's campground (605-267-3075). There is a clear, sandy area, and a road leads to the shore. The primitive campsites are sheltered and shaded, and it is a short walk to the RV campground where the shower house is located. If you need a break or a change of pace, you can rent an air-conditioned room and make arrangements for a day or evening raft float. The owners, Mike and Joan Miller, are great hosts.

Below St. Helena Bend the river widens you will work your way around Audobon Bend, and then the river narrows again at mile 788. The forested area at the point on the left is Myron Grove, and just a bit farther down on the right you will see Bow Creek. The National Park Service recently purchased an area here for river access and primitive camping. If you stay left as you come around the point, you will pass the Highline ramp at mile 787 (42.77192/-97.12118). One mile farther downriver is the upstream end of Goat Island. Also known as Jake's Island, this island is 3.5 miles long, heavily wooded, publicly owned, and a popular site for shore picnics and camping. You can pass this island on either the north or south side.

If you stay on the south (right) side of the island, you will come to the Brooky Bottoms access and ramp at mile 785 and a steak house that may be reopened with private campsites. If you stay on the north (left) side of the island, a good channel runs close along the island for about 2 miles. Then you will have to work toward the left shore. The Clay County Park and ramp (mile 780.8 left; 42.76597/-97.00336) is 1.7 miles from the downstream end of Goat Island. There is a vault toilet here and a parking area. About a half mile north on the access road, there is a well-shaded public campground. It is my understanding that if you are floating the river, you can stay overnight near the ramp as long as you set up off to one side. There is good cell phone reception here.

The river widens significantly below the Clay County ramp; you will encounter shallows, and the channel can be difficult to follow. A mile after leaving the ramp, you have to cross over to the point on the opposite (right) shore.

This section of the river is the North Alabama Bend. Once you round the point, you need to follow good water back to the left side. When I paddled this stretch in 2003, I reached the left shore near mile 778 and then stayed close along shore until rounding the point at Mulberry Bend. After paddling under the Highway 19 bridge, I worked over to the right shore and passed the Mulberry ramp at mile 775.2 (42.71482/-96.94343), where there is a vault toilet, a picnic table, and camping. Because this ramp is on the outside of the bend, the current is swift and it can be difficult to pull out.

Once you are around Mulberry Bend, you should stay right and watch for snags. At mile 773 you begin to round Vermillion Bend, and in another mile,you should angle toward the Vermillion River on the other side. Watch for shallows here. There are homes along the shore below the confluence. You have rounded Vermillion Bend when you pass mile 769, where the river narrows dramatically. In the next 2 miles you will pass an area known as Ryan Bend. Here, however, the river has taken a shortcut by carving across the base of the land forming the old point of the bend. Kate Sweeney Bend follows, starting at mile 767. If you stay to the right, you will come to the Indian Hills ramp at mile 765 right (42.68075/-96.80866).

Below the Indian Hills ramp, the river is relatively wide and there are extensive areas of shallows and sandbars; stay right until the river narrows, then cross over to the left shore to get to Burbank ramp at mile 763.4 (42.66594/-96.78688). Ionia Bend follows, and then the river turns hard to the south around Elk Point Bend beginning near mile 760. An access point is planned on the Nebraska side of this bend. Once you are around Elk Point Bend, you may have to angle to the opposite (left) shore for about a mile, and then angle back to the right shore to pull out along the shore at the Ponca State Park observation area (mile 753.8 right; 42.60710/-96.71601).

Near the observation point, there is a shaded tent-camping area. As you approach the shore, you will see a fence that separates the observation point from a parking lot. There is no easy way to get ashore here; you will have to get your boat and gear up a steep sandy bank. This will take some effort, but it can be done. Watch out for a barbed wire fence buried in the sand. A short walk inland is a primitive campground with a vault toilet, picnic tables, and good shade. A drinking water fountain is just up the road that leads to the boat ramp. The Ponca State Park's boat ramp is about 0.4 mile farther down the shore (right; 42.60710/-96.71601); the main campground is above the riverfront (402-755-2284).

This is a beautiful 1,400-acre park with more than 20 miles of trails and 2 miles of shoreline. You can see lots of wildlife here including deer, turkeys, bobcats, foxes, and raccoons. Forest species include bur oak, basswood, elm, and walnut. Near the center of this park is the 380-year-old Old Oak Tree. If for no other reason, you should stop here to pay your quiet respects to this tree that was, as the park's web page advertises, "a sapling 24 years before the Mayflower landed at Plymouth Rock."

From Ponca to Sioux City, it is about 22 miles–an easy day's paddle with good current. About a half mile below the Ponca ramp, the river narrows; on the right, you will begin to see the remnants of the effort to channelize the river for barge traffic. Here, tightly lashed pilings were driven into the river bottom and their bases covered with riprap. These are the remainders of river containment efforts that have been abandoned. The piles are skeletons of their former selves, with cable that hangs loosely from their thin, worn waists.

Watch the right shore carefully as you get about 3.5 miles from the Ponca ramp. Just before the river widens briefly, you should see the ACE river mile 750 sign. The Rosenbaum Area Public Water Access is on the left, below mile 750. I was unable to locate a ramp, but I did note some nice potential campsites along this shore. There are sandy beaches and thick woods along both sides of the river in this area. Below mile 748 there are cabins and trailers, and a small ramp on the left near mile 747. Three miles farther down, as you round a bend, you will see cabins and homes on the left. There is a private ramp here with a security light on a pole. From here you will paddle about 6 miles around a bend. At mile 738, on the left, you will see Dakota Dunes, a high-end residential development with trophy homes lining the riverfront.

As you approach Sioux City, I suggest you stay to the right, along the Nebraska shore. There can be considerable boat traffic here, especially on the weekend. The Big Sioux River joins the Missouri on the left at mile 734. As you pass this confluence, you will be able to see traffic on Interstate 29 and the Highway 77 bridge. The Sioux City Municipal Boat Dock is on your left at mile 732.6. You will see the Scenic Park take-out after the bridge, on the right. If you paddle just beyond the ramp, you will see a sandy area where you can pull out. This is the day-use area of Scenic Park. A quarter mile down the shoreline is a small inlet that you can paddle into. The campground headquarters is on the right. This is a very nice campground, with a friendly staff, good shade, and hot showers. This is a good place to stop; the staff here will always try to make room for paddlers.

SECTION 3: THE CHANNELIZED LOWER MISSOURI (RIVER MILE 732 TO MILE 0)

Sioux City, Iowa (~ mile 732), to the Missouri River confluence (mile 0)

- **River miles:** 732
- **Difficulty level:** Medium
- **Typical time to complete:** 24 to 31 days

A river without islands is like a woman without hair. She may be good and pure, but one doesn't fall in love with her very often.

Mark Twain, as quoted in *Mark Twain, His Life and Work*, by Will Clemens

The first time you paddle on the Channelized Lower Missouri, you quickly come to understand that you are riding a different beast. As explained in the Channelized Lower Techniques section, the river has been engineered for

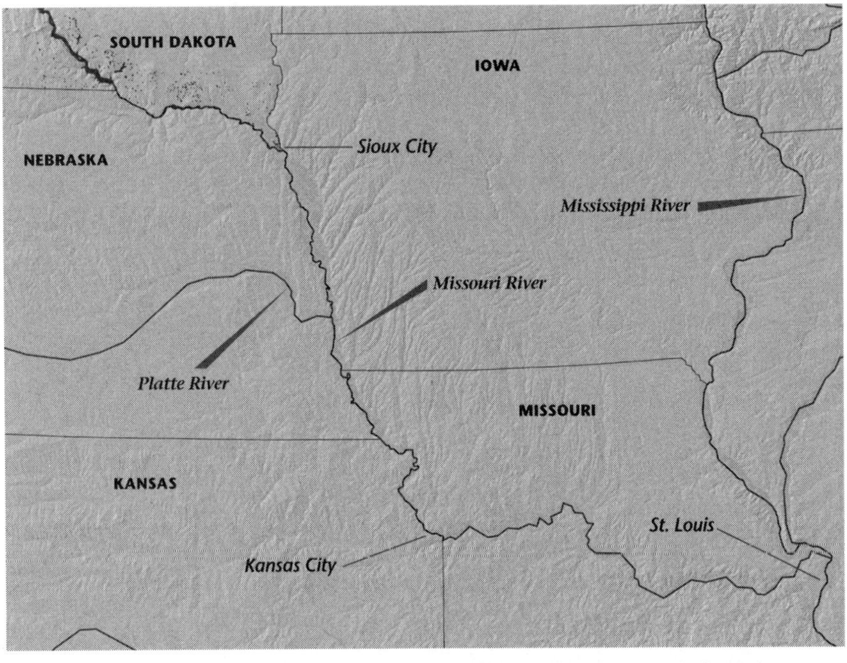

Map 3.0: Section 3—The Channelized Lower Missouri from Sioux City, Iowa (mile 732) to St. Louis, Missouri.

barge traffic. The Army Corps of Engineers (ACE) maintains a channel that is 300 feet wide and 9 feet deep. The river meanders considerably, and the main channel always swings to the outside of each bend. Riprap (crushed rock) walls line the outside bends, and wing dikes stick out perpendicularly from inside bends. Stay in the main channel, except to avoid barges. Channel markers and crossing beacons mark the main channel; because approaching barges must stay in the channel, you will know exactly where they are going to be when they pass. You can plan where you need to be to get out of their way and position yourself to minimize buffeting by considerable wakes.

Beginning with this section, you will see mile marker boards on a fairly regular basis. So you'll know, with precision, where you are and how far it is to the mouth of the Missouri river at its confluence with the Mississippi. If you are not careful, you might find yourself paying too much attention watching for the next mile marker. In essence, you may become fascinated with watching the trip odometer roll backward, counting down your progress toward the finish. From Sioux City to Omaha it is 105 miles; you will drop slightly more than a degree of latitude by the time you arrive at Omaha. From a bigger picture standpoint, from Sioux City to Kansas City you will continue to drop serious latitude but not longitude. Only when the river arrives at Kansas City does the flow finally make a sustained turn to the east, to ultimately cross the state of Missouri and reach the confluence.

This is actually a very nice section to paddle. The current is generally good, so you should average between 5 and 6 mph for this section without much effort. There is actually little barge traffic to worry about, at least until you get below Omaha. There is only modest powerboat boat traffic, and there are just two towns of consequence along the way. There are a number of ramps where you can pull out and, if necessary, camp. Also, there are some sandbars where you can camp, but you will find them less frequently, as is the case above Sioux City. There are still long stretches of water where you can paddle for hours without seeing anyone. And you will see a variety of waterfowl in and about the slack water below the dikes. Deer browse along the shore; you may also see raccoons, foxes, and a host of other creatures.

The main concern on this section is snags, as discussed in the Techniques section. Stay well away from buoys, bridge piers, and wing dams. These elements frequently snag tree limbs and sometimes tree trunks. The area in front of snag fields–tangled piles of branches, logs, and other debris–is hazardous to your health. Stay in the main channel. Also, when approaching a ramp, watch for a wing dam immediately above the pullout. Most ramps have an upstream wing to create slack water at the ramp and to divert debris.

Information/Maps/Resources

As mentioned in a previous section, Nebraska has a website (www.ngpc.state.ne.us) that provides useful material for Missouri river paddlers where you can get information about parks, campgrounds, and ramps. You might also order from the Iowa Department of Natural Resources website (www.iowadnr.com) the *Iowa Stream Fishing & Canoe Guide,* which includes three maps showing the locations of 17 boat ramps along or near the Iowa side of the Missouri River. This publication is 144 pages long and printed on newsprint; the Missouri River maps are of poor resolution.

Two ACE Omaha District publications are useful: *Missouri River Navigational Charts–Sioux City, Iowa, to Kansas City, Missouri* (1991) and *Aerial Photos (1995) of the Missouri River–Ponca State Park to Rulo, Nebraska* (June 2002), and can be ordered online by following links at www.nwo.usace.army.mil. The USGS Missouri River InfoLINK site at http://aa179.cr.usgs.gov/photos_2000/ provides access to high-resolution air photos of the river from "Sioux City Iowa to the Mouth at St. Louis, Missouri." These images are compressed in the MrSID format and should only be downloaded if you have a high-speed connection. The MrSID viewer can be downloaded by following links at www.lizardtech.com.

For the section between Sioux City and the Missouri state border, I used primarily the current *Iowa 2004 Transportation Map,* available free at any Iowa Welcome Center. This map accurately depicts the river's winding path and shows the locations of bridges that you will encounter. You should obtain a copy of the brochure, *Missouri River Boating Information,* published by the Washington Missouri Boat Club (www.washingtonmo.us and click on "boater info.; 888-792-7466). This publication lists information about ramps and docks by mile mark and details about amenities including gas availability. Primarily intended for power-boaters but useful to paddlers, the information provided is generally accurate, except for a few mile marks incorrectly assigned to locations.

To view photos of many ramps, read brief descriptions of facilities and nearby services, and for information about cell phone signal strength, see Richard Lovell's website at http://missouririvertrips.com. Richard has floated just over half the distance from Gavins Point Dam to the confluence with the Mississippi and provides photographs of almost every ramp.

Suggested Readings

Eighteen Lewis and Clark campsites are in this section. Information about what transpired here during the outbound trip (July 28 to August 20, 1804) can be found in Vol. 2:423–496 (*Journals,* [Moulton, ed.]). Return trip event detail (September 5 to 7, 1806) can be found in Vol. 8:350–353. Context about events can be found in Stephen Ambrose's *Undaunted Courage,* in chapters 12:150 and 32:401–402.

Information about life in this section in the 1850s can be found in *Forty Years a Fur Trader on the Upper Missouri,* by Charles Larpenteur. His chapter 15, "Fort Vermillion, Little Sioux, and Ponca Post," relates information about making passage from St. Louis to the Ponca area above Sioux City.

SEGMENT 3.A: Sioux City, Iowa (~ mile 732), to Omaha, Nebraska (I-680 bridge; mile 626.4) *(Maps 3.A–3.A.3)*

- **River miles:** 105.6
- **Difficulty level:** Low
- **Typical time to complete:** 5 to 7 days

Paddler's Notes and Cautions

Assuming a Sioux City start at either the Scenic Park ramp or from the shore below the campground, you should begin angling to the outside bend along the left shore. As explained in the Channelized Lower Missouri Issues and Techniques section, outside bends are typically lined with riprap, and the main channel runs along them. Dikes stick out from a turn's inside bend, and sharp-edged rocks piled to create these dikes can be submerged and difficult to see. Stay in the main channel. Read and follow the signage. Buoys are frequently out of position; do not rely on them and give them wide berth.

At mile 731 left you will see the Floyd River confluence; you'll paddle under a railroad bridge and, in about a mile, see Sergeant Floyd's Monument (~ mile 729.7) on a bluff overlooking the river. You cannot get to the monument from the river; there is no easy landing along the shore since busy Interstate 29 blocks the way, and there is no trail up the side of the bluff. Console yourself with the fact that you are paddling around Floyd Bend. As you continue on, you will paddle under the I-129 bridge and then under a natural gas pipeline bridge that crosses the river almost exactly at the 728-mile

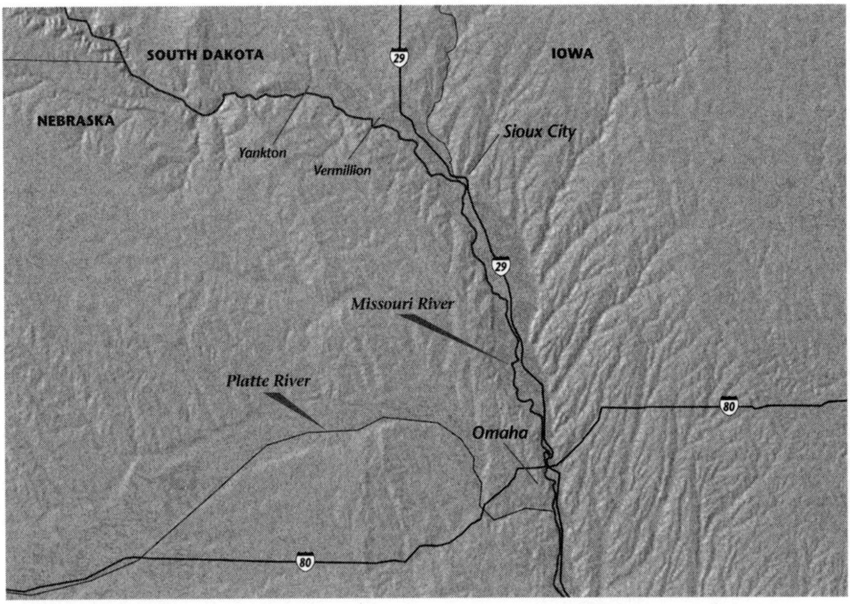

Map 3.A: Sioux City, Iowa (~ mile 732), to Omaha, Nebraska (I-680 Bridge; mile 626.4) Because of good current, this segment is a relatively easy float; barge traffic is modest, and there are numerous ramps where you can pull out in the event of high water. Below Omaha, at the Platte River confluence, the river can rise more than 5 feet overnight after stormy weather.

mark. As you paddle beyond this area, you should pinch your nose and breathe through your mouth; when I paddled through here there was one pipe dumping a foul-smelling yellow liquid into the river. I gagged when I got my first whiff of it. Up to this point I had paddled nearly 1,600 miles on the Missouri River; this was the first place where I saw what clearly smelled like some kind of toxic liquid pouring out a pipe into the river.

Once around Floyd Bend, you will come to the Cottonwood Cove ramp at mile 725.6 right. The Sioux City airport is on the opposite side of the river. From here, you will work through a series of gentle bends, most about 3 to 4 miles long. Pay attention to the crossing beacons; when you reach a crossing beacon on the shore that you are paddling on, locate the crossing beacon on the opposite shore and aim for that mark. On the right, about 0.3 mile above the Wheatland River Access ramp (mile 722 left; 42.36266/-96.41565), there are a couple sandy and level places where you could pull over in the lee of the wing dams. Three miles beyond the ramp, you will cross under the first of two power lines (mile 718.8); the second is a bit more than a mile downstream. You will pass two large power

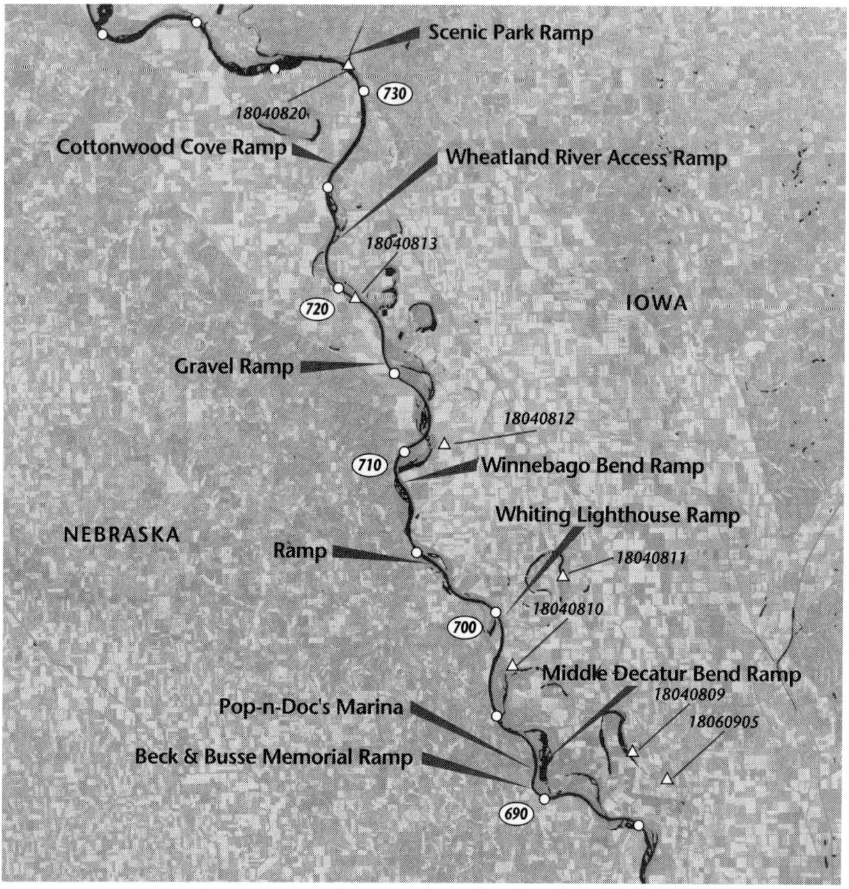

Map 3.A.1: Sioux City, Iowa (~ mile 732) to mile 690.

plants on the left. These stations are along the outside bend; they both have shoreline buildings with intake and output pipes sticking out into the river. Stay to the right side of the main channel as you pass these structures.

Just below mile 716 on the Nebraska side (right) is a gravel ramp (42.28981/-96.36926). The Winnebago Indian Reservation begins on your right near mile 714.5; Winnebago Bend begins near mile 710, and the Winnebago Bend Access ramp is on the Iowa side (left) at mile 708.7 (42.20985/-96.35943). Several homes line the shore near the ramp. Just above mile 707 left, the Winnebago Reservation ends and the Omaha Indian Reservation begins. You will work through Upper, Middle, and Lower Omaha Mission Bends. As you approach Lower Omaha Mission Bend, there is a ramp on the right (mile 704.5; 42.15516/-96.33696). In about 4 miles, you will reach the 700-mile mark, about half a mile beyond that is the Whiting Lighthouse ramp on the left (mile 699.3; 42.11331/-96.26851). This is one of the few privately owned ramps on the Iowa side; I was told there is a small marina here and fee camping. About a quarter mile downstream as you round the bend, there are some possible campsites on the right. From here it is about 8 miles to Decatur.

You will see the Decatur highway bridge as you round the bend near mile 692. The Omaha Reservation ends on the right about half a mile before the bridge. The Decatur Bridge is a toll bridge. It is the only Missouri River crossing for more than 30 miles up and down the river. A quarter mile before the bridge is the Pop-n-Doc's Restaurant and Marina (402-349-5193). To put in here, stay to the right and watch for a cut that leads into a nicely sheltered harbor (mile 691.2 right; 42.01086/-96.24173). Just above the ramp is a very popular bar and restaurant with a big deck overlooking the harbor. The restaurant opens at 5 P.M. Wednesday through Friday, and at 11 A.M. on the weekend. I give you this detail because this is a good place to stop. If at all possible, time your trip to stop and get a meal. I paddled in here during a weekday in the early afternoon. The place was not yet open, but I met Bob Hutton, one of the owners; he got me a cold drink and we talked about the river. He was very helpful and provided me with useful information. This is a paddler-friendly stop.

Just across the river from Pop-n-Doc's, on the Iowa side before the bridge, is the Middle Decatur Bend Access ramp (mile 691.2 left). A quarter mile below the bridge, on the Nebraska side, is the Beck and Busse Memorial Recreation Area ramp (right; 42.00402/-96.24382), which has a nice campground with shower houses. There is a fair amount of traffic on the bridge, and you will hear some of the noise at the campground, but you can easily walk to the marina or into town where there is a gas station and convenience store, and the Green Lantern Restaurant, which serves good steaks. The Decatur Bridge has an interesting history. Before the bridge's construction was completed, the river shifted course, leaving the span crossing dry land. Eventually the ACE rerouted the river to pass under the bridge.

As is the case elsewhere, there are dikes along the inside bends of turns below Decatur. Level areas and sandy beaches sometimes develop below some of these dikes, and this is the case along the inside bend of the turn after mile 689. If you want to pull into one of these areas, use caution. If you look carefully, you should be able to determine how far the rock extends; stay well away from the tip. Once you are downstream from the dike, turn your bow into the

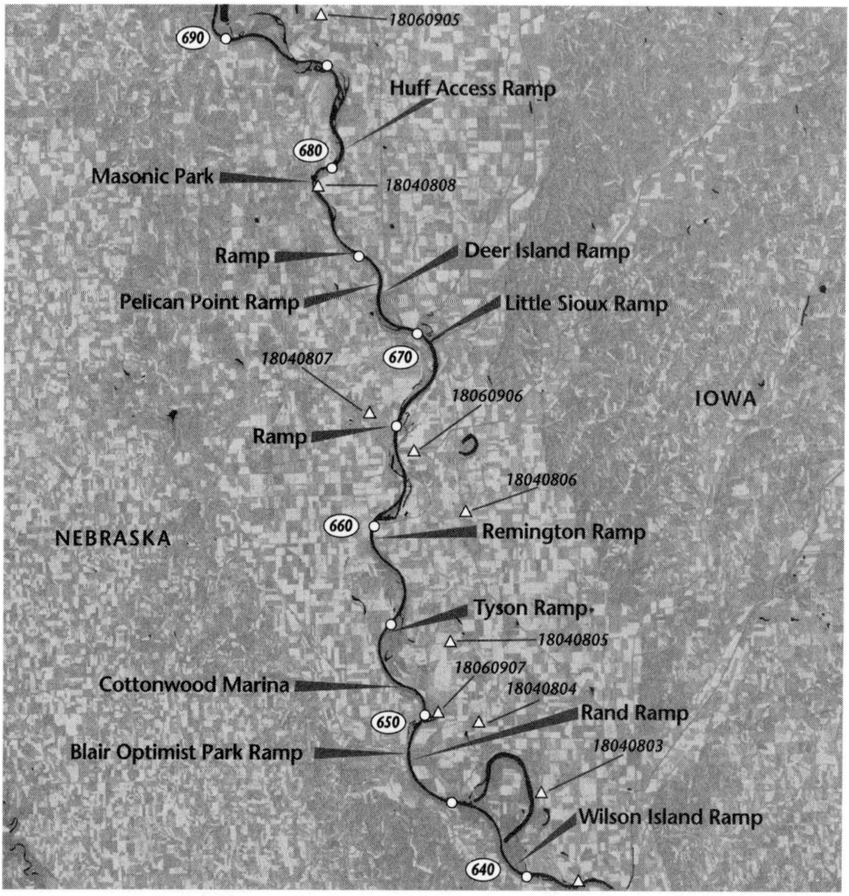

Map 3.A.2: Mile 690 to mile 640.

current and use the back eddy to bring you to the slack water below the dike. Below mile 686, you will see cabins on the left; across on the right is another inside bend with potential pullouts and emergency campsites.

There is supposed to be a channel below mile 683 on the left that leads to a ramp at Louisville Oxbow Lake. I did not see it. About 2 miles down the river, however, is the Huff Access ramp and campground (mile 681.1 left; 41.92486/-96.13478). This would be a nice place to camp if you needed to stop. Farther downstream on the right, you will see Masonic Park (mile 678.4), and at mile 675 right, there is a ramp. At mile 672.7 right is the Pelican Point Recreation Area ramp (41.83368/-96.11161). This area has water, a shelter, primitive campsites, picnic tables, and fire rings. There is also poison ivy, so stay in the mowed areas. If you are lucky, the mulberry tree right above the ramp will be in fruit. Less than half a mile downstream on the Iowa side is the Deer Island Access ramp (mile 672.3 left; 41.82780/-96.11176). A couple miles downstream, the Monona Harrison Ditch enters from the left; less than a mile from that, you will see the confluence of the Little Sioux River (mile 669.3 left). The Little Sioux Access ramp is just down from the river's mouth (mile 669.3 left; 41.80233/-96.06672). Four miles downstream on the Nebraska side, there is a ramp (mile 665 right).

The Soldier River joins the Missouri River from the left exactly at mile 664. Less than 5 miles down on the left is the Remington (Mondamin) Access ramp (mile 659.7; 41.68661/-96.12094). The Tyson Island State Wildlife Refuge begins on the left near mile 656. The Tyson Access ramp is at mile 654.4 left (41.62270/-96.11569). Recent dredging by the ACE in this area has created what locals call the "Missouri River Party Cove" at mile 653 left. Powerboat traffic is considerable in this area on weekends, so be prepared for boat wakes. The Cottonwood Marina (402-293-3122) is on the right at mile 651 (41.58807/-96.09180). There is a restaurant and bar here with an ATM machine, and a nice campground with shaded sites. After the marina you will round California Bend, and the Blair bridges will come in sight. The Blair Optimist Park ramp is just before the railroad bridge on the right (mile 648.4; 41.55216/-96.09673). At the park, there is a shelter and a bathroom with water. Across the river on the Iowa side is the Rand Access ramp (mile 648.3 left; 41.55084/-96.09633). I spoke with two Blair City Water Department workers who told me that swimmers have drowned near the Rand ramp and that it was closed. The Highway 30 bridge is just downstream from the railroad bridge. The town is about 2 miles to the west on Highway 30.

Desoto National Wildlife Refuge begins just after mile 645. The east side of this refuge features a nearly 8-mile-long oxbow lake. Oxbow lakes are the stems and pieces of abandoned river channels, and are formed naturally when flooding cuts a new channel across a natural bend. Oxbows were also formed as the river was straightened for barge navigation after 1945. You will see an observation point at mile 643.7 left, and pass the lower end of the oxbow lake at mile 642 left.

A mile downstream on the left is Wilson Island State Park, with a ramp and nice campground with amenities (mile 641; 41.47848/-96.01456). About 0.8 mile farther downstream, also on the left, a road comes to the river's edge. You could pull out here if necessary. At mile 639.6 there is a ramp on the Nebraska side (right; 41.47100/-95.98909). I was told this was the Fort Calhoun ramp,

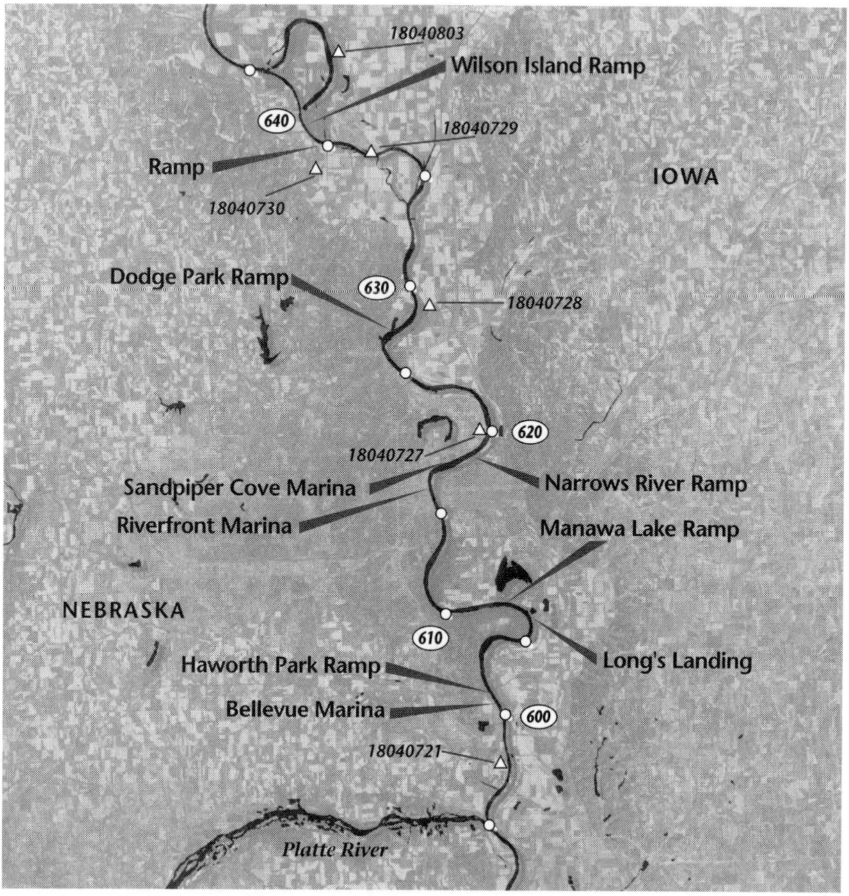

Map 3.A.3: Mile 640 to mile 595 below Omaha.

but I have been unable to confirm this. On your right at mile 637.8, you will see the Boyer Chute, a 3-mile-long channel that cuts across the base of Boyer Bend. No boats are allowed in this channel. Snags and fallen timber sometimes block the channel; if a good current is moving through it, you could be pinned against these strainers.

As you work around Boyer Bend, the Boyer River joins the Missouri at mile 635.3 left, and the downstream end of the chute is on the right at mile 633.6. Just below this on the left is Goose Haven, where there are some cabins and a private ramp. From here, it is about 5.5 miles to the Dodge Park Marina at mile 627.5 right.

The Dodge Park ramp (41.35713/-95.94963) is just below the marina entrance channel. I suggest you stay here, because paddling beyond Omaha to a place you can camp may take more than four hours. If you stop, there are two options. There is a nice campground at Dodge Park, but unfortunately it is a good hike from the boat ramp. If you stay at this campground, you will have to find a secure place to leave your boat. You might ask for suggestions at the concession stand and fueling dock just down the shore from the ramp. The second option is to paddle to the marina and ask if you may leave your boat there overnight while you stay at the campground or make other arrangements. The marina manager is John Niksick (402-444-5916) and the marina caretaker is Dick Strehle (402-444-4675). This well-run marina is a paddler-friendly stop; the management understands the fact that the park setup is less than ideal for paddlers. Dick has assisted paddlers on numerous occasions. This is a secure facility, the entrance gate is closed at night, and there is a shower in the bathroom near the docks. If you ask for permission to use the shower, the request will usually be granted.

That night Dick and I went out to dinner at a local roadhouse. Besides talking about the river, we spoke at length about issues faced by paddlers at Dodge Park and similar facilities. He appreciated the fact that paddlers want to camp by their boat and that there are few official areas where this is possible. Dick pointed out that the paddling community has not communicated its needs to the folks that design ramps. It turned out that his son, Kevin, is a landscape architect who has designed parks and other recreational facilities including boat ramps. We both agreed that the situation could be improved with a minimal investment and some tweaking of existing ramp sites. The next morning, before I left, we had coffee. Dick made a phone call to his son, explained that I was a paddler, and related the gist of our conversation about facilities for paddlers. I spoke with Kevin, and we agreed to remain in contact with the intent to see if we could incorporate paddler's needs into the design of an upcoming ramp project. I was heartened by this discussion; there is no question in my mind that the Missouri will see more paddler traffic. The development of one or two model areas that are paddler-friendly–having room off to one side for manual launch and coming ashore, a source for drinking water, and a nearby overnight floaters camping area–would do much to help demonstrate the best practices for minimizing environmental impacts and ensuring compatibility with the activities of other users.

Just below mile 627 right is the entrance to the Coast Guard station and moorings. Here you may see some of the Coast Guard's Missouri River fleet, including the buoy tender responsible for setting and replacing the red and green buoys marking the main channel. The ACE Missouri River Project office is also here. The I-680 bridge is at mile 626.4.

SEGMENT 3.B: Omaha, Nebraska (I-680 bridge, mile 626.4) to Kansas City, Kansas (Kaw River ramp, ~ mile 367.5) *(Maps 3.B–3.B.6)*

- **River miles:** 258.9 miles
- **Difficulty level:** Low
- **Typical time to complete:** 7 – 10 days

> *The taste for country displays the same diversity in aesthetic competence among individuals as the taste for opera, or oils. There are those who are willing to be herded in droves through 'scenic' places; who find mountains grand if they be proper mountains, with waterfalls, cliffs, and lakes. To such the Kansas plains are tedious. They see the endless corn, but not the heave and grunt of ox teams breaking the prairie. History, for them, grows on campuses. They look at the low horizon, but they cannot see it, as deVaca did, under the bellies of the buffalo.*
>
> ALDO LEOPOLD, *ROUND RIVER*

The Platte River joins the Missouri about a dozen miles below Omaha, easily adding another mile-an-hour to the current. From this point on, you should be averaging 5.5 to 6.5 mph without too much work. From the big picture, by the time you reach Kansas City you will have dropped more than 3 degrees of latitude. Not much to look forward to? Well, if you look at the map you will see that once you get to Kansas City, you have made just about all the southerly progress that is necessary; the confluence's latitude is less than a third of a degree farther south. Of course, longitude is another story. When you get to Kansas City, at about 94.5 degrees west, your easterly progress from Sioux City's longitude is a modest 1.8 degrees. This changes after Kansas City, where the river turns hard to the east. From this point on, every morning you will paddle toward the rising sun, and in the afternoon the sun will be at your back. You gain daily reductions in longitude, and each day's effort brings you closer to the confluence's longitude of 90 degrees west.

Between Omaha and Kansas City, there are a few very nice towns; most are located where a bridge crosses the river. You will still paddle long stretches where you will see little evidence of settlement. The river shore alternates with

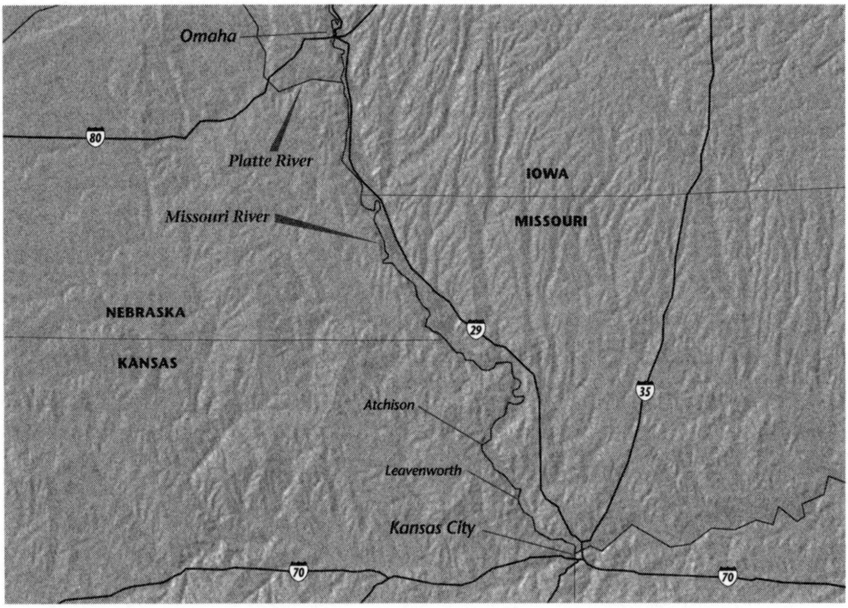

Map 3.B: Omaha, Nebraska (mile 626.4), to Kansas City, Kansas (mile 367.5). Expect barge traffic in this segment and be prepared for rapid increases in river level associated with rivers and streams that dump storm-related floodwaters into the Missouri River.

groves of forest and farm fields. The land is well watered–too well watered, in fact. Drainage structures, rather than irrigation hardware, are featured along the river's edge. If you have paddled the Missouri through the badlands of the Dakotas, the contrast is a 180-degree difference.

Water levels on the river can change considerably on this section. You need to be mindful of this fact. Summer thunderstorms bring torrential rains, and it is not unusual for the river to rise 3 or 4 feet after a big storm. If you are not going to camp above a ramp or at a campground, you need to select a site with some elevation. Look for recent evidence of flooding, and camp above the high water line. After high water, many sandbars are plastered with a thick coat of muddy sediment; until this washes away or dries out, these areas are not good campsites.

Information/Maps/Resources

As mentioned in previous sections, Nebraska has a website (www.ngpc.state.ne.us) that provides useful material for Missouri River paddlers where you can get information about parks, campgrounds, and ramps. From the Iowa Department of Natural Resources website (www.iowadnr.com), you might order the *Iowa Stream Fishing & Canoe Guide.*

Two ACE Omaha District publications are useful: *Missouri River Navigational Charts–Kansas City, Missouri to the Mouth* (1991) and *Aerial Photos (1995) of the Missouri River–Ponca State Park to Rulo, Nebraska* (June 2002), and can be ordered online by following links at www.nwo.usace.army.mil.

For the section between Sioux City and the Missouri state border, I used the current *Iowa 2004 Transportation Map*. Once I reached Nebraska City, just north of the Iowa and Missouri border, I relied principally on the *Lewis & Clark Bicentennial Lower Missouri River: A Guide to Recreation & Visitor Safety*. This is an outstanding publication. There are 12 maps in this publication; each covers about 50 river miles. The maps are well designed and provide accurate information about river safety, navigation, boat ramps, and the location of public land. This guide was published in October 2002; copies are not easy to locate, but all pages of the guide can be downloaded as Adobe PDF files at the Kansas City ACE Lewis and Clark Bicentennial Commemoration website (http://www.nwk.usace.army.mil/lewisandclark/map-2.htm). Some additional riverside facilities have been added since the publication of this guide; I have included information about these in my commentary and on my maps.

Another useful publication is the Missouri Department of Conservation's map titled *Upper Missouri River*. This map shows the area from the far northwest corner of the state to Kansas City. It contains information about public land and access points along the river, and which of these allow camping. This map was printed in November 2000. A sister publication, *Lower Missouri River,* covers the river from below Boonville (near mile 175) to the confluence with the Mississippi. To my knowledge there is no map for the middle section. You should also obtain a copy of the brochure, *Missouri River Boating Information,* published by the Washington Missouri Boat Club (888-792-7466). This publication lists information about ramps and docks by mile mark and details about amenities including gas availability. Although primarily intended for powerboaters, the information provided is also useful for paddlers.

To view photos of many ramps, read brief descriptions of facilities and nearby services, and for information about cell phone signal strength, see Richard Lovell's website at http://missouririvertrips. Richard has floated just over half the distance from Gavins Point Dam to the confluence with the Mississippi and provides photographs of almost every ramp.

Suggested Readings

Twenty-nine Lewis and Clark campsites are in this section. Information about what transpired here during the outbound trip (June 26 to July 27, 1804) can be found in Vol. 2:323–423 (*Journals,* [Moulton, ed.]). Return trip event detail (September 10 to 14, 1806) can be found in Vol. 8:355–360. Context about events can be found in Stephen Ambrose's *Undaunted Courage,* in chapters 12:147–150 and 32:402.

Steamboat traffic figures large in the early history of this area. One of the best sources for information about piloting on the Missouri is Donald Jackson's *Voyages of the Steamboat Yellow Stone.* Jackson provides an account of the 1833 voyage of the steamboat *Yellow Stone*'s passage through this area when it was struck by a cholera epidemic.

Additional sources of information about the area's natural history and cultural landscapes include Don Pierce's *Exploring Missouri River Country,* and Brett Dufur's *Exploring Lewis and Clark's Missouri.* The latter provides an updated reference to the towns and historic places along the river, as does the *National Geographic's Guide to the Lewis & Clark Trail,* by Thomas Schmidt.

Paddler's Notes and Cautions

It will take at least four hours to paddle through Omaha. There are a few places where you can take out, but no established places to camp. If you want to spend a day or two looking around the city, you might make arrangements to leave your boat at one of the marinas. If you do not have a support vehicle, you will have to work out transport. If you do not know anyone in Omaha, a hotel shuttle might pick you up at a marina, or you can call a cab or rent a car. If you do stay in Omaha, you should visit the Henry Doorly Zoo. This is one of the best laid-out and most interesting zoos that I have ever visited.

Just below the I-680 bridge (mile 626.4), you will pass the M.U.D. Water Works Intake on the right. Somehow this name is appropriate, but it must horribly complicate marketing efforts. After this you will paddle by Omaha's working riverfront, past a series of power plants, bulk materials handling dockage, and barge terminals. Stay to the center of the channel. If you see smaller towboats pushing barges, give them lots of room to maneuver. Because of the possibility of traffic, it would be a good idea to have your kayak spray skirt or canoe bow cover in place.

When you reach mile 624, you will start around a 7-mile-long bend in the river. The Omaha airport, Eppley Field, is on the right. At mile 623.3 right, there is a small ramp that provides the airfield with access to the river. Given airport security–related issues, you should probably not stop here. Instead, continue paddling about 4 more miles around the bend to the Narrows River Access ramp at mile 619.2 left. You will see a tan water intake building just after this at mile 619, followed by an abandoned railroad swing bridge. The Iowa side span is now permanently open, resting on its pedestal paralleling the shore. Because the channel is on the left descending side, this structure is judged not to be a hazard to navigation and the structure does not have to be removed.

After mile 618 right are Freedom Park, the Anchor Inn, and the Sandpiper Cove Marina. There is a restaurant at the Anchor Inn. A quarter mile before the marina, you will see a submarine on blocks parked on the shore next to a larger navy ship. These vessels were brought up the Mississippi and Missouri to this inland resting place. Both appeared in shipshape condition and would be worth an inspection. As I paddled by these vessels, I could not help but think that either would be dwarfed by a battleship such as the *Missouri,* but that it is still nice to know that the citizens of Omaha maintain at least a limited naval presence along their waterfront. With respect to the sub's operation, the 9-foot depth of the main channel would be an issue.

The channel to the Sandpiper Cove Marina (617.6; 41.27510/-95.90462) is on the right, about a quarter mile beyond the submarine. A relatively narrow channel leads to the marina; look for a Phillips 66 gas sign at the entrance. There are docks and a ramp here (402-346-8883). Beyond the marina you will have an impressive view of the Omaha skyline. If it is at the dock, you will pass the *River City Star,* a modest-sized excursion steamboat. The Riverfront Marina (404-444-5916) is at mile 616.4 right. Currently, you can dock here for free between 10 A.M. and 4 P.M. Monday through Friday; otherwise you pay $5 per hour and $50 for an overnight stay. You will have to tie up at a boat slip; there is no place to pull out for canoes or kayaks. If you have not practiced such a boat exit or entry, now would probably not be a good time. Pull in if you want to look around Omaha's newly developed riverfront. There is an impressive sculpture dedicated to the American worker, and good access to the historic Old Market area. Ric's Café, an upscale, on-the-river eatery, is right next door, as is the new National Parks Service building, where you can troll the lobby for brochures and maps.

In the next few miles, you will paddle under four bridges: the I-480 bridge at mile 616, a railroad bridge just above mile 615, the I-80 bridge near mile 614,

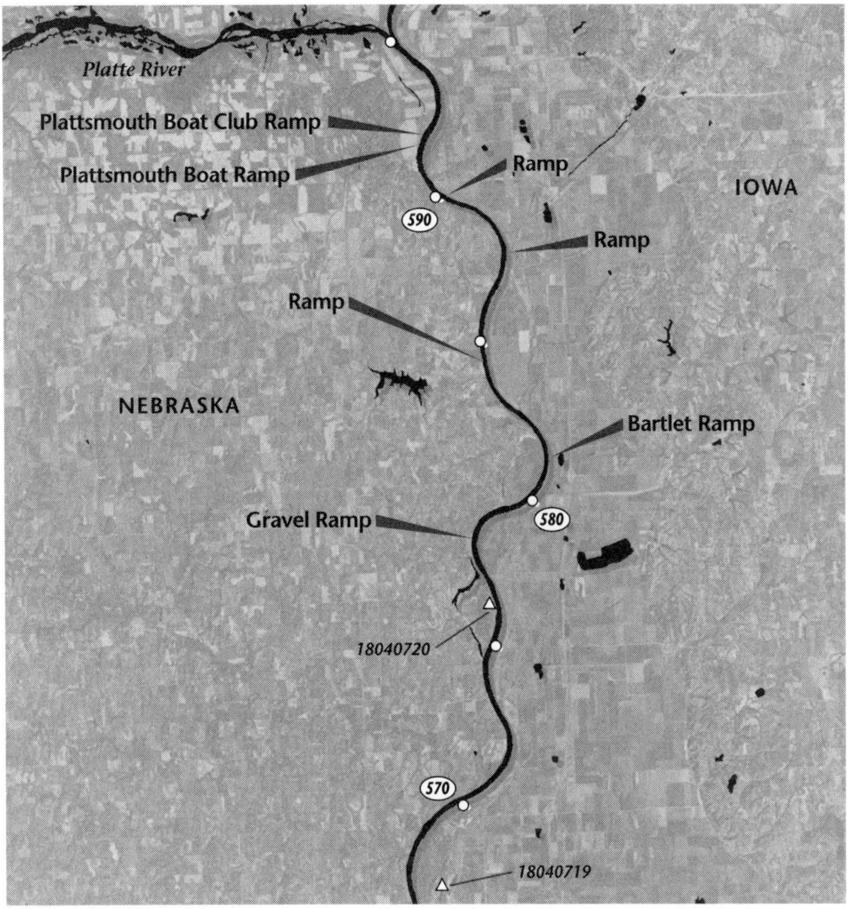

Map 3.B.1: Platte River (mile 595) to mile 568. (Note: See Map 3.A.3 for miles 626 to 595.)

and the Highway 275 bridge at mile 612.2. About 4.5 miles down from this last bridge, on the left, is the Manawa Lake river access ramp (mile 607.4; 41.18890/-95.86408). Manawa State Park is more than a mile to the north of this ramp, so the campground there is not an option. The Long's Landing Recreation Area is on a bend near mile 606.5 left (41.18415/-95.84613; these GPS coordinates are derived from imagery, as a towboat's passage interrupted my mapping efforts). You will paddle by the Omaha Power and Light plant (left) as you round the tip of this bend, and in another mile or so the river turns to the west. As the river turns to the south, you will begin to work around the Bellevue Bend. After you paddle under the Highway 370 bridge, you will see the Haworth Park Recreation

Area ramp on the right at mile 601 (41.13348/-95.87694). The Bellevue Marina is just downstream at mile 600.7 right (41.13075/-95.87404). This is a 200-slip, floating-dock marina in a well-protected harbor with a launch ramp. The 600-river-mile mark is about 0.6 mile downstream.

The Platte River empties into the Missouri at mile 595 right. The channel is on the right as you approach the confluence. If there has been recent flooding, there may be a lot of debris exiting the Platte, so approach this area with caution. Watch for snags below the confluence as you enter Upper Plattsmouth Bend. The Plattsmouth Boat Club ramp is at mile 591.7 right (41.01653/-95.86753), and just below this is the Plattsmouth Boat ramp (591.7 right; 41.01476/-95.86869). The town of Plattsmouth is about 0.8 mile to the southwest from the ramp. Below mile 591, you will pass under a natural gas pipeline bridge, then a railroad bridge, and finally the Highway 34 bridge. One-half mile after the bridge is a ramp on the left (mile 590; 40.99473/-95.86138); another Iowa side ramp is 2.5 miles farther downstream (mile 587.5 left; 40.97244/-95.82877).

When I stopped at Plattsmouth, a fisherman told me that there had been some heavy rains to the north, and that the river would be rising shortly. I checked NOAA weather radio, and the forecast was for heavy thunderstorms. I had started the day at Dodge Park, at the north end of Omaha City, and had so far paddled 36 miles. I decided to start looking for a campsite on a bank well above the river. I paddled well beyond the bridges because I did not want to listen to train and truck noise all night. It took a while to locate a good campsite, but I eventually found a site up a sandy bank on the left just above mile 586 right (40.95203/-95.83761). This site was about 6 or 7 feet above the river, and there were some large logs and tree branches on the ground that had been deposited during spring floods. I set my tent close by these for shelter from the wind. This site was a good one; it got me the elevation I needed, was sandy, and had shelter that would have protected me from high winds. There was a lot of thunder that night, but the main storm missed me. I was able to sleep well because I knew that I had a good campsite.

One thing about this site bears mentioning. As I got out of the water to pull my kayak ashore, I splashed some water on myself to cool down. I immediately felt a burning sensation on my back and shoulders–almost like sparks from a campfire. There was something in the water that caused this, but I have no idea if it was a chemical or biological agent of some sort. I only know that it was an instantaneous irritant. I rinsed off with some of my drinking water and the burning disappeared. This may have been caused by some chemical being dumped in the river at Plattsmouth, or by some nearby agricultural activity.

About 1.5 miles downriver on the right, you will see a large, white grain elevator. Just before this is a boat ramp (mile 584.7 right; 40.93315/-95.84104). Below mile 584 you enter Calumet Bartlett Bend. After a mile or so, on the left, you will see an area where sections of the bank have been cut to add habitat along the shoreline. The intent here is to provide a structure behind which fish can find slack water to rest or feed and perhaps places to spawn. The Bartlet Access ramp is at mile 580.9 left (40.88753/-95.80938). Three miles beyond, as you are rounding Pin Hook Bend, you will come to a low, cleared area along the right shore (mile 577.5) that would make a good rest stop or emergency pullout. Wa-Con-Da Lake is just west of the river for the next mile or so.

Fourteen miles downstream is Nebraska City. About a mile before town, you will see large grain elevators on the right. The Riverview Marina State Recreation Area ramp is at mile 563.2 right (40.69113/-95.84822). There is a shelter and a bathroom with water near the ramp, but the full-service campground is a good distance away. The entrance to the marina is just down from the ramp. This is a site where, with just a little work, a very nice floater's camp might be established. While I rested here, a pickup drove up and two men in Lewis and Clark reenactor's costumes got out and walked down to the ramp. I introduced myself to them, and it turned out that they were with the Discovery Expedition of St. Charles, the group that was coming up the river in replica vessels. I explained that I was an honorary member of their group, that I had come down from Three Forks, and that I would provide them with information about the river ahead when I arrived at their downstream camp. One of the men was crew leader Scott Mandrell (a.k.a. Meriwether Lewis). Scott told me that the group would be at Brownville in a day or so, and I told him I would probably meet them there.

The Highway 2 bridge is 1.5 miles downstream from the Riverview ramp. Between mile 560 and 559, there are a few places along the left shore where you could find a campsite. At mile 554.5 left is the Hamburg Mitchell Access ramp, where you might camp. This ramp is 0.8 mile above the Iowa border with Missouri; when you see the 553-mile mark, Missouri is on your left. When you paddle across the border, it is about 175 river miles to Kansas City.

I started to look for a campsite after I got past the Hamburg Mitchell ramp, but I could find nowhere to pull out for the next several miles. Eventually, as I approached Lower Barney Bend at mile 548, I saw some trailers and a ramp

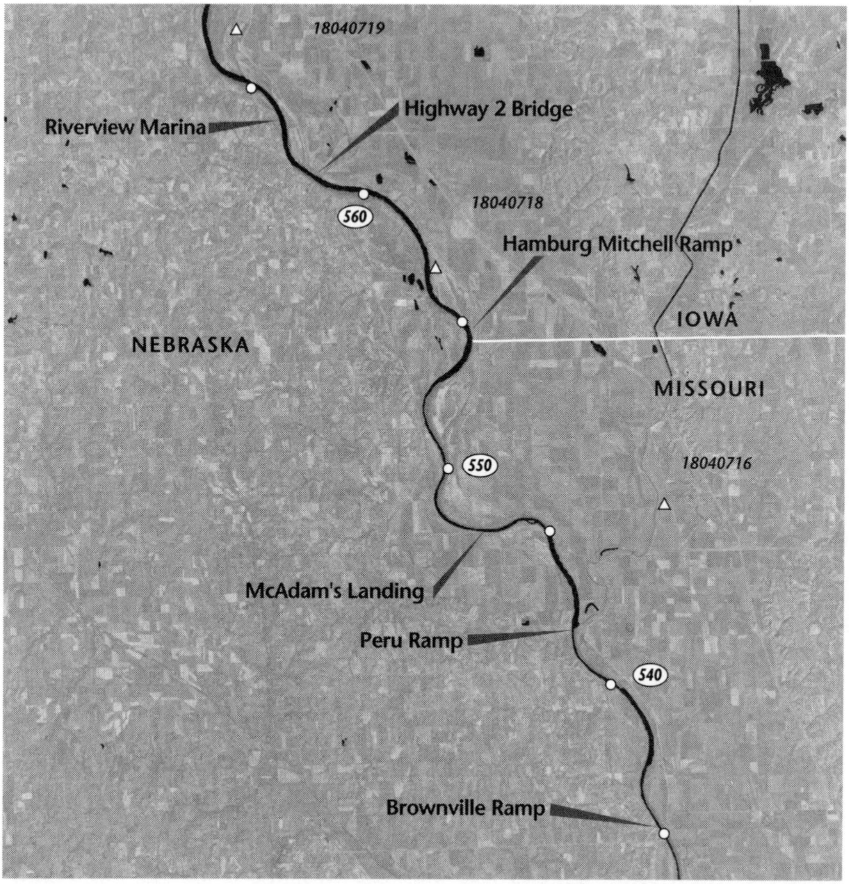

Map 3.B.2: Mile 565 above Riverview Marina to Brownville ramp (mile 535).

on the right. There were some men working on an outboard motor along the shore; as I passed them, I said hello and asked them if they knew where I could find a place to camp. They said I could camp "right here." A very fast current was running along the right shore since it is on the outside of the bend. By the time I slowed down and turned around, I was downstream from the ramp. I paddled mightily against the current to get back to the ramp but could make no progress. I decided that I would have to paddle across the river to get to an area of less current. Just as I started to do this, one of the men called out that I might find a place to pull out just a bit downstream. This was good advice. I drifted backward with the current until I was just past some rocks jutting out into the channel and then slipped into the shore just below them.

It turned out that I had put in at the river camp known to locals as McAdam's Landing (mile 547.6; 40.52388/-95.75266). I introduced myself to what turned out to be an outstanding bunch of river rats: Bob and Sarabeth McAdams, Carl ("Windy") Iske, Brian Kerr, and Bill Lewis. They helped me with my gear, found me a chair, and got me a starter beer, and we ended up talking about the river for the next several hours. Sarabeth and Brian went out for more beer and a couple of pizzas for dinner. Everyone in this group was a NASCAR fan, and early on in the evening one of them remarked about my resemblance to Dale Ernhardt. As far as they were concerned, I was a dead ringer for him. Brian remarked that his jaw dropped when I got out of my boat and he got a good look at my face. Everybody agreed that the similarity was not a bad thing since there is a tremendous reservoir of respect for "The Eliminator." But from the standpoint of hospitality, I am convinced that virtually anyone coming off the river would receive a welcome. There is an ethic here: River rats look after other river travelers. You will find that many locals, such as this group at McAdams Landing, welcome Missouri River adventurers. If you need a place to camp, or simply to fill your water jugs, all you have to do is ask for assistance and you will probably get the help that you need.

During our conversation, I explained that I was working on a guidebook for paddlers for the entire Missouri River, starting from the headwaters and finishing at St. Louis. We went over my maps, and I made notes about ramps downstream and camping spots based on their information. We talked about the river, drank beer, and slapped mosquitoes. Windy explained that he typically did all his boating upstream; that way if he lost power the current would bring him back to his dock. Bob said, "You have to respect this river, use common sense, and don't ever think you are too good. I am 67 years old, and I've been on this SOB all my life. I've been lucky. It doesn't want to take anybody, but you make mistakes and it will get you." We ended the night talking about fishing and about the 1993 flood that had nearly washed away the trailers high up from the shore. "There were a lot of refrigerators floating downriver that spring," Bob said.

Below McAdams Landing, on the right between mile 545 and mile 543.5, is one of the few places where the state of Nebraska is on both sides of the Missouri River. A several-square-mile piece of Nebraska that resembles the end of a dog bone juts into the Missouri. This "overage" is the result of a straightening of the river that left a big chunk of Nebraska on the "wrong" side.

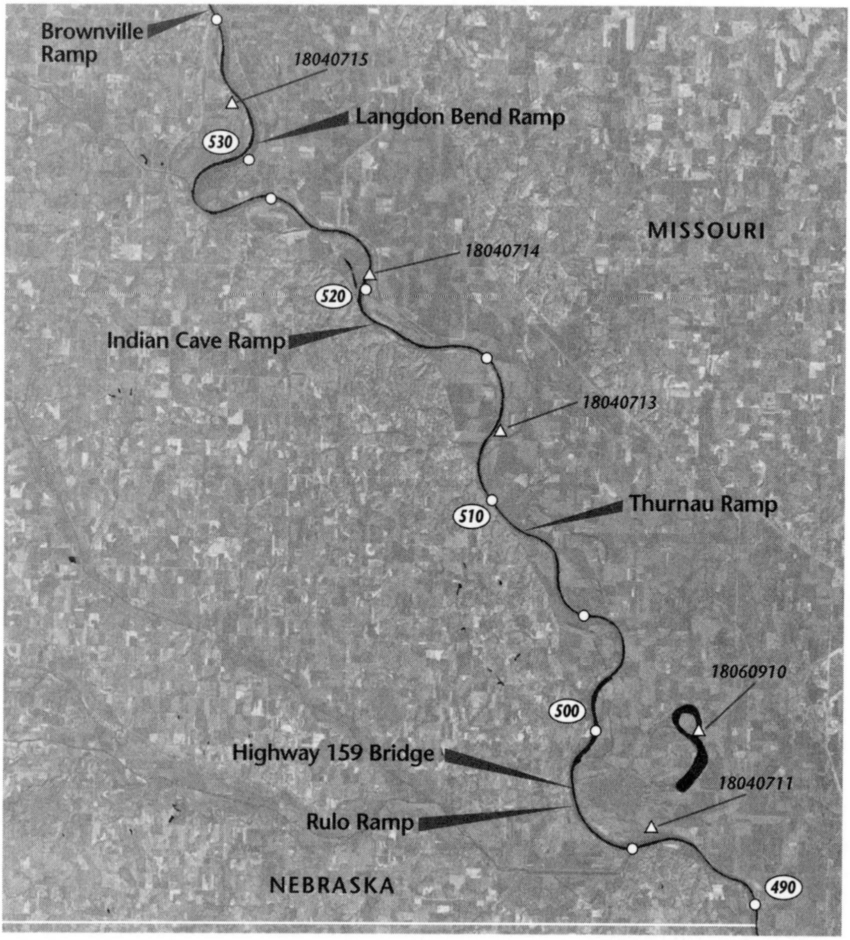

Map 3.B.3: Brownville ramp (mile 535) to mile 490, near the Nebraska border with Kansas.

Partway down this section at mile 544.3 right is a cabin with a private ramp. Just before mile 542 on the right is the Peru ramp (~ 40.48439/-95.69732), and the Nishnabotna River joins the Missouri on the left.

About 7 miles downstream on the right is the town of Brownville. After crossing under the Highway 136 bridge, you will see a ramp on the right (mile 535; 40.39883/-95.65309). Above the ramp is the Brownville State Recreation Area, where there is drinking water, shaded campsites, picnic tables, shelters, vault toilets, and a floating restaurant. The recreation area is home to the Meriwether Lewis Dredge Museum, which is actually a large ACE riverboat that has been pulled up into "dry dock" and retired from service. I recommend that you stop here and take a tour of this vessel. From the upper deck you can look out at the Missouri to enjoy a riverboat captain's view of the river. If you do stay here, try to get a ride into town to visit the arboretum and the local winery.

As I paddled under the Brownville Bridge, I saw the Discovery Expedition's keelboat and two smaller pirogues tied to a floating dock. Before I began my 2004 summer expedition, I contacted this St. Charles, Missouri–based Lewis and Clark Expedition reenactment group, offering to assist them with maps and intelligence about the river farther upstream. My assistance was welcomed; I was made an honorary member of the Discovery Expedition, and we agreed that I would meet them at some point as I worked my way downstream to provide a briefing about conditions they would encounter. I pulled my kayak out at the ramp, walked to the reenactors camp, and introduced myself to one of the crew, explaining that I needed to report to the commanding officers. Eventually I sat down at the mess tent with Peyton "Bud" Clark (a.k.a. William Clark). I summarized current conditions at ramps, talked about facilities, and described some of the difficulties that they would face making passage on the reservoirs upstream. I expressed my concern about how dangerous Lake Oahe might be, and we talked about the seaworthiness of their vessels. During our conversation, Jim Rascher (a.k.a. Ruben Fields), who built the boats at the group's St. Charles Boathouse, joined us.

Before my conversation with Bud and Jim, I was seriously concerned that these Lewis and Clark reenactors might be in over their heads–literally and figuratively–on the Missouri River, and that the group's reception at some of the Indian reservations might not be entirely hospitable. Bud explained that contacts had been made with tribal leaders and that the boats planned to fly each tribe's colors as they passed by the reservations. He and the leadership of the effort clearly understood that calling the 200-year anniversary a "celebration" is inappropriate from the standpoint of American Indian sensibilities. Members of the party want their effort to be understood as a reenactment and not a celebration. Whether this respectful approach will allow unimpeded passage remains to be seen; until you have spent time in or lived near reservations, you do not truly appreciate that these are separate nations. When you paddle the Missouri River through certain reservations, you are a foreigner, and to some an unwelcome guest.

Overall, I came away from the meeting feeling better about the effort. These two crew members were sensitive to other-than-mainstream views of the

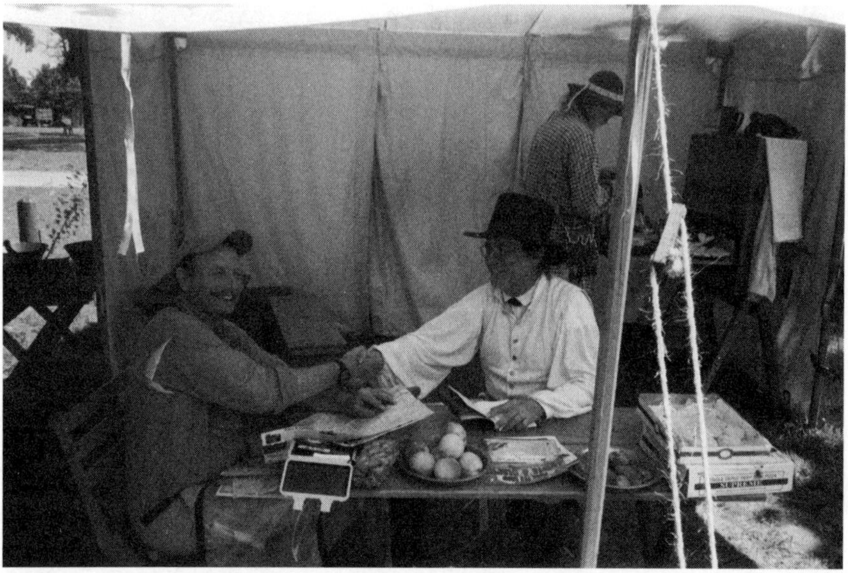

The author with Peyton "Bud" Clark, the William Clark reenactor with the Discovery Expedition of St. Charles.

changes that occurred in the expedition's wake. In addition to knowing their history and having a real passion to get it right, they showed a respect for the river's powerful ability to surprise and upset the best-laid plans. Before I left, we shared a quick lunch and I promised to send maps and "sailing directions" as I finished them. Bud asked me to consider joining the crew at some point, and Jim gave me his "Rubin Fields" business card along with a message to pass on to his friends at the Discovery Expedition Boathouse in St. Charles. I promised him I would pass on his message.

The Cooper Nuclear Station (a.k.a. power plant) is on the right at mile 532.6; you will see the plant's power line towers as you approach. After you cross under the suspended power line, you enter Langdon Bend where at mile 530.6 left, you will reach the Langdon Bend ramp (40.33899/-95.62205). Just below mile 529, I met Rob Carpenter, an independent filmmaker paddling upstream in a canoe, literally following in the wake of the Lewis and Clark reenactment. Rob was taking footage of the river and talking with local residents about their impressions of the reenactors' passage. We talked for a while, and I learned that Rob had made a downstream Missouri River passage a couple of years ago. We exchanged information about good stops that we had made.

When you meet a fellow traveler on the river, it is a good idea to spend some time comparing notes.

As you work your way around the U-shaped bend, you will see the Nemaha River confluence on the right just below mile 528. Hoot Owl Bend observation point is on the left at mile 525.3 (40.314/-95.61782), but the bank is quite steep and a landing did not appear possible. Indian Cave State Park (402-883-2575) is along the right shore for at least 1.5 miles, but there are few possible places where you might camp. The Indian Cave ramp is at mile 518.3 right (40.25577/-95.54052). It has a place off to the side where you can pull out your boat; there is a vault toilet here. A trail leads from the ramp area to a special-use area where you can camp. If you paddle 0.25 mile beyond the ramp, you will see this camping area as a clearing on the right where you can put ashore. According to park superintendent Tom Morrison, you will have to hike about 2 miles to a developed site to get water.

The Thurnau State Wildlife Area ramp is about 9 miles downriver at mile 508.7 (40.16884/-95.45731). There are no facilities here other than a vault toilet, but you can camp here. Below the ramp is a good catfish hole, so you may see locals fishing along the shore. A fresh catfish dinner is a nice change of fare, so if you camp here try your luck. Below the Thurnau ramp, there are several ACE remediation sites; once these stabilize there may be good campsites along this stretch. The Tarkio River confluence is at mile 507.6 left. There is a sheltered area at the river's mouth and a level area at the shore nearby. Since this is private property, you will need to get permission to come ashore. Anglers at the Thurnau ramp told me about this landing; they said the folks owning the area are good people and might allow access if asked.

As you come around the bend at mile 499, you will see the Rulo bridges. Stay right as you paddle under a railroad bridge and the Highway 159 bridge, and you will see the Rulo ramp at mile 497.8 right (40.04995/-95.42118). There is no room along the side of this ramp for your boat, so if you want to stop here, look for an area just below the ramp where you can pull out. But be careful–there is deep mud along the shore. Above the ramp is a gravel lot and vault toilet that was in the worst condition of any that I experienced on my entire expedition.

There are some small cottages and trailers nearby where you might ask for water to refill your jugs. The Camp Rulo River Club is the big building near the entrance to the ramp area. I was told that this was a good restaurant, but it was closed when I walked by it on my way into town. Downtown Rulo is modest; there is a post office and a bar restaurant. The rest of the downtown looked closed and boarded up. The bar was open, and I got a nice home-cooked meal accompanied by a big Mason jar filled with iced tea. This bar is an original and is worth the ten-minute walk into town; you will see an outstanding collection of old-time local brew beer bottles along the wall and a double-barreled shotgun hanging from the wall behind the barkeep. The shotgun is probably not necessary for crowd control since the food is served in big portions, drinks are cold, and the people are friendly. I got good cell phone reception across the street from the bar.

Three miles below Rulo, at mile mark 495 right, is the Big Nemaha River confluence and the upstream border of the Iowa Indian Reservation, which then runs for almost a mile along that shore. Just below mile 490 is the 40th parallel, which serves as the dividing line between Nebraska and Kansas. There are 325 as-the-crow-flies miles from this point to the Missouri confluence, but since you are not a crow, you will have to paddle nearly 500 miles to get there. Even though the river is channelized, there are still many long S-shaped river bends ahead. Returning to what's more immediate, there are numerous wing dams in this area, so pay close attention and stay in the main channel. At higher water levels you will probably hear water breaking over these features before you see them. Also, watch for bald eagles; I saw a pair here that might have had a nest in one of the large cottonwoods near the river.

The White Cloud ramp is at mile 488.1 right (39.97902/-95.29465). There is a bathroom with running water near the ramp, a fish cleaning station, and a Lewis and Clark information shelter. You can camp here for a modest fee, but there is little shade. The White Cloud Grain Company is nearby, and there is considerable truck traffic on the nearby highway. I walked into town and found it pretty vacant; I would have said the downtown was abandoned except for signs advertising a huge flea market that is held every year.

As I was resting in the shade of the bathroom near the ramp, Roy Ivy, a White Cloud resident, joined me. From Roy, I learned that there was a bank with an ATM in town and a soda machine across the street. That was about it, except for the flea market, which brings in thousands of shoppers every year. We talked about the town and Roy filled me in on the history of rivalry between White Cloud and Rulo boys. In the old days, fights between the young men of these riverfront towns occurred on a regular basis. This was a place where you grew up tough; according to Roy, "You could get in a fight at Rulo, but you could get killed at White Cloud."

Eleven miles below White Cloud is the Payne Landing ramp (mile 477 left;

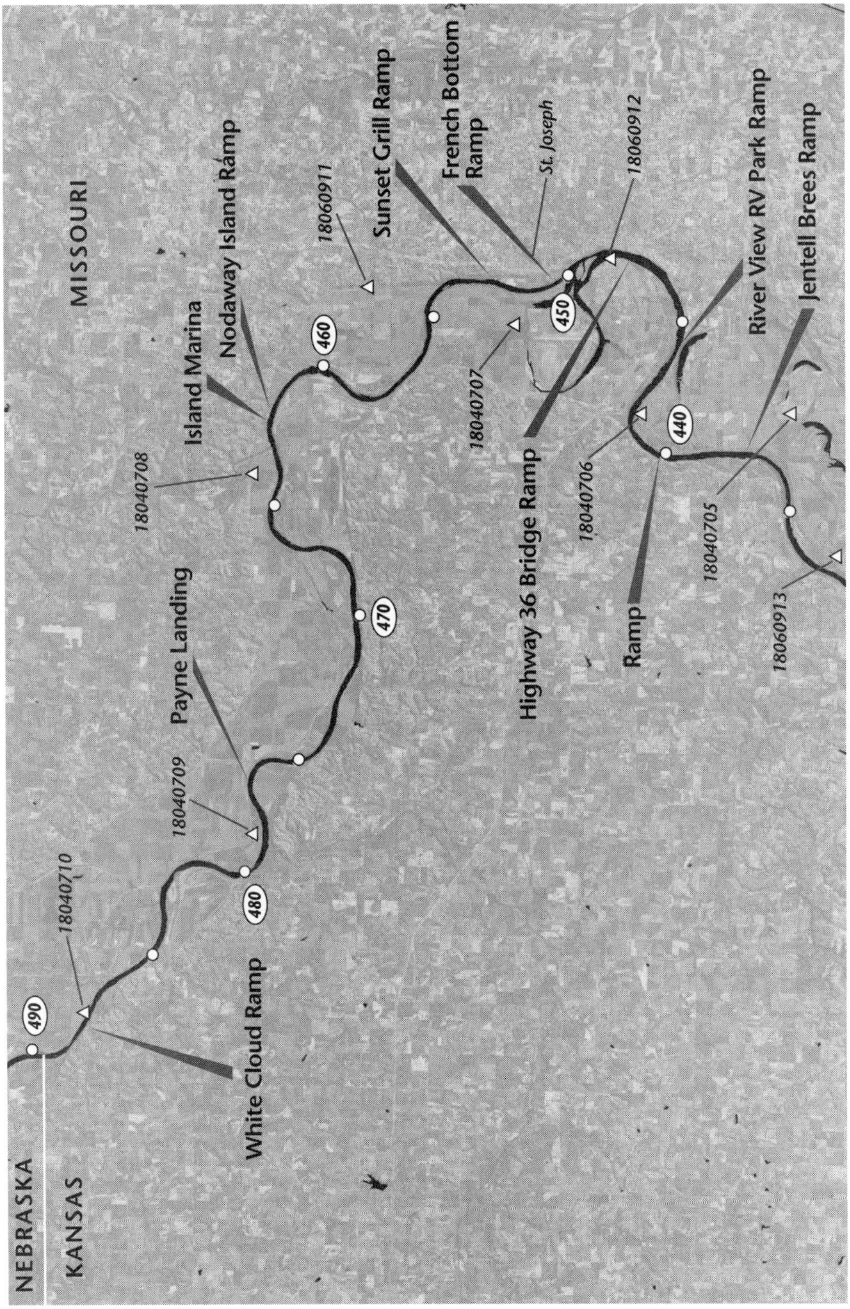

Map 3.B.4: Mile 490 near the Nebraska–Kansas border to mile 435 below the Jentell Brees ramp (mile 437.3).

39.90776/-95.16104). There is no vault toilet here, and if it has recently rained, there will be mosquitoes. The best campsite is at the high area on the right as you look up the ramp. I camped here because I was unsure if I would find a decent campsite farther downstream and because it would make for an easy next day paddle to St. Joseph.

Below Payne Landing you will round a bend and then travel east for several miles before the river resumes serious meandering. Below mile 472 there are some small trailers on the left, and you will begin a long stretch where remediation efforts have been applied to sections of the right bank. Less than 9 miles farther, you will come to the Nodaway River confluence. At mile 462.5 left, you will see the recently reopened Island Marina (39.90255/-94.95877; 816-475-2010), where there is a small sheltered bay with a dock and fuel station, and a nice level shore where you can pull out. I recommend stopping since there is a convenience store with soda, beer, ice, and groceries, and a nice deck that overlooks the river. At the counter I met Mel Hart, who was very helpful and who told me about the history of the place. During the flood of 1993, the marina was damaged extensively and the operation closed. This past year, repairs had been made and the business reopened. Nearby, there are RV and tent sites, and a special area may be created for paddlers. Mel told me that paddlers have stopped in here before and he always tries to accommodate them. His advice to anyone setting out on the river is, "Be careful." Depending on your carrier, you may be able to get cell phone reception here.

The Nodaway Island ramp (mile 462.2 left; 39.90162/-94.95263) is about 0.3 mile down the left shore from the marina. You will see large stone blocks that serve as barriers along the shore, no shade, and a vault toilet. From here, it is about 10 miles to the upstream side of St. Joseph, where you can expect to meet sand-and-gravel barge activity. Have your spray skirt or your bow cover in place. The Sunset Grill ramp (mile 452 left; 39.80202/-94.87741) is right before the establishment's dock. The ramp is not in service but will work for paddlers. I stopped here and rented a cottage for the night because I heard the restaurant was good, I needed to resupply, and I wanted to look around St. Joseph. The Sunset Grill and Speed Liner Lounge is definitely upscale and the food is good. The accommodations are expensive, but if you speak with the manager and there is a vacancy or last-minute cancellation, you might get a room for a reduced rate. Behind this eatery is the location of the former Speed Liner Boat Works, where classic wooden speedboats were constructed. If you do not have transportation, you will have to take a cab to get to town.

While I was here Steve Campbell, another distance paddler, found me and we spent some time together. Steve was paddling up the river on a sit-on-top kayak. We spent a couple hours comparing notes about places with good facilities and talking about the river. Steve is one of the owners of The Rivermen, a whitewater rafting business in Fayetteville, West Virginia. He was paddling the river in sections, having to return to his guide business periodically. His support team consisted of his mom and dad, who occasionally joined him to replenish his supplies and give him a shuttle to his truck. Steve, a veteran paddler in excellent shape, was making between 15 and 20 miles a day against the current. His choice of a sit-on-top for an upstream effort is instructive. He explained that as you work against the current, you frequently have to line your boat to get beyond sections of fast current and past wing dams. With a sit-on-top, he said he can "just hop out, tow, and then hop back on and start paddling."

St. Joseph is a truly unique river city from the standpoint of attractions that paddlers might find interesting. It's an eclectic combination; there is something here for just about everyone. Besides the Albrect-Kemper Museum of Art, you might not want to miss the Robidoux Row Museum (built in the 1840s by the city founder), the Pony Express Museum, the Society of Memories Doll Museum, or the Glore Psychiatric Museum (nationally recognized as one of the 50 most unusual museums in the country and featured on Jimmy Buffet's "Radio Margaritaville"). There is also the Jesse James Home Museum, on the site where Jesse was shot and killed. The museum features artifacts from Jesse's grave when he was exhumed in 1995 for DNA tests. According to the tests, there is a 99.7 percent chance that it was Jesse in the grave. Getting a little bizarre here? Well, there always is the Stetson Hat Factory Outlet, where you can get a really nice straw hat. That old baseball cap really does not provide adequate protection from the sun.

From the Sunset Grill, you will paddle about 9 miles to get past St. Joseph. A second boat ramp is on the left just after the Sunset Grill ramp, and at mile 450.7 left you will paddle by the St. Jo Frontier Casino. The French Bottom ramp is at mile 450.5 left (39.78075/-94.87678). There is no toilet here and this is probably not a place to camp. Near mile 448 you will pass under a railroad bridge followed by the Highway 36 bridge with a ramp underneath (right; 39.74877/-94.86001). For the next 3 miles you will pass the industrial underbelly of St. Joseph, by a shore lined with barge docks, material transport machinery, and processing structures. Near mile 446, you will pass the

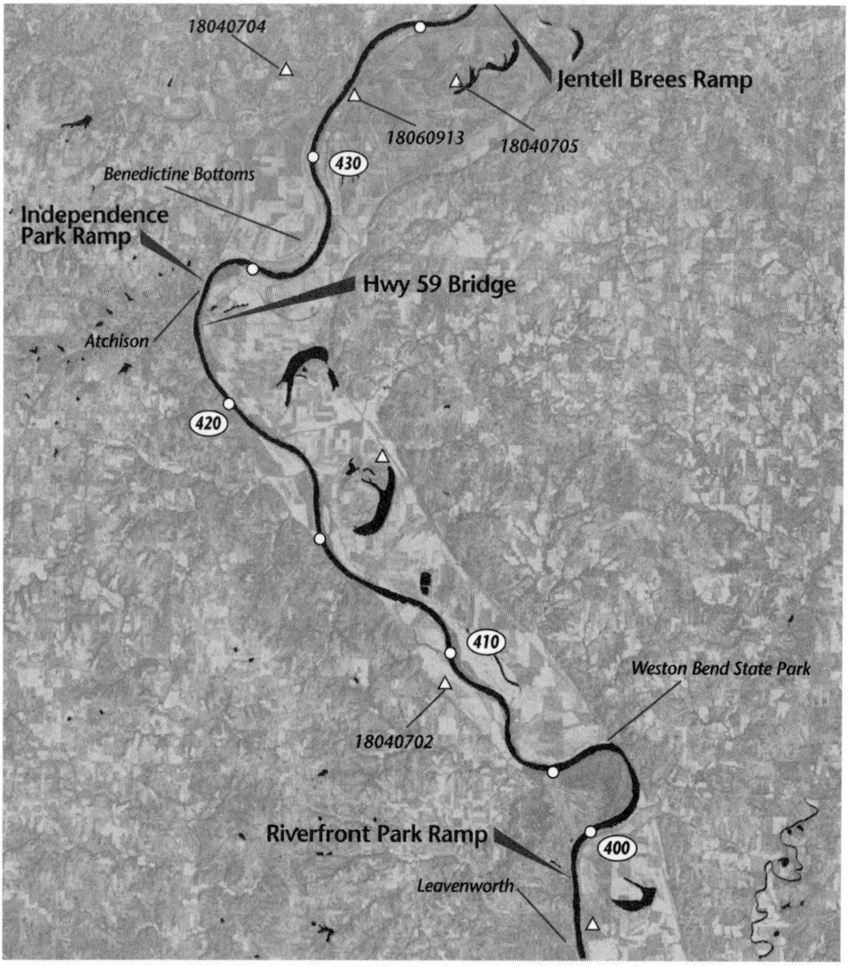

Map 3.B.5: Jentell Brees ramp (mile 437.3) to Leavenworth, Kansas (mile 397.6)

stockyards and then come to the Flathead Fishing Club ramp at mile 444.6 left (39.90245/-94.90245). The River View Retreat & RV Park ramp is at mile 444.3 left (39.72471/-94.90897; 816-233-1974). Paddlers are welcome here, although tenters will have to rough it, as there are no facilities except for a fully furnished "retreat house" that is available for rent. This location is about 5 miles from the city's attractions, so if you don't have a vehicle you will need to take a cab into town. At mile mark 444 left, you will pass the St. Joseph Outboard Motor and Yacht Club ramp and dock (39.72712/-94.91625).

Once you are beyond these ramps, you pretty much are past St. Joseph. As you work around the next bend, you will come to the Wathena River Access ramp (private) at mile 441, and then to what appeared to be a public ramp near Walnut Creek, just above mile 440 right (39.73426/-94.97012). About 3 miles downriver is the Jentell Brees Access ramp (mile 437.3 left; 39.69146/-94.96747). There are no facilities at this area, but there is a nice sandy area just upstream from the ramp, where the Lewis and Clark reenactors camped. From here it is about 14 miles to Atchison, so this is a good place to rest or stop.

Before you get to Atchison, you will pass Benedictine Bottoms beginning near mile 428.5 right and continuing almost all the way to Atchison. This area has a decidedly wild and tangled appearance that perhaps will give you a good sense of what a section of natural river bottom would look like. Just above mile 424 right is the Independence Creek confluence near where the Lewis and Clark Expedition camped on July 4, 1804. Atchison's Independence Park, on the right before the bridges, has two ramps: the first at mile 423.2 right (39.56791/-95.11133) and the second at mile 422.9, about 0.2 mile down the riprap-lined shore. I pulled out at the first ramp, which turned out to be functioning as a very efficient sediment trap; the lower end was covered with deep mud and getting my boat up was a messy exercise. It is about half a mile from here into town, so you probably should pull out at the second ramp to cut this distance in half. There is a bathroom with showers nearby.

There is no "official" camping here but Jerry Hicks, the Riverfront Redevelopment Project inspector for the city of Atchison, told me that a place can be arranged for paddlers. This town is paddler-friendly; everyone that I met here was extremely helpful. Atchison is the birthplace of Amelia Earhart, and has a huge festival in her honor on the third weekend in July. If you can, time your stop to make this event; you will hear great music, see airplanes perform aerobatic maneuvers over the river, and watch spectacular fireworks at night. When I pulled in at the ramp, I was offered a ride into town by John and Gail Meranda. I explained that I was working on a guidebook and they took me to the Visitor Information Center, located in the restored Santa Fe Depot. The center is also a museum, with a large collection of railroad memorabilia, old guns, and Amelia Earhart's personal effects. I suggest that you get a copy of the *Visitors Guide & Map,* and a meal at one of the local restaurants. If you have no transportation, consider taking the trolley, which provides a narrated tour of Victorian mansions and other historic sites.

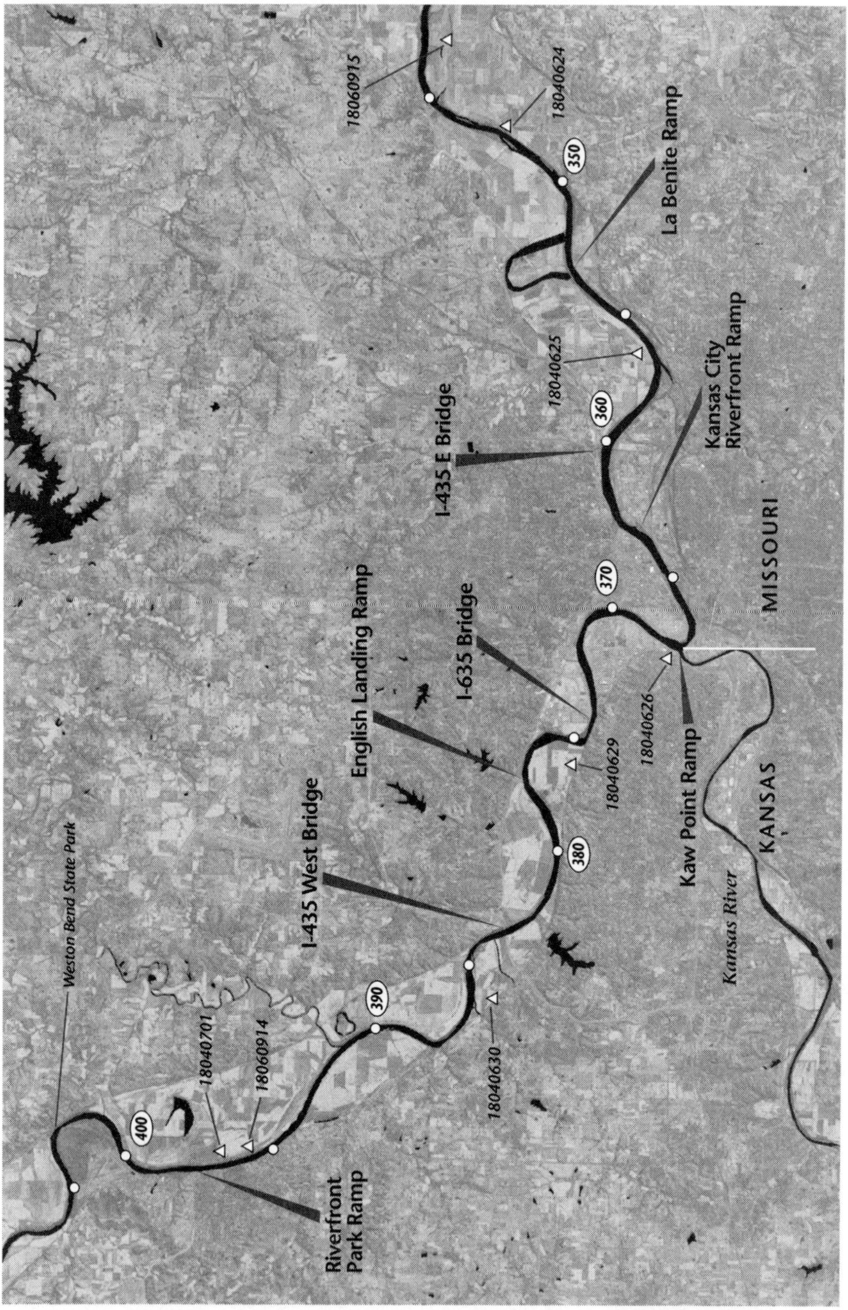

Map 3.B.6: Leavenworth, Kansas (mile 397.6), to the Kansas City area and downstream to mile 345.

I looked around for a good breakfast place and found the Paolucci Restaurant and Lounge on 113 South Third Street. While I was eating breakfast, I met Jerry Hicks and Ray Clem. Ray had been down at the riverfront and saw my arrival. We talked about the river, and Ray told me a horrific but instructive story about canoeing on the Missouri and being hit by a powerboat. A woman passenger was killed and his wife was severely injured. There was suspicion that the powerboat operator may have been drinking before the accident, but no evidence was produced to confirm this. Ray's take-to-heart message was that paddlers need to be extra careful wherever powerboats are running the river; they don't see you, much like some auto drivers don't see motorcyclists. I took Ray's advice to heart. As I paddled away from Atchison, I pulled my boat horn from my life vest pocket and tucked it under an elastic cord on the deck in front of me.

After Independence Park you will cross under the Atchison railroad bridge and the Highway 59 bridge, and then paddle by Whisky Creek just below mile 421. At mile 418.5 left is a small, unmarked river access (39.51245/-95.07707), and just below this is Sugar Creek. As you continue downriver, you will

Author's campsite below Leavenworth, Kansas, at mile 395 left. This campsite had good elevation, offering safety in the event of an overnight rise in river level.

paddle under power lines at mile 410.4 and then come to the Weston Bend State Park, which has a path to the shore near mile 403 (39.39193/-94.88831). You can camp here and there is a vault toilet, but I could see no easy pullout. I suggest that you continue on to Leavenworth.

The Leavenworth campground is on the right just before the bridge; however, the very busy Union Pacific Railroad line runs nearby. If you want to camp, the best site is just before the campground that has riprap along the bank. As you approach, you will see a creek on the right, followed by a level area with a small clearing among the trees. You can pull your boat in here and look over the site. The Leavenworth ramp is just after the Highway 92 bridge at mile 397.6 right (39.32898/-94.90971). Just below the ramp is the Coast Guard facility, where you may see a buoy tender docked.

I began looking for a campsite after Leavenworth because I wanted to be away from train and highway noise. The forecast called for heavy thunderstorms, so I looked for a campsite with some elevation. I settled for a campsite on a high sandy area on the shore, just below mile 395 left (39.29317/-9489243). This campsite was a good 6 feet above the river and gave me the height that I needed in case the river rose quickly.

Missouri's Platte River joins you from the left just above mile 391; on the right shore is the Kansas State Penitentiary Farm. Keep paddling. After mile 389 you will see the crossing beacon sending you over to the right; get to the right quickly, as the inside area of this bend is very shallow and snag filled. At mile 384 you will pass under power lines and see the I-435 bridge ahead. Parkville's English Landing ramp is downriver at mile 377.4 left (39.18549/-94.68129). This is a nice park with water, bathrooms, and shelters, but there is no camping. One 60-plus-year-old upstream paddler told me that when he tried to camp here, the police forced him to take his tent down and told him to clear out. He had to get back on the river at night, which can be very hazardous. This paddler had come down the Ohio and was working his way up the Missouri; he had stayed at countless parks where authorities were willing to make an accommodation. Parkville was the unhappy exception. Stop here maybe for water but nothing more. Parkville gets my vote as the most paddler-unfriendly park in America.

On the left, about half a mile below the Parkville ramp, is the Missouri River Boating Association ramp (mile 376.5 left; 39.18166/-94.66574). As you continue around the bend, you will see Intercontinental Engineering and Manufacturing's huge orange crane on the left. This structure seems delicately balanced and looks everything like a world-class piece of sculpture designed to welcome boaters to the city of Omaha. As you work around the next bend, you will see the I-635 bridge just above the 374 mile mark, farther down you will pass under the Highway 69 bridge and then begin to work your way around Kaw Bend. You will get a nice view of the Kansas City skyline and paddle by the downtown airfield on the right. I did not know the airport was here, and as I paddled by mile 369, a World War II B17 lifted off and roared right over my head. Stunned by its sudden appearance and the roar of its engines, I almost rolled my boat. A few minutes later a B24 took off from the same runway. I later learned that rides were being offered on these planes, formerly of the Confederate Air Force, now flying as the Commemorative Air Force.

As you work your way past the airport, there are sandy areas along both shores. Ahead you will see the mouth of the Kansas River. Stay right and enter this river to get to the Kaw Point ramp (mile 367.5 right; 39.11572/-94.61160). I paddled up to this ramp and met Mike Calwell, a member of Friends of the Kaw (www.kansasriver.com), a group dedicated to restoring the Kansas River. It turned out that he is one of the people responsible for getting this facility built. Mike is a paddler, and we had lunch together and then toured the facility. There are bathrooms here, but they are usually locked at night. The Lewis and Clark reenactors camped here, as did the original expedition, and there is a nice walkway along the point. I discussed with Mike the need for a "paddler's rest stop," and he agreed that one is necessary. Until an alternate area is designated, paddlers can camp overnight at a small and secluded site on the point. Security is an issue, but Mike told me that the gate to this facility is closed at night and there is a watchman near the entrance.

When you get to Kaw Point, you will need to look at the time and the weather and make a decision whether to camp or continue on. It is about 15 miles through the city to a ramp where you can camp. Once you get around the Kansas River Bend, you will enter the Kansas City Reach, which angles to the northeast for about 7 miles. The right bank is steep and funnels a headwind right at you. Paddling can be very difficult. Besides the Kansas City Riverfront ramp at mile 363 right (39.13748/-94.54205), there are few, if any, places where you can pull over. Beyond Kaw Point, the first opportunity to camp is at the La Benite ramp at mile 352.7 (39.16739/-94.39468). So carefully consider the best course of action.

SEGMENT 3.C: Kansas City, Kansas (Kaw River ramp, ~ mile 367.5), to the Missouri's confluence with the Mississippi (mile 0) ***(Maps 3.C–3.C.8)***

- **River miles:** 367.5 miles
- **Difficulty level:** Low to medium
- **Typical time to complete:** 12 to 14 days

You have very good current on this cross-state stretch of the river. If you stay in the main channel and are not plagued by headwinds, you should easily average around 6 mph. I paddled about 5 hours each day and averaged about 30 miles for the 12 days I was on the river. I took my time, and stopped to look around and meet people at a number of small towns along the way. I recommend that you factor in a couple extra days to explore some great places on this section. Besides historic riverfront towns, the Katy Trail runs along more than half the length of this section, beginning at Boonville, near the center of the state, and extending to St. Charles at the far eastern end of the state.

There are few developed campgrounds with showers along the way. But

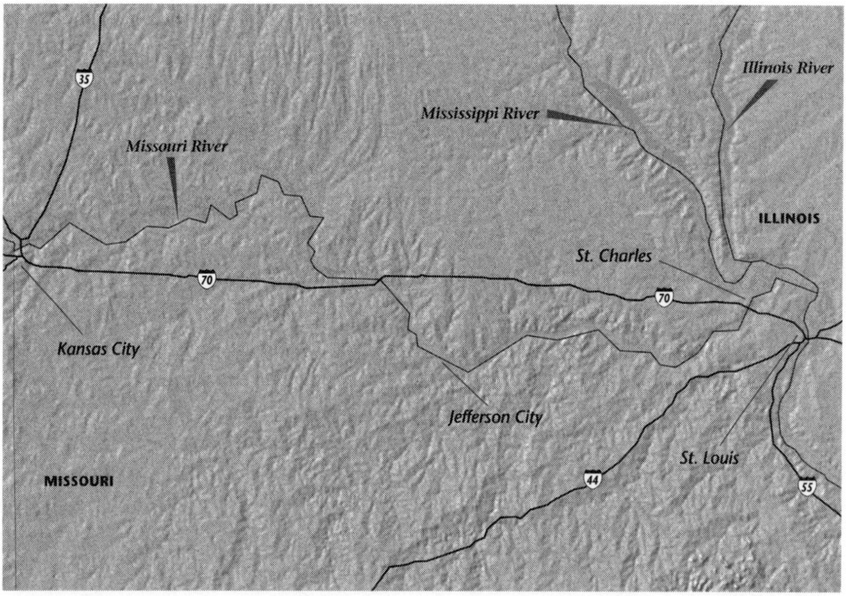

Map 3.C: Kansas City, Kansas, (Kaw River ramp, ~ mile 367.5) to the Missouri's confluence with the Mississippi (mile 0)

drinking water and supplies are generally not an issue, as there are towns along the way where you can replenish. Many towns have nice bar/restaurants with good food, libation, and local knowledge. Missouri has vineyards, and many of the state's wineries produce excellent wines. At the end of a day's paddle, a nice red would make that freeze-dried meal-in-a-bag truly palatable.

Since there is barge traffic on this section, you will need to be prepared to deal with large wake issues. As explained in the Techniques section, your job is to stay out of their way. Since they stay in the main channel and follow the crossing signs when they come to bends in the river, you can predict exactly where they will be as they pass you. They cannot stop or swerve to avoid you, so stay out of their way. Find a sheltered area and point your bow into the waves generated by their wake. You will also see a dredge or two operating at one side of the main channel. Give these vessels wide berth, and keep your eyes open for towboats shuttling barges back and forth from the dredges.

Finally, if water levels are down, there are several long-established sandbars along the way where you can camp. When you stop in at any riverfront town, you should be able to locate a local river rat to find out about where folks camp downriver. You will enjoy fewer mosquitoes at these locations.

Information/Maps/Resources

For this section I relied exclusively on the *Lewis & Clark Bicentennial Lower Missouri River: A Guide to Recreation & Visitor Safety,* as described in the previous section. Some additional riverside facilities have been added since the publication of this guide; I have included information about these in my commentary and on my maps.

Also useful is the Missouri Department of Conservation's map titled *Lower Missouri River,* which covers the river from below Boonville (near mile 175) to the confluence with the Mississippi.

Suggested Readings

There are 40 Lewis and Clark campsites in this section. Information about what transpired here during the outbound trip (May 14 to June 25, 1804) can be found in Vol. 2:323–423 *(Journals,* [Moulton, ed.]). Return trip event detail (September 15 to 22, 1806) can be found in Vol. 8:355–360. Context about events can be found in Stephen Ambrose's *Undaunted Courage,* in chapters 12:147–150 and 32:402.

Although it was printed more than 20 years ago, Don Pierce's *Exploring Missouri River Country* remains a good source for detail about the area's natural history and cultural landscapes. Pierce provides mile-mark referenced information that is very useful to voyagers. Two more recent books by Brett Dufur are excellent sources: *Exploring Lewis and Clark's Missouri* and *The Complete Katy Trail Guidebook,* 7th Edition. The former contains much information about the area's natural history in addition to material from Clark's journal entries. This author is clearly a river rat, and this is a book that you want to take with you on the river. Dufur's book on the Katy Trail is definitive. Since the 225-mile-long trail runs along the river at many places, information regarding B&Bs, camping, and places to eat is very helpful. The historical information about communities, interviews with residents, stories, and anecdotes also make for good reading.

Paddler's Notes and Cautions

When you make the turn east below the Kaw ramp, you enter the state of Missouri and begin the paddle along the Kansas City (Missouri) Riverfront (see Map 3.B.6). Unfortunately, the folks designing the riverfront did not create any easy paddler's access to the City Market and Steamboat *Arabia* Museum. If you want to stop, you have to watch on your right as you pass the riverfront for a set of concrete stairs coming down to a set of poles driven into the levee near the water's edge. The current is fast here and the riprap chunks are large; if you want to come ashore, be careful. You should chain your boat to one of the poles for security, and probably have someone keep an eye on things. The City Market's selection of fruit and groceries is outstanding, and the *Arabia* museum is right next door. Visit this museum; it is one of the best of its type that I have seen anywhere in the world.

As you continue along the riverfront, you will paddle under a host of bridges as you work past Kansas City. The Kansas City Riverfront ramp is on the right just above mile 363 (39.13748/-94.54205); beyond this, your next pull-out is a bit more than 10 miles downriver at the La Benite ramp, just after the Highway 291 bridge, on the right at mile 352.7 (39.16739/-94.39468). Camping is permitted; there is a vault toilet and good shade. I did not camp here, but a paddler that I talked with said the campsites were nice.

Once past La Benite, you leave Kansas City behind. Just below mile 349 you will paddle under a power line, and 4 miles downriver you will pass the Independence Power Plant with its orange and white chimney (mile 345.4). On

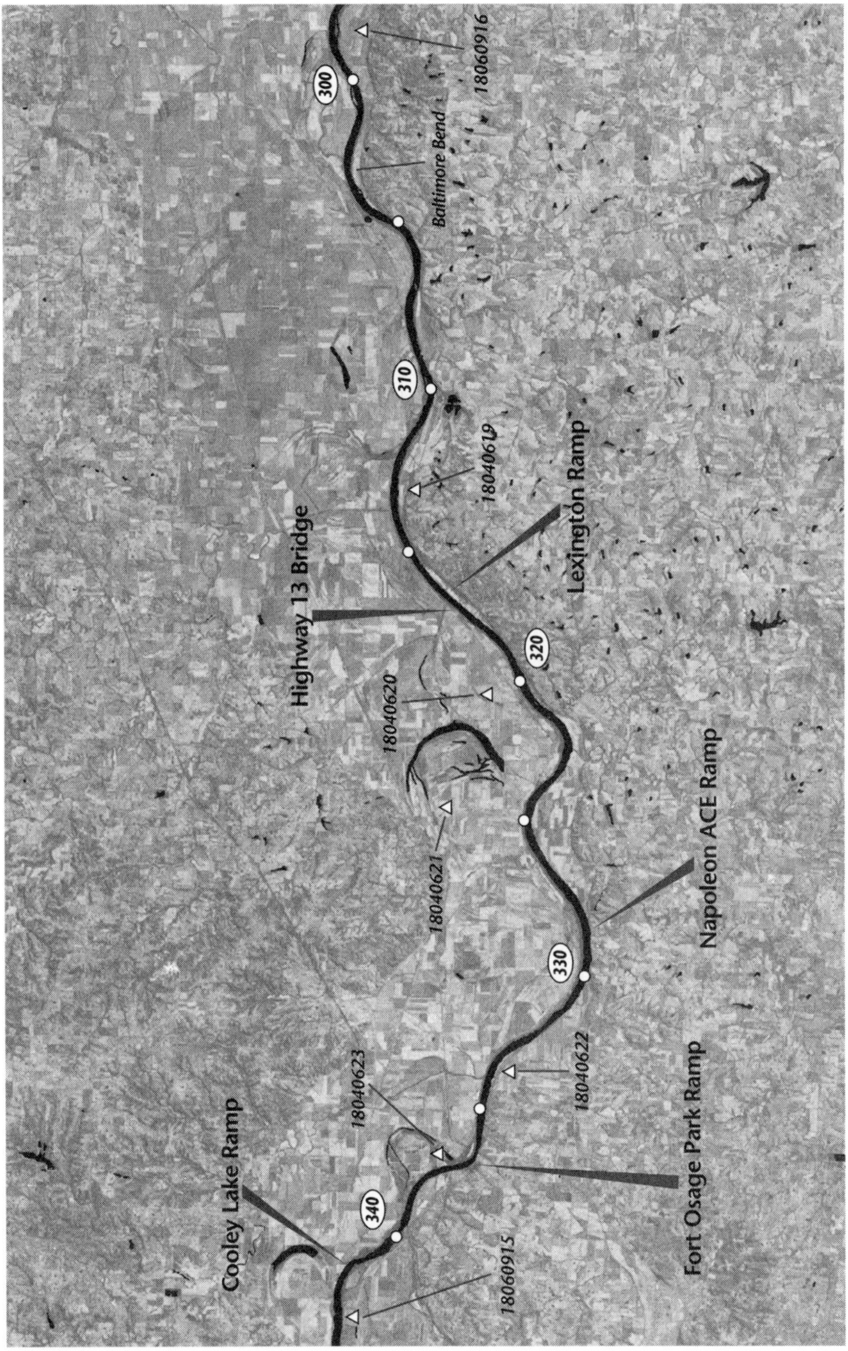

Map 3.C.1: Mile 345 below Kansas City to Baltimore Bend at mile 297.

the left at mile 341.2 is the Cooley Lake ramp. There are wing dams immediately above and below this ramp so take care when landing. At high water these structures are difficult to see; swing wide before you turn in to the ramp but keep an eye out for the downstream wing. I spoke with anglers here who told me that many boats have lost their lower units on these wing dams. There is a vault toilet here.

The Little Blue River mouth is at mile 339.5; just below is a park with some level areas near the shore. I did not see a ramp here, although the navigation chart shows one below the confluence. From here you will work around Jackass Bend, the site of the first of six units of the Big Muddy National Fish and Wildlife Refuge. This unit has more than 500 acres and currently can only be accessed by the river. The U.S. Fish and Wildlife Service hopes to preserve and restore portions of the Missouri River floodplain and its fish and wildlife habitats, and to provide compatible public uses. The idea is that there will be a series of refuges ("a string of pearls") along the river. Although you can fish, hunt, bird watch, and hike here, camping and overnight use is prohibited. Perhaps, as a friend suggested, there might be a permit system initiated to allow paddler "overnights" and assist impact assessment.

The Fort Osage ramp is at mile 337.3 right (39.18969/-94.19117). There is a gravel ramp just before the concrete ramp where you can pull out. Fort Osage, constructed in 1808, has been restored and is a short walk up the hill. Near the ramp you will see a metal gate that opens into a mowed grassy area; enter here, walk up the first slope, and follow the trail to the right. This will lead you to a wide path that winds up to the fort; do not try to bushwhack up the hill because it is thick with poison ivy.

This is not a designated camping area, but I camped just inside the gate, near the shore. I wanted to visit the fort, but it was closed when I arrived. In exchange for the campsite, I spent an hour picking up cans, bottles, and trash around the ramp. As I was unloading, I met a group of local river rats who visit the ramp on a regular basis to fish and watch the river. We shared a few beers and talked about the fishing. I learned that an 84-pound blue catfish was caught here a year ago, and this year's catches included a 54-pound flathead and a 60-pound blue. We talked about hazards posed by snags floating downriver after storms and dangers associated with trying to anchor in the river. Just recently a new boat had been lost when it snagged a buoy line and was pulled under by the strong current. Before the group left, one of them took my water jugs to a nearby house and filled them.

As I finished setting up my tent, Rex and Debbie Godfrey walked up and we talked for a while. I explained that I was working on a guidebook, and we talked about places along the river. Later that evening they returned with some homemade soup, sandwiches, a bag of chips, and two sodas. I enjoyed the meal and thanked them for their kindness. That night a bunch of teens showed up at the ramp, drank beer, and tossed rocks from the levee into the river. I was out of view and they did not know I was there. Eventually they packed off and I got to sleep. Places like this ramp can be local youth hangouts; it is always a good idea to locate yourself, and your boat, out of the traffic pattern.

The following morning, Jim McCandless–a member of the group I had met at the ramp the night before–brought me a large coffee and an egg-and-ham breakfast sandwich that he'd cooked. He told me about the 1986 run he made up the river to Yankton, South Dakota, in a 16-foot, flat-bottom boat. Jim, in finest river-rat tradition, educated me about the finer points of fishing for "cats." Here is what you need to know: When the creeks rise after a storm, sand toads wash into the water; these are among the favorite foods of catfish. From mid-June to late July, the mulberry trees are in fruit; find a tree hanging over the river and fish just downstream, as there will be catfish in the shallows just along the shore. Trotlines, or set lines, with 10 to 30 hooks, are put out where snags won't drag them away. They can be baited with goldfish, chub minnows, or "Extra Sticky" stink bait on treble hooks. Flatheads taste best; blues get oily when the river warms up.

Before I left that morning, we loaded the garbage that I'd collected the evening before into Jim's truck so he could take it to the dump. Fort Osage had been a very good stop; if you do pull in at this ramp and you meet any locals, ask them if they know Jim; if they do please pass on my regards. As is the case everywhere, you'll meet many good people along the river, hear great stories, and learn a good deal if you approach folks respectfully and listen carefully.

The town of Sibley is about half a mile south of the ramp; after you pass the Sibley Power Plant, you will paddle under power lines and then the railroad bridge. At mile 334 left you will see Fishing River, and at mile 328.6 right you will come to the ACE ramp at Napoleon. Floaters can camp overnight at the small park before the ramp, but there is a railroad line nearby so there will be some noise. I spoke with ACE environmental coordinator John Skelton at the Napoleon office. We went over my maps and he gave me good information about places downstream. We talked about a number of issues including barge traffic, cell phone reception, and the lack of campsites along the shore at high water. John said that cell phone reception is spotty at best and that carrying a marine radio is a good idea. He explained that there are marine band repeaters up and down the river so coverage is good, and that barges monitor channels 16 and 13. If you want to communicate with a barge coming your way, it is best to use channel 13 since the other frequency is for emergencies.

After Napoleon is, appropriately, Wellington (mile 323 left); Waterloo lies between them (I kid you not; check the map). Across the river from Wellington and about 1.5 miles inland is Sunshine Lake, said to have been a getaway destination for gangsters such as Dillinger and Capone in the 1930s. After you pass Sni-A-Bar Creek on the right at mile 321, you will enter Bootlegger Bend where during Prohibition there was a still on an island. The Peckerwood Club, said to be the first Missouri bar to get a liquor license after Prohibition, still stands on the shore before Lexington. Before it was closed, this was the place to get a beer and fried or hot-spiced catfish. I was told that patrons, who ranged from mob leaders to the likes of Stan Musial and Joe Lewis, were greeted at the door with the salutation, "How you doing, peckerwood?"

The old Highway 13 (Lexington) bridge is at mile 317.4, and the Lexington ramp is on the right at mile 316.5 (39.19579/-93.88467). Stop here; a new ramp area has been developed and features a Lewis and Clark observation point and a vault toilet. Floaters are welcome to camp overnight. There is history here. In 1852, the steamboat *Saluda* exploded just offshore, killing virtually everyone on board. Eighty-three bodies were recovered. During the Civil War, the Battle of Lexington was fought nearby. In town you will see a cannonball embedded in a courthouse pillar and a memorial to those lost on the *Saluda*. It's a mile walk into town, but chances are someone will offer you a ride. The downtown is small, but there are bars and restaurants, a public library with Internet access, and an ATM machine at the bank. Besides an Irish bar and a Mexican restaurant, there is the Franklin Hole Family Pub, my dining choice. When I walked in and sat down, I was treated like family; the pork tenderloin sandwich was outstanding. After my meal, I introduced myself to the owner, Brian Eads, who was a member of the band Rampage, a group that played all over the United States in the 1970s and opened for some big names in the concert business. The pub's walls are lined with autographed photographs of rock stars.

A new highway bridge is being constructed just south of town, which will no longer bring traffic through downtown Lexington. Because this is a principal route from northern Missouri to Branson, there is local concern that downtown business may suffer as traffic diminishes. Efforts are underway to develop a long-term strategy to maintain the flow of tourists into town. If the information I got from a fisherman at the ramp is correct, the town has gained a reprieve. The new bridge's completion has been delayed because the sections built from each side did not line up correctly when it came time to install the span connecting them at midriver. Somehow there was a mismeasurement; efforts are underway to correct the mistake so the elements will align and the bridge construction will be completed.

About 5 miles after you pass under the new bridge, there is a small boat ramp on the right (~ mile 311). This is probably a private ramp. As you approach the crossing beacon at mile 309.6 right, you will see a possible campsite on the left. Near mile 307 there appeared to be possible campsites on both sides of the river. Dover Station is just below mile 306, along the Union Pacific Railroad tracks, which you can see from the river. At mile 304 you have started around Baltimore Bend; in 1.5 miles on the left, you will see the upstream end of the Baltimore Island Chute. This is an area where considerable mitigation work has taken place, and some potential campsites appear to be developing on the right shore. Near the chute's downstream end is mile marker 299; if you average 30 miles a day from this point, you will arrive at the confluence in ten days.

The Port of Waverly Park ramp is at mile 293.5 right (39.21354/-93.51623), just before the Highways 24 and 65 bridge. There are shelters, camping, and a bathroom with running water; however, the railroad line runs close by. If you walk up the hill to the highway and head south for a couple of blocks, you will arrive at a convenience store. The Lucky Lizard pub is next door. It was early afternoon when I landed at Waverly, so I got a ride from a fisherman up to the pub for a meal. The walls inside were decorated with some impressive hunting and fishing trophies. The menu advertised hot wings that are "Melt Your Lips, Thermonuclear Steamin', Screamin', Drop Your Pants and Jump in the River Hot!" Thinking that this would be a tough instruction to follow once I was back in the cockpit of my kayak, I asked the barmaid what was the house favorite; she suggested the pork tenderloin sandwich. It turned out to be massive and very tasty. I recommend this as another good place to stop.

After my meal, I visited the convenience store and bought some granola bars and sports drinks, walked back to my boat, and pushed off. A new bridge is being constructed just downstream from the old one; a second ramp is on

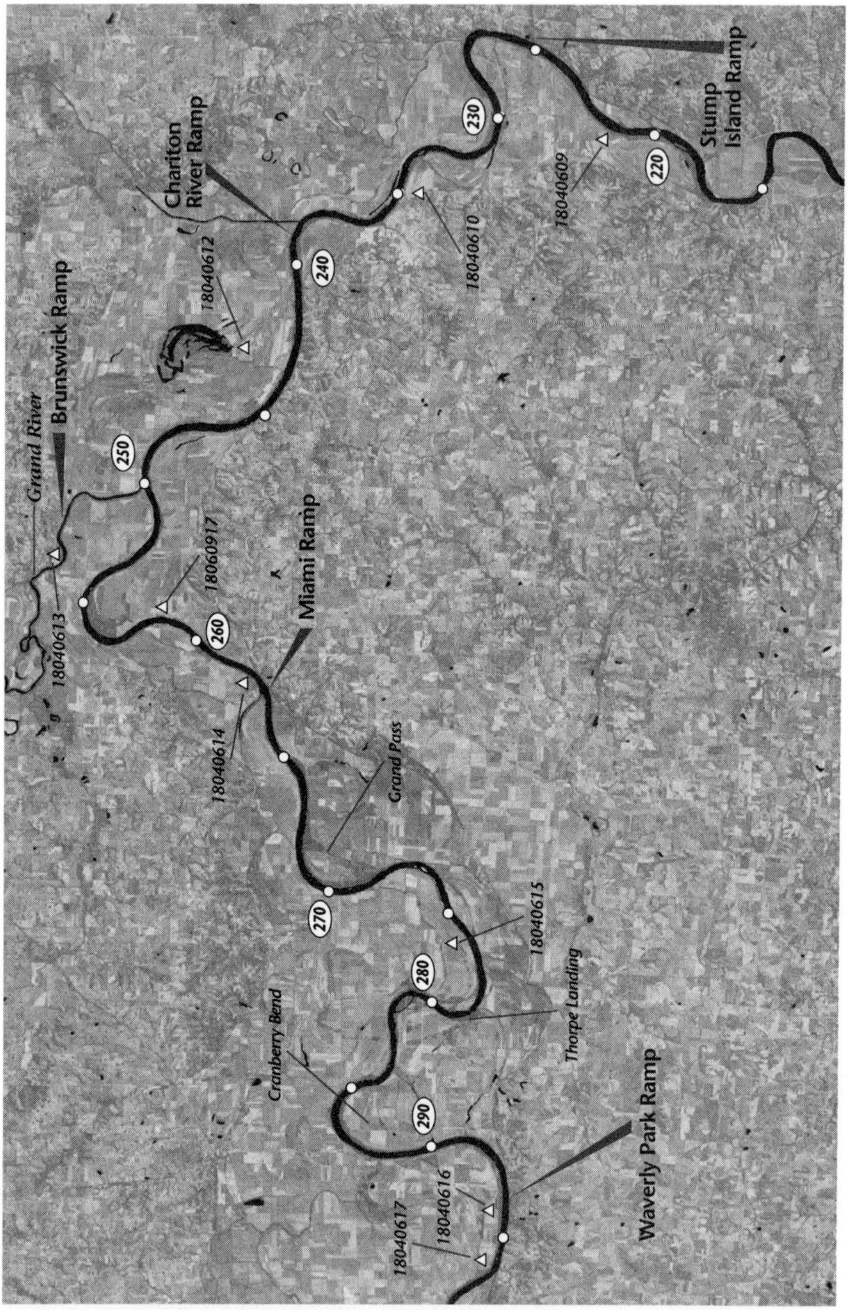

Map 3.C.2: Mile 295 above the Waverly Park ramp to mile 220 below Glasgow's Stump Island ramp.

the right nearby, probably associated with the construction activity. This ramp may be temporary. Once you leave Waverly, you will approach the Big Muddy Refuge's Cranberry Bend Unit, which consists of an 85-acre parcel with 0.5 mile of riverfront starting at mile 291 right, and a second 468-acre parcel also with 0.5 mile of shoreline starting at mile 281 right. As you round the bend before the second parcel, you will see Hills Island Chute on the right; stay left in the main channel, chutes can be lined with snags. At the time I paddled by (July 2004), it did not appear that you could get through. As I was working through this area, I kept my eyes open for possible campsites but saw few. Eventually I found a small access cut in the bank at mile 278.3 right. I pulled in here because it was getting late and I had paddled almost 40 miles.

I searched for a local landowner to ask for permission to camp but could find no one, so I set my tent up close to the shore. Later I met John Thorpe, who was farming land nearby. I explained that I was just set up for the night and would not have a fire. John said it was no problem and that this was one of the few spots along this section of the river where you could pull out and have a safe place to camp, because the water level could rise 4 or 5 feet in a matter of hours. We talked about the river, about the crops, which looked pretty good, and about his sons, who were also farming just up the road. The bottomland area farmed by the Thorpe family was extensive; almost all the crops that I could see were part of the operation. Before we parted, John wished me luck and warned, "The channel just around the bend gets very narrow; the river there moves real fast so be careful. Lots of people have drowned in this river. Treat it with respect." Before I launched my kayak the next day, I took a minute to write down John's parting words so I could pass them on.

At mile 272 right, you will come to the Grand Pass Conservation Area, which is some 8 square miles of bottomland with a riverfront that extends to mile 265.7, a distance of 6.3 miles. Camping is permitted, but I saw few places where you might pull out. There is camping at the Miami ramp at mile 262.9 right (39.32603/-93.22814), but you will have to ask for water at one of the nearby houses. The St. Cloud Restaurant, on Highway 41, is a 0.75-mile walk to the south. You can get a good lunch here; there is a salad bar, the burgers are thick, and there are ice-cold bottles of sports drinks in the cooler by the register. If it is a hot day, this is the place for a midday break.

After you push off from the Miami ramp and cross under the Highway 41 bridge, there is a long stretch with limited places to pull out. You will have to paddle almost 23 miles to get to the next ramp. The river winds to the north for almost 8 miles before turning to the southeast near mile 255. About 4 miles up the Grand River at mile 250 left is a ramp at the town of Brunswick. Continuing down the Missouri, there is a private pullout on the right before mile 243, a power line after mile 242, and a new ramp at mile 239.1 left (39.31499/-92.96331). This ramp was under construction when I camped here in late July 2004. The bottom of the gravel ramp was thick with mud, so I hope the alignment is "reengineered" before the concrete gets poured. There is a vault toilet, but no water. This is a popular place, and at night the parking lot sees some traffic; if you camp here try to set up off to the side. I did not have any problems when I stayed here; it's just smart to keep a low profile. There is a fair amount of poison ivy growing on trees in the area, so be alert. According to a local I talked with, the name of this ramp is at issue, but if you refer to it as the ramp above the Chariton River, folks will know what you are talking about. Another option for a campsite is at a sandbar on the right about a mile below the Chariton River mouth. Remember, however, that at higher water levels, such sandbars will not be an option.

As you approach the bend below mile 229 above Glasgow, be prepared for barge traffic. Just after you paddle under the railroad bridge and then the Highway 240 bridge, you will see the Stump Island ramp (mile 226.2 left; 39.21993/-92.84911). There is a campground, a bathroom with a shower house, and shelters with electrical outlets where you can recharge your cell phone. The camping area is downstream from the ramp, so once you have scouted out the area, you can paddle from the ramp downstream to the shore near your campsite. This is a good place to stop; there is a hot shower, the town is convenient, people are friendly, and you can get cell phone reception up the hill in town. From the campground, it is a short walk to Charlie's Quick Check grocery where you can resupply. And if you need help carrying your purchases, they will give you a ride back to the campground.

Below Glasgow you will paddle about 8 miles to the south before you reach the start of an 8-mile-long S bend containing two more "pearls" in the Big Muddy Refuge string. The upstream refuge is the 2,014-acre Lisbon Bottoms Unit, which begins just above mile 219 left. The Lisbon Chute is at mile 218.1 left. Depending on conditions, it may be possible to enter the chute opening and take out at a sandy area on the right. Snags and debris can pile up along the opening, and you should not attempt to enter if there are any obstructions. The downstream end of this chute is near mile 215 left, and the refuge unit ends just below mile 213 left.

The Jameson Island Unit is 1,871 acres; it begins at mile 215.5 right and

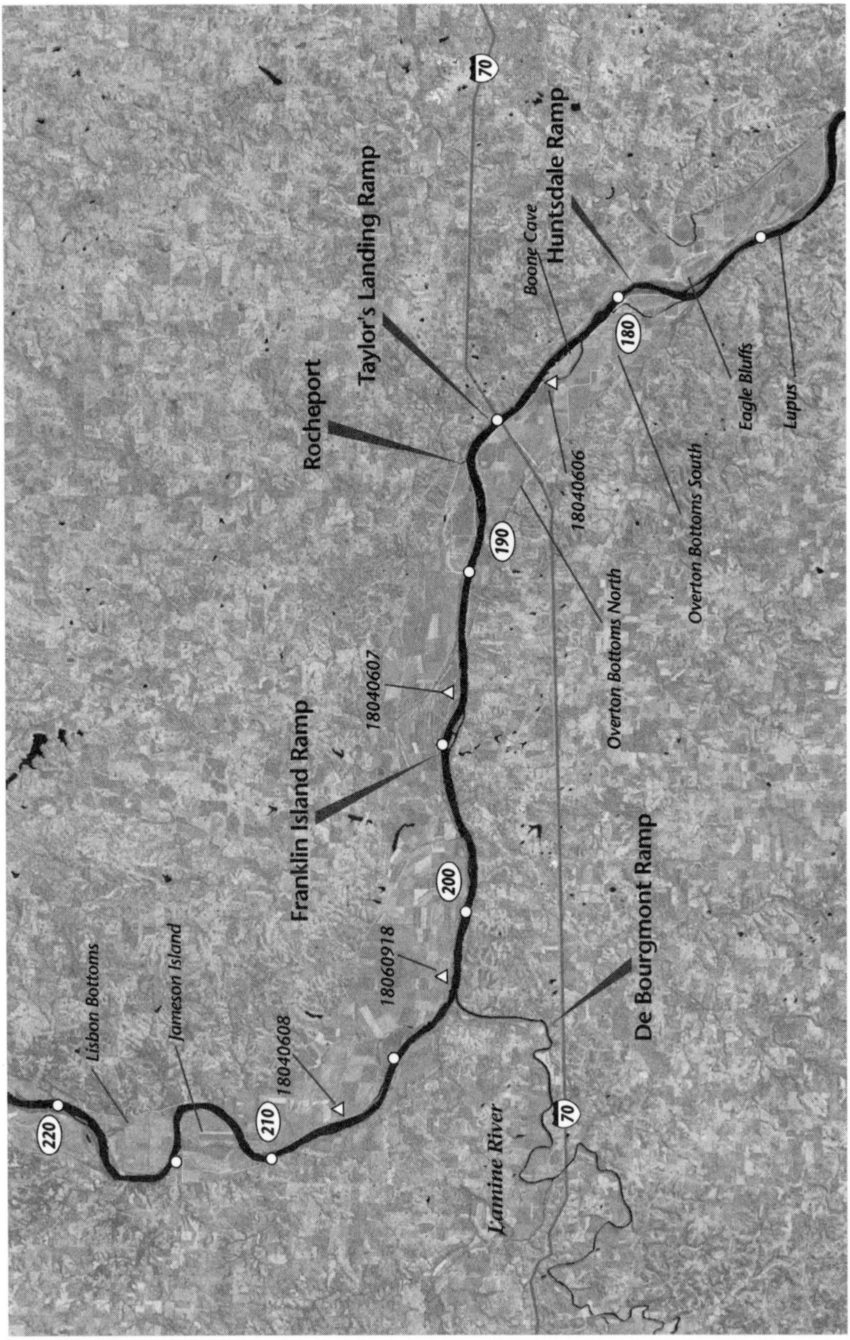

Map 3.C.3: Mile 220 above Lisbon Bottoms to Lupus at mile 175.

extends to mile 210.4 right. Depending on water levels there may be sandbars where you might camp, but make sure to pick a site with good elevation. Water levels can rise quickly with heavy upstream rain. At mile 211 you will enter Arrow Rock Bend. About a mile inland is Arrow Rock State Historic Site, but there is no river access. I started looking for a campsite after I passed mile 210 because bad weather was approaching; I could not find any campsite until mile 205 left, where I pulled out at a level graveled area next to a large drainpipe. This was an "emergency camp" (39.00651/-92.88262); I set up here because lightning was starting to strike uncomfortably close and I had to get off the river.

There are times when you have to take the first available pullout wherever you are; you do not have the luxury of scouting for the best camp, and every additional minute you are on the river increases the risk of being struck by lightning. That night it rained hard off and on, and the river rose considerably. I had pulled my kayak well up the bank after I came ashore; it was a good thing. Do not neglect to haul your boat well out of the water and secure it to a tree or stake driven securely into the bank.

After a hard rain, the river's current will increase as tributaries dump storm flow into the river. After I paddled past the Lamine River at mile 202.5 right, I could feel the extra speed of the current. You will see a railroad bridge that crosses this river as you paddle by. The De Bourgmont ramp is 3 miles up this river, and there is a vault toilet but no camping. A couple of miles below the Lamine confluence is the river-mile 200 mark; a good place to take stock. Just ahead is Boonville, where the Katy Trail crosses the Missouri and parallels the river all the way to St. Charles, which is about 30 miles from the Mississippi. So if your intent is to finish at the Mississippi, you are on the homestretch. If you average 30 miles a day, which you should easily be able to do, you will be at the Missouri confluence in a week. Headwinds and weather may add a couple more days, and you may decide to add a day or two to spend time at one of the river towns along the way. Or you may just opt to slow the pace a bit to enjoy the scenery for the next 100 miles; handsome rock bluffs line much of the river, and an extensive effort is underway to restore large areas of the river's floodplain.

Just before mile 197 you will pass under an old railroad bridge and then pass Boonville on the right, but there is no easy access to the town. This would make a great stop, but there is no place to land and a railroad runs right along the shore. About a mile after you pass under the Highways 40 and 87 bridge, you will come to the Franklin Island Access ramp at mile 195.2 left. The current can be fast along this ramp so you will need to use care if you are going to land here. The water just below the ramp is quite deep, and this is a favorite place to fish for blue catfish. According to one fisherman, "Goldfish are about the best bait, but the local bait shop is charging an arm and a leg for them; so get them at the pet store where they are cheaper."

About half a mile downriver from the Franklin Island ramp, you will see a mitigation site on the left. Here the riverbank has been incised to facilitate the river's propensity to create floodplain. Ultimately, this area may self-restore to a more natural state that supports a more diverse flora and fauna. As you paddle along mitigation sites, you will be observing the first signs of changes that will ultimately result in a much more natural-appearing shoreline. Whether the floodplain rehabilitation effort will provoke the intended ecological responses–enhanced reproduction and recruitment of target species–is very much an open question. Scientists working at these sites will tell you that we have much to learn about habitat use and function at different life stages of targeted species, and about the timing of life events in relation to changes in river hydrology. And, being good scientists they will tell you that it will be a long time before the data will allow us to state with confidence how the changes set into motion will play out. I am okay with that, but my seat-of-the-kayak perspective is that any alterations to the "barge canal" appearance of the river certainly make things more pleasing to the eye.

Below these mitigation sites the river runs generally east before bending to the southeast at Rocheport. The large section of the Overton Bottoms Refuge Unit begins at mile 188 right and extends along the shore for 3 miles. Before mile 190 left there is an old house with a small ramp; 0.25 mile after this you will see a crossing sign. After you angle to river right, you will begin to work around Diana Bend. At mile 187.3 left, there appeared to be possible campsites on sandy level areas. As you approach Rocheport Bend, you will see a sand and gravel operation on the left. Just before the dock and barges is Moniteau Creek, which leads to Rocheport. I did not paddle up this creek, but I later talked with Brett Dufur, owner of the Mighty Mo Canoe Rental (573-698-3903; www.mighty-mo.com) and Pebble Publishing Bookstore, about the area. Brett told me that there is a ramp about 0.8 mile up the creek, but that the best place for paddlers to take out or put in is on the right at the first bridge. Rocheport is a good stop. There is Brett's bookstore, of course, and also a number of nice restaurants. For current information about Rocheport, see the town's website at www.rocheport.com. About a mile down the Katy trail, and up a path with switchbacks to the top of the bluff, is the Les Bourgeois

Winery's A-Frame Wine-garden. The view is spectacular and should be enjoyed with a good glass of wine or other beverage. Brett told me that it is possible to land below the winery, climb the bank, and make your way to the trail leading up the bluff. You may see canoes and kayaks at the pullout.

After you round Rocheport Bend, you will see the I-70 bridge downstream. The Taylor's Landing ramp is before the bridge at mile 185.2 right (38.96078/-92.54796). There are no facilities here, and the area is not designated for camping. However, I have been told that paddlers overnighting are not forced to leave. Just above the ramp on the upstream side, there is a nice level area in the trees where you can rest in the shade. After you cross under the I-70 bridge, the Overton Bottoms South Unit begins on the right; you will see extensive mitigation work along the shore until the end of the refuge at mile 178. On the left you will see high bluffs and the Katy Trail running along their base.

At mile 182.6 left you will see a small spring flowing from the riverbank. I was told by a well-informed official not to drink from this or any spring along the river because of possible pollution issues. Daniel Boone's Cave is on the left, but there is no easy access from the river.

Five miles below the bridge, on the left at mile 180 (38.90852/-92.47965), is Katfish Katy's Campground (573-447-3939). You will see picnic tables at campsites along the shore, and you can find places to land near them or pull out at the Huntsdale ramp. There's a red depot building about one-eighth mile from the ramp where you can arrange a campsite. There are vault toilets, water, and campsites with nice views of the river. As you work around the next bend, you will see a nice sandbar on your right; if you are thinking about camping, continue on for another 1.5 miles around the next bend to an even better sandbar for camping. This sandbar is known to locals as California Island (mile 177.5 left), and is the scene of a mini-Woodstock-style river rat reunion every summer. If you have the good fortune to arrive the day of this event, stop here for a spectacular night of live bluegrass and blues music and outstandingly good karma.

The Eagle Bluffs Conservation Area begins on the left after mile 178 and extends to mile 170. An observation point is at mile 175.7 left; there is no landing and the shore is lined with riprap. The town of Lupus is at mile 175 right; you will see a railroad bridge crossing a creek just before a section of shore where residents moor their boats. You will see some sets of wooden stairs leading up to the town. Don Pierce notes in his book, *Exploring Missouri River Country,* that Lupus was originally called Wolfe Point "but when posta authorities would not permit the name Wolfe, the town's name was changed to

Lupus, Latin for wolf." Just below Lupus, there is a long wing dam that sticks out toward the main channel; when you paddle away from the town, head directly out to the main channel to avoid this wing dam.

Five miles below Lupus, as you work around Plowboy Bend, is Cooper's Landing (mile 170.2 left; 38.81605/-92.38340). Watch for the wing dam just above the ramp. Here, you can camp, shower, wash clothes, listen to live bluegrass or river blues music on the weekend, and eat killer barbecue ribs at Randy Slater's Mo River Rib Shack. If there is a must-stop on the Lower Missouri River, Cooper's Landing is it, plain and simple. You will find the owner, Mike Cooper (573-657-2544), to be very helpful and a good source of information about the river. "Coop's Landing" has a convenience store and is a good beverage stop. It is a popular place and is busy on weekends, but Mike will do everything he can to see that you are squared away. If conditions are right, you will see an incredible sunset from the spectator's gallery above the ramp.

I had intended to take a day off at Cooper's Landing, but decided instead to stay an additional day for the Blue Moon party on California Island. I met David Stevens, Captain Kirk McFaddin, and a host of other rats, and spent a Saturday morning helping them set up a large tent and other equipment at the site. We pooled some money and made a run for beverages, food, and ice, and late that afternoon after I pulled together some gear for an overnight, I got a shuttle to the island. There was live music, cold beer, and dancing in the sand. It was a beautiful, clear summer night with a full moon; when folks got too warm they got wet to cool down. The next morning the river rats served breakfast under the big tent. This was a river-community celebration; the sandbar's shore was lined with boats of all sizes, and there must have been 250 people present. It was a fine way to celebrate life along the river. Every summer this reunion is held, whether there is a blue moon or not.

When I left Cooper's, I paddled with Bryan Hopkins, an environmental education specialist with the Missouri Department of Natural Resources. I'd met Bryan at a Missouri River conference where I made a presentation. Bryan is an experienced paddler and outdoorsman who has built his own kayaks. He has good knowledge about this section of the river. We both share the conviction that the river will one day be discovered by the paddlesport community, and that it will become the paddler's equivalent of the Appalachian Trail. Over the course of the day, we talked about what might be done to make the river more paddler-friendly, and we agreed to work together to establish better facilities for paddlers along the river.

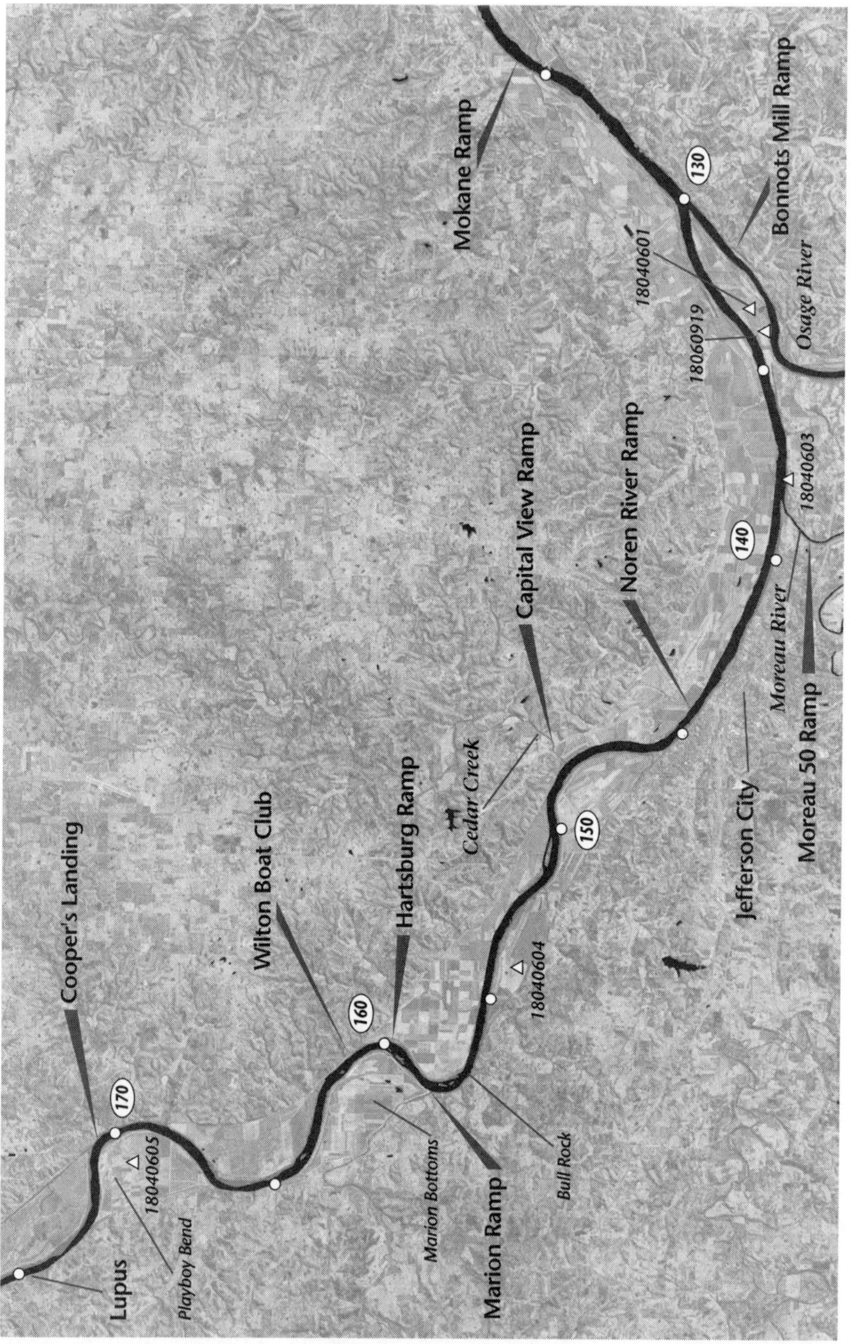

Map 3.C.4: Mile 175 at Lupus to mile 125 at the Mokane ramp.

About 1.6 miles downriver from Cooper's is Big Bonne Femme Creek on the left. When I paddled past, I looked the confluence area over; it appeared that you could pull out along the nearby shore. The mouths of streams and creaks often have a sand or gravel flat where you can land; however, these can be dangerous areas after a storm. Flash floods are not uncommon. The Marion Bottoms Conservation Area and Mitigation Site begins near mile 164 left and extends for 6 miles around the bend. The town of Wilton is on the left, just after Little Bonne Femme Creek near mile 162. In *Exploring Missouri River Country,* Pierce notes, "the large cemetery visible from the river is filled with the dead of two boatloads of immigrants stricken with smallpox here." The Wilton Boat Club ramp (private) is at mile 161 left (38.72284/-92.34876), and just over a mile downriver is the Hartsburg ramp at mile 159.8 left (38.70743/-92.34075). There are no facilities at the Hartsburg ramp.

The Marion Access ramp is at mile 158.1 right (38.69039/-92.36342). This is a pretty stop where you can camp and use a vault toilet. Below this ramp, there are several sandbars that might serve as campsites. At mile 156.3, you will see Bull Rock, also known as Sugar Loaf Rock or Moniteau Rock. I was told that the size of this "projecting rock" was reduced during the construction of a rail line near its base. The Bull Rock Historic Site is on the hill above, as is the Native Stone Winery & Bull Rock Brewery (573-584-8600). When I spoke with the owner, Larry Stauffer, he told me there is a mile-long trail from their establishment to the Bull Rock and a place just upstream where paddlers can land. Larry cautioned that there is a wing dam near the landing that paddlers will have to negotiate. If you want to make this stop, it might be helpful to call ahead to find out about the landing's current status.

Below the rock is a ramp at mile 154.7 left that I believe is private. About 4.1 miles farther down on the left are sandbars that may offer good campsites (mile 150.6). On the left at mile 148.7, you will see an out-of-service Amoco Oil loading dock; below this is the entrance to Cedar Creek at mile 148.3 left. A half mile up this creek is the Capital View ramp, which was closed in 2004. Bryan had arranged for his wife to pick him up here and to bring a couple bottles of water for me. I decided to camp nearby, as we had paddled 23 miles and the next sure place to camp was Bonnots Mill some 20 miles farther down the river. Although there is a ramp about a mile up the Moreau River, 10 miles farther, I'd been told that the Moreau's mouth might be hard to locate and that there were shoals nearby. My plan for the next day was to paddle past Jefferson City, do about 30 or 35 miles in total, and camp at either Chamois or Portland.

When we approached Cedar Creek, Bryan pointed out a wing dam above the creek's mouth and warned me about the very strong current present above our turn in. I held back to watch him navigate the obstacle; he swung wide around the tip of the wing dam and then expertly turned his boat up into the current and into the slack water below the dam. I followed his lead and we both paddled up the creek. As we paddled we talked about "flying" carp and the danger that they pose to paddlers. These fish–silver and bighead species–rest in the slack water near the shore below wing dams and other obstacles to the current. They can be hazardous to your health because their response to being startled is flight. Real flight. They launch themselves into the air and can do real damage if they run into you. At 12 to 15 pounds, the average-sized carp weighs as much as a bowling ball and moves about as fast. If one hits you, it can knock you unconscious and out of your boat. Outboard motor noise seems to especially trigger the flight response, but paddlers should also be wary. When I paddled out the next morning, I startled a large carp that went airborne and crossed the bow of my boat looking like a low-flying cruise missile.

As you round the bend at mile 146, you will enter the Jefferson City Reach. You will paddle under a power line, and then, just before the Highways 63 and 54 bridge, pass the Noren River Access ramp (mile 144 left; 38.58898/ -92.17912). After the bridge, the channel angles to the left side; there appeared to be no easy place to put ashore near the center of the city. A mile farther down the channel begins a crossing to the right; you will aim toward the crossing marker at mile 141.6. The Missouri State Penitentiary is nearby. The Moreau River mouth is at mile 138.3; the Moreau 50 ramp is 1.75 miles up this river just before the highway bridge. I did not stop at Moreau, but camping is permitted; there is no toilet.

A mile below the Moreau River, on the left, there appeared to be some possible campsites, and near the crossing beacon at mile 137 right there is a concrete ramp. The navigation chart labels this area as "Ewing Landing," which is probably a private ramp. At mile 136.2 right you will see a crossing sign indicating that the channel shifts to the left. I took a bit longer than I should have to begin my crossing and was surprised by the rocks of a wing dam at mile 135.5 right. This was a wake-up call for me to pay closer attention.

The Osage River confluence is at mile 130 right. The Bonnots Mill ramp is about 2 miles up this river; there is camping and a vault toilet. Below the Osage confluence there are numerous sandbars where you might camp if the river is down. Most of the possible campsites are on the downstream side of wing dams; if you do camp here, pick a campsite on the left side since the railroad runs along the right. The first of two Big Muddy St. Aubert Island Units extends on the right from mile 126 to 125. The Mokane ramp is at mile 124.6; there is no toilet or camping here; however, there is a very nice grassy area in the trees on the downstream side of the ramp where you can rest in the shade by a fire ring. You will find good cell phone reception if you move around a bit. The only downside to this site is a very loud siren that will scare the bejesus out of you if you are resting here at midday. I assume the siren will also start wailing in the event of fire or tornado.

Below the Mokane ramp, the second St. Aubert Island Unit begins at mile 122 right and extends for a mile down the shore. The Auxvasse River joins the Missouri on the left at mile 120.6, and just below mile 119 on the left someone has created a landing by making a cut in the riverbank. The Chamois ramp is at mile 117.9 right; there is a new campground with RV and tent sites, water, and a park with shelters. Just below the town is the Chamois Power Plant, and a power line stretches across the river at mile 116.6. About a mile down on the left is the Callaway County Nuclear Plant's intake structure. The Portland ramp is at mile 114.2. This is a private ramp that can be used by the public. I camped here and I recommend this stop; there are shady campsites off to the side, and the Riverfront Bar and Restaurant is within sight of the ramp.

The Riverfront Bar is air-conditioned and serves meals; order the giant cheeseburger or the catfish sandwich and a mega-order of fries. Add a cold soda or brew or two, and there is no better way to sit out a "bake-you-completely-well-done" hot July afternoon. Captain Kirk McFaddin, well known up and down the river, told me about this bar and restaurant when I stayed at Cooper's Landing. He was right about this being a must-stop for river rats; with the exception of a dented NASCAR fender on one wall and some other racetrack paraphernalia, the decor inside the bar seems a good half-century old. The bar itself is a classic, the pool table is antique but functioning, and the barmaid manages the ebb and flow with grace. You cannot create this kind of atmosphere; here there is a patina that has built up slowly, layer by layer, over more than a half century. It is unfortunate that so few places like this survive. On your way out, look on the bar and you will see a large glass jar with money in it; this is the ramp fund. Money goes to repair the ramp, spread an occasional load of gravel in the parking area, and efforts to control the ever-present poison ivy. So drop a few bucks into the jar.

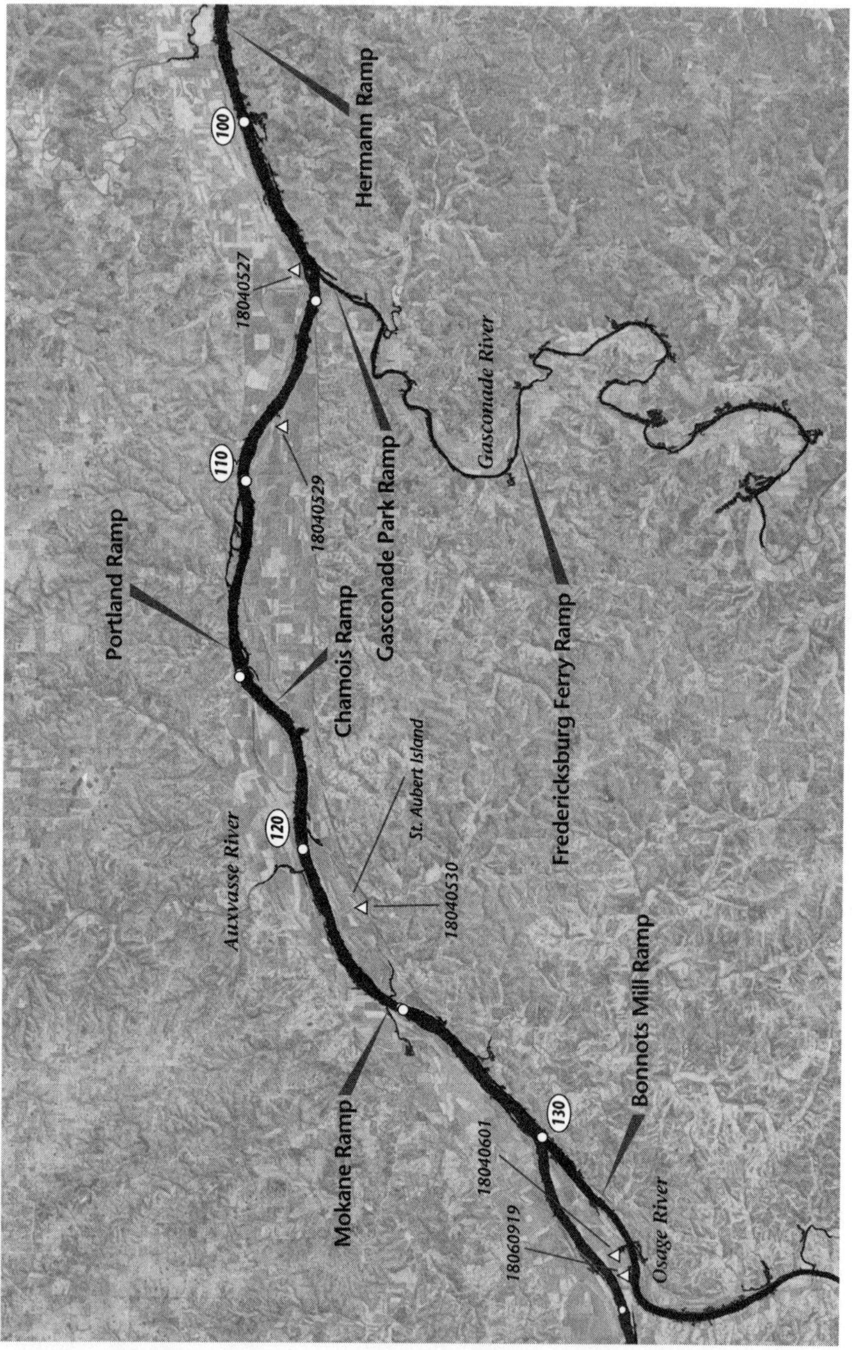

Map 3.C.5: Mile 135 near the Osage River mouth to mile 98 near the Hermann ramp.

When I left the bar, it was late afternoon but still blazing hot. I returned to the ramp and got my gear to set up camp. As I was removing the deck bag from my kayak, an old black-and-white collie walked slowly down the ramp and waded into the water. He stopped and, without lifting his hind leg, relieved himself into the river. He then continued down the ramp until he was shoulder deep, made several turns like you would see a dog do before lying down in tall grass, and then exited the water clearly several degrees cooler. Walking over to me he paused, sniffed me, shook himself covering me with a spray of river water, and walked back up the ramp. I could not help but think that if it is possible for a dog to be a river rat, this is how it's done.

One last thing about Portland: According to Don Pierce, in 1866 a blue catfish was landed nearby that weighed 315 pounds. This is thought to be the biggest fish ever taken in the Missouri River. Today, a really big catfish (a "supercat") is near the 100-pound mark. At Omaha's Dodge Park, I saw a blue that weighed an estimated 80 pounds; it was nearly 5 feet long. I cannot imagine how big one almost four times that size would be. If there were still some behemoth cats in the river, any dog wading into the water to cool off might be rolling the risk dice.

Below Portland you will cross under a power line after mile 114; about half a mile after this you will see a small ramp on the left (mile 113.4; 38.7099/-91.70241). There were two tents pitched under a shelter near the ramp when I paddled by. This is along the Katy Trail, so it may be a fee campsite or a private camp. Immediately after this ramp is a crossing beacon marked mile 113. This mile mark does not appear accurate. In any event, the Tate Island Mitigation Site begins on the left near the beacon and extends for about 3 miles downriver. This is a pretty area; the island has sandy shores and is heavily wooded, so it might make for nice camping or exploration. However, there are pilings that fence off most of the shoreline making it almost impossible to find a place to land. In any event, at about mile 110 you will see the Grand Bluffs on the left, another very picturesque section of the river. As you paddle here, it is easy to forget that you are on the channelized Missouri River (unless a barge materializes from around the bend ahead).

After mile 110, the Bluffton Quarry is on the left; there is a landing here and a road nearby. Some 5 miles farther down, you will come to the Gasconade River on the right (mile 104.4). The Gasconade Park ramp is 0.6 mile up the river on the right. You will paddle past an ACE boatyard, under a railroad bridge, and under the Highway 100 bridge before you see the ramp. There is a vault toilet, camping, and minimal shade. I walked into town and found the Dewdrop Inn closed. I saw a man working in his garage and asked for permission to fill my water bottles; we talked briefly and he told me that the inn was "kind of an off-and-on thing, mostly closed." At one time Gasconade was a thriving town and an important boatyard, but that industry had died. There are some very nice houses in town, and many smaller homes have been fixed up and painted. Most of these sport FOR SALE signs, so there has been some real estate speculation underway. Just above the boat ramp, a huge home has been constructed with several garage doors at ground level that look appropriately sized for personal watercraft. So goes the neighborhood.

Use caution when you return to the Missouri at the Gasconade River mouth; there may be a lot of debris trapped in the eddies. When I exited, the water was really swirling carrying some very big snags. From here the 100-mile mark is about 4.5 miles. After that point you will begin working on a double-digit countdown. For perspective, if you were to turn around and paddle up the Missouri from this mile mark, the counter would not turn to a four-digit reading until you began rounding Big Bend, a three-day paddle from Pierre, South Dakota. For me this 100-mile mark was an especially important marker for my expedition. I had paddled the river from Three Forks, Montana, and now the end was truly within sight. Also in sight, in fact overhead, at the 100-mile mark is a power line. So you will know exactly when you move into double digits.

The Hermann Riverfront Park ramp is after the Highway 19 bridge, at mile 97.7 (38.70813/-91.43508). Hermann is a historic town, established in the 1830s by German immigrants. Home of the Stone Hill Winery, trendy shops, and numerous B&Bs, everything is very quaint. There is no camping here, but there is a grocery store nearby. You want to stop here because Dallas Kropp's K&S Bait and Fish is above the first ramp. Like his father, Dallas has lived on the river all his life. He has assisted many paddlers and is a river rat's "rat" who has truly forgotten more about the river than any of us will ever learn. I stopped in and we talked for an hour. Dallas knows the Missouri; he has strong opinions about it and will tell you that you had better respect its power and know what you are doing when you get on it, whether you are a paddler or a powerboat operator. He will tell people that you do not get on this river without wearing a lifejacket. He's a great source of information and local color. If you do drop in on him at Hermann, make sure to send him a card when you get wherever you are going. He likes to keep track of paddlers who have visited.

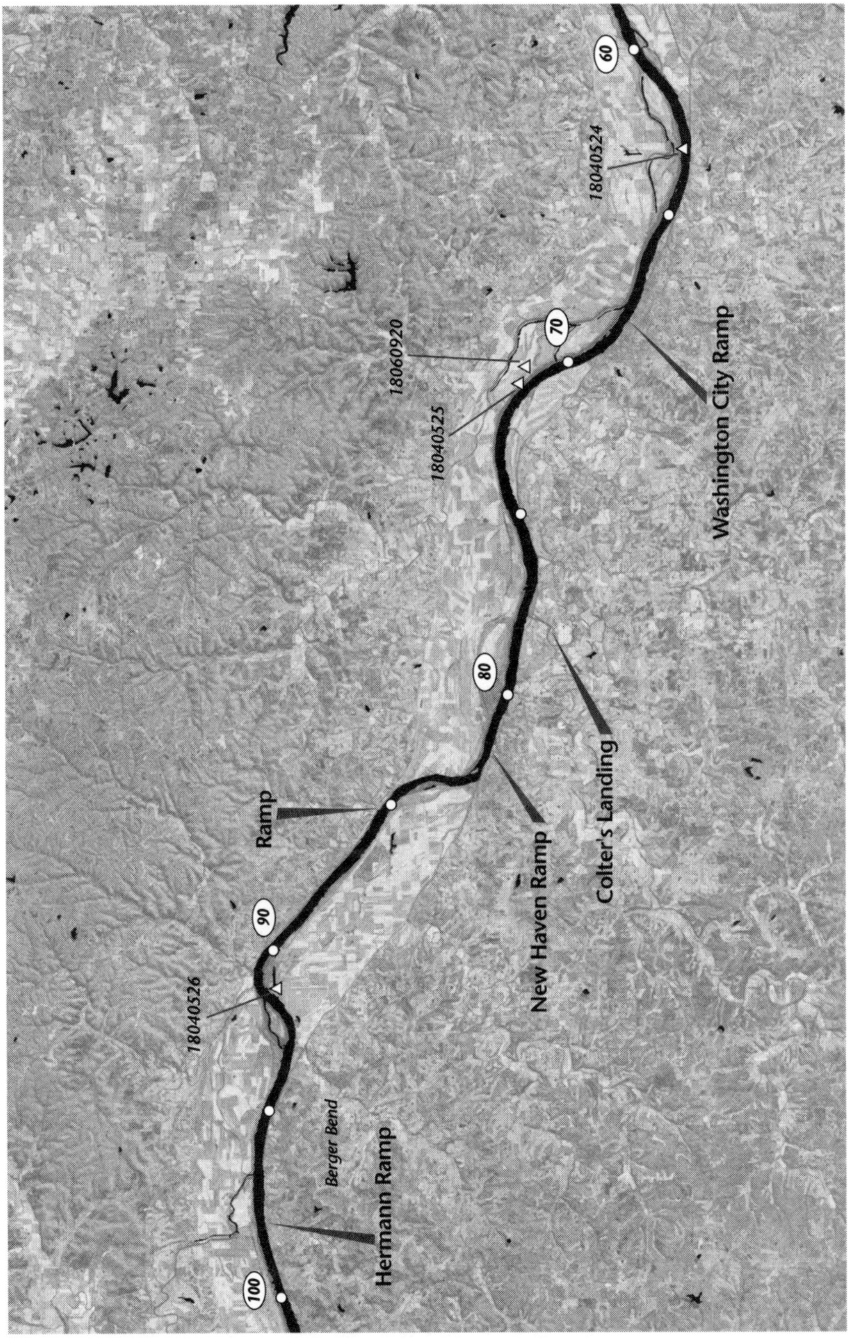

Map 3.C.6: Mile 100 above the Hermann ramp to mile 60.

About 5 miles below Hermann, there is a nice sandbar on the left (mile 92.9), and just after mile 90 you will see the mouth of Lost Creek, also on the left. As I paddled through this area, a bad thunderstorm moved in; I started looking for a campsite shortly after Lost Creek, but was unable to find anything even remotely acceptable until I spotted a set of wooden stairs along the bank at mile 86.5 left (38.66895/-91.25830). I beached my boat in a downpour and struggled up a slick mud bank to the base of the stairs. At the top was a grassy, level area and a path to the Katy Trail, which was a short distance inland. There was a house nearby, but I could find no one to ask for permission to camp. Because of the heavy rain and lightning, I returned to the clearing and set up my tent. Late that afternoon, as the storm was moving away to the southeast, the landowner came by to put out some setlines for catfish. I explained that I'd been forced off the river by the bad weather, and he said absolutely no problem and that he knew what it was like to be on the river in bad weather. By early evening, the water in the nearby creek was raging with floodwater. This was instructive to see; when I'd landed, there was barely a trickle of water flowing; later there was a 4- or 5-foot-deep torrent of muddy water boiling out into the river.

Because the bank was so steep and slick with mud, I had difficulty pulling my boat as high out of the water as I thought necessary. I secured it to a tree with a long line, and to keep track of how fast the water was rising, I pushed the end of a long stick into the shore at the water level to serve as a gauge. Twice during the night I got up to shine my flashlight on the stick to check conditions. My boat was okay in each instance, but by the next morning the water had risen almost 2 feet. After I got back on the river, I passed a home with a ramp at mile 85.5 left and a very nice ramp with a gravel parking area at mile 85 left. The latter might have served as a better place to pull out during the storm the day before; however, I did not know about this ramp. Three miles down from this ramp, there is an excellent-looking sandbar on the left (mile 82).

The New Haven ramp is at mile 81.4 (38.61453/-91.21044). You will see boats docked along the shore before the ramp. There is a restroom nearby with water and a place near the ramp where paddlers are permitted to camp. I got here early in the morning and set out on a search for a cup of coffee. I asked a man who turned out to be Ralph Haynes, owner of the Riverfront Mercantile, where I might get some coffee, and he suggested that I go into Aldo's Italian Restaurant to see if Aldo had a pot on. He said that even though

Aldo's doesn't open until later, the door would be unlocked and I probably could get a cup of coffee there. I found the place, knocked on the door, saw a light on in the kitchen, and walked back to the kitchen entrance. I introduced myself to Aldo and asked if I could get a cup of coffee. Aldo said, "Sure, I'll put on a pot." There had been flow up through one of the drains, so he and a worker were cleaning and disinfecting the kitchen floor. With the task finished, Aldo joined me at the bar and we drank coffee together. I explained a little about my trip and then Aldo talked a bit about the restaurant business. Before I left I thanked him for his hospitality and told him that someday I'd be back to enjoy a meal. If the timing works out, have a meal at Aldo's; I am sure it will be good. Tell him that you are a Missouri River paddler and that you learned about his place in this guidebook.

Another place you should visit in New Haven is the Riverfront Mercantile (573-237-5100; www.rfm-g.com). It's hard to characterize this place; perhaps it's enough to say "good spirits, art, and music." Ralph's business card states, "Value-priced Wines/Craft Brews & Imported Beer/Familiar and Exotic Spirits," but this only hints at what's inside the store. The walls support a host of museum-grade artifacts; there is an art gallery, a music room, and wine racks with an extensive selection of Missouri wines. On Saturday evenings there is, as Ralph puts it, "live acoustic music, mostly bluegrass, traditional, blues, and jazz, followed by an open jam." At Ralph's recommendation I purchased a bottle of Montelle Winery's Cynthiana (vintage 2001), which turned out to be an excellent wine. I recommend that you stop in and spend some time talking with him; if you want lodging for a night he can suggest a B&B or help you get set up at the recently refurbished Central Hotel overlooking the river (573-237-8540; www.centralhotelhn.com).

Less than 4 miles below New Haven is Boeuf Creek (mile 77.8 right). Pierce writes, "Early settlers, apparently seeing many buffalo along its banks, called the river Rivievere aux boeuf–River of Beef." About 1.5 miles up this creek is the Colter's Landing ramp with a vault toilet and no camping. According to Pierce's book, John Colter, one of the Lewis and Clark Expedition's most renowned members, was buried in 1813 at a graveyard on the bluff between Big and Little Boeuf Creeks. Unfortunately, Colter's gravesite no longer exists for reasons that Pierce explains:

The Missouri Pacific Railroad dug a tunnel through the bluff under Colter's grave when its tracks were first extended westward in 1855. In 1926, a railroad company began putting in double tracks and rather than enlarge the tunnel, it cut away a large portion of the bluffs. Before the local people were aware of what was happening, the shovels digging out the bluffs had devoured the whole graveyard. The remains of Colter and the other settlers buried on Tunnel Hill now are part of the track bed of the Missouri Pacific.

The mouth of Little Boeuf Creek is at mile 76.7 right and the old Missouri Pacific Railroad tunnel is just upriver. As you paddle between miles 77 and 76, you might tip your hat to Colter's shade. If you need to find a campsite, there is a good sandbar at mile 76.7 left, across the river from Little Boeuf Creek.

The Washington City ramp is at mile 68.3 right (38.56132/-91.01035), less than 0.75 mile before the Highway 47 bridge. Inside the long wing dam above the ramp is a small marina. This is a nice day stop; there is a good bar and restaurant just across the railroad tracks that run between the river and the town. Washington City is the home of the Gary Lucy Gallery (www.gary lucy.com). Much of Lucy's art is of a historical nature, focusing on life during the steamboat era and things Lewis and Clark. A gifted painter, he has an eye for detail, and his paintings are historically accurate. Because you have been on the river and have paid attention to the play of water, wind, and light, you will notice that he gets it right.

I landed here at noon on the day that presidential candidate John Kerry's train was scheduled to stop. The ramp area was closed off for security, and as I climbed out of my kayak I was questioned by police. After I produced ID, established my harmlessness, and expressed a desire to see Kerry, a policeman escorted me to the train station where I was searched and then allowed to wait three hours at the reception area along a low chain-link fence with some veterans and their families. It turned out that I was in the front row, and I eventually had the opportunity to shake Kerry's hand and get a double pat on the shoulders from him. He's impressive in person, and he connected with the crowd. At one point after he got back on the train platform, he put his arm around his wife Teresa, pointed to the river, and spoke to her. Later, when he came out for an encore, he explained that he had told his wife that this was the river that Lewis and Clark had paddled up, fighting an incredible current and enduring great hardships.

After the campaign train pulled away, I was permitted to walk back to my kayak on the ramp. I passed a Kansas City bomb squad truck and two ambulances where men in peeled-down chemical suits were being treated for what appeared to be heat exhaustion. Stopping for Kerry's visit had taken much longer than I thought, and it was late afternoon when I got back on the river.

While at the ramp I'd listened to the NOAA weather report and learned that it had rained heavily to the west. So I knew that the river level would be rising and that I should find a good campsite with some elevation. I spoke with an officer of a patrol boat being taken out of the water, and he told me there was a sandbar along the left shore after mile 60 where I could camp.

When you get information about possible campsites downriver, it's best to confirm as many details as possible. I asked a few questions to help me locate the site and learned that it was between two wing dams and that I would see a 4- or 5-foot sand cut bank with a trail leading up to a grassy area. I also learned that the officer was a boater and that he was a member of the Washington Missouri Boat Club (www.washmo.org). He gave me a copy of the group's *Missouri River Boating Information* brochure, which provides mile-marked location information about ramps, docks, and fuel for powerboat operators. Armed with reasonably good information about where I would find the campsite and what it would look like, I paddled away from the Washington City ramp.

It was late afternoon when I left, but there was a good current. About 5 and 1.5 hours of paddling miles downriver, I paddled under a power line a little before mile 63 and then found the campsite. The information about looking for a small, sandy path leading up and rounding down the top edge of the cut bank was critical in finding the location (mile 59.5 left). Although I had good elevation for my tent, I could not get my kayak as high up the bank as I would have preferred, so I ran the bowline up the bank and tied it to a tree. I again pushed a stick into the shore at the waterline so I could see how much the river was rising. By the next morning the river had come up about a foot.

Downriver from this campsite, on the left before mile 58, are a series of nice-looking sandbars where you might camp. On the right about half a mile below this is the Labadie Bottoms Power Plant. After the power plant the river widens a bit, and you paddle through a beautiful stretch of river. The Augusta (or Klondike) ramp is at mile 56.3 (38.58202/-90.81927). According to a fisherman that I spoke with, there is water here and a vault toilet. There also is a nice area where you can pull out less than 0.2 mile down the shore from the ramp. There are two more ramps on the left within the next mile; both may be private, and locals know one of these as the "Duck Club ramp." A mile farther down, you enter St. Albans Bend, where between mile marks 53 and 52 left is a long sandbar where you can camp and enjoy an outstanding view of the St. Albans Bluffs. Tavern Cave, visited by Lewis and Clark in May 1804, is after mile 52 on the right. Pierce provides information on how to locate this historic spot:

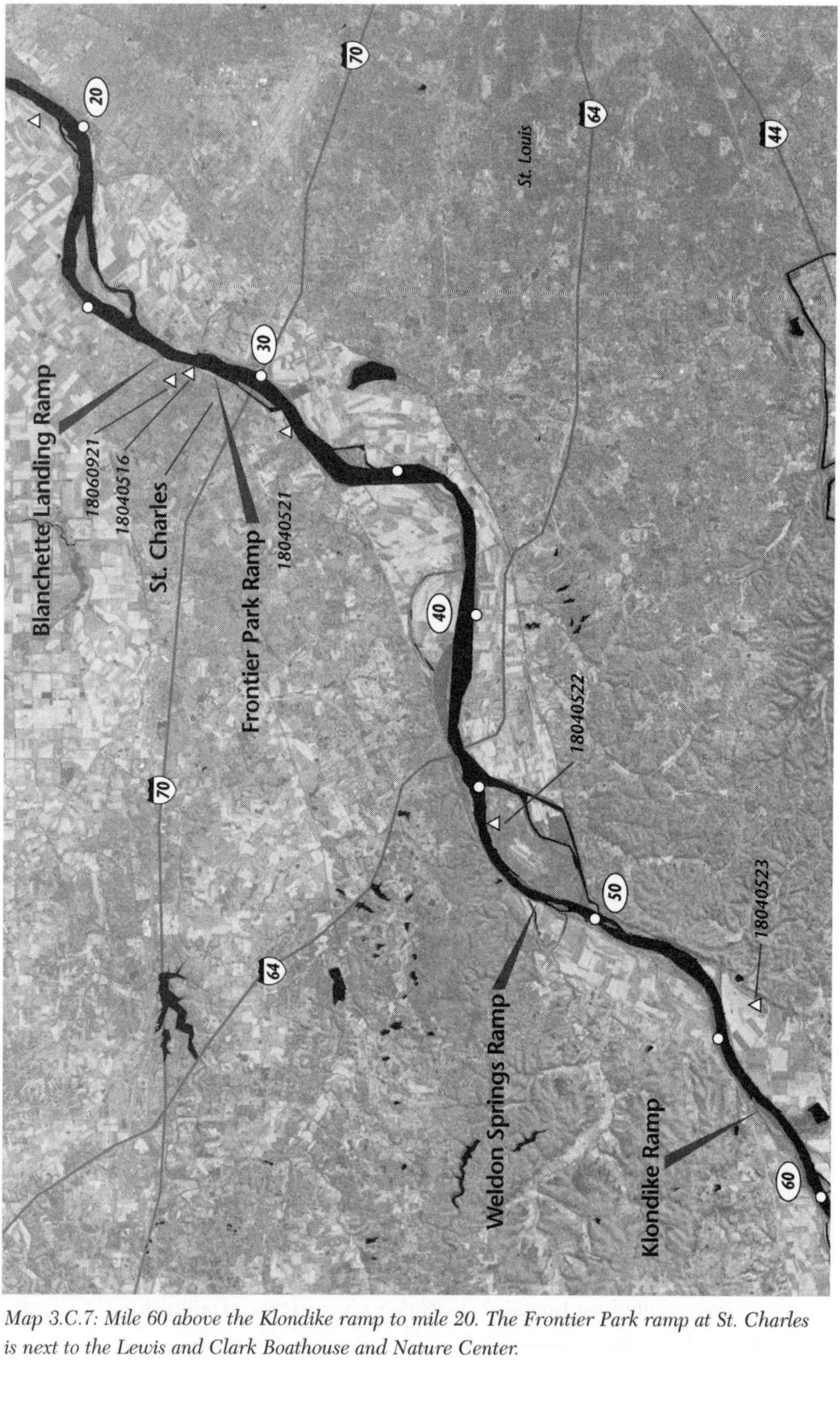

Map 3.C.7: Mile 60 above the Klondike ramp to mile 20. The Frontier Park ramp at St. Charles is next to the Lewis and Clark Boathouse and Nature Center.

The cave is not visible from the river now, partly because the river has cut into its bed in the intervening years and partly because the blasting of the railroad tracks above the cave dumped a large amount of debris in front of the cave. To reach the cave, pick out the white bluff face distinctly lower than the rest of the bluff faces. That low bluff is actually a scar left by blasting for railroad tracks. The cave is just below the tracks and the scar on the bluff. If you miss the cave and find yourself on the railroad tracks, look along the tracks for the mile 38 sign. The cave is below that (Exploring Missouri River Country, p. 241).

At mile 49.5 right you will pass the upstream end of the Centaur Chute, which marks the beginning of the Howell Island Conservation Area that extends to the chute's outlet, about 4.5 river miles downriver. The Weldon Springs Ramp is at mile 48.6 left. Here, there is good cell phone reception and a vault toilet, but no camping. At this point you should pause and look over the map. It is less than 50 miles to the Missouri/Mississippi confluence; the next public ramp is at Blanchette Landing at St. Charles at mile 27.5. There is no camping at Blanchette Landing. In fact, to my knowledge there is only one designated camping area–Sioux Passage County Park at mile 11–between Weldon Springs and the confluence. Unless you plan on landing at St. Charles, have arranged lodging, and have a place to store your boat and gear, the first certain place to camp is on a sandbar off Pelican Island, near mile 17. Other campsites will be available if water levels are low, but you can always count on Pelican Island, which is almost 32 miles downriver from the Weldon Springs ramp. Assuming that you average a little over 6 mph on this stretch, you are looking at another five hours of paddling to reach the Pelican Island sandbar. So when you get to Weldon Springs, consider the time of day and the weather; if you are headed for the confluence and it is late in the afternoon or the weather is sour, you may need to scout around for an adequate campsite.

After Weldon Springs, you will paddle under the Highways 61 and 40 bridge at mile 44. From this point on, you should be prepared for more frequent barge traffic. There is a sand and gravel operation on the right immediately below the bridge, and you will encounter similar operations farther downriver. Expect some traffic associated with dredging operations. After the bridge there are few places where you can pull out and make an emergency camp. If a southeast wind is blowing when you round the bend at mile 41, the paddling for the next 5 miles may be difficult. I had a stiff headwind as I worked through here and had to hug the shore as best I could. Wing dams, of course, complicate the effort to stay out of the wind, as does the need to stay in the channel, which swings back and forth as the river meanders.

At mile 32.6 you will pass under a new highway bridge, and 0.2 mile below this on the left is a small ramp that is about the size used by crew-rowing teams. About 3 miles farther down is the Interstate 70 and U.S. 40 bridge (mile 29.5). Before you reach this bridge, you will pass the Riverport Casino Center on the right. After the bridge you will pass the Ameristar Casino on the left; if you want to visit St. Charles, you need to be along the left shore. You will pass the Lewis and Clark Boathouse and Nature Center before you come to the Frontier Park ramp at mile 28.9 left. This ramp is right before a large floating dock. Just before the ramp, in front of the boathouse, is a low sandy area where you may want to leave your boat. However, I suggest you land at the ramp first to look things over.

River voyagers are always welcome at the boathouse; on the ground floor there is a working boatyard, and there's a fine little museum upstairs. This is the home base of the Discovery Expedition of St. Charles, the nonprofit group undertaking the Lewis and Clark reenactment in period costume on a replica keelboat and two pirogues. As an honorary member of the expedition, I provided the crew with early drafts of sailing directions for the river above Sioux City, Iowa. I'd met the crew three weeks earlier at Brownville, some 500 miles upstream, and provided information on conditions upstream. I went up to the museum to deliver a message from Jim Rascher ("Rubin Fields") to Mimi and Darold Jackson and found Jim there. Or, I should say, he found me. I did not recognize him out of costume. Jim gave me a tour of the facility, and then we loaded my boat and gear into his truck and transported it to the boathouse for storage while I stayed in town.

The Historic District of St. Charles is another good stop; it is an easy walk from the boathouse. Perhaps your first stop should be at the visitor center, where you can get a visitor's guidebook and map. Besides the historic architecture, there are many good places to eat on South Main Street. Steve Kinzy, a friend who works at the St. Charles Environmental Science Research Institute office took me to dinner at the Trailhead Brewing Company after I gave a presentation about how I was using his company's mapping software to assist my navigation and record data. The Trailhead features handcrafted beers brewed on the premise, and for someone who had been on the river for an extended period of time, the name seemed most appropriate.

It is an easy day's paddle from St. Charles to the confluence. After the Highway 370 bridge, you will come to the Blanchette Landing at mile 27.5 left

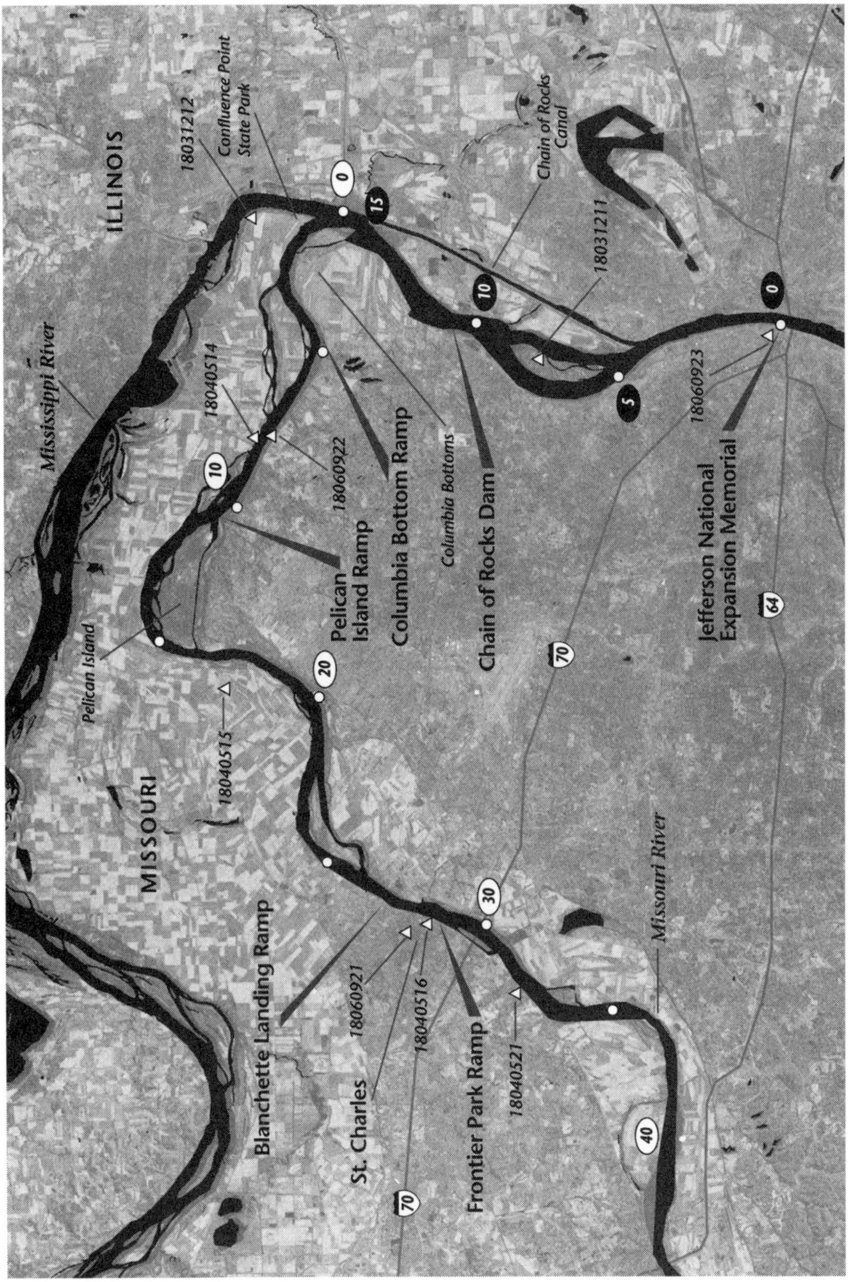

Map 3.C.8: Mile 40 to the Missouri River confluence with the Mississippi at mile 0, showing St. Charles and St. Louis. Mississippi 5-mile marks are shown in black; the Chain of Rocks Dam above St. Louis is a hazardous feature that must be portaged.

(38.79304/-90.47340), where there are toilets but no camping. A half mile down the river is a railroad bridge and another highway bridge; beyond this things get more scenic. The Bryan Island Chute is on the right at mile 26.3; it joins the river again near mile 22. About a mile after the upstream end of the chute, you begin around Cul De Sak Bend; just beyond mile 24 there was a sandbar where there may be a campsite. At mile 20.7 right, there is a private ramp, and below mile 20 there are triple power lines overhead. Sunset Park is on the right below mile 20, but motorcycles were racing on trails near the river's edge when I passed, so I'd avoid stopping at this park. At mile 17.3 there is a ramp with a nice level area nearby; this is private but you might get permission to land in an emergency. Just downstream, also on the right, is another sand and dredging operation. After you pass this operation, you will begin to round Pelican Bend. At mile 16.4 you will pass the Car of Commerce Chute on the right, and after this is about a quarter mile of excellent sandbar where you can camp. Farther around the bend, there is another nice-looking sandbar at mile 14.2 right. At mile 12.6 left, there is a private ramp that is protected by a very long wing dam that runs in front and extends well below the landing.

Just below the mouth of the Car of Commerce Chute is the Pelican Island ramp at mile 10.5 (38.85986/-90.27109). This ramp was supposed to be open, but it was closed when I paddled up to look it over in August 2004. Its lower end was solidly caked with thick Missouri River mud. After this ramp, it is a 2.5-mile paddle to a railroad bridge and then the Highway 67 bridge, the last bridge you will paddle under on the Missouri. Fort Bellefontaine, founded in 1805, is above Coldwater Creek, near mile 7 right. A bit farther down on the right, you will see several trophy homes and then cross under a power line. Below mile 5 right you will pass an old ramp, and at mile 3.5 right is the Columbia Bottom ramp (38.82452/-90.16344).

Stay left for the last 2 miles as you approach the Missouri River mouth. The upstream side at the mouth is the Edward "Ted" and Pat Jones Confluence Point State Park. The "official" Missouri confluence (mile 0) is near the middle of the Mississippi River, where the Missouri channel joins the Mississippi channel. For the moment, your destination is mile 0.7 left, the Confluence Point (38.81612/-90.11954). After you pass the point and the line of riprap that extends from it, turn left and paddle a short distance up the Mississippi shore. Once you are out of the Missouri's flow, you will be in slack water. It may be muddy, so land wherever it looks best. Walk to the marker at the point, stand on it, give thanks, and maybe have someone take your picture. You have arrived.

The Confluence Point State Park has a vault toilet and is a day-use area; there is no water. However, if you intend to paddle on to St. Louis and need to overnight here, or if you are a day early for your shuttle, you can camp along the shore to the north as long as you are a good distance away from the footpaths and make an effort to not be obvious. There are often long lines of weathered barges moored just offshore just above the point, so the addition of your seasoned craft to the area nearby is totally in character.

SEGMENT 3.D: Confluence Point State Park (mile 0.7) to the Arch at St. Louis *(Map 3.D.1)*

- **River miles:** 16
- **Difficulty level:** Moderate
- **Typical time to complete:** 1 day

If you send a damned fool to St. Louis, and you don't tell them he's a damned fool, they'll never find out.

MARK TWAIN, *LIFE ON THE MISSISSIPPI*

From Confluence Point to the St. Louis Arch waterfront area is about 16 miles. Less than 5 miles downriver from the confluence is the Chain of Rocks, a rocky area and below-water dam that stretches across the Mississippi. Unless you are an experienced whitewater paddler with an absolutely "bombproof roll" and have a knowledgeable guide, you must portage this feature along the Illinois side. Below this hazard, the next 5 miles are barge free; after that barge traffic reenters the river after using a canal to bypass the Chain of Rocks. For the last 4.5 miles, you will need to be alert for river traffic and for tow barges maneuvering around docks along the shore. Then you will arrive near the Arch where you can easily pull ashore. There are fee parking lots right along the river's edge where you can meet your ride.

Information/Maps/Resources

For this section, I used Map 1 (River Mile 0 to 52) in the *Lewis & Clark Bicentennial Lower Missouri River: A Guide to Recreation & Visitor Safety*. As described in the previous sections, this 2002 publication contains 12 maps and each covers about 50 river miles.

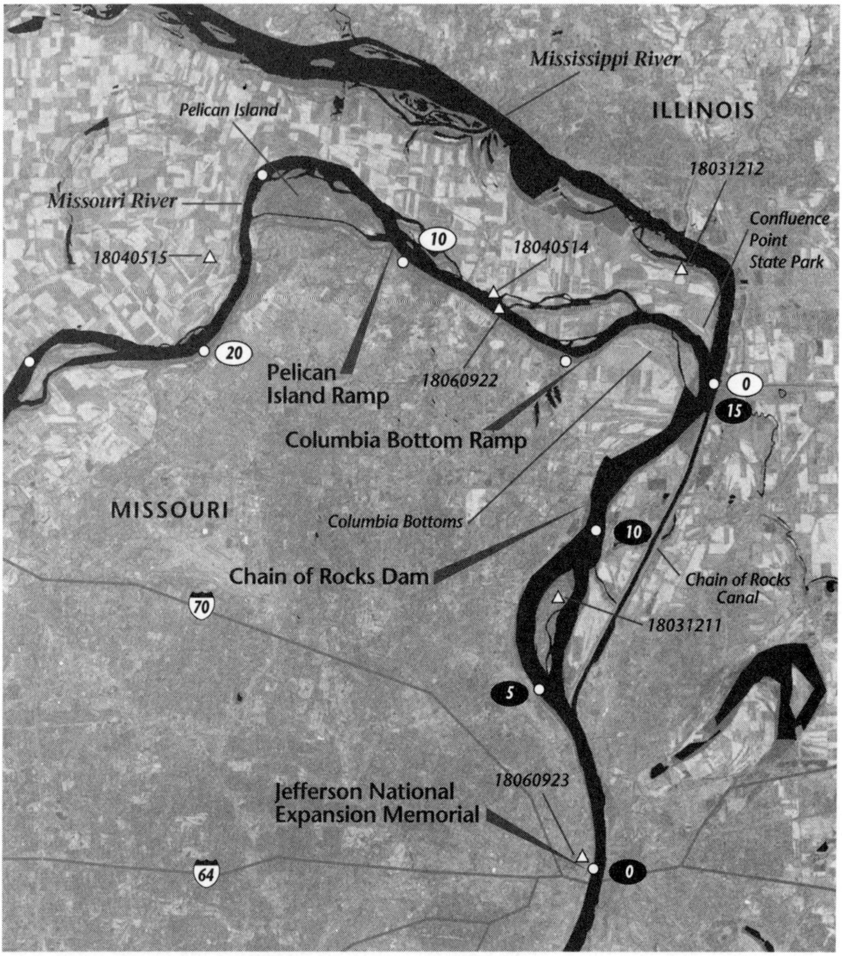

Map 3.D.1: Mile 25 to the Missouri River confluence with the Mississippi, showing St. Louis. Mississippi 5-mile marks are shown as black numbers in circles; the Chain of Rocks Dam near mile 10 above St. Louis is a hazardous feature that must be portaged.

Useful information about the Chain of Rocks is available from the National Paddlesport Center at http://streamtech.org/site/ed-ventures/chainrocks.html, where you will find detailed information about this hazard and photos.

Suggested Readings

Camp River Dubois is located about 2 miles to the north of the confluence. The expedition quartered here from December 12, 1803, to May 13, 1804, prior to starting their way up the Missouri. Information about what transpired here during this period is found in Vol. 2:130–226 (*Journals,* [Moulton, ed.]). The expedition returned to St. Louis on September 23, 1806. Details regarding this event are found in Vol. 8:370–371. Context about events can be found in Stephen Ambrose's *Undaunted Courage,* in chapters 10:123–137 and 32:403–405.

Paddler's Notes and Cautions

I paddled this section with Bryan Hopkins and Scott Meyer, who both work with the Missouri Department of Natural Resources. I had paddled previously with Bryan from Cooper's Landing to Jefferson City, and I had asked him to gather information about the best way to navigate past the Chain of Rocks area. Bryan gathered several air photos of the feature and talked with white-water kayakers who frequent the rapids. Scott is a photographer who came along to get some photos for an article about paddling on the river.

At the southeast corner of the parking lot at Edward "Ted" and Pat Jones Confluence Point State Park, you will see a trail leading up the levee and into the woods along the east side of the park. This trail leads to the shore of the Mississippi River where you can launch. You must portage your gear to or from the parking lot as driving on the levee is prohibited. There may be long lines of barges moored just off this shore, but there is little current so this is a safe starting point. As soon as you get below the confluence point, you will pick up the strong Missouri River current. The Missouri's actual 0 river mile mark is about 0.6 mile to the southeast from the point. But this area is "Tow Barge Central," in the lane used by barges entering and exiting the Chain of Rocks Canal, which runs on the Illinois side. If there is no traffic, you can swing out into the main channel and get near the 0 mark by angling for the Cahokia Creek Diversion Channel, a canal that you will see entering the Mississippi on river left about 0.7 mile from the confluence point. However, the Chain of Rocks Canal is a mile below this also on river left, and barges exiting the canal can surprise you.

For purposes of describing the 15-mile paddle to St. Louis, I have designated Missouri's river mile 0 confluence as Mississippi river mile 15 (all Mississippi river mile markers are italicized), which is the distance remaining to the take-out near the Gateway Arch (see Map 3.D.1).

At mile 15 right, there is an island with many nice campsites. The downstream end of this island is near mile 14; the canal entrance is on the other side of the river. At mile 13.8 right there was a nice sandy shore that would make an excellent campsite. After this you should angle over to the left and stay left as the upcoming portage is on that side (see Map 3.D.1). You will pass under the Interstate 270 bridge at mile 10.8; about 600 yards after this is the Old Chain of Rocks Bridge. Stay left; watch for wing dams. Paddle under the bridge; you will see two water intake structures at midriver and the rapids below them. Stay left. After about 200 yards you will see a sandy area on the left and two large rusty brown circular structures capped with cement. The Chain of Rocks portage take-out is at the sandy area immediately before these features (mile 10.3; 38.75656/-90.17160). There is a parking lot just above the shore, and the portage to a sandbar below the rapids is about 50 yards. If water level permits, you can walk out on one or both of these structures and view the rapids. High water associated with flooding will make this portage more difficult.

If you think you can run this whitewater, think again. As the National Paddlesport Center's description states, these features can be quite hazardous:

Looking west across the Mississippi at the Chain of Rocks Dam at mile 10.3 above the St. Louis take-out. This section has Class III features with "extras," including rebar and steel beams. The portage around this extremely hazardous area is river left, at a sandy area immediately above two large rusty brown circular structures capped with cement (see Map 3.D.1).

Screen capture of an image generated by The National Map interactive mapping service (http://nationalmap.gov) showing the Chain of Rocks area on the Mississippi river above St. Louis, about five miles below the Missouri River Confluence. Images like this can provide critical information about portage routes around dams.

Class III features.... There is a nasty low head dam in the middle of the shoals 100 yards or so below Blockhouse but above the other play features. "Oil Can Hole" is a dangerous life-threatening hole that is difficult to rescue from....Do not paddle without a knowledgeable guide as there is rebar, steel beams....

Rebar can spear you or snag your boat. And your touring kayak or canoe offers little protection in the event of a collision with the sharp end of a steel beam. The object is to get to the Arch, not to be bent into the shape of one around a piece of construction debris or a sharp-edged boulder. Unless you are an experienced whitewater paddler with all the appropriate gear and have a local guide, do the portage.

The main channel below the portage is on the right; there is a ramp at mile 8.8 right (38.74308/-90.9325), but the surrounding area has personal security issues. A half mile below on the left is Mosenthein Island, which is almost 3 miles long and reachable only by boat. Here you can safely put ashore at a sandy beach. You will cross under a power line just before coming to the down-

Upstream portage take-out above Chain of Rocks Dam at mile 10.3 left above St. Louis. This portage is less than 50 yards long; it is the shortest and easiest of all portages between the Missouri headwaters and St. Louis.

stream end of the barge canal at mile 4 left; watch for tow barges entering and exiting this channel. Less than a mile after the canal is the first of several bridges. For the next 4 miles you will see a great deal of barge-related activity along the waterfront. Just above the Martin Luther King Bridge is the docked ship *Admiral,* a fabulous art deco–design vessel that serves as the President Casino. Below this is Laclede's Landing, which extends along the riverfront to the Eads Bridge. This is a good place to exit; the shore is gently sloped pavement and there is a fee parking lot (mile 0.2 right; 38.63040/-90.18137). You can literally back down to the river and load your boat and gear. The Eads Bridge is at the north end of the Jefferson National Expansion Memorial, home of the Gateway Arch and Museum of Westward Expansion.

If you want, you can paddle another 0.4 mile to land closer to the Arch, before the Gateway Arch Riverboats Dock. However, the parking areas along the shore at that location are sometimes closed. The Arch is an easy walk from Laclede's Landing, which is a nine-block historic area and home to restaurants, cafes, and nightclubs with live music including ragtime, blues, jazz, and rock. To celebrate the conclusion of your river expedition, you might consider an educational visit to the Morgan Street Brewery on Second Street, or get a good meal at Skeeter's Eatery on First Street. And, of course, there is good cell phone reception in St. Louis.

AFTERWORD: ON FINISHING THE ENTIRE DISTANCE

> *I must warn you of one thing. You have become a different person in the course of these years....Perhaps you have hardly noticed it yet, but you will feel it very strongly when you meet your friends and acquaintances again in your own country: things will no longer harmonize as before. You will see with other eyes and measure with other measures. It has happened to me too, and it happens to all who are touched by the spirit of this art.*
>
> EUGEN HERRIGEL, *ZEN IN THE ART OF ARCHERY*

If you have made the distance from Three Forks to St. Louis, what have you accomplished? I've talked with several paddlers who have made the trip and reflected on these conversations for common themes. What follows is a distillation of experiences.

First, you have made more than just a river passage. With or against the current, you have learned to read the river well enough and that new lessons are always just ahead. Now you have learned to move in cooperation with the twined currents of wind and water. For so long you sat at the air/water interface, subject at times to brutally uncooperative flows of energy that support the environment. You have learned flexibility and greater patience, and have experienced long periods of silence. You watch the sky and water; you pay attention to the rustle in the brush. You watch for snakes. You forever look and see elements of your world differently. In addition, it is fairly safe to assume that you have become a river rat.

Second, you understand that any day on the river can be at once a test and a lesson. You have had time to sort out which is which. You may find that you are quieter, and that you look more carefully at faces. You appreciate signs of weathering–the crows feet and undereye tracks of those who have spent time outside. You, and fellow voyagers, will forever have Missouri River mud in your veins. You know more profoundly than anyone reading a historical account, looking at the river on a map, or driving along a highway, what a long passage is truly like on this river.

Third, after you return, people hearing about your adventure will ask you what it was like. How to reply? A meaningful response is difficult. It is hard to know where to begin and what to say. Sometimes I'll respond with something like, "It was a hell of a trip" or "It was a wonderful trip." But it is impossible to relate accurately the texture of my passage. I cannot get it right, not yet at least. Perhaps I'll someday assemble the right combination of anecdotes to give those asking a glimpse of the beauty, the silent endless miles of Dakota barrens, the sweat, the mud, the discovery of a single tree for shade, the burning heat and cotton mouth of thirst, the unrelenting bastard headwinds, the shoulder pain that you mentally can no longer numb, the terror/joy of racing with a storm tailwind up then down huge waves at an insane velocity, and the full-body cry of relief when the dam at the end of a 250-mile-long reservoir comes into sight. All these things have to be wrapped into the telling. Many of the elements of my experience surface briefly in this guidebook. But I still am distilling lesson and meaning; I suspect this is going to continue for a very long time.

Finally, what you may find on the "afterback" is that you have moments when your eyes unfocus, and you suddenly cast back, with micro-precise clarity, to somewhere on the river, with the sound and light perfectly right. Some of these flashbacks are to places you had no idea that you'd remember. Yet some kind of registry was etched as you paddled. Perhaps you carry this river with you, forever.

So what do we learn? Surely after you make this trip your being is changed. You understand patently that paddling the Missouri River is not an "achievement," at least as some may think of that term. You understand that you do not conquer or bag this river, as some might think about a successful ascent of an Adirondack high peak. Successful passage is earned because you approached the river with respect, or because you learned to respect this river early along the way. Your passage was aided by prudence, reasoned judgment, good seamanship, the kindness of strangers, and, if you are honest about it, luck. Your skills were tested and honed every day you were on the river. You were a quick enough study of the river's lessons so that you did not repeat often your errors.

If you start at Three Forks and you paddle the 2,300-some miles to St. Louis, you finish. In the end, you paddle one last stroke, turn the nose of your boat up into the current, and come to shore near the Arch. And that's it. But you finish this river understanding that it granted you passage.

Acknowledgments of Assistance

2002 Fort Benton, Montana, to West Whitlock, South Dakota

Charleen "Pete" Elliott; Upper Missouri National Wild and Scenic River monument manager Gary Slagel and Wade Brown of the BLM's Livingston, Montana Office; Les Donezal of Canoe Montana; Don Sorensen and Jim Griffin at the Virgelle Merc and Canoe Co.; Montana Mountain Men–Bill Hammer, Bob Garritson, Jerek Garritson, Lyle Schwope, and Montana Mountain Woman Nancy Krekeler; river pilot Mike Nottingham; BLM park rangers Aaron Bradley and Matthew Danzer; paddlers Dave Weichel and Joe McCormick; Kipp Recreation Area BLM host Jack Conner; USFWS Charles M. Russell Refuge's Bill Berg and Jo Ann Dullum, wildlife biologist; Dave and Tara Waterson of the Fort Peck Marina; ACE Fort Peck Dam manager Roy Snyder; ACE Williston project manager Kasey Beekler, park ranger Jeff Keller, and the entire staff at the Williston, North Dakota office; Bruce and Debbie Erickson of the Tobacco Garden Resort and Marina; Captain Mike Quinn and his better half, Cissie; Kelvin, Laura, and Corey Heinsen of the Dakota Waters Resort; Kit and Fay Henegar of Captain Kit's Marina; Lake Sakakawea State Park manager John Tunge; USACE Garrison Project Office park ranger Linda Phelps and outside maintenance foreman Chuck Phelps; Cross Ranch State Park manager Dennis Clark and Arik Spencer, park interpreter; Chuck Suchy, South Dakota musician; bikers Bill and Renee Willey and Ken and Linda Ware; Bill and Dina Butcher and Cecily Cook; Kevin and Leeann Turnbow and Dee DeBell of Bismarck's Southport Marina; Jim and "Super-Chef" David Castillo of the Huff Bar and Grill; ACE park ranger Don Hatfield of the Beaver Creek Recreation Area; Ken and Diana Moser of the State Line Resort; Bob and Tess Shadwell of the Point of View Resort; Don Barr, fishing guide; Dean Ulmer, stockman; Jerry and Janice Frailing of Mobridge's Bridge City Marina and Resort; SDGFP Indian Creek Park manager Ryan Persoon and Caroline Iverson, ranger; Catherine "Katie" Zerr; Lynnard and Catherine Spiry, Jim and Nard Spiry; SDGFP (West Whitlock) district supervisor Jerry Gray and conservation foreman Lee Kinney; West Whitlock Recreation Area campground host Leroy Quast; Monty, Nancy, Tracy, Casey, and Corey Cronin of the West Whitlock Resort, and walleye guides Gary LaFurge, LeRoy Madsen, LeRoy Deneke, Joyce "Hawkeye" Olson, and the rest of the good folks saving me a seat at the counter.

2003 West Whitlock, South Dakota, to Sioux City, Iowa

Mark Albers, American Rivers; Brad and Charla Garret; Ken Johnson and Sarah Kindropp at Sunset Lodge, Bush's Landing; John and Nancy Hoffman and Gene and Alice Paull of the Pike Haven Resort; Rodney Vaughn, USACE Omaha District Big Bend Project natural resource management specialist; Dennis and Norva Rausch; Pat

Buscher, park supervisor, Oahe Downstream Recreation Area; Stephanie Brandl and Jeff Winge, cyclists; Perry Griffith, and Lisa Etzkorn at Degray Campground; Thomas, Karen, Kyle, and Dillon Treloar at Joe Creek; John, Jason, and Carla Smith and other family members at West Bend Campground; Reid Smith; Camille Azure; Larry Hoffer, Reed Sanderson, and Brandon Bacon, ACE Big Bend Dam/Lake Sharpe Project; Carl Holmgren and Bruce LeMere, "Big Ride" cyclists; John and Helen VanWeyh, Downstream Campground hosts; Chris Hausman; Leonard Andera; Brian and Jeanine Keiner of Keiner's RV Campground at Elm Creek; Ken and Jackie Dooley of Dock 44 Marina at Snake Creek; Dave Enkc, SDGFP district park manager, Snake Creek Recreation Area; Dan and Nita Foster at Platte Creek Campground; Thomas Curran, ACE operations manager, Fort Randall Project; the Wolkens and Sorensens, with special thanks; Jon Corey, SDGFP park supervisor North Point Recreation Area; Dan Hemphill, Rick Faber, Bruce Moss and Bill and Karen Naley for portage and fellowship; David Becker, ACE operations manager Gavins Point Project; George Berndt, NPS park ranger at Lewis and Clark Visitor Center; Rex and Janet Anderson, hosts at Nebraska Tailwaters; Bruce Barton and Bryan Gasper; and Chris Hausmann.

River Master Jim Peterson; MRE river rats: Chad Cadwell; Matt "Perk" Perkins, Matty Heard, Payton Brown, Rodrigo Campos, Tony Demma, RJ Fitsimmons, and Steve Feimer, Government Research Bureau, USD; Mike Feimer, Dakota Claims Service; Bruce Barton, USD; Bob Gregone; Harlow Hatle; Dr. Spencer and daughter Karyn; Bonnie Sorensen, Linda Sorensen, Tom Luther, and Toby's Chicken.

2004 Three Forks, Montana, to Fort Benton, Montana, and Sioux City, Iowa, to St. Louis, Missouri

Doug Monger, state parks administrator, Montana Fish, Wildlife and Parks; Ken McDonald, special projects bureau chief, fisheries division MFWP; Julie Kleins, Rich and Annette Their at Headwaters State Park; Al Anderson of The Canoeing House at Three Forks; also at Three Forks, Dave and Norma Miller and Marie Powers, Slice of Heaven Bakery; Sonny Weldon, Toston Dam host; Ron Lloyd, Silo's Campground host; Rick Langguth and family; Bill and Kathy Frazier, Yacht Basin Marina; Bob Berge and Dean Culwell, Coast Guard Auxillary; Laurie Simms, True North Sailing Club; Frank and Bonnie Nance, hosts at Riverside Campground; Bill and Jean Anderson of Stevensville, Montana; Tim and Doris Crawford, Gates of the Mountains Marina; Marty Williams, Dearborn Country Inn; Terry and Pam Curnow of Cascade; Rocky Infanger, campground manager and the rest of the staff at Holter Campground; Kay Ruh and Bill Bartlett, distance paddlers; Gil and Linda Payne, MRCC; Jill Jackson, director of library and education services at Lewis and Clark Trail Heritage Foundation; Sandy Bramlette, D&S RV Park and Palace barkeep; and Bill Hammer for the shuttle from Fort Benton back to Three Forks.

For assistance on the second leg of the trip I wish to acknowledge assistance from

Jack Wardell, parks and recreation director of South Sioux City, Nebraska; James Riis, program administrator, SDGFP Wildlife Division; MRE personnel including Sarah Stamp and Robin Morgan; upstream paddler Dick Silvestri; Mike and Joan Miller of the Missouri River Rafting Company; Peyton "Bud" Clark; Robert Carpenter, "Fighting the Current"; Shirley and Ralph Lawrence at Thurnau Landing; Roy Ivy, White Cloud; Roy Clem, Jerry Hicks, and John and Gail Meranda at Atchison, Kansas; Mel Hart, Island Marina; Bob and Judy Hutton, Pop-n-Doc's Restaurant, Decatur Marina; Sean Cleary, MDC wildlife management biologist; riverman Steve Campbell of Fayetteville, West Virginia; Kim Penner, USACE Kansas City district geographer; Mike Calwell, a brother waterman; Vic and Ellen Miles and Alan Caldwell, Kansas City hosts; Jim McCandless and the men at Fort Osage landing; Rex and Debbie Godfrey; John Skelton, ACE Napoleon office; Bob and Sarah McAdams, Bill Lewis, Brian Kerr, and Carl "Windy" Iske at "McAdam's Landing"; Brian Eads, Franklin Hole Family Pub, Lexington; John Thorpe, below Cranberry Bend; Officer Becki Bulls and Ranger Tim Haller at the Big Muddy National Refuge.

I also wish to acknowledge assistance from Brett Dufur, Rocheport; Mike Cooper of Cooper's Landing; David Stevens, Captain Kirk, and Randy Slater; Roxann, Copper, and Sadie Menning; Lupus residents James Denny, Lewis and Clark Bicentennial Commission historian and Doug Elley, environmental specialist with the MDNR; Joe Engeln, assistant director for science and technology, MDNR; Steven Sheriff, MDC biometrician; Duane Chapman, research fishery biologist, USGS Columbia Environmental Research Center; Ritch Nelson, state wildlife biologist, USDA-NRCS Nebraska; David Bedan, Audubon Missouri; Jack Finley, UMC graduate student; Oz Hawksley; Dallas Kropp at Hermann; Ralph Haynes and Aldo Alu at New Haven; local police officers and Secret Service officials at Washington City; Tim Long and crew at Weldon Springs; Stephen Kinzy and Michael Klepper, ESRI-St. Charles; and Captain Jim Rascher, Daryl and Mimi Jackson, and all members of the Lewis and Clark Discovery Expedition of St. Charles, Missouri.

Bibliography and Suggested Reading

Aczel, Amir D. *The Riddle of the Compass*. San Diego, CA: Harcourt, Inc., 2001.

Ambrose, Stephen E. *Undaunted Courage*. New York: Touchstone (Simon & Schuster, Inc.), 1997.

Badovinac, Trapper. *Fly Fishing Montana's Missouri River*. Helena, MT: Farcountry Press, 2003.

Barbour, Barton H. *Fort Union and the Upper Missouri Fur Trade*. Norman, OK: University of Oklahoma Press, 2001.

Beal, Merrill D. *I Will fight No More Forever: Chief Joseph and the Nez Perce War*. Seattle, WA: University of Washington Press, 1966.

Bechtold, Chris. *A Current Adventure: In the Wake of Lewis and Clark*. Choteau, MT: Arnica Publishing, 2003.

Botkin, Daniel B. *Passage of Discovery*. New York: The Berkley Publishing Group, 1999.

Bryson, Bill. *A Walk in the Woods*. New York: Broadway Books, 1998.

Cline, Andy. *The Floater's Guide to Missouri*. Helena, MT: Falcon Press, 1992.

Dufur, Brett. *Exploring Lewis and Clark's Missouri*. Show Me Missouri Series. Rocheport, MO: Pebble Publishing, Inc., 2004.

–. *The Complete Katy Trail Guidebook*. 7th Edition. Rocheport, MO: Pebble Publishing, Inc., 2003.

Duncan, Dayton. *Miles from Nowhere: Tales from America's Contemporary Frontier*. Lincoln, NE: University of Nebraska Press, 2000.

–, *Out West*. Lincoln, NE: University of Nebraska Press, 2000.

Drury, Keith. *A Guide to Canoeing the Missouri River*. Marion, IN: Premiere Publishing Company, 1999.

Fanselow, Julie. *Traveling the Lewis and Clark Trail*. Guilford, CT: The Globe Pequot Press, 2000.

Fifer, Barbara, Vicky Soderberg, and Joseph Mussulman. *Along the Trail with Lewis and Clark. 2ed.* Helena, MT: Farcountry Press, 2002.

Fischer, Hank, and Carol Fischer. *Paddling Montana*. Helena, MT: Falcon Publishing, 1999.

Fletcher, Colin, and Chip Rawlins. *The Complete Walker IV*. New York: Alfred A. Knopf, 2002.

Fredston, Jill A. *Rowing to Latitude: Journey's Along the Artic's Edge*. New York: North Point Press, 2001.

Gillespie, Michael. *Wild River, Wooden Boats*. Stoddard, WI: Heritage Press, 2000.

Glickman, Joe. *The Kayak Companion: expert guidance for enjoying paddling in all types of water from one of America's top kayakers*. North Adams, MA: Storey Books, 2003.

Grossman, Elizabeth. *Adventuring along the Lewis and Clark Trail*. Sierra Club Adventure Travel Series. San Francisco, CA: Sierra Club Books, 2003.

Hafen, LeRoy R., ed. *Fur Traders, Trappers, and Mountain Men of the Upper Missouri*. (Bison Book ed.) Lincoln, NE: University of Nebraska Press, 1995.

Harlan, James D., and James M. Denny. *Atlas of Lewis and Clark in Missouri*. Columbia, MO: University of Missouri Press, 2003.

Hawksley, Oz. *Missouri Ozark Waterways*. Jefferson City, MO: Missouri Department of Conservation, 1997.

–, *A Paddler's Guide to Missouri: Featuring 58 Streams to Canoe and Kayak*. Ed. Joan McKee. Jefferson City, MO: Missouri Department of Conservation, 2003.

Heat-Moon, William Least. *River-Horse: the logbook of a boat across America*. New York: Penguin Books, 1999.

Herrigel, Eugen. *Zen in the Art of Archery*. New York: Vintage Books (Random House), 1999.

Hoganson, John W., and Edward C. Murphy. *Geology of the Lewis and Clark Trail in North Dakota*. Missoula, MT: Mountain Press Publishing Company, 2003.

Jackson, Donald. *Voyages of the Steamboat Yellow Stone*. Norman, OK: University of Oklahoma Press, 1987.

Jacobson, Cliff. *Expedition Canoeing: A Guide to Canoeing Wild Rivers in North America*. 3rd edition. Guliford, CT: The Globe Pequot Press, 2001.

Jensen, Richard E., and James S. Hutchins, eds. *Wheel boats on the Missouri: The Journals and Documents of the Atkinson-O'Fallon Expedition, 1824-26*. Helena, MT: Montana Historical Society Press, 2001.

Kellar, Tony. *Camping and Cooking With the Bare Essentials*. Mission Hill, SD: Four Winds Publishing, 2004.

Kipling, Rudyard. *From Sea to Sea and Other Sketches*. The Collected Works of Rudyard Kipling: Vols. 17 & 18 of 28. New York: AMS Press, Inc., 1941.

Larpenteur, Charles. *Forty Years a Fur Trader on the Upper Missouri*. Bison Book Edition. Lincoln, NE: University of Nebraska Press, 1989.

Leopold, Aldo. *Round River; from the Journals of Aldo Leopold*. Luna B. Leopold, Ed. New York: Oxford University Press, 1993.

Lopez, Barry H. *About This Life*. New York: Alfred A. Knopf, 1998.

Lourie, Peter. *In the Path of Lewis and Clark: Traveling the Missouri*. Englewood Cliffs, NJ: Silver Burdett Press, 1996.

—-. *On the Trail of Lewis and Clark: A Journey Up the Missouri River.* Honesdale, PA: Boyds Mills Press, 2004.

Maximilian, Alexander P. *People of the First Man: Life Among the Plains Indians in Their Final Days of Glory: The Firsthand Account of Prince Maximilian's Expedition Up the Missouri River, 1833-34.* Eds. David Thomas and Karin Ronnefeldt. New York: E.P. Dutton & Co., Inc., 1976.

–. *Maximilian, Prince of Wied's, Travels in the Interior of North America, 1832-1834.* [Parts 1-3/Vols. 22-24] Early Western Travels 1748-1846 Series. Ed. Ruben Gold Thwaites. New York: AMS Press, Inc., 1966.

McKee, Joan, ed. *A Paddler's Guide to Missouri: Featuring 58 Streams to Canoe and Kayak.* ["Based on and expanded from *Missouri Ozark Waterways* by Oz Hawksley"] Jefferson City, MO: Missouri Department of Conservation, 2003.

Miller, David A. *Call of the Headwaters.* Kearney, NE: Morris Publishing, 1999.

Monahan, Glenn, and Chanler Biggs. *Montana's Wild and Scenic Upper Missouri River.* 2nd ed. Anaconda, MT: Northern Rocky Mountain Books, 2001.

Moulton, Gary E., ed. *The Definitive Journals of Lewis and Clark.* (Nebraska Edition) Vol. 2-8. Lincoln, NE: University of Nebraska Press, 2002.

Mullen, Tom. *Rivers of Change – Trailing the Waterways of Lewis and Clark.* Malibu, CA: Roundwood Press, 2004.

Neihard, John G. *The River and I.* Lincoln, NE: University of Nebraska Press, 1997.

Peck, David J. *Or Perish in the Attempt: Wilderness Medicine in the Lewis and Clark Expedition.* Helena, MT: Farcountry Press, 2002

Pemberton, Mary Ann. *Canoeing in Northern Missouri.* Jefferson City, MO: Missouri Department of Natural Resources, 1978.

Pierce, Don. *Exploring Missouri River Country.* Jefferson City, MO: Missouri Department of Natural Resources, ca 1982.

Plamondon, Martin II. *Lewis and Clark Trail Maps: A Cartographic Reconstruction, Vol. 1 Missouri River between Camp River Dubois (Illinois) and Fort Mandan (North Dakota) – Outbound 1804; Return 1806.* Pullman, WA: Washington State University Press, 2000.

–. *Lewis and Clark Trail Maps: A Cartographic Reconstruction, Vol. 2 Beyond Fort Mandan (North Dakota/Montana) to Continental Divide and Snake River (Idaho/Washington) – Outbound 1805; Return 1806.* Pullman, WA: Washington State University Press, 2002.

Russell, Jerry, and Renny Russell. *On the Loose.* New York: Ballantine Books, 1969.

Schmidt, Thomas. *National Geographic's Guide to the Lewis & Clark Trail.* Washington, DC: National Geographic Society, 1998.

Schneiders, Robert K. *Big Sky Rivers: The Yellowstone and Upper Missouri.* Lawrence, KS: University Press of Kansas, 2003.

–. *Unruly River: Two Centuries of Change Along the Missouri.* Development of Western Natural Resources Series. Lawrence, KS: University Press of Kansas, 2002.

Schultz, James W. *Floating on the Missouri.* Helena, MT: Riverbend Publishing, 2003.

Seidman, David. *The Essential Sea Kayaker.* 2nd edition. Camden, ME: Ragged Mountain Press (McGraw-Hill), 2001.

Sobel, Dava. *Longitude: The True Story of a Lone Genius Who Solved the Greatest Scientific Problem of His Time.* New York: Penguin Books, 1995.

Steinbeck, John. *Travels with Charley; In Search of America.* New York: Penguin Books, 1980.

Thompson, Curt. *Floating and Recreation on Montana Rivers.* Kalispell, MT: Thomas Printing, 1993.

Thorson, John E. *River of Promise, River of Peril: The Politics of Managing the Missouri River.* Lawrence, KS: University Press of Kansas, 1994.

Twain, Mark. *Following the Equator.* Reprint edition. Mineola, NY: Dover Publications, 1989.

Online Sources for Government Publications

Abbreviations

ACE	U.S. Army Corps of Engineers
BLM	U.S. Department of Interior, Bureau of Land Management
USGS	United States Geographic Service
USFWS	United States Fish and Wildlife Service
SDGFP	South Dakota Game Fish and Parks
NGPC	Nebraska Game and Parks Commission

General Information – Entire Missouri River

Current water conditions: http://waterdata.usgs.gov/sd/nwis/rt

Omaha District: www.nwo.usace.army.mil/html/Lake_Proj/index.html

USGS Water Watch: http://water.usgs.gov/waterwatch

ACE Northwestern Division, Missouri River Basin

"Water Management Information": www.nwd-mr.usace.army.mil/rcc

University of Montana Lewis and Clark Education Center:
www.lewisandclarkeducationcenter.com

Missouri River Information Center (Yankton, South Dakota): 1-866-285-3219;
www.nwo.usace.army.mil/html/Lake_Proj/infocenter.html
www.nwo.usace.army.mil/html/Lake_Proj/portage.html

Online Sources for Imagery

The National Map: http://nmviewogc.cr.usgs.gov/viewer.htm

Terraserver: www.terraserver.microsoft.com

USGS Columbia Environmental Research Center

Hi-resolution air photos from Fort Randall Dam to Springfield, South Dakota

http://aa179.cr.usgs.gov/1999_Photos/ftrandal_spg/index.htm

Hi-resolution air photos from Sioux City to the mouth at St. Louis, Missouri: http://aa179.cr.usgs.gov/photos_2000/

University of Montana Lewis and Clark Education Center: Satellite Imagery of Entire Missouri River: www.lewisandclarkeducationcenter.com

GPS Navigation and Tracking

Garmin GPS website: www.garmin.com

Lat/long Converters: www.directionsmag.com/latlong.php or
www.fcc.gov/mb/audio/bickel/DDDMMSS-decimal.html

Air-Trak Corporation: www.air-trak.com

The Upper Upper

Montana State Tourism: www.discoveringmontana.com
Charles M. Russell National Wildlife Refuge (USFWS)
P.O. Box 110; Airport Road
Lewistown, MT 59457
406-538-8707; http://cmr.fws.gov/

Bureau of Land Management (state office)
Montana/Dakotas State Office
5001 Southgate Drive; P.O. Box 36800
Billings, MT 59107
406-896-5000
www.mt.blm.gov/faq/index.html
www.mt.blm.gov/faq/maps/index.html (map ordering)

Missouri Breaks Wild and Scenic River
Bureau of Land Management
Airport Road; P.O. Box 1160
Lewistown, MT 59457
406-538-1900
www.mt.blm.gov/ldo/fbtrip.html and www.mt.blm.gov/ldo/fbframes.html

Montana Department of Fish, Wildlife, & Parks
1420 East Sixth Avenue
Helena, MT 59620
406-444-2535; www.fwp.mt.gov

Important Upper Upper Websites and Phone Numbers – Mile 2321 to Mile 1895

Missouri Headwaters State Park: 406-994-4042
Yacht Basin Marina, Canyon Ferry Lake: 406-475-3440
Gates of the Mountains Marina, Holter Lake: 406-458-5241;
 www.gatesofthemountains.com
Holter Lake Lodge: 406-235-4331
Holter Lake Recreation site: 406-235-4314

Dearborn Country Inn: 406-468.2007
Badger Motel, Cascade: 406-468-9330
Great Falls Portage Assistance arranged by Medicine River
Canoe Club (MRCC): 406-452-7379; 406-727-2762;
406-452-6946; 406-268-2300 (PPL)
Lewis and Clark Trail Heritage Foundation, Inc.: 1-800-701-3434;
www.lewisandclark.org
Carter Ferry: 406-734-5335
D&S RV Park, Fort Benton: 406-622-5104
Upper Missouri River Wild and Scenic Visitor Center
(Fort Benton) 406-622-5185
Virgelle Ferry: 406-378-3194
Virgelle Mercantile: 406-378-3110; www.paddlemontana.com
James Kipp State Park: 406-538-7461 (Lewistown BLM Office)

The Dammed Upper

North Dakota State Tourism: www.ndtourism.com
South Dakota State Tourism: www.travelsd.com
Nebraska State Tourism: www.visitnebraska.org

North Dakota Game & Fish Dept.
100 North Bismarck Expressway
Bismarck, ND 58501
701-221-6300
www.state.nd.us/gnf/
www.state.nd.us/gnf/boating/boatramps.html

North Dakota Parks & Recreation Department
1424 West Century Avenue; Suite 202
Bismarck, ND 58501
www.ndparks.com/

South Dakota Department of Game, Fish and Parks
523 East Capital Avenue
Pierre, SD 57501
605-773-3485; 605-773-3391 (parks)
www.sdgfp.info/Parks
www.sdgfp.info/Parks/Regions/LocatorMap.htm

Nebraska Game and Parks
P.O. Box 30370
Lincoln, NE 68503
402-464-0641
www.ngpc.state.ne.us
http://mapserver.ngpc.state.ne.us/website/gpc_land/viewer.htm

Lewis and Clark Visitor Center, Yankton, South Dakota
Missouri National Recreation River
National Parks Service, Department of the Interior
402-667-2550; www.nps.gov/mnrr/pphtml/camping.html

Important Dammed Upper Websites and Phone Numbers – Mile 1895 to Mile 732

Fort Peck Marina: 406-526-3442
Ace Fort Peck Lake Project Office: 406-526-3411
Fort Peck Recreation Area, West End Campground: 406-526-3411
Fort Peck Dam Manager: 406-526-3411
Fort Union Trading Post National Historic Site: 701-572-9083
Fort Buford State Historic Site: 701-572-9034
ACE Williston Office: 701-572-6494
Lewis and Clark State Park: 701-859-3071
Tobacco Garden Campground: 701-842-6931
New Town Marina: 701-627-3900
Indian Hills Resort: 701-743-4122
Dakota Waters Resort: www.dakotawaters.com; 701-873-5800
Sail Sakakawea Charter Service: 701-748-6111
Captain Kit's Marina: 701-487-3600
Bayside Marine; 701-654-7446
Lake Sakakawea State Park: 701-487-3315
Garrison Dam (ACE office at Riverdale): 701-654-7411
Garrison Dam Powerhouse (projected releases): 701-654-7441 ext. 3200
Missouri River Lodge: www.moriverlodge.com/index.htm; 701-748-2023
Matah Adventures, Mandan, ND: 701-663-0054
Lewis and Clark Canoe and Kayak Rentals: 701-462-8635
Fort Mandan, ND Lewis & Clark Interpretive Center: 701-462-8535; www.fortmandan.com

Cross Ranch State Park: 701-794-3731
Broken Oar Bar and Grill: 701-667-2159
Southport Marina: 701-258-0158
Fort Lincoln State Park: 701-663-9571
Huff Bar and Grill: 701-663-3376
Walker Bottom and the Prairie Knights (Casino) Marina: 701-854-7777
State Line Resort: 701-336-7765
Point of View Resort: 605-889-2326; www.pointofviewlodge.com
Country Camping RV Park, Mobridge:
Bridge City Marina: 605-845-9129
Indian Creek Campground: 605-845-7112
West Whitlock State Park: 605-765-9410
West Whitlock Resort: 605-765-9174
Sunset Lodge, Bush's Landing: 605-264-5480
Pike Haven Resort: 605-264-5465
Oahe Marina and Resort: 605-223-2627
Oahe Downstream Campground: 605-223-7722
Oahe Dam Visitor Center: 605-224-5862
Down's Marina, Pierre: 605-224-5533
Dakota Adventures: 605-224-6572
Farm Island Campground: 605-224-5605
West Bend Recreation Area: 605-773-2885 (Farm Island)
Big Bend Dam Powerhouse: 605-245-2331
Left Tail Race Campground, Big Bend Dam Project Office: 605-245-2255
North Shore Bait and Tackle: 605-245-2707
Rank's Service: 605-245-2531
Cedar Shore Resort, Chanberlain area: 605-734-6376
American Creek Marina, Chamberlain: 605-734-5692
Keiner's RV Kampground, Elm Creek: 605-734-6826
Dock 44 Marina, Snake Creek: 605-337-3005
Snake Creek Recreation Area: 605-337-2587
Platte Creek Campground: 605-337-2587 (Snake Creek)
Fort Randall Dam: 605-487-7845
Randall Creek Campground, below Fort Randall Dam: 605-487-7046
Lewis and Clark State Park: 605-668-2985
Lewis and Clark Marina: 605-665-3111

Tailwaters Campground, Nebraska side, below Gavins Point Dam:
1-877-444-6777

Lewis and Clark Visitor Center, Nebraska side, at Gavins Point Dam:
402-667-2550

Missouri River Expeditions: www.missriverexp.com; 605-360-2646

Missouri River Rafting Company & Campground: 605-267-3075

Ponca State Park: 402-755-2284
www.ngpc.state.ne.us/parks/guides/parksearch/showpark.asp?Area_No=143

Sioux City Municipal Boat Dock: 712-224-5043

Scenic Park, South Sioux City: 402-494-7543

The Channelized Lower

Nebraska State Tourism website: www.visitnebraska.org

Iowa State Tourism website: www.traveliowa.com

Kansas State Tourism website: www.accesskansas.org

Missouri State Tourism website: www.missouritourism.org

Nebraska Game and Parks
P.O. Box 30370
Lincoln, NE 68503
402-464-0641; www.ngpc.state.ne.us

Iowa Department of Natural Resources
Wallace State Office Building
Des Moines, IA 50319
515-281-5145; www.iowadnr.com

Kansas Department of Wildlife and Parks
Office of the Secretary
1020 South Kansas
Topeka, KS 66612
785-296-2281; www.kdwp.state.ks.us/main.html

Missouri Department of Natural Resources
P.O. Box 176
Jefferson City, MO 65102
573-751-3443; www.dnr.mo.gov

Kansas City ACE Lewis and Clark Bicentennial Commemoration
www.nwk.usace.army.mil/lewisandclark/map-2.htm
Nebraska Lewis and Clark Bicentennial Commission Boating Information:
http://www.lewisandclarkne.org/boatinginfo.php
Lewis and Clark in Missouri website: www.lewisandclark.state.mo.us
The Discovery Expediton of St. Charles, Missouri: www.lewisandclark.net
Washington Missouri Boat Club: 888-792-7466;
www.washingtonmo.us (click on "Boater Info")
Richard Lovell's Missouri River website: http://www.missouririvertrips.com

Important Channelized Lower Websites and Phone Numbers – Mile 732 to St. Louis

Information on flying carp:
www.cerc.usgs.gov/pubs/center/pdfDocs/Asian_carp-2-2004.pdf
Whiting Lighthouse Marina: 712-458-2066
Pop-n-Doc's Restaurant and Marina, Decatur: 402-349-5193
Cottonwood Marina, above Blair: 402-426-2440;
www.omahariverfront.com/cottonwoodmarina
Desoto National Wildlife Refuge: 712-642-2772
Dodge Park Marina, Omaha: 402-444-5916/402-444-4675;
www.ci.omaha.ne.us/parks/Marina/npmarina.htm;
ACE Missouri River Project Office, Omaha: 402-453-0202
Sandpiper Cove Marina: 402-346-8883; www.sandpipercovemarina.com
Riverfront Marina: 404-444-5916
Bellevue Marina: 402-293-3122; www.bellevue.net/parks.htm
Riverview Marina State Recreation Area: 402-873-7222
Brownville State Recreation Area: 402-883-2575;
www.ngpc.state.ne.us/parks/guides/parksearch/showpark.asp?Area_No; 36
Indian Cave State Park: 402-883-2575
Island Marina, above Nodaway Island Ramp: 816-475-2010
Sunset Grill and Speedliner Lounge, St. Joseph: 816-364-6500
River View Retreat & RV Park, St. Joseph: 816-233-1974
Kaw Point, Kansas City: www.kansasriver.com (Friends of the Kaw);
see also www.kansasriver.com/21kawpoint.htm
ACE Napoleon Office: 816-240-8131
Big Muddy Wildlife Refuge: 573-876-1826
Mighty Mo Canoe Rental, Rocheport: 573-698-3903; www.mighty-mo.com

Les Bourgeois Winery: 573-698-2133
Katfish Katy's Campground: 573-447-3939; www.katfishkatys.com
Cooper's Landing: 573-657-2544
Native Stone Winery & Bull Rock Brewery: 573-584-8600; www.nativestonewinery.com
Riverfront Bar and Restaurant, Portland: 573-676-3271
K&S Bait and Fish, Herman: 573-486-3488
Riverfront Mercantile, New Haven: 573-237-5100; www.rfm-g.com
Central Hotel, New Haven: 573-237-8540
Gary Lucy Gallery, Washington: 636-239-6337; www.garylucy.com
Washington Missouri Boat Club: 888-792-7466; www.washingtonmo.us (click on "Boater Info")
Lewis and Clark Boathouse and Nature Center, St. Charles: 636-947-3199
Chain of Rocks Dam information (National Paddlesport Center): http://streamtech.org/site/ed-ventures/chainrocks.html
Jefferson National Expansion Memorial/Gateway Arch and Museum of Westward Expansion: www.nps.gov/jeff/index.htm
Morgan Street Brewery, Laclede's Landing St. Louis (free wireless internet access): 314-231-9970; www.morganstreetbrewery.com/welcome.htm;

Index

M

N

Y

About the Author

David L. Miller is Distinguished Teaching Professor and Chair of the Department of Geography at the State University of New York's College at Cortland. For the past ten years, he has served as Director of the College's Geographic Information Systems Lab, where he teaches computer mapping, Global Positioning System navigation, and physical geography.

Photo by Eline Haukenes at the Missouri River confluence.

An experienced paddler, he made his first long-distance wilderness canoe trip in 1968. In the spring of 2002, he began the first of three summers kayaking solo down the 2,321-mile-long Missouri River. Articles on his expedition and the technology that he carried have appeared in *Pocket PC Magazine, The Professional Surveyor,* and *The Small Craft Advisory*. A member of the Discovery Expedition of St. Charles, he has served as a "forward scout" for that organization's bicentennial reenactment of the Lewis and Clark Expedition's voyage up the Missouri River.

Professor Miller is a member of the National Association for Search and Rescue and a member of the Lewis and Clark Trail Heritage Foundation. He has served as an equipment tester for Sierra Designs. In the years to come, he'll be spending some part of every summer on the Missouri, updating this guidebook, meeting old friends, and making new ones.